INPUT–OUTPUT TECHNIQUES

INPUT-OUTPUT TECHNIQUES

PROCEEDINGS OF THE SECOND HUNGARIAN CONFERENCE ON INPUT-OUTPUT TECHNIQUES

AKADÉMIAI KIADÓ, BUDAPEST 1976

The Second Hungarian Conference on Input–Output Techniques was organized by the Mathematical, Economic, Planning and Statistical Sections of the Hungarian Economic Association and its Branch in Baranya county, as well as by the Statistical Committee of the Hungarian Academy of Sciences

Translated and supervised by

GY. HAJDU and J. RÁCZ

ISBN 963 05 0891 5

Printed in Hungary

CONTENTS

OPENING SESSION

FIRST SESSION

STATISTICAL PROBLEMS OF THE CONSTRUCTION OF INPUT–OUTPUT TABLES

SECOND SESSION

STATISTICAL PROBLEMS OF THE APPLICATION OF INPUT–OUTPUT TABLES IN PLANNING

THIRD SESSION

SOME METHODOLOGICAL PROBLEMS OF THE APPLICATION OF INPUT–OUTPUT TABLES IN ECONOMIC ANALYSES

FOURTH SESSION

MATHEMATICAL PROBLEMS IN THE CONSTRUCTION AND APPLICATION OF INPUT–OUTPUT TABLES

OPENING SESSION

SOME IDEAS CONCERNING THE INPUT-OUTPUT METHOD

(Introductory address)

by

ISTVÁN HUSZÁR

The concrete economic situation of Hungary and the plans for the coming years are just now being discussed at another forum by the leaders of the nation. There decisions will be made which will determine the course of our economic development for several years, both from a strategic and a tactical point of view. I would like to start by calling attention to this parallel discussion.

The organization and the control of the economy are reflected in a series of decisions taken at various levels of economic life. It is decisions that determine the volume of output to be achieved, that influence the financial and income processes, and that, by way of shaping prices, influence the market, or, more precisely, the supply and demand. It is a common feature of theirs that they have an effect on, and bring about changes in, the substance of the economy. Therefore, they must rely on a firm basis. They assume a thorough knowledge of the substance and the laws of motion of the economic processes to be influenced or regulated.

Economic models are important tools for gaining knowledge about the economic processes and thus helping in the preparation of decisions. Having separated the substance of the processes from their less essential features, the economic models present these processes as a complicated chain of causes and effects. The more we have succeeded in grasping the substance of the economic process, and the simpler we can formulate its laws of motion, the more valuable will our model be and the more efficiently will our model-constructing activity help the difficult and tiresome work of preparing decisions. And this is the point where the objectives of the two discussions meet. On that other forum, the leaders of the country hope to make sound decisions to keep our economic life healthy and to promote the fast development of our national economy. Here we make efforts to facilitate the difficult and tiresome work of decision-making and to provide the leadership with all the tools that may promote making well-founded and correct decisions.

This conference deals with a special category of economic models: the input–output models. We will examine their usefulness in terms of both economic investigations into past situations and projections into the future, suggesting ways of improving the construction of the model while also seeking new utilization areas for input–output techniques.

Allow me to avail myself of this opportunity to outline some thoughts related to the present — mainly Hungarian — problems of the general theory of statistical economic models and, within that, especially those of input–output models. Having read a number of the papers submitted, I believe, and I am sincerely glad for it, that these thoughts will not be unfamiliar to those present, nor do they pretend to be original. Yet, due to their topical nature, I would like to emphasize these ideas in the given situation. Their topicality emerges from two aspects. On the one hand, nowadays definite efforts — and, let us add, claims — are made to develop a closed and consistent system of statistical information. On the other hand, both the economic control agencies and economic researchers urge the elaboration of comprehensive models, since the efficiency of their work would be significantly improved by a uniform interpretation of the economic processes which help to create a possibility for influencing and regulating the economy in an all-round manner. Therefore, the time has come to also reconsider the input–output models in this context.

According to one of the definitions, input–output analysis is "an attempt at accounting for the phenomena of general equilibrium in the empirical analysis of production".

I think it should be emphasized right here that this rather widespread definition incorrectly restricts the role and importance of input–output models. The origin and the spreading of this conception might be explained by the fact that the input–output method first appeared everywhere as a statistical table describing interindustry relations empirically and independently, and this has remained its most general usage to this day. However, one must not equate the statistical balances of interindustry relations and the input–output method of economic analyses (this is not intended to underrate, but rather to appreciate the balances). Input–output analyses are models capable of much more than mere empirical descriptions. They enable us to interpret interrelations between empirical input and output data, to reveal cause and effect relations in the different plan variants which we may derive by changing the system of constraints, and to disclose the conditions and the likely consequences of the possible decisions.

Input–output tables, as statistical ones, can also be conceived of as an element of the system of national economic balances (accounts). They are an organic part of the macro-economic national accounting system which aims at providing a comprehensive and consistent framework for systematizing the most important indicators of the national economy. Within this systematically elaborated and ordered set of data, input–output tables fulfil a very important function. They give the inputs and the outputs in a breakdown by industries. As a by-product, they offer a possibility for linking gross and net output directly with final demand. The other elements of the system of national economic balances do not make this possible. (To avoid any misunderstanding, it must be pointed out that input–output tables cannot only be constructed on a national economy level but can also be worked out for a single enterprise. Those expounded above are — *mutatis mutandis* — valid also in the latter case.)

Thus, the input–output model — as a logical construction interpreting the balance of interindustry relations — relies, statistically, on the data contained in the national accounting system. In this respect, the extent of its possible improvement depends on the extent to which the latter may be improved. In other words, progress in any one field of economic analysis has a developmental effect on the methods of other fields. In this context all the problems of data collection, processing and grouping which generally emerge in connection with the national accounting system are to be examined.

At present the statistical accounting of distribution (turnover) seems to be the least satisfactorily treated in the input–output tables. If there is a demand for a step forward in the field of statistics, this is where it is the most expedient to improve the available data and to increase the reliability of accounting.

However, it is very difficult to find the place of the input–output model in the system of models which, as it has developed so far, consists of extremely heterogeneous elements and comprises the most diverse tools of economic analysis from the purely theoretical constructions through econometric models to normative programming procedures.

Three major groups of input–output models can be distinguished: (1) the *production*, the static variant of which explains the output of industries by starting from intermediate consumption (the dynamic variant takes into account capital formation too when explaining the volume of output); (2) the *financial-income model*, which defines relations between the value of goods and services and the primary inputs, i.e., between the value and the income components; and finally, (3) the *price model*, which relates the changes in the prices of products and services to the industries turning out the product or providing the service. Input–output models are characterized by great originality both in their approach and in their choice of subjects. They constitute an autonomous category among the economic models, i.e. they cannot be identified with any other type. In spite of this, there some similarity can be shown in both the econometric and the programming models.

Each variant of the input–output model has some features relating to the simplest econometric models and can be considered as a very simplified linear model. Simplification is employed here in the determination of the parameters of the system of equations, in the handling of the variables and in the identification of the explanatory variables. The parameters are derived from empirical data by very simple means. Although increasing the popularity of the input–output model, this procedure reduces the theoretical value of its parameters in comparison to the value of those of the econometric model. Furthermore, the deterministic nature of the usual, open and static input–output model definitely reduces the prognostic value of such a model in comparison with a similar econometric one which, in addition, also involves probability theory. With the help of regression analysis, however, it is also possible to estimate the parameters of the input–output models, if a series of tables is available. Therefore, input–output models are able to compete with the highest quality econometric models in this respect, while retaining their evident advantage of being more detailed. In other words, when complemented by considerations relating to probability theory, input–output models correspond to econometric models with highly favourable properties, and so, with their greater detail, they would have essential advantages over the present econometric models.

The application of considerations of probability theory in input–output models assumes the existence of a series of tables consisting of comparable elements, but these are usually not available. The difficulties are further increased by the fact that the mass of information has been continuously increasing and its analytical processing threatens to overburden our present computer capacity. Therefore, from a practical point of view, the conception which instead of seeking a solution fully acceptable from the theoretical aspects, tries to combine the advantages of the econometric and the input–output models is of major importance. Namely, on the one hand, it improves certain crucial parts of the input–output models by including some aspects of probability theory and, on the other hand, it complements certain parts of the econometric model with an input–output model.

It is a characteristic of the input–output model, as it is, that it explains the relation between input and output only from the aspects of the intermediate consumption, while failing to account for changes in the technological equipment of production. This is especially the case with static input–output models. Consequently, open static input–output models are only used for short-term prognoses. When working out medium- or long-term plans, the use of input–output models involves considerable risk. The difficulty can be overcome by making the model more dynamic, using any of several possibilities. In the simplest case, the coefficient system of the model is brought up-to-date by means of opinions given by specialists. This, however, means that the model departs from experience to some extent, and becomes a theoretical deterministic model. Another possibility consists of estimating the trend of changes in the coefficient system from a time series of input–output tables. This procedure is, of course, very uncertain and hence unsatisfactory. Namely, in the majority of cases there are alternative curves available, since various functions can be simultaneously applied when examining the data relating to the past. Finally, the movement of the coefficient system can also be estimated with the aid of regression techniques. In this case, an econometric model is implicitly used for helping to estimate the expected movement of the coefficient system, examining its changes as a function of the changes in the stock of fixed assets.

All this clearly shows that one of the most important tasks to improve the input–output model is to make it more dynamic. If we require it of the input–output model that the scope of its prognostic power should not only be short-term, but also cover a longer period, we cannot escape this task.

Finally, I would like to mention some theoretical interrelations between programming procedures and the input–output model. As regards its substance, it is a programming model without constraints and without an objective function. That is, it is a model of "unlimited resources and possibilities". By this formulation I would like to call attention to the fact that the results derived from an input–output model must be checked both in respect of the limited nature of resources and in respect of the obtainable objectives. But — and this is the other aspect of the problem — we should also examine whether it would be really impossible, in theory, to develop the programming procedure in a manner that, as a result, both the system of constraints and the objectives could be determined in their full complexity, i.e., as a set of interrelations of the economic growth. Furthermore, could such a system of models really not offer more to decision-makers from a practical point of view, could it not facilitate the survey of a greater number of alternatives, by supplying solutions which better conform to the ever changing economic situation?

To conclude, while the participants at this conference will doubtlessly be able to report on valuable results of research, we must admit that the possibilities are by no means exhausted yet. I hope that the conference will provide incentives and useful ideas for future work in this field.

OPENING ADDRESS

by

JÓZSEF NAGY

In the name of Baranya county, acting as host on this occasion, I should like to welcome the chairman, István Huszár, Secretary of State and President of the Central Statistical Office and all participants of the Input–Output Conference. Allow me to extend the greetings of the Baranya county committee of the Hungarian Socialist Workers' Party and, as the chairman of the Baranya county branch of the Hungarian Economic Association, to express my pleasure that the conference is being held here.

Baranya county, and in particular the town of Pécs, has been a pillar of culture and the arts for a long time. Besides the four institutions of higher education in the town, the University of Economics opened a branch here a few years ago. The Baranya county organization of the Hungarian Economic Association was the first county organization in the country and it has been very active ever since. Further professional training of economists in the county has thus been ensured. The rich programme of the county organization testifies to the fact that economy mindedness is gaining an ever greater ground here. This is why we were particularly glad to hear that this conference would be held in Baranya county.

It is known that we have been using input–output tables for almost fifteen years. During this period the study of economics has attained considerable results in Hungary as regards the elaboration, application and the analysis of these tables. Input–output tables have been playing an influential role in national economic planning, in the elaboration of the price system as well as in the analysis of economic relations and processes.

Although there are economists more competent than myself to evaluate the important role that input–output tables play in the central control of the economy, I would like to refer in a few words to such problems of regional management which are, or can be, indirectly related to the subject of this conference. It is known that the leaders of a region can only perform efficiently in economic policy if they utilize up-to-date methods of economic analysis within the framework of the present system of controls.

Although an administrative unit cannot be considered a closed economic one, we are of the opinion that the leadership of a region must have a comprehensive analysis of the on-going economic activity in order to be able to follow the development of the economy, the effect of economic incentives and the implementation of the economic policy of both the party and the government. In other words, the leadership must know how its area fits in with the growth pattern of the whole of the economy. Since the leaders of an area are not only responsible for production, but also for utilization and for supplying the population with material goods and cultural services, we believe that they have to examine developments in production and consumption simultaneously, combined with their interrelations on a regional level.

In the various economic control agencies of the county, above all in the County Directorate of the Central Statistical Office, economic analyses have been prepared which, rising above the limited viewpoints of some enterprises and branches, aimed to examine the economic life of the county in an all-round manner. We can mention here, for example, the investigation of economic efficiency, which has been initiated by the Economic Research Institute and which has also been worked out from regional aspects. Furthermore, the various regional or county balances of purchasing power, manpower or of products as well as energy balances drawn up for a region could be mentioned. These comprehensive studies help the economic leaders of the county to be informed. In certain cases they were most helpful in attaining concrete decisions. In spite of this, the economists in the county did not, or rather could not, apply such methods of analysis which would have provided the minute details of the relations among the individual productive branches within the county. Nor could the above-mentioned analyses elucidate the economic relations of the county as a territorial unit to its environment and to the whole economy. It was partly due to the fact that the regional scheme of the input–output tables is still in its early stage and partly that our information system is not yet able to provide all the data necessary for the practical application of such a scheme.

The programme of this national conference deals with some problems of regional product flows too. I would be glad if the discussions could further the solution of this problem. It would be useful to place greater emphasis on this problem in the future in the appropriate sections of the Hungarian Economic Association as well as in its county organizations. In the course of such discussions we could agree on a regional model which might then be used in practice.

*

I hope the Second Conference on Input–Output Techniques can work undisturbed and with success within the ancient walls of the Castle of Siklós, with its historical atmosphere. I hope that the lectures and contributions will further the development of economics and help in the methodological improvement and practical application of input–output tables. With these thoughts, I now declare this Second Conference on Input–Output Techniques open.

THE IMPORTANCE OF INPUT-OUTPUT TABLES AND HOW TO IMPROVE THEM

by

ALBERT RÁCZ

Input–output tables and the various models derived from them occupy a central place both in modern planning and in economic analysis. This has not come about overnight. It has been the result of a short but very intensive development. Therefore, when we now wish to evaluate the importance of input–output tables in the economy and wish to outline the directions of further development, we should examine these tables in their development from their start up to the present. We can only judge the present realistically and lay a firm foundation for the future if we have a thorough knowledge of the past.

The construction of input–output tables and analyses relying on them has been going on for 15 years in Hungary. These one and a half decades were characterized by the seeking of various ways and means, and the result of the work materialized in a constant improvement of the tables. In the statistical sense, development meant that a growing number of the elements describing interindustry relations could rely on collections of data. Thus it has become possible to substitute for the expert estimates relying on relatively uncertain bases with data of empirical observations in a growing number of fields. In respect to economic theory this progress meant that the tables became more diversified Tables constructed recently enabled us to approach and analyse several economic aspects which had been inaccessible by previous ones.

Compilation of input–output tables started in Hungary in 1959. The first tables were drawn up for the year 1957. These presented the production relations among industries in a breakdown of 39 sectors, among which 32 related to industry and the remaining seven represented the following branches of the national economy: construction, agriculture, transport, communications, domestic trade and foreign trade. These tables were of an explicitly experimental nature. Both the statistical information basis and the techniques of accounting used served to give information on the difficulties and problems emerging in the course of constructing an input–output table. The computations provided a basis for creating a system of statistical data collection which would feed into the construction of an input–output table of satisfactory accuracy and quality suited for analytical purposes. At the same time, through the mathematical processing of these experimental tables and with the help on input–output models, there was an opportunity to gain an insight into fields of analyses that had been inaccessible through earlier analytical methods.

Utilizing the experience gained with the experimental table, the next table was drawn up for 1959. It meant progress compared to that for 1957 not only in its size (productive activity in the national economy was broken down into 95 sectors, of which 82 represented industry) but it also contained qualitative improvements as regards available statistical data. The special data collection for compiling the table and the rational adaptation of the existing data collections were successful. The table for 1959 already possessed the qualities which made it suitable for solving the more complicated tasks of economic analysis and of planning problems.

This table was followed shortly by a third one covering 1961. This had 54 sectors, among them 47 industrial ones. The fourth, compiled for 1965, comprised 83 sectors, with 68 industrial ones. The fifth table related to 1968; its sectoral breakdown essentially coincided with that for 1965.

Besides the reviewed, so-called large models, a series of small tables were also compiled. First with 13 sectors for the years 1959–1964, then with 16 sectors for 1964–1966 and 1965–1968. These small input–output tables were intended to meet a double need. First, they were meant to make up for the lack of large models for the interim years. Second, we wanted to ensure comparability over a period of time mainly by issuing these small tables. They proved useful and for many kinds of computation, analysis and planning the small tables were sufficient or sometimes even desirable.

Both the small and the large tables relying on the empirical data of statistics can be called *general-purpose* input–output tables. These tables served to characterize the whole economy and constituted a basis for computations and analyses on a national level. It is necessary to emphasize this fact, since, in the meantime, with the spreading of input–output methods, also some partial and special fields have needed input–output tables. The general-purpose input–output tables were able to satisfy these demands only to a restricted extent and, therefore, work has started to compile the so-called *special-purpose* input–output tables.

In the last decade much experience has accumulated in connection with the compilation and use of general-purpose input–output tables. Thus, we are in a position to draw up a balance of this work. In the following I am going to review the positive and negative features that — in my opinion — characterized these tables. It must not, however, be forgotten that this is done on the basis of our present knowledge and experience. We intend to utilize the experience of earlier tables in the construction of future ones.

The positive features are as follows:

1. It may seem to be a formal feature, yet I consider it important that input–output tables relying on statistical figures are regularly drawn up in Hungary. True, real regularity would mean tables at equal intervals and conforming to various needs, first of all to those of planning. But it must be added that this "irregularity" was partly caused by practical needs.

It should also be noted that each of the Hungarian fact tables were drawn up and published in a relatively short time, namely, within two years. Being aware of the labour intensity and the complex work-connections required for the compilation of input–output tables and knowing international practice, I believe it will not be immodest to list this among the results.

2. I consider it very important that general-purpose tables are closely linked to the statistical information system. This means, on the one hand, that their compilation and structure are based on the statistical information system, and on the other, that input–output tables themselves are an organic component of this system. Thus, the reliability of these tables is firmly founded.

3. During the ten years of their existence, the compilation and use of input—output tables helped to improve statistical methodology and disclosed many concepts that had not been used in other fields. Demands developed for new types of information, like export and import data elaborated by branches of origin and by users, observing the direction of industrial sales, etc. It was in this period that notions like "final use", "direct and cumulated input indicators" became known.

4. It proved to be useful practice to regularly work out some data closely linked to the basic table, e.g., those on the input of assets and labour. Beyond the technological relations, or rather with their aid, this provided an opportunity to determine also the branch and national-level indicators of assets and labour engaged.

5. Still much remains to be done for ensuring the multi-facet comparability of these tables, but the results hitherto achieved are promising. The publication of the time series of small tables, and the conversion of the 1965 table into the system of the 1968 model were useful for comparison.

6. The experience gained in compiling an investment matrix for 1959 and a 1961 table of net turnover tax was also useful. Such compilations should not only be made for single years far from each other, but also at regular intervals.

7. Finally, it was also useful that, beginning with 1959, the tables were constructed in several variants (A, B and C), depending on the method applied for accounting imports. The tables were complemented by a publication including their mathematically processed data (viz. technological and inverse matrices) and of various indicators worked out from the model (showing the shares of cumulated wages, labour and asset in the net production value).

The negative features are as follows:

1. Outsiders are usually struck first by formal features. Such is the sector nomenclature of the tables; this formal feature, however, is at the same time the medium of their contents. The difference in nomenclature in each table made it difficult to use the tables. Further, it also hindered comparisons, analyses and the elaboration of basis series for the purpose of planning. In the past, the number of sectors was determined by the availability of information, by the system of branch classification valid in Hungary, and, in the first years to no small extent, by the mathematical and computational facilities available. In the future, a series of tables with a stable sector nomenclature should be created in order to ensure the basic formal requisite of comparability.

2. Comparability of the tables over a period of time was also difficult because there were also some methodological differences in the tables relating to different

years. This was, of course, partly justified, since the improvement of methods involved some changes. I feel that today our methods are sufficiently stabilized to enable us to work out a longer series of comparable input–output tables.

3. Knowing what present practice needs, it may be mentioned as a deficiency that only the basic input–output tables were published. When constructing input–output tables, we used many kinds of information which would also be useful for the users of the model. Such are, for example, data on stocks, trade margin, commercial turnover, activities outside the principal production profile of the branches, etc. In the future, these basic documents should be made available in an adequately arranged form to those interested.

4. Today, it is also clear that the use of the model was difficult, particularly in the first years, due to the fact that although it relied on statistical information, it did not consistently fit into the entire system of statistics. In recent years, there has been some advance in this field. The objective is to achieve full consistency, since the needs of economic analysis and planning can only be satisfied in this way. Within the possibilities of methodology and statistical information, full consistency should be realized at the earliest possible date.

The evaluation of the last ten years' work cannot be restricted to reviewing the general-purpose statistical tables only. On their basis, and linked to them, input–output analyses were used in a wide field. Also, plan tables for the national economy and for individual branches were constructed.

First of all the attempt should be mentioned which aimed at exploring interindustry relations in certain narrower fields of the national economy. Such branch tables were compiled for the heavy industry, for metallurgy and engineering, for the construction industry and for the "food economy", i.e., agriculture and food industry. Recently, some input–output tables relating to individual enterprises also appeared mainly in the field of agriculture, and attempts were made to compile so-called regional input–output tables for the geographically defined areas of the country. Thus, from the general-purpose input–output model a whole system of models has been developed, showing further details for partial areas of the economy.

This particular method of accounting for interindustry relations offered advantageous possibilities for planning. Planning soon could rely on these possibilities and, besides the fact-tables, several input-output tables were compiled for the purposes of short-, medium- and long-term planning. The starting point of these tables were again the statistical tables constructed on an empirical basis, but their compilers took also into account the past trends as well as their own ideas about how, according to realistic considerations, future developments would influence interindustry relations.

If we were to conclude here our reasoning on the importance of input–output tables, what has been said so far would suffice to draw the conclusion that input–output tables, as a method, have proved their viability during the 15 years of their existence. They have proved to be an efficient tool in both economic analysis and planning, as it has been palpably testified by the fast growth of their system both in the field of empirical statistical tables and in that of planned ones which anticipate the future.

Development has, of course, not been limited to the original input–output tables, but it has also spread to other fields. Various input–output models have been derived from the original ones. The practice of model construction which was initially intended to formulate equations expressing interbranch relations in terms of physical quantities, later, more frequently and with a growing intensity, also attempted to determine such relations in terms of value, in the form of the so-called price models. The models interpreting relations between physical quantities were further developed to exploit the possibilities opened up by the fact that we had succeeded in writing up the interbranch relations between final demand and gross output. The earlier used "balance accounts" or even the econometric models had not provided any opportunity for that. Recently, however, with the financial control of economic processes pushed to the fore, growing emphasis is being given to such model-like approaches of the interbranch relations which would formulate the ratios between the price of a product and its various value components in a breakdown according to branches or even groups of products. These efforts are embodied in the various price models and the so-called models of money circulation. It is justified and reasonable to assume that new conceptions of economic policy aiming to influence economic processes indirectly will cause accelerated development in this field as well. This is the more expectable since it seems that the new input–output models can provide better opportunities for working out the so-called financial, income and price models than the old ones did for the formulation of quantitative interrelationships.

Relying on all this, the conclusion might be drawn that the input–output tables and the various models derived from them showing quantitative, financial, income and price interrelationships are indispensable tools of contemporary economic analysis, planning and control. It was especially the new conceptions of economic control that opened up rather broad perspectives for them.

*

The importance of input–output tables in present economic activity and the expected fast rate of development force us to keep pace with progress by preparing our statistical tables and by stating the expectable trends of economic development in every important field. We have to construct our tables so that we can satisfy the requirements as they arise either from the aspect of economic analysis or from that of planning. Only in this way can we perform really useful, intelligent work. In outling the major development trends of input–output tables, I will first make an attempt to define the fields which, in my opinion, should be essentially developed in the future, then I shall try to formulate the possibilities of development, and finally I will write about our intentions to meet the growing requirements by solving some statistical problems.

1. Input–output tables as an accounting system must first of all be consistently fitted into the general accounting system of the national economy, into the system of the so-called national accounts. Though this seems to be a formal requirement, it is important since the practice of economic analysis and planning increasingly assumes, and even requires, the existence of a consistent system which is able to create a full-scope account of economic processes. In this conceptual system, identical denominations must denote identical contents, and the individual elements of the system should mutually and unequivocally correspond to one another. Therefore, in the future, we intend to consider the input–output tables as *a component of the system of national accounts* (which, from this formal point of view, is an ordered set of data). From the viewpoint of input–output tables this involves that

a) its classification system conforms to that of national accounts and thus its system of tables becomes stabilized;

b) there is a mutual and unequivocal correspondence between the individual elements of the system of national accounts and the input–output tables; in other words, the system of national accounts sets a consistent frame for the input–output tables in its accounting;

c) the identically denominated items in the system of national accounts and the input–output tables must have the same contents and they must also agree numerically.

However, it should be emphasized that a strict observance of this latter formal requirement relates only to the general-purpose input–output tables which are to be drawn up annually. In case of the models to be derived from the input–output tables, we wish to continue preferring the more important requirements of model construction (homogeneity, uniform valuation, etc.) to this formal requirement, even at the latter's expense. We have to do this because otherwise — though formal numerical agreement would be ensured — the analytical and prognostical value of our models would diminish to a great extent. Thus, in the case of large input–output tables, to be prepared at longer intervals, it may sometimes occur that some items deviate from the system of national accounts, provided that such deviations are justified by the requirements mentioned above.

Of course, deviations are intended to be few and the number of "bridges" by which transition is possible from input–output tables to other tables of the system of national accounts (and vice versa) should be as few as possible. We know, however, that such deviations will occur. Therefore we think it important to ensure consistency also in the system of input–output tables by processing and publishing the most important data necessary for the users (mainly planners). I think here of data relating to employment, assets, investments, return of turnover taxes, customs duties, etc.

It should also be clear that, beyond the construction of a uniform national-economic accounting system, model construction also raises a few requirements which substantially determine the improvement of our work related to the compilation of input–output tables. This may be one of the causes for the differences between certain data in the input–output tables and those in the system of national accounts.

2. From the aspect of the input–output model which describes the interbranch relations of production, first of all the requirement of full coverage arises. There was a time when we restricted our observations of economic processes to the so-called sphere of material production, in accordance with the ideology prevailing at the time. The interrelationships of the so-called non-productive sphere with the sphere of material production were not represented in the input–output tables explicitly. This simplification cannot obviously be maintained any longer. We intend to grasp the economic processes and the mutual interaction of the branches in their entirety. At most we can say that, in the case of a relatively not very developed economy, the neglect of the non-productive sphere was permissible for practical reasons. In the past, this did not lead to great errors. In the present, however, and particularly as regards the future, this method can no longer be followed. The branches of the so-called non-productive services have had an increasing role in our economy. We have sufficient reason to suppose that the input–output models which treat the quantitative relations among the economic branches would become sources of error if in the construction of their tables we continued to neglect the non-productive branches.

In the future we shall need input–output tables that are worked out according to both conceptions. Therefore, we compile our input–output tables in a way that the interbranch relations could be interpreted in both the MPS and the SNA system.

This extension of the input–output tables is made possible by our new national accounting system, which accounts for both the material and the non-material activities. Its categories and accounting methods are already stabilized, ready for application in the construction of the new input–output tables.

3. Another essential requirement arising from the aspect of balance construction is to draw up an input–output table that enables the treatment of income flows. This means, essentially, that an input–output table should be compiled which decomposes the price sum of products and services for final demand breaking them down, by branches, according to value components like wages, depreciation taxes, etc. There can be no doubt that this model is of outstanding importance if we intend to influence the economic processes primarily through financial regulators. As a matter of fact, this is the substance of our present economic policy.

This model raises the problem of delimiting the branches in the construction of the input–output tables. Incomes and financial processes can only be interpreted for organizations but not for activities. Income as such always occurs at an organization unit, and it can also be withdrawn from such a unit. Enterprise incomes cannot be unequivocally divided up by "activities"; it is only by proportionate division that the incomes of the various activities can be approached.

Plausible as it is to formulate the existing and stable production interbranch relations in terms of activities (i.e., independently of organizational structure) it is similarly plausible that for the investigation of financial and income flows we need such an input–output model which is classified according to *organizations.**

Thus, it is necessary to build up the input–output tables according to *two cross-section classifications:* activities and organizations. These two types of tables are necessary not only for analysis and model building, but also for planning. Namely, the annual and the medium-term plans are prepared according to organizations, while long-term plans are drawn up according to activities.

4. When analysing or planning financial and income processes, pricing deserves particular attention, since it has acquired considerable role in the new system of economic control and management. The approximation of the price problems and their analysis with the aid of input–output tables present several difficulties. Our earlier results, which have been obtained with the aid of input–output tables drawn up either purely according to activities or to organizations, were of highly debatable value. Namely, the price problem is a Janus-faced one. Directly, the price components appear in the framework of an organizational unit (enterprise, etc.), since the factors of price formation can only be interpreted if the unit is taken as a whole. But the price itself explicitly attaches to some individual product or service. In other words, cost and income as elements in price formation only appear in the framework of an organizational unit taken as a whole, and they can only be divided up between individual products and services by rather arbitrary methods. On the other hand, a price may be attached to an individual product or service, and no individual price is able to characterize the price situation of an individual organization if it involves more than one product or service.

This may induce one to consider the construction of such tables where the nomenclatures would differ on the sides of output and input. That is, the columns of the tables would mean organizational units (or groups of these), making it possible to account the price components correctly and unequivocally in the individual branches. The rows of the table, however, would mean products and services (or groups of these) in as much detail as possible. This would permit the assignment of prices to products and services in an unequivocal and theoretically correct way.

* The meaning of the terms "activity" and "organization" in this context could be explained by the following example. When interpreting, say, the building industry (or an individual enterprise belonging to it) as an "organizational unit", this would include every activity performed by it, i.e., not only the building activity proper but also that of wood processing (making doors, windows etc.), the production of certain building materials, the activity of shops repairing machines, as well as many other activities. When, however, we want to distinguish the branches by "activities", "construction industry" would be comprised of only the building activities proper, and all other activities performed by its enterprises have to be attached to the wood industry, to the production of building materials, to engineering, and so on. (At the same time, building activity performed by other branches has to be treated under "construction industry".)

The construction of such a model raises, of course, many problems. By increasing the number of the products and services to be considered in the rows of the table, the required amount of labour is multiplied. Difficulties arise also in its mathematical handling, since the system of coefficients of the model based on this input–output table could no longer be arranged in a quadratic matrix.

Considering these difficulties, it seems to be expedient to look for some compromise that would both improve the prospects of analysis against the models applying purely either the principle of organization or that of activity and fit into the present development programme. Such a transitory solution could be provided by the construction of the so-called "activity-by-organization matrices". Here, the inputs would appear in the columns delimited by organizations, whereas the outputs would be shown in the rows meaning activities. This type of input–output table would ensure an adequate possibility for accounting the price factors. At the same time, its rows would interpret the assigned prices (or price index numbers) according to activities rather than to the outputs of the existing organizations. By assigning prices or price index numbers to activities, this type of interpretation takes a medium position between the accounting by organizations and that by products. In so far as the product pattern does not show serious fluctuation in the short run, this solution seems to be satisfactory. It should be stressed, however, that the lack of corresponding sums for the rows and columns in this type of input–output table raises problems in the mathematical handling of the model.

In spite of these difficulties, we should make an attempt to construct an input–output table which, even at the cost of some compromises, could be suited for meeting the requirements of a price model. One could hardly defend a viewpoint which would give up all hope of investigations in this field, when price policy is one of the most important ways of influencing and regulating economic activity.

5. The next problem is how to make the tables dynamic and suited for comparisons over time and space. All input–output tables applied presently, as well as the models derived from them, are of a static character. They provide information for a given period on the interbranch relations, the proportions between production values and final outputs, on the primary inputs and on their relation to the price sums of final demand. But these tables tell us little about the development of the economic processes. The present state of things is isolated from the past. Thus, we must try to explain a given stage of development by starting from this stage itself. However, the present can only be understood fully if we know the past, just as the guaranty of a reliable forecast for the future is the full knowledge and understanding of the present. Many important factors of development can only be recognized after a certain time, and they can hardly be felt within a short period. That is why, besides the static models which are satisfactory in the short run, there is an increasing need for dynamic models which are able to describe the process of development.

Models explaining development can be constructed according to various approaches. Actually, the number of various dynamic models corresponds to the number of ideas regarding the relevance or irrelevance of the various factors acting over time as well as the effects they are exerting. It is clear, therefore, that during the creation of dynamic models, subjective thinking and imagination have a greater role to play than in the case of static models, where the system of constraints, though simple, is rather strict.

So far only a few initiatives have been made to construct dynamic models, and there is no such model which having been subject to extensive investigations and discussions, could claim the approval of the majority of Hungarian economists. Thus, it would be a mistake to force any of our "home-made" models on the experts working in some other economic field. The initiatives made by the Institute of Economics and the Central Statistical Office can only be regarded as a first step along this path.

Progress needs to be made in this field in two directions. The construction of a dynamic model that would meet with the general consensus of both theoretical workers and statisticians should be encouraged.

In theory, all initiatives which intend to make the input–output model more dynamic should be supported. Opportunity is to be given for the discussion of the theories, for the exchange of opinions, in order that a theoretically correct and practically feasible model should be born.

In the practice of model construction, future requirements are to be anticipated. We are convinced that input–output models made dynamic will be increasingly needed in the future and therefore we are making efforts that the indispensable elements of *every* dynamic model should be available by the time of decision. In our opinion, one of these elements is the so-called investment matrix which is necessary for each dynamic model, independently of its special structure. We wish to compile the investment matrices regularly, i.e., simultaneously with the construction of the input–output tables which describe current relationships.

Of course, making a model dynamic presupposes the existence of time series consisting of static input–output tables. Namely, in order to be able to explain the developments over time, we need such input–output tables on the grounds of which we can trace the strengthening or weakening of interbranch relationships. Against such a series of tables, two requirements must be raised. First, the *structural* changes taking place over time should be eliminated from them. Therefore, the data of a comparable series should be grouped according to activities rather than organizations. Second, besides the tables based on current prices, a series of tables based on "constant" or "comparable" prices also have to be constructed, i.e., tables where the individual rows reflect the changes in volume.

I should like to stress, however, that even a dynamically comparable series of tables can serve general purposes only. These general-purpose input–output tables have to be converted according to the needs of the various users. At present, it does not seem clear what kinds of comparable table series are needed and — this is perhaps even more important — which are the problems that require investigations at constant and which at current prices.

6. The elaboration of a system of regional input–output tables should also be continued. This work is highly important for both regional planning and the economic control performed by local authorities. In Hungary, there are differences among the levels of economic development in the various geographic areas and this brings about differences in both the economic and the cultural levels of the population.

The input–output tables elaborated for Vas county (see the study by Kovács, Csepinszky and Novák) may be regarded as the first initiative. Though it is the first, we expect much from it. It will certainly give answers to a number of methodological and other questions. It should be decided, however, what the nature of these regional input-output tables should be and to what extent they should correspond to or may deviate from the national tables. Further, it should also be examined how far the counties (i.e., the administrative units) may be considered as "regions". Finally, the questions regarding the organization of data-collecting should be taken into account too.

*

Let us now sum up what is to be done in order to improve the work relating to the construction of input–output tables and models.

We intend to compile the next two input–output tables for 1972 and then for 1975. Both will present the economic processes in a breakdown by 80–100 sectors. As usual, different types of tables will be constructed according to the various ways of accounting imports.

As regards their system of accounting, these tables will be closely linked to the system of national economic balances.

Beginning with the tables relating to 1972, also the various fields of "non-productive" activities will also appear in the tables besides those of the sphere of material production.

The tables will be aggregated according to activities, organizations and also considering both activities and organizations.

Beyond the current interindustry relations, attempts will be made to trace and account the interrelationships of investments as well.

For the purposes of comparison over time, a series of input–output tables are needed.

A dynamic input–output model that can be applied in practice has to be elaborated too.

The planned improvements of the general-purpose input–output tables based on statistical figures are expected to make our models more suitable for practical use; we wish to provide assistance to economic analysis and planning by elaborating and developing them.

FIRST SESSION

STATISTICAL PROBLEMS OF THE CONSTRUCTION OF INPUT-OUTPUT TABLES

Chairman

DR. ALBERT KISS

SOME STATISTICAL ASPECTS CONCERNING THE COMPILATION OF THE 1968 INPUT-OUTPUT TABLE

by

MRS. ÉVA KOÓS

The Central Statistical Office has regularly compiled input–output tables relating to material production every two or three years since 1959. These tables are grouped according to 60–80 sectors. Their primary aim is to state, for a given year, the movement of the social product and the interindustry relations in both production and final use, furthermore to provide basic information for the future construction of input–output models to be used in economic analysis and planning.

In this decade the method of compiling input–output tables has much improved and their statistical basis has been founded and organized better than before. For compiling the table for 1957 we could only rely on statistics generally available at the time, while from 1959 on, the requirements made by input–output tables have increasingly been taken into account in the collection of statistical data.

The implementation of this system brought about several changes also in the method of compiling this table. Its compilation was difficult due to the important changes in the accounting system and in the related statistical report sheets. Consequently, the preparatory work had to be performed, both relying on the practice of earlier years and in consideration of the changes due to the new system of economic control and management.

A work as complicated and complex as the above preparations consisted in making the table for 1968 comparable to those drawn up for 1959, 1961 and 1965.

With all this, of course, it took longer to compile the table. In the following we are going to survey the major methodological steps we took as well as the conceptual problems that occurred during the construction of the input–output table for 1968. As a matter of fact, we shall not mention the general problems of compiling input–output tables, as we assume these to be known.

1. THE CONCEPT OF MATERIAL PRODUCTION

Similarly as to its predecessors, the 1968 input–output table also comprises the branches of material production. In the new accounting system, however, those services are also accounted for within the output of the branches of material production, which are performed by the organizations of these branches, e.g. services performed for social institutions, rent revenues of housing estates, receipts from rentals, etc. In principle, these should not be comprised in the gross production value of the individual branches. In practice, however, the magnitude of such activities is relatively small and they need not be separated.

2. CLASSIFICATION BY BRANCHES

According to the new system of classification, the 1968 input–output table comprises two new sectors. Namely, forestry has been separated from plant cultivation, to figure as a separate sector, and water management has been transferred from the non-material sphere into the scope of material production. "Other agricultural activity" is no longer an independent sector; the value of this activity has been distributed among engineering, plant cultivation and water management. A considerable part of the "other productive activities" has been transferred to the non-material sphere, the remaining ones (mainly the collection of wastes) being classified in the corresponding sector.

3. "CLEANING OF PROFILES"

Whereas statistical accounting is made according to the "organization principle", input–output tables are compiled according to the "activity principle". This difference necessitated the "house-cleaning of production profiles", that is, the separation of certain activities which are performed by an organization but, according to their nature, belong to another sector. This extends now to almost every sector of the input–output table. Although the necessity of separating such "foreign activities" increased in some fields in 1968, there was also a decrease in some other fields owing to certain changes in the bookkeeping system.

In the input–output tables of 1957, 1959 and 1961, *construction activity* was separated only from three industries (coal mining, electric energy, and extraction of oil and natural gas), as well as from agriculture, transport and home trade. In the 1965 table, not only construction was separated from every sector, but *industrial activities* were also separated from metallurgy and engineering, and the production of refractory materials was transferred from metallurgy to the sector of brick production. Beyond the activities listed above, the industrial branches were already "cleaned" also of *transport* and *trading* activities in the 1968 table. However, owing to the bookkeeping regulation introduced that year, only such "foreign activities" could be separated the products of which were sold by the enterprise itself, for, since 1968, only these have been counted into the output value, whereas earlier the total product of the "foreign activities" was considered as output, independently of the fact whether they had been sold or used within the same enterprise. Thus, in 1968, those construction activities performed by enterprises which *did not* belong to the building industry could not be separated, as they were performed on their "own account" and not for sale.

In compiling the 1968 table we also dispensed with separating "foreign activities" when their value was fewer than 1 per cent of the gross output of the sector in question or, regardless of its percentage, when it was fewer than 50 million forints. In 1968, no "foreign activities" were separated from the industrial sectors, since only the engineering branches reported such activities and even these were more or less related to the main activity. (However, in order to achieve homogeneous sectors, a "cleaning" of industrial profiles is intended in the table planned for 1972.)

4. THE ACCOUNTING OF WASTE AND REFUSE

The method of registering waste and refuse has been a recurring problem. In the tables for earlier years, the value of recycled waste figured in the sector under "other productive activities", that is, it was considered to have been turned out by that sector. Beginning with 1968, the activities performed in this sector have been divided between the other sectors. Thus the use of waste had to be accounted for in the 1968 table in a different manner. The only starting point was the value of waste and refuse utilized by the enterprises as it figured in their annual balance sheet. On the assumption that, in the absence of recycling, the industrial consumption of raw materials should be increased accordingly, we added this value to the consumption of raw materials (and, consequently, also to the gross output) of those sectors which utilize waste and refuse. As regards the origin of waste and refuse by sectors, we applied estimations corresponding to their nature. In the course of distributing the value of output, the increase which thus occurred was accounted for as "changes in stocks".

Below, we wish to emphasize a few methodological changes which became necessary in compiling the 1968 table partly because of the new accounting rules and partly owing to some other changes.

5. EXPANSION OF THE SCOPE OF ACTIVITIES ACCOUNTED

Distinct from earlier tables, the result of the activities of a sector is expressed as the value of its social product. In addition to the basic activity of a sector, this value also includes the value of the activities which belong, according to their nature, to some branches of the economy, as well as the value of research and development, of organizational, planning and other activities, and also the value of the materials sold, etc.

6. THE ACCOUNTING OF RENEWALS

One of the most significant problems of comparability was the change in the methods applied for accounting renewals. Beginning with January 1, 1968, renewals, as an item of final use, ceased to exist; it is now accounted as an item of the current cost of the sector where it occurs. Accordingly, the sum of depreciation allowance is diminished by the former replacement fund.

7. THE ACCOUNTING OF TURNOVER TAXES

The input-output tables compiled so far have been drawn up at current producer prices. The price of most products also included the turnover tax levied on them. The rates of the turnover tax in the price differed according to buyers. However, the tax always appeared in a direct manner, that is, in the transactions between the buying and the selling sector, or the selling sector and the final consumer. In 1960, owing to various considerations in price policy, the points at which the turnover tax is levied were displaced. Now a considerable part of it is levied in the sector of home trade:

Branches of national economy	Turnover tax receipts in			
	1965		1968	
	million Ft	per cent	million Ft	per cent
Industry	27,591	91.6	6,804	22.8
Construction	165	0.5	106	0.4
Agriculture	—	—	772	2.6
Transport	742	2.5	434	1.5
Trade	1,327	4.4	21,769	72.7
Other	304	1.0	—	—
Total	30,129	100.0	29,885	100.0

In order to make the two tables comparable, the 1965 table had to be transformed considerably according to the methodological principles valid for 1968. However, the question of comparability of the 1968 table not only arises in connection with the input–output tables of earlier years, but also in respect to the system of national accounts (economic balances) for 1968. In the next paragraph, some related problems will be dealt with.

8. INPUT-OUTPUT TABLES IN THE SYSTEM OF NATIONAL ACCOUNTS

It is worth while to deal in somewhat greater detail with the methodological differences between input–output tables and the "system of national accounts" which comprise a set of statistical balances as well as tables systematizing the processes of social reproduction on a macroeconomic level. The balances of the social product and of national income, as well as input–output tables themselves, are parts of this system. Therefore, the basic data of these accounts must be in a close relationship with one another, and, if there are differences due to methodological deviations, these must be explainable numerically. The differences in question are as follows.

1. The balances of the social product and national income are compiled according to activities, that is, all activities of the branch, foreign to its main production profile, are separated and transferred to their relating sector. The same principle has to be asserted also in compiling input–output tables. In practice, however, this principle could not be fully implemented, partly owing to the lack of adequate data and partly because we had to consider whether the amount of labour needed was proportionate to the expected result, that is, whether it was worthwhile to separate foreign activities of a value of 1–2 million forints, (Ft) and, as a consequence, to elaborate a host of data on inputs, distribution, employment, fixed and circulating assets, etc., most of which should have been estimated. Still, in order to render the sectors as homogeneous as possible, 31 sectors were "cleared" of 83 foreign activities. (See the following aggregated table.)

As we did not apply the principle of "classification by activities" rigidly, the sums for the individual branches of material production in the balance sheets of the social product and national income do not aggree exactly with the relative data in the input–output table. These differences, however, do not impair the equality of the marginal figures in the three tables.

2. A further difference was caused by the fact that the units of observation in the balance of the social product were different from those in the input–output table. The former is a balance aggregated to the *main branches,* while the sectors of the input–output table are, as a rule, industrial branches, sometimes even sub-branches or individual activities (e.g., foundries). This entails a difference also in the *cumulation* figures, thus causing the value of the social product in the two tables to deviate. In the 1968 table, such differences in cumulation were caused, e.g., by the separation of briquetting from coal mining, of foundries from metallurgy, of asbestos-cement production from the lime and cement industry, etc.

Let us now examine the characteristic features, i.e. the structure and the mathematical processing of the input–output table for 1968.

It breaks down the national economy into 83 productive sectors. Of these, 68 are industrial, 5 relate to construction; agriculture and transport are represented by 4 sectors each, while trade falls into 2 sectors. The size of the table was determined by the general requirements raised by planning and analysis and at the same time we tried to ensure a maximum extent of comparability with tables of earlier years, too.

All data in the table were calculated from two separate sources. For the inputs, the statistics on the consumption of raw materials, for the distribution, the sales statistics were used. As a result of this double approach, at first each cell of the table contained two figures; in about 75 per cent of the cells, their difference did not exceed 10 per cent, and it reached 20 per cent only in 5 per cent of the cells. To clear up the causes of such differences and establish relatively accurate figures was the most time-consuming procedure in constructing the table. There were cases when the data submitted by enterprises had to be checked; for this, sometimes the results of statistical surveys were used.

Separation and transfer of "foreign activities" in the input–output table of 1968

Separated from sectors \ Transferred to sectors	Engineering	Building materials industry	Chemical industry	Light industry	Food industry
Mining	—	—	—	—	—
Metallurgy	—	—	—	—	—
Engineering	—	—	—	—	—
Building materials	—	—	—	—	—
Chemical industry	—	—	—	—	—
Light industry	—	—	—	—	—
Food industries	—	—	—	—	—
Construction	364	441	—	225	—
Agriculture	905	600	170	—	910
Forestry	—	—	—	769	—
Water management	—	—	—	—	—
Transport	1,510	—	—	—	—
Trade	1,107	273	214	1,268	976
Total	3,886	1,314	384	2,262	1,886

In the case of earlier input–output tables, this collation process had been continued until a single figure was found which could be considered the most correct one in view of all the circumstances examined. In compiling the 1968 table, we requested such a degree of accuracy only where the difference between the two figures exceeded 5 per cent. In cases where the difference was smaller, the collation of the intermediate inputs was performed with the computer using the so-called RAS method. Before undertaking this mechanized collation, the primary input and final demand figures were rendered final, thereby determining about 60 per cent of the elements figuring in the block of intermediate inputs. The computer programme of the RAS method was written in a way not to alter any element by more than 5 per cent.

The 1968 input–output table was elaborated in two variants; moreover, also a matrix of imports was worked out, relying on foreign trade statistics. The mathematical processing of both variants has been completed, so the technological coefficient matrices, the inverse matrices, the matrices of the distribution coefficients as well as the different indices regarding the direct and cumulated ratios of wages, employment, fixed and circulating assets, and the consumption of imported materials are all available.

The 1968 input–output table and the data derived from its processing were published in 1970. In the same year, the publication "Input–output tables for 1965–1968" appeared in which the national economy was presented in a breakdown by 14 sectors, at 1968 prices, and according to the organizational constructions prevailing in 1968. A variant of the 1965 input–output table was published

(Gross output values, million forints)

Construction	Agriculture	Forestry	Water management	Transport	Trade	Total
717	—	—	—	46	129	892
—	—	—	—	—	53	53
510	426	—	—	—	148	1,084
—	—	—	—	—	—	—
264	—	—	—	—	—	264
440	—	—	—	—	285	725
—	—	—	—	213	1,453	1,666
—	—	—	—	—	182	1,212
4,190	—	—	—	1,187	656	8,618
143	—	—	—	—	—	912
2,362	—	—	—	—	—	2,362
2,463	—	—	—	—	—	3,973
252	183	—	—	42	—	4,315
11,341	609	—	—	1,488	2,906	26,076

in 1971, which considered the methodological changes introduced in 1968, at 1968 prices, and in 83 sectors.

It can be seen from this survey on the major problems of the compilation, comparability and mathematical processing of the 1968 input–output table that the changes in the methods of accounting, bookkeeping and statistics, due to the reform of Hungarian economic control and management, caused much difficulty for those who constructed this table. Nevertheless, as it was compiled for the first year of this reform, it occupies an important place within the series of input–output tables.

SOME QUESTIONS OF ACCOUNTING INPUT AND DISTRIBUTION RELATIONS IN THE CONSTRUCTION INDUSTRY AND SOME PROBLEMS OF DATA COLLECTING FOR AN INPUT-OUTPUT TABLE ON CONSTRUCTION ACTIVITIES

by

Mrs. ZSUZSA HUSZÁR

At the present stage of Hungary's economic development, increasing attention has been paid to the interrelationship between the various productive branches, and the different activities aimed at maintaining the fixed assets of investment. At the same time, in view of the relative insufficiency of investments in the non-productive sphere, it has become most urgent to set up such a uniform theoretical and practical approach which, with the utilization of available resources and considering both the productive and non-productive spheres, would ensure the optimum efficiency of the national economy as a whole.

In the period from 1968 to 1970, the share of construction in the country's total investments exceeded 50 per cent, partly as a result of the change in the price ratios in 1968. The value of the activities performed by the construction industry (inclusive of the costs of making projects and of the activities of the investors themselves) amounted in 1965–1967 to 51 per cent of all investments. This share was 56 per cent in the average of 1968–1970, and amounted to 57 per cent in 1970. These increasing proportions, as well as the difficulties connected with the re-grouping of capacities within the construction industry and the necessity of shortening the time for completion, emphasize the importance of further research with the aid of mathematical methods to make our investment policy more flexible.

When assessing the role of the construction industry in the national economy, it is also important to consider that about one fifth of all building and fitting work carried out in this country is of a maintenance nature and that this proportion is likely to grow in the future, partly under the influence of preference in prices and partly due to a long-time neglect of maintenance of state-owned and private residential buildings as well as of public utilities.

In view of all this, it became necessary to review and analyse the data on the construction industry in order to include them in the nation-wide input–output table planned for 1972. Input–output tables usually present the construction industry in four sections (surface construction including private housing; civil engineering; fitting industries; planning institutes), and this classification is likely to be used also in the 1972 table. This grouping can be accepted mainly from practical considerations, but with the condition that the collecting and

Table 1

Structure of the gross social product of the construction industry by activities and organizations (1970)

Organizations	Surface construction	Civil engi-neering	Fitting	Projecting*	Total
	(percentages)				
State-owned construction enterprises	44.9	58.5	71 1	2.9	47.9
Construction cooperatives	10.5	—	28.9	1.2	9.2
Socialist construction industry	55.4	58.5	100.0	4.1	57.1
Private builders	17.2	—	—	—	11.9
Construction industry proper	72.6	58.5	100.0	4.1	69.0
Projecting institutes*	—	—	—	95.9	3.6
Construction and projecting proper	72.6	58.5	100.0	100.0	72.6
Building and fitting activities performed by other branches of the national economy	27.4	41.5	—	—	27.4
Total	100.0	100.0	100.0	100.0	100.0

* Including also the organizations of and the activities performed by the investors serving the implementation of investments.

processing of data should be organized with a view to ensuring a subsequent desaggregation, according to the special requirements of the construction industry.

Namely, as regards the input structure of the industry, various effects create situations which are more complicated than with most other branches. In view of the diversity of input structures within each sector, the practicality of the above fourfold classification seems questionable. Input structures may differ widely even within the same sector, as a result of differences in technology and location of the building sites (e.g., soil conditions, transport distances, etc.).

Apart from these differences, in a table where the data are grouped according to the character of activities, the contents of each sector will be heterogeneous (from the point of view of input structures) also because it summarizes the activities of large-scale, state-owned, construction enterprises, of construction cooperatives and of private builders.

By summing up the economy-wide building activities according to the above four sectors, in 1970, the shares were 69.1 per cent for surface construction, 20.5 per cent for civil engineering, 6.7 per cent for fitting and 3.7 per cent for the the projecting institutes. It has to be noted that about 40 per cent of the aggregated activities of surface construction and civil engineering were carried out either by other branches of the national economy or by private builders, and regarding the input structures of these two groups we have to rely mostly on estimates.

Table 2

Percentage shares within the output of the construction industry, of maintenance activities and those belonging to other branches of the national economy

Sectors of the construction industry	Maintenance	Activities belonging to other branches of the national economy
Surface construction	17.2	6.3
Civil engineering	22.5	3.5
Fitting	35.3	2.8
Average of the three sectors	19.7	5.4

Within the total output of "construction industry proper", it seems to be useful to examine the shares of two particular kinds of activities which show very different input structures, namely, those connected with the maintenance of already existing buildings and those which, by their nature, belong to some other branch of the national economy (e.g., to the industry of building materials, to the wood-processing industry, etc.).

The structural proportions observed in 1970 within the output of the construction industry resulted from the development in previous years which was different for each sector. Thus, for instance, the rate of growth of building and fitting organized or performed by other economic branches doubled in five years compared to the activity of the state-owned enterprises belonging to the construction industry. Another change was that, whereas maintenance amounted to 25.5 per cent of all performance of the construction industry proper in 1965, this share was reduced to 19.7 per cent by 1970. During the five years from 1966 to 1970 the structure of the various types of new investment changed, too.

From the brief discussion above we may get an insight into the circumstances giving such a system of indices which characterize the internal relationships of the construction industry. This may provide a reliable basis only for short-term analyses and planning.

Some other factors affecting the technological coefficients of the construction industry also confirm this assumption. For instance, such is the rapid progress in technology (light structures, panels, the industrialized prefabrication of materials like mortar, concrete, road-building materials, the use of prefabricated piping). In other words, the extent to which the materials produced by the construction industry's own factories are replacing the traditional ones raises the question of the variability of technological coefficients. The significance of this is indicated by the fact that in 1970 more than 20 per cent of the materials used by the socialist construction industry were produced in its own plants. Mention should be made of the particular ways of accounting self-produced materials, too. Up to 1967 the output value of the construction industry, as a branch of the

Table 3

A breakdown of labour inputs within construction investments, according to the functional types (percentages)

Construction types	1965	1970
Industrial	9.9	11.4
Agricultural	7.7	11.0
Trade and warehouses	6.0	6.3
Administration, education and welfare	9.5	8.8
Residential	32.3	29.4
Roads	7.3	6.9
Railways	5.1	3.3
Waterways and bridges	4.7	3.6
Transmission lines	7.5	8.6
Other buildings	10.0	10.7
Total	100.0	100.0

national economy, was accounted in a "cumulated" form. The value of building materials produced within the construction industry figured twice in its output. From 1968 on, this double accounting has been eliminated. At present, the value of self-produced materials figures only in the value of the buildings where they were built-in, and it is included in the output only when these materials are sold to an organization outside the construction industry. (In 1970 the latter item amounted to nearly 5 per cent of the total output of the construction industry.)

Due to the particular features of construction (namely, that it is performed at different building sites, or the special conditions of storing, invoicing and cost-accounting of materials, etc.) analytical bookkeeping records also the self-produced materials at "gross" (producer) prices. As a result, reports of building enterprises on the use of materials, serving as a basis of input–output tables, contain double accounts on certain materials, e.g., in addition to the value of self-produced panels, the value of cement, etc. used in their production appear in the total. This double accounting is then eliminated by a further step of calculation, in order to show the value of materials used as it has to appear in the annual balance sheet of an enterprise. The difference, however, is shown only as a global figure. In order to obtain a figure cleared of double accounting for the input of each material, it is necessary to start from the total industrial output of each building material produced by the building enterprise itself, and then to divide it up according to whether it has been used within the enterprise (and for what purpose), or has been sold (and to whom). Since, unlike the general practice in the other branches of industry, the building enterprises are bound to record the value of products they themselves produce and use up also at accounting prices, we may ask them for the data of production and realization which are necessary for shaping a reliable input structure.

In the following, let us touch on a few questions of accounting that are worth mentioning in this context.

An object of our special consideration was the accounting of semi-fixed assets, (i.e., tools having a purchase price of less than 2,000 forints apiece and other "expendable supplies" used in the production process). Such inputs represent about 4 per cent of all costs of the socialist construction industry, and the stocks belonging to this category amount to more than 20 per cent of all its stocks. According to the planned instructions on the statistical accounting of materials, the enterprises have to report on the amount used of the assets belonging to this category (i.e., either scrapped or finally built-in). This instruction has made it easier to get a reliable accounting of the distribution of semi-fixed assets as well as of the changes in stocks in the various branches.

The registration of transport costs was made easier to some extent by the uniform system of accounting introduced in 1968. Thereby, the former practice of increasing the value of the building materials by an "average rate" of transport costs was eliminated. (Up to 1968, for the purposes of input–output tables, the transport costs of building materials were only estimated, by subtracting a sum proportionate to the prescribed norms of transport costs from the given values which included the "average transport costs".) At present, the actual transport costs of building materials are shown as a separate cost, and can be unequivocally stated on the grounds of the annual balance sheets. They amount, on the average, to 15 per cent of the total input value of materials used by the building industry. Problems arise, however, on how to select the transport costs of the materials which have been bought from enterprises trading with means of production (see P. Szikla's study in this volume), as these costs are included in the prices invoiced by such enterprises. In the case of materials, for which the official "List of Building Components and Prices" determines the transport cost as a separate element of pricing (e.g., bricks, stone, etc.), the estimate may be based on these prescriptions. However, in some cases (e.g., metallurgical and engineering products), the list does not show the transport costs separately, so we must start from the accounts of the distributing enterprises in order to estimate the transport costs on the basis of rates varying by products.

Although the accounting of inputs is to some extent easier since the data suppliers use uniform accounting prices (based on the above-mentioned official "List of Building Components and Prices"), there are still some minor price differences left (amounting to 1–2 per cent). A similar problem arises also in connection with the use of materials obtained from demolitions. The guidelines for accountancy in the construction industry permit the valuation of such materials within wide limits (up to 100 per cent of the original purchase price). Thus corrections of input values entailed with the use of materials obtained from demolitions can be made only after checking each group of material input against the resources. Estimates of this kind may, in some cases, be checked by the analysis of sample figures obtained from selected data suppliers.

The rows of the input–output table show the distribution of output of the construction industries, and within this they also indicate the investment outputs. In 1968, 78.3 per cent of the outputs of building and fitting served investment purposes. For practical analysis, the investment structure is obtained from the input–output table of investments. The compilation of this table is very time-consuming and requires a special knowledge of each field concerned. In view of the special requirements in relation to construction industry investments, we should like to set up a system of data collection which would indicate the distribution of building investments of the state-owned building enterprises from 1971 on and of the whole socialist construction industry (i.e., construction cooperatives also involved) from 1972 on, according to branches and construction types.

The data obtained in this way and complemented by building investments performed by other branches, will ensure a relatively reliable assessment of the data in the rows of the input–output table which is compiled to show the distribution of outputs.

Of course, these data must match the ones provided by the investors (as the latter ones are also figuring in the table). In order to achieve this, a double checking of the data on building investments is performed. When this kind of data collection and checking is carried out for each year, we shall be able to draw interesting conclusions about the "market conditions" of building investments.

Summing up what has been said here on the building industry, I wish to emphasize that, in view of the heterogeneity of the activities and the important role of other economic branches in this industry, future investigations based on the analyses of input–output tables should rely on a desaggregation of sectors (in order to obtain more homogeneous groups) and on a more exact assessment of the building activities which are performed by other economic branches. This requires the re-grouping of organizations within the construction industry; as regards the other branches of the national economy, their building activity should be detached from their other activities, and complementary information should be gained from them on the origins of at least the most important inputs of their building activity. Information about the nature and origin of such inputs is urgently needed, because up to now we have not had detailed accounts as regards the construction by other branches. It has now turned out that the share of materials and equipment produced by metallurgy, machine industry and chemical industry has been rapidly increasing in the inputs in these fields as well.

Although the input–output table of the construction industry drawn up according to activities is clearly very important for decisions which aim to achieve economic equilibrium, attention has also to be paid to the tables constructed according to organizations, as they reflect the circumstances resulting from the rapid changes in technology and in the use of new materials.

The possibilities offered by input–output tables for analysing and planning economic processes might be increased by improving the conditions for the compilation of more accurate tables. The ideas suggested here were intended to serve this purpose in the field of the construction industry.

STATISTICAL PROBLEMS OF CONSTRUCTING INPUT-OUTPUT TABLES FOR AGRICULTURE

by

ISTVÁN HAJDU and MRS. RÓZSA SZIKSZAI

In the economy-wide input–output tables compiled by the Hungarian Central Statistical Office, agriculture is generally represented by two sectors: crop growing and animal husbandry. Detailed tables of an explicitly agricultural character have been drawn up for 1959, reflecting the agricultural conditions before the large-scale socialist reorganization and for 1968, showing the present social and economic structure.

Contemporary methods of economic planning and management require complex economic analyses revealing the details of the interbranch relations of agriculture. At present, the bulk of agricultural production is done on large-scale socialist farms (state-owned or cooperative) which are able to fulfil the requirements of bookkeeping, statistical regulations and the supply of data. In spite of this, the analysis of relations between the various producing branches still seems to encounter several difficulties. Many questions of principle and methodology will have to be clarified before an agricultural input–output table satisfying the diverse requirements can be compiled.

In the following we shall raise some of the problems connected with the compilation of such a table, namely those which concern accountancy and methodology from the aspects of statistics. We emphasize this because we believe that, whereas the theoretical principles discussed by this conference are generally valid, the methodological questions should be treated in the light of the particular features of the individual branches.

DELIMITATION OF AGRICULTURE AND ITS BRANCHES

The first problem consists in deciding whether the lines between the branches of the national economy should be drawn according to the organizational status of the individual productive units or according to the nature of their activities. Essentially, the activity of agriculture consists of crop growing and animal husbandry. There are, however, economic units belonging to agricultural organizations which are separated from the farms engaged in these activities and serve their production only indirectly. There is, for instance, a state-owned enterprise engaged in soil amelioration. Such organizations undoubtedly belong to agriculture, their inputs serve productive purpose, but their product is only indirectly embodied in the yield of wheat, apples, etc. Even an agricultural farm may perform services (e.g., ploughing) for other farms, thereby acquiring an income which will be included in its production value.

When trying to separate agricultural data according to "activities", there are two alternatives:

a. neglecting independent accounting, we show the inputs with the agricultural branch which takes advantage of the activity in questions; and

b. in addition to the two main categories of crop growing and animal husbandry, we introduce a third for "other agricultural activities".

When compiling the 1968 input–output table of agriculture, we chose the second alternative, because the data used in the block of primary inputs could be interpreted more unequivocally, and it was easier to divide the inputs of fixed capital and live labour. The inputs of these "other agricultural activities" were shown in the sector where their sales income was realized, and the latter were divided among the users' branches.

Another particular problem of separating activities and productive branches also arises because each agricultural farm has several kinds of produce. No farm can specialize exclusively in the production of cereals, apples or eggs. Thus, the grouping of productive units cannot be made in the way applied, e.g., in industry. In agriculture, the grouping according to activities takes place not by aggregating *production units* of a similar specialization but by aggregating the data relating to their different *products*. Thus, the data on the output of the various agricultural branches and on its distribution have to be elaborated by products or product groups.

The distinction of data within the various branches represented in a given farm is complicated by the fact that, generally, bookkeeping does not separate farm costs and incomes by branches. In most farms production costs and income distribution can only be shown if the farm is regarded as a whole and its non-agricultural activities are also included. Thus, if inputs by branches are wanted, one cannot rely only on the data of the annual balance sheets and instead he must resort, in the first place, to data on farm statistics for the calculation of certain specific indices, like the consumption of seeds or fertilizers per hectare, that of fodder, and so on. Also the products sold to agriculture by other branches of the national economy are available as a single sum. For dividing this sum among the various branches of agricultural activity, one must again rely on the above-mentioned statistical observation. It is relatively easier to follow the distribution of the output produced by the various agricultural activities since production balances are annually drawn up for most agricultural produce, and these clarify which products were used within the farm itself and which were marketed (the latter ones are broken down also by purchasers).

At the same time, the calculation of the block relating to primary inputs, i.e., that of income distribution among the various agricultural activities, is highly problematical. There are many debated questions, among others, whether only crop growing should be debited with the land tax or animal husbandry should have a share too and how the wages (or the incomes of cooperative members) could be differentiated according to the various agricultural activities. We could obtain a more satisfying picture if the calculation of production costs became more general and more reliable also in the farming cooperatives. What is more, there is almost nothing to rely on when we want to separate the incomes of small-scale producing units (household plots and individually owned small farms) according to the various agricultural activities. We have divided the "wage-type incomes" of these small units according to the inputs of work-days but even the distribution of the latter was obtained by calculation.

Finally, there is the problem as to how many agricultural activities should be distinguished and what criteria should serve for their delimitation. Agriculture produces a very large number of goods, which have to be aggregated into groups in order to ensure the manageability of the input–output table. Our table for the year 1959 divided agriculture into thirty-three sectors; the 1968 table contained twenty six; in the table planned for 1972, only fifteen sectors will be distinguished.

The forming of groups or sectors may be done in view of several considerations: according to the purposes of final use, the methods of cultivation, the botanical and zoological classification of crops and animals, or by the classification of a "product list" applied for various administrative purposes, etc.

We tried to choose the classification that seemed most suitable to determine inputs unequivocally both in the already compiled input–output tables and in those which have only been planned. Our sectors include such items as bread grain, grain for fodder, raw fodder, vegetables, fruits, etc., or in animal husbandry: cattle, pigs, poultry, etc. Also certain technical considerations recommended this kind of classification. For instance, it is easier to assess the inputs of "cattle-breeding" as a whole than to divide them between the activities producing beef-cattle and milk. We consider this type of classification to be justified also by economic considerations, however, this does not exclude the possibility of applying other classifications when some special purpose has to be served.

When taking decisions on the grouping of agricultural products and activities, one has to bear in mind that not only production but also certain "complementary" data must be divided in the same manner (e.g., the output per work-days and fixed assets, etc.). If our classification is overelaborated, the division of such complementary data will likely raise additional problems.

THE RELATIVE PROPORTIONS OF SOCIAL SECTORS IN AGRICULTURE

Except for agriculture, the state-owned sector represents the predominating, characteristic socio-economic formation in all branches of Hungary's economy. In agriculture, cooperatives constitute the bulk of large-scale units and, within the whole of agriculture, a substantial role is still played by small units (household plots worked by members of farming cooperatives and "auxiliary farms" belonging to people employed in other branches of the national economy). The farming methods, the systems of accountancy and the forms of income distribution are different in the various social sectors, and this makes it difficult to apply the general principles consistently in our calculations.

It has already been indicated that accountancy and statistical practice are different in the state-owned and the cooperative farms, although there is a certain tendency towards uniformization. As regards the small farming units, there is no accountancy; the statistical surveys that are taken are irregular and cover different spheres like production patterns, the structure of inputs and outputs. Moreover, the forms of income distribution, the proportions between consumption and accumulation and even the producer prices are different in the three social sectors of agriculture.

Therefore, apart from the data of agricultural statistics, we must resort to several other sources in order to make our calculations more reliable, e.g., to household budget surveys, to the data of free-market turnover, to investment statistics and to the statistics of sales prices. This means that a whole set of preliminary calculations have to be performed before drawing up an input–output table. The most important data have to be grouped according to social sectors and checkings or economic estimates have to be performed in other cases.

The question emerges at this point whether it is possible to characterize agricultural inputs and outputs by the data of its largest socialist sector (i.e., farming cooperatives). In our opinion the particularities of each social sector are so different that none of them could give a realistic picture about the relations prevailing in agriculture as a whole. Of course, a single social sector may be analysed separately.

As a result of the different particularities of the social sectors, agricultural input–output tables are very labour consuming, in particular when current prices (varying by sectors) are to be applied. This is one of the reasons why we do not compile them for each year.

THE ROLE OF CENTRAL PURCHASES AND OF DISTRIBUTING TRADE IN AGRICULTURAL INPUTS AND OUTPUTS

Agricultural farms in general hardly have any direct relations with industry, except the food industry. Part of the products sold by agriculture arrives at other productive branches and the population through the central purchasing organizations as intermediators, the rest is sold directly to the population. The means of production are sold to agriculture by various trading enterprises. This intermediary role of trade has not been represented in our tables of agriculture. Only the price margin of the products purchased from or sold to agriculture figures in the sector of trade.

Let us deal briefly with producer prices in agriculture. Agriculture sells its products through several channels. Accordingly, the same product may have different sales prices simultaneously. Even the state-owned purchasing organizations may pay different prices, according to whether the product is bought under a contract at a previously fixed price or without a contract. The price of the same product sold on the "free market" may again be different. Finally, there are "accounting prices" for stating the value of the products used within the farm itself and the changes in stocks.

Since the balance must reflect the actual process of realization, all actual prices have to be taken into consideration when calculating the various input and output items. For instance, the production of wool and certain other goods is subsidized by the state. In such cases, agriculture provides a value higher than what will figure in the costs of the processing industry. There are also examples of the inverse case, e.g., the price of petrol and diesel oil paid by agriculture is, as a result of subsidization, lower than the industrial producer price. Also, the prices of exported goods are problematic, since these are different in the bookkeeping of agricultural units and in the foreign trade contracts. Another problem is connected with the valuation of consumption in kind, i.e., of goods produced by the farms and consumed by people employed there. This part of production has to be valuated at producer prices. But since the food consumed by the rest of the population is valued at retail prices, the share of consumption of goods received in kind within the total, as well as the total itself, is underestimated.

The clearing up of such problems is necessary for the subsequent analysis of the input–output table. Therefore, it is important to improve our next tables by providing a "matrix of price margins" which will reveal the extent and the causes (e.g., state subsidy or other external factors) of the differences between the prices received by the suppliers and those paid by the consumers.

INPUT-OUTPUT TABLES AS A NEW SOURCE FOR ANALYSING THE FOOD ECONOMY*

by

PÉTER SZERDAHELYI and GÁBOR UDOVECZ

THE INFORMATION BASIS OF THE FOOD ECONOMY

The economic reform, the new system of management, introduced in our country, which includes an increased utilization of economic regulators serving the indirect control of production and consumption, had an important side effect, namely, an increased demand for information. Both the producing units and the controlling authorities wanted more data; the former about the "market" situation and the profitability of their production, the latter about the effects exercised by the indirect regulators, i.e., about the behaviour of the producers. The preliminaries of economic decisions and the estimates on their expectable effects require information of an ever increasing diversity in every field, and the food economy is no exception.

The inclusion of the whole of the "food economy" into a system subjected to uniform control and management involved several difficulties just in this respect. It is not easy to satisfy this "craving for information". In our field, primary information obtainable from the various units of production is necessarily heterogeneous, since the character of agriculture, as a producer of basic food materials, widely differs from that of the processing industries in respect to both technology and organization. This relates to all measures, regardless of their being expressed in physical units or monetary terms. The controlling organs of the food economy can use the primary data supplied by the producing units only for analysing the activities directly concerned. As regards the whole of the production process which consists of several vertical stages, information can only be obtained from a further analysis of the primary data. In other words, the central authorities, in the first place the Ministry of Food and Agriculture, must rely on "secondary information". The analysis of economic phenomena on a nation-wide level requires a certain uniformity of the measures relating to the various agricultural and industrial fields within the food economy; in many cases, their comparability with the measures relating to the other productive branches of the national economy must also be ensured. This requirement has to be particularly emphasized when plans covering the whole of the food economy are to be drawn up. For such purposes, a very substantial body of information may be provided by the combined input–output table of the whole food economy.

This input–output table supplies highly useful information, first of all by creating a uniform or quasi-uniform accounting system for the vertically connected sectors. Further, the associated mathematical apparatus is an up-to-date means

* Agriculture and food industry combined.

of economic analysis. Even though the possibilities offered by mathematical methods are not as yet wholly exhausted by our researches, it is beyond doubt that computations and analyses of this new type may substantially help the experts who deal with the central control of the food economy. This fact is also expressed by the decision of the ministry that input–output tables are to be drawn up periodically, in order to provide this new type of information.

THE 1968 INPUT–OUTPUT TABLE OF THE FOOD ECONOMY

a) STRUCTURE OF THE TABLE

The Centre for Statistics and Economic Analysis of the Ministry of Food and Agriculture started to compile input–output tables at a time when there was no previous experience to go by. The first crucial problem was to define the sectors. Regarding the number of sectors, "maximalist" requirements were advocated both by those wishing to utilize the table and by some experts. At the same time, there was a severe limitation to desaggregation, due to the lack of certain data and to the uncertainty of the experts' estimates which were used instead. In this preparatory stage of our work, we had to take into consideration the sector nomenclature applied in the economy-wide input–output table compiled by the Central Statistical Office. In particular, we were obliged to retain the nomenclature of the sectors outside the food economy.

In the end, our input–output table of the food economy included 26 sectors for agriculture and 14 sectors for the food-processing industries. We were given a free hand to classify agricultural production but, as regards the processing industries, we had to apply the classification used in the table of the Central Statistical Office. Some of the activities relating to the rest of the national economy, shown in the economy-wide table, are represented in our table in an aggregated form, while others were divided according to their importance for the supply of agriculture or the food-processing industries or for the utilization of agricultural products and food. These shares had to be estimated on the grounds of the economy-wide input–output table in which agriculture was only globally represented. Finally, 35 sectors not belonging to the food economy were included in our table.

It is a particular feature of our table that the consumption by the peasantry is shown separately within final use and that a separate table was constructed to show the non-agricultural activities pursued by agricultural farms.

b) THE DATA USED IN THE TABLE

The input–output table of the "food economy" was elaborated simultaneously with the economy-wide table of the Central Statistical Office. Substantial work was additionally required for classifying the outputs and inputs of agriculture according to the special structure of our table. This work was successfully performed by the experts of the agricultural department of the Central Statistical Office. Thus, one of the basic conditions of our future work with input–output tables is to do it in close coordination and cooperation with the Central Statistical Office, as this entails substantial savings of energy at almost every stage of calculation.

ECONOMIC ANALYSES RELYING ON THE INPUT–OUTPUT TABLE

The compilation of a detailed input–output table of the food economy relating to 1968 allowed us to undertake certain macro-economic analyses that could not have been performed otherwise. It became possible to reveal the interconnections of the "food economy' with the rest of the national economy, as well as those existing within the food economy (e.g. between the production of basic materials and their processing). Further, it was also possible to analyse vertical integrations within the food economy and to calculate and interpret the relative indices of direct and cumulated wages and depreciation.

Investigations based on our input–output table helped to reveal many particular features of interindustry relations which were either not known or not proven numerically before. In the following, we shall present some of the important findings of these investigations.

a) EXTERNAL RELATIONS OF THE FOOD ECONOMY

Agriculture and food industry are known to be branches complementing each other, the former supplying the basic materials processed by the latter. Thus, the activities of the food economy may be clearly delimited from other economic activity. They represent more or less "closed" production cycles in so far as their products are only insignificantly used by other productive branches. Apart from internal use, their production mostly serves the purposes of final consumption either by the population or for export.

Also, the input relations of the food economy are of a particular nature. The food industry purchases 69 per cent of its home-produced inputs from domestic agriculture. Hungary's agriculture relies extensively upon purchases from external (mainly industrial) sectors. Thus, the food economy is "open" when considered in respect to agriculture, that is, the effect of other economic branches on food production is expected through the branch where basic materials are produced, viz. through agriculture. Accordingly, most tasks of increasing and improving food production fall on industry. Since in the past the supply to the food economy of up-to-date equipment and materials did not receive sufficient emphasis among the development objectives of industry, a certain structural change seems necessary for this purpose; more exactly, the development of production in certain industries must be brought into harmony with the needs of agriculture.

Imports by the food economy are relatively low. They consist mainly of machinery for agriculture, and raw materials for the food industry that cannot be produced, or not efficiently, by domestic agriculture. But the bulk of imports needed by the food industry belongs to the first group, consisting of industrial products. Most of these serve the purposes of crop growing. In 1968, about 30 per cent of the industrial products needed by the food economy were such which could only be purchased from abroad.

b) INTERRELATIONSHIPS WITHIN THE FOOD ECONOMY

The relationship between agriculture and the food industry may be considered as the basic condition for creating vertical cooperation. The relations among the vertically connected sectors are the closest and the probability of building up integrated organizations among them is the highest, where the extent of their interrelations is the greatest.

In some vertical production chains within the food economy, these interrelations are very close. In many of them, 80–90 per cent of the output (serving intermediate inputs) released by a material-producing sector are sold to a single processing sector. On the other hand, with but a few exceptions, any processing sector of the food industry gets about 80 per cent of its material inputs from agriculture.

Another feature of the relationships within food industry is that they are unidirectional. There is practically no feedback from the processing sectors to the material-producing ones. This is due partly to the nature of the activities in question and partly to the present low level of vertical cooperation.

The close ties within the food economy are also reflected in the high proportion of intra-sector relations, i.e., of outputs which are used within the very same sector where they were produced. This proportion amounts to about 30–40 per cent of the gross output of agriculture.

c) ENGAGEMENT OF ASSETS IN THE FOOD ECONOMY

In 1968, the food economy produced nearly 30 per cent of the gross output, while it engaged only 22 per cent of the assets of the productive sectors. In other words, the relative capital intensity of the food economy was lower than the average of the productive sphere. (It is practically equal to that of the total industry without the food industry.) However, the 63 per cent share of fixed assets in the food industry within the sum of both fixed and working assets is much lower than the figure valid for the whole industry (78 per cent).

When comparing the relative amounts of (fixed and working) assets engaged in the material-producing sectors of the food economy and in its processing sectors with the analogous two groups of industry, it turns out that in both groups the measures are lower in the food economy. The fact that, in spite of this, the average measure of the food economy is practically equal to that of the whole industry is due to the food economy's higher share in the production of more capital-intensive materials.

Taken by sectors, the amounts of fixed and working assets engaged for producing one hundred *forints* worth of output vary rather greatly, despite the fact that the two main groups of agricultural production, crop growing and animal husbandry, show almost identical measures. Within these main groups, however, there is considerable dispersion. In general, the highest measures occur in the sectors where production is carried on at deficits or is bringing very low rates of net income.

As regards the food industry, on the average the sectors which process the products of crop growing employ about 2.5 times as much of fixed and working assets for producing a unit of output than the sectors which process animal products. Therefore, the amount of additional investment required for developing the various branches of the food industry may differ enormously.

The conspicuously low capital intensity of the branches of processing animal products may be illustrated by the fact that, for instance, in 1968 the meat industry engaged only Ft 17 worth of fixed assets and Ft 10 of working assets per Ft 100 of production value. This phenomenon deserves particular attention because one of the major objectives of the present economic policy consists in developing meat production. Thus, even with substantial further investments, the meat industry would be far from becoming a capital-intensive branch.

d) MEASURES OF DIRECT AND CUMULATED INPUTS

The measures of cumulated inputs, computed with input–output techniques, show at an economy-wide level the value of materials, equipment, live labour, etc. used in the various phases of production. That is, they show the numerical value of not only the inputs directly occurring in a certain phase of production (represented in the table by some given sector), but also those which were made in other sectors in order to ensure production in the sector in question; in other words, all of the efforts that had to be made by the national economy for creating a certain kind of output. In this sense, they represent a novel type of information which, in combination with the indices of direct inputs, allow the activities performed by the various sectors in a vertical chain of production to be appraised from two different aspects.

As regards the input of materials both direct and cumulated, the processing branches are more material consuming than those producing the basic materials. The share of home-produced materials (related to the value of gross output) is highest in the industries processing animal products (meat, milk, poultry, eggs, etc.) and the next highest shares occur in the canning and baking industries. In agriculture, it is only cattle-breeding that shows a value exceeding the average measures of both direct and cumulated material inputs.

It is remarkable that the relative difference between cumulated and direct material inputs is higher in agriculture than in the food industry. It follows that plans aimed at extending agricultural production (when assessing only the direct inputs required for the extension) will be less accurate than they were in the former case.

The cumulated inputs of industrial products used by the food economy are, in most sectors of the table, proportional to the cumulated inputs of all home products. The difference between direct and cumulated inputs is remarkable in the case of industries processing milk and poultry, in the baking industries, in agriculture, and in the case of cattle breeding. These branches show measures lower than the average as regards direct inputs of industrial products whereas, concerning the cumulated inputs of these products, their measures are higher than average.

In view of the shortage of investment resources, it is highly important to know the total amount of fixed assets which is necessary for the extension of a given sector. In other words, we have to state the cumulated capital intensity of the various activities.

According to our calculations carried out on a national economic level, the additional amount of fixed assets required for the planned growth of a given processing sector is several times greater than what is directly required within the sector itself. The major part of the cumulated investment is needed in the sector or sectors which produce the basic material. For example, the wine, milk and canning industries belong to the most capital-intensive branches of the food industry, although their "direct" capital intensity is average or even lower. The difference is due to the very high capital intensity of the branches supplying materials.

Our computations regarding the cumulated engagement of fixed assets show that, from the total of fixed assets ensuring the final output of the food industry, 73 per cent was employed in "foreign" sectors, mostly in agriculture. In the case of some sectors of the food industry practically all these "external" fixed assets belong to a single sector of agriculture.

Consequently, the coordination of the production and processing of materials in the food economy could — and should — take place already at the time when investment decisions are made.

The food economy is relatively labour intensive due mostly to agriculture. About 90 per cent of the cumulated labour-inputs of agriculture are covered internally. At the same time, agriculture greatly contributes to the cumulated labour inputs of other branches too. For instance, 39 per cent of the cumulated labour inputs in the final consumption, and 32 per cent of those in the export production are of agricultural origin.

The danger of "inaccuracy" mentioned in connection with material inputs does not occur in the case of labour inputs, as most of these are provided within the sector in question. Yet, when the extension of a branch of the food industry is planned, the increase in labour inputs needed in the branch supplying the material for processing should be considered. This may require ten times as much labour input in the sector producing the basic material than what is needed in the processing sector. Therefore, development plans must take into consideration the increase of labour inputs in the sectors which produce the materials.

SOME IDEAS ABOUT THE USE OF INPUT–OUTPUT TABLES

A further development of our work with input–output tables requires efforts to be made in the following directions.

1. It is possible and necessary to extend the utilization of information obtainable from input–output research; this is understood to mean a more extensive use of up-to-date computation techniques (programming, equilibrium analyses, medium-term forecasts, etc.).

2. A requirement voiced by many experts is aimed at an additional refinement (desaggregation) of sector classification, regarding both the food economy itself and its related "foreign" sectors. This highly justified requirement will have to be reckoned with in the future, the more so since the central and intermediary controlling agencies are increasingly specialized and the people working there obviously strive for creating a special system of information.

3. Some of our ideas aim to promote the development of such a system of information that would permit the progress of the food economy and its interrelationships to be observed. That is to say, input–output tables based on the same principles will have to be drawn up within certain periods.

INPUT-OUTPUT TABLES RELATING TO SOCIALIST FARMING UNITS

by

LORÁND NAGY

Socialism creates favourable conditions for operating production units, but at the same time it requires that they be examined from a national economic aspect. Meanwhile, however, motivation in production, i.e., personal incentives and profitable enterprise production, also have to be asserted. Recent developments in economic research and analysis have contributed considerably to the possibility of satisfying both requirements and revealing the laws and interrelations within the economy.

One of the methods recently introduced for this purpose consists in compiling input–output tables relating to the *individual units* of production.

Formerly, input–output tables were drawn up mainly on a national level, to reveal the interrelations between the productive branches.

The idea to compile input–output tables for individual farms, too, primarily arose due to the subtle interrelations among the diverse productive processes within agricultural farms (a fact well known to practical experts, yet only insufficiently systematized so far).

THE SIGNIFICANCE AND PRACTICAL USEFULNESS OF INPUT–OUTPUT TABLES

An input–output table relating to a farm gives answers or at least suggests possible solutions to almost every economic problem arising on a farm. Its uses and main advantages consist of the following.

Showing the interbranch* relations of all inputs and outputs, it reviews in a single table all the economic activities performed. Thus, farming is broken down to its elementary activities, any of which can be examined either statically or dynamically by tracing the elements from the very beginning up to the output of the final product. This is a very great advantage of an input–output table over traditional accounts.

It shows the share of the various elements in the total of inputs and outputs.

It states the cost level of each branch, and the share of the various cost elements within it.

* In this paper, the term "branch" is understood to mean a distinct kind of agricultura activity, like wheat growing, milk production, etc.

It shows the profitability of the individual branches as well as their contribution to the profits of the farm as a whole.

It reveals the amounts of intermediate inputs and shows how these change during the production process. The degree of efficiency with which a product is transformed into another, or labour input into products, is also clarified by the input–output table. This analysis is highly important for the correct appraisal of farming activities not only on a branch level but also from the aspect of the national economy as a whole. Thus, besides providing material for further economic analysis, it provides a basis for checking both the efficiency of agriculture and the adquateness of prices.

Further, it shows how cultivated land, the most important factor of agricultural production, is utilized and with what degree of efficiency. By assuming that the land used for various purposes represents the inputs of this factor, it is possible to separate those parts of the land which serve for the output of marketable products, for fodder (to be used within the farm but realized through the products of animal husbandry), or for other internal purposes of the farm. It is the proportion between costs and yields that characterizes the efficiency of land use.

Such an analysis helps to develop the right proportions in land use, in order to improve farm profitability (e.g., how much of the land should be utilized for directly marketable products and how much for the internally used ones).

An input–output table reflects the interrelations between a given farm and the rest of the national economy. The farm's purchases and sales can be shown not only in their entirety but also according to the various branches of farming activity, and so the national economic performance of each branch can be stated separately.

Furthermore, an input–output table is also suitable for examining the way in which labour input has been used, as the proportion between labour input and capital formation in each branch of farming can be easily stated. As a result, labour management on a farm can be judged from the national viewpoint as well.

Part or the whole of the labour input performed on a farm is usually transformed into capital within the farm itself. This process can be followed in every branch of farming. Obviously, the degree of its efficiency is relevant not only to the producing unit but to the whole national economy as well.

The data, expressed in terms of value, which characterize the interrelations of the branches as well as their effects on each other and on the national economy, can only be evaluated correctly if the data of the related physical units are also provided. These obviously necessary data can be found in farm accounts or farm statistics. Research on farming operations can only succed if we are able to relate the economic phenomena to both the physical and the biological factors. These interrelations are very complicated and difficult to show. Input–output tables are very useful here, as they help to understand the hidden *causal relations*. To achieve further results, these analyses may be complemented with mathematical methods, which can be applied easily in the case of input–output tables.

THE STRUCTURE OF THE INPUT–OUTPUT TABLE

Our analytical methods were built up according to the principles of the usual input–output tables. We aimed to present the production processes in agricultural farms, to express the exchanges in terms of value, and to interpret them from an economic point of view.

The data for our input–output table were taken from the bookkeeping (including appendices) of the farms as well as from their statistical accounts. Although we were able to find all the necessary data, they were sometimes grouped in a way unsuitable for our purposes. If the bookkeeping vouchers and the statistical accounts had been originally grouped in a way directly applicable to our analyses, the compilation of our input–output table would have required much less work.

The main condition for analysing farm activities correctly is that the data expressed in terms of value should be consistent with those accounted in physical units. In other words, the data expressed in physical units should be available (for each branch) in a breakdown so as to express the efficiency of use and transformation of the various material inputs; at the same time, the data expressed in terms of value should reflect the same efficiency from an economic point of view.

The set-up and the contents of farm balances of inputs and outputs necessarily differ according to the character of the farm examined, only the principles are invariable. This character of the accounts permits analysing the activities of each farm in due consideration of their particular features.

The following are all presented in one table (given at the end of this paper): intermediate flows of products between the branches, the purchases and sales from and to the rest of the national economy, including also those connected with the non-agricultural activities pursued by the farm, and the investments made in the given year.

The table shows the yields by branches. These represent cumulated yields, including the values of products both sold and used internally for current production or investment. The major part of the cumulated yields is used (or consumed) internally. The realized outputs consist partly of sales and partly of the net increase of stocks. With this grouping, double accounting is eliminated.

Inputs, made from own or purchased products, are also broken down by branches. They also appear in a cumulated form, but double accounting can again be eliminated. The final sums of the yields and the inputs show their proportions by branches.

The use of labour input and capital (materials and equipment) is shown separately, so that input whose conversion into capital has taken place on the farm itself might be segregated from the rest. In this way, the total amount of live labour used on the farm can also be shown by branches.

THE ANALYSIS

An input–output table in itself is simply the systematical review of the production processes, but the analysis of its data is another task.

Our table permits various analyses. We cannot enumerate here all the possibilities, as the questions to be answered by the analysis vary according to the particular features of each farm.

The widest field of farm production to be analysed consists in revealing the agronomic problems hidden behind the value figures and in stating how the various physical quantities have been produced and used. Here the indices of efficiency are combined with those of profitability.

We have also calculated the amount of fodder consumed by the various branches of animal husbandry, and the ratios at which each kind of fodder was converted into other animal products. Starting from the production costs and the yields, we have ranked the fodder cultures, and calculated their substitution coefficients as well as their relative values. Relying on these findings, every farm may check the efficiency of its fodder cultures, its feeding schemes and, in general, the technologies applied in its animal husbandry.

Our table clearly reflects the relationships between crop growing and animal husbandry. Unlike traditional bookkeeping methods, it shows not only the total material consumption, but also the shares, expressed in terms of value, of various plant cultures through which they contribute to animal husbandry.

The table also clarifies the interrelations between the agricultural and non-agricultural activities pursued on a farm. The output value and the cost structure of each non-agricultural activity are shown too.

In order to make comparisons between various farms, or to evaluate the activity of a farm during a certain period, the input and the output data may be converted to per-hectare quantities and values, or they may be related to product units of animal husbandry. Such calculations open the way for more thorough analyses.

There are still many further fields which can be analysed. For instance, we have compared cumulated and non-cumulated production as well as net income, and separated the costs according to the major cost groups.

Another calculation by which we expressed the production costs in the quantities of the product itself also deserves attention; in other words, we have stated the percentage of each product which was needed to cover its own production costs at current prices.

Efficiency investigations are made to decide whether it is on the input or the output side where the activities of the various branches of a given farm should be improved. If such an examination shows that a given branch is operated more or less efficiently, yet its profits are insufficient, then the adequateness of the prices has to be questioned. In this case, the input–output table can be used as a model for estimating the expectable effects of a suggested price change.

The main advantage of input–output tables relating to individual farms consists in the availability of all the data in a single table, so that any kind of analysis can be carried out if needed. When the data are systematically registered in this form, analyses and case studies require much less work than they would if the necessary figures had to be collected for each case from the bookkeeping accounts.

Let us add that analyses based on input–output tables also permit us to examine and appraise to economic activity of each farm as a separate unit, as well as to measure its progress in the course of years.

Relying on the analysis of input–output data, it would also be possible to choose "representative" farms for each agricultural region of the country, in order to reveal the special requirements and possibilities of regional development.

THE INPUT–OUTPUT TABLE OF THE METALLURGICAL AND ENGINEERING INDUSTRIES

by

ZSIGMOND KOSTYÁL

Since about 1960 the various organs of economic control and management have increasingly urged the creation of a method that would make it possible to review and analyse the external and internal relationships as well as the mutual effects in the field of metallurgy and engineering, as regards both economic accounting and planning. These industries consist of very heterogeneous branches, the internal and external relations of which are highly complicated due to efforts aiming to save labour inputs by rational specialization and interenterprise cooperation.

The exposition, analysis and appraisal of the production relations with the aid of a very detailed input–output table seemed desirable for several reasons.

a) It is possible to do a comparative analysis of branch activities, eliminating the distorting effects caused by differences in the verticality of production.

b) With such an analysis and by measuring the indirect effects, it is possible to forecast and estimate the expectable consequences of decisions which aim to change the structure of the branches.

c) Checking the consistency of medium-term plans becomes possible (as regards both the internal proportions of the various outputs and the use of fixed assets and materials).

d) The possibilities and the efficiency of interenterprise cooperation can be analysed.

e) It is possible to assess the outputs of individual products, product groups, components, etc., and also the interindustry relationships required for their output.

f) By considering every important effect, it is possible to forecast the expectable efficiency of a decision on development as well as to tell what complementary development measures will be required.

g) Long-term plans for large enterprises can be developed — or checked — on the basis of the most important economy-wide indices.

When we started our work in 1966, we could only guess the significance of the above-mentioned fields of analysis and planning. Since then, the new system of economic control and management introduced in 1968 has confirmed the necessity of preparing a detailed input–output table for metallurgy and engineering, which can help in solving the everyday tasks and problems of economic activity.

In 1966 the National Board for Technological Progress commissioned a working team to investigate the possibilities of drawing up an input–output table for the metallurgical and engineering industries. On the recommendation of this team, the Ministry of Metallurgy and Engineering ordered the table to be drawn up for all fields under its supervision.

The team proposed that the sectors should be built up according to the nature of the activity of each economic unit, rather than according to their organizational affiliations, that the table should be based on an open and static model and should be drawn up on the basis of input data, and further, that it should be closely connected to national accounts (balances). Moreover, the proposed nomenclature of the sectors was also elaborated. According to this, the sectors contained product groups which covered all the products and activities of metallurgy and engineering. There were 81 groups of products in the sphere of the engineering industries and 14 groups of metallurgical products. The rest of the national economy was represented by a further 18 sectors, that is, aggregates different from those in the national accounts were used. Thus, the total number of sectors amounted to 113.

On the recommendation of the National Board for Technological Progress, the Ministry of Metallurgy and Engineering started to organize the supply of data. Later on, this system was revised in accordance with the new circumstances created by the reform of economic control and management. Preparatory work required the solution of many problems, most of which were caused by the fact that the necessary data had to be taken from the enterprise's annual balance-sheets where they were shown in the form of aggregates. These data had to be broken down according to the product groups figuring in our nomenclature (in the case of some enterprises, it means 8–10 product groups). Supplying some other data not directly related to the input–output table had to be organized (e.g., employment by groups of workers and employees; work-hours performed; average annual value of fixed and working assets, etc.). Moreover, since the table was intended to be used to assess foreign-trade efficiency too, the values of exports and imports had to be shown also in foreign currencies, e.g., roubles or dollars.

In the stage of revising the data-collecting system (made necessary by the economic reform), it became clear that the amount of work to be done needed a specialized institute. Thus, the Institute for Industrial Economics and Business Organization was commissioned to collect, revise and process the data. When, in late 1970, the detailed input–output table was ready, the same Institute was asked to make some analytic studies about the table. The first volumes of this work have already been published.

*

We are going to mention here some problems that emerged in the course of compiling the table.

It had to reveal the interrelations both within the sectors of this industry and with the rest of the national economy. Therefore, the sectors have been grouped according to activities — i.e., possibly homogeneous "product groups" — rather than according to the organization principle. As a result, in the case of individual enterprises many of the interrelations got lost, as some of the products are used within the enterprise.

The manufacturing of diesel engines may be mentioned as an example. It was important to know the total output and the total input of this line of production, its relationships with the users and the suppliers, and so on. However, enterprise bookkeeping shows separately only the data of those engines which have been sold. So, a special solution had to be found to cover the total production of engines.

The manufacturing of nuts and bolts, a problem still present, is another good example. Since most of our enterprises manufacture these products for their own use, their production does not appear in the accounts.

According to the prescriptions for supplying the data in the case of a product or product group appearing as a separate sector in the input–output table, not only the products sold by the enterprise but also those used within it had to be reported as "final products". Furthermore, whereas in the bookkeeping accounts the latter is generally evaluated on the basis of "direct production costs", for the purposes of our input–output table they had to be evaluated at a "calculated price", obtained by adding a proportionate part of "indivisible costs" and profits to the direct costs. This method resulted in some double accounting, but it could be eliminated at both the enterprise and the product level on the basis of data obtained from a questionnaire.

A special case of this problem emerged, for example, when an enterprise manufactured some "semi-finished product" which it used in the production of the *same* sector into which this semi-finished product belonged (e.g., cog-wheels built into a driving gear).

In this case, the cost structure in the input–output table had to be modified, and so the wages, other costs, profits, etc. calculated for the semi-finished product figured as "costs of material" of the final product.

We wish to emphasize that the necessity of applying this method was due to our classification by *activities* and not by *organizations*, since the table was expected to provide data relating to, e.g., the amount of screws manufactured and the product groups for which they were used, or the amount of cogwheels used by the various sectors (products), and so on.

When forming the sector nomenclature, it was an important requirement that the products belonging to a given sector should represent a homogeneous, or nearly homogeneous, group from the point of view of production technology. However, the input structure of the sectors had to be similar too, in order to enable us to draw some conclusions valid for the sector as a whole, particularly as regards its inputs. Hence, both technical and economic considerations had to be taken into account when forming the nomenclature.

As it was not possible to collect data covering all activities in the metallurgical and engineering industries, in many fields we had to rely on sample surveys. The data thus obtained were then modified to match the figures in the national input–output table compiled by the Central Statistical Office for the year 1968.

The checking of the collected data was laborious, for the data were supplied by 211 state-owned enterprises and by the National Association of Industrial Cooperatives (with regard to industrial cooperatives). The checking of data was done in several steps. The main data (sales value by enterprises, costs, total output, employment, etc.) had to be collated with the annual statistics reports and then the sector data, obtained by generalizing the samples, had to be made consistent with those in the national input–output table of the Central Statistical Office. The next step was the regrouping of activities according to our nomenclature. Finally, after having cross-checked the marginal values, the breakdown of sector data by product groups was controlled relying on the logical interrelationships contained in the questionnaire. This was followed by the correction of the incidental inaccuracies.

A special problem emerged from the fact that our table had been constructed from the side of inputs. Namely, only a part of the enterprises and cooperatives belonging to the metallurgical and engineering industries supplied data, and the engineering activities of the trading enterprises could not be included; the data collected on the sales of the enterprises could only be used as points of orientation. Therefore, we had to collate the data of the Central Statistical Office relating to the inputs of metallurgical and engineering activities of non-metallurgical and non-engineering enterprises with those which we obtained from the enterprises, and in this way it became possible to give useful estimates for the purposes of our input–output table. The input data of the Central Statistical Office told us about the amount of inputs originating from metallurgy or engineering. By comparing these data with the value of sales of metallurgy and engineering received from the rest of the national economy, we were able to form a picture about the sales structure of our industries. Similar corrections had to be carried out with regard to the inputs of metallurgy and engineering purchased from the rest of the national economy.

The input–output table of imports was drawn up in a combinative way, for our enterprises could not supply all the information needed. Their data had to be complemented by those provided by the Ministry of Foreign Trade and by the trading enterprises, in order to allow us to carry out the necessary corrections.

When analysing and utilizing the data in our table, especially when comparing the various product groups, it has to be taken into account that due to the sector nomenclature we used, the size of the sectors varies greatly.

The first input–output table of metallurgy and engineering is to be considered as an experiment. Some of the problems arising from the particularities of our industries seem to have been solved, while others, e.g., those connected with the accounting of imports or with the different sizes of the sectors, require further research. Nevertheless, elaboration of this first table may be considered successful.

The question arises whether the interdependencies revealed by the 1968 table as well as the conclusions that may be drawn from them remained valid for the subsequent 3–4 years.

As regards the totality of these industries — and even their major subgroups — the answer is in the affirmative. However, as regards smaller units, individual products or product groups, particularly when decisive changes in technology were introduced in the meantime, the conclusions must be subject to certain reservations. Nevertheless, in the period which has elapsed since 1968, no such changes have occurred that will hinder the utilization of information or lead to a false orientation.

Our results are published piecemeal; each publication relates to a selected point of view and contains both texts and complementary computations. So far the following five studies have been planned:

1. Providing a general view about the themes that can be analysed on the basis of the input–output table as well as carrying out some large-scale analyses.

2. A detailed analysis of the production relations in the metallurgical and engineering industries (their internal cooperation, their connections with the rest of the national economy, the degree of the concentration of these relations, etc.).

3. Study of demand for intermediate inputs and the capital intensity of these industries, the proportions between their inputs and outputs, outputs and employment, wages, imports, etc.

4. The relationships of these industries as regards final demand.

5. Their foreign-trade relationships (interdependencies between exports and imports; efficiency of exports, etc.).

Even our first table has inspired various ideas about its utilization, especially in the field of planning.

Such was, for instance, the checking of the consistency between the interdependencies obtained for 1968 and the growth rates planned up to 1975. This is especially important, for in this way it is possible to correct some mistakes in coordination at the beginning of the Fourth Five-Year Plan (1971–1975).

Relying on these studies, it becomes possible to compute the most important technological coefficients (at both branch and enterprise levels). It turned out, for example, that in the case of most sectors the decisive part of the inputs of materials — frequently 70 to 80 per cent — is supplied by fewer than 10 sectors. The conclusion drawn from such calculations may help to eliminate the shortages in certain materials.

The usefulness of our table as a tool for supporting efficiency computations and assessing the coordination requirements of any development conception can hardly be overestimated.

Since we have elaborated our tables in two versions (according to the different ways imports are accounted), it is possible to carry out analyses with regard to the anticipated effects of structural changes in every field and stage of production — including the amounts of the means of production and labour that will be released or additionally needed, the changes in national income, etc. Thereby opportunities are open for a selective policy of industrial development in the sphere of the metallurgical and engineering industries.

Finally, the table also enables us to calculate the efficiency of the structure of production and of exports, the amount and structure of necessary imports, the expectable effects of price measures, etc. All these computations are highly important in our present economic situation. The input–output table of the metallurgical and engineering industries can only provide the basic data for such calculations, but it certainly creates a strong incentive for such research by the simple fact that it makes the essential data available.

THE SPHERE OF TURNOVER IN INPUT-OUTPUT TABLES

by

PÉTER SZIKLA

Input–output tables are used most frequently for stating the technological coefficients of production. The analysis of these coefficients needs the so-called "production" table. However, it is the relationships of turnover, i.e., direct purchases and sales between the various sectors, that appear on the "surface" of economic life.

The so-called "turnover sphere" plays an important role in the sales and purchases of the productive sectors (centralized purchase of agricultural products, the purchase and distribution of certain means of production, domestic wholesale trade and foreign trade). When constructing an input–output table of the production type, the turnover sphere is disregarded, as if the products were sold by the producer directly to the consumer. As the methods and techniques used for eliminating the turnover sphere are little known, the present study is going to deal with them.

It is one of the basic principles in the construction of an input–output table to approach it from two sides, if possible. In fact, we have to construct two tables; the first including the sector inputs (appearing in the columns of the inner square and of the right wing), the second containing the distribution of outputs by sectors (appearing in the rows of the inner square and of the lower wing). Thus, in the first approach every field of the inner square contains two figures, which usually differ to some extent.

Let us examine, e.g., what the a_{ij} element means in the two tables which have been constructed from the points of view of input and distribution, respectively.

Seen from the side of inputs, a_{ij} means what sector j uses from the products of the sector i, regardless of whether these have been produced domestically or imported, and whether they have been purchased directly from the producing sector or not.

Although there are statistics on the use of materials in Hungary, they show individual import items only for a few important materials, and make no distinction as to whether the material has been purchased by the processing enterprise directly from the producer or through the intermediary of a trading organization.

From the side of distribution, a_{ij} means the sum of the following items:

1. the products of sector i directly sold to sector j (direct transfers);
2. the sales of the turnover sphere of the products of sector i to sector j;
3. the amount of imported products belonging to the "production profile" of sector i, purchased by sector j;
4. the amount of products belonging to the "production profile" of sector i but used by sector j from its stocks previously purchased.

In principle, the figures relating to total inputs, on the one hand, and to the sum of the four distribution items, on the other, should be identical. When they are equal or show but a small difference, there may be assumed no failure in either principle or methodology. Small deviations may be tolerated, as they are due to the technical and methodological differences among the various statistical sources. In such cases, the input figure should be considered to be more reliable and accepted. Any larger deviation, however, indicates some error that must be cleared and corrected.

The major problems connected with the statistical sources of the items in question are as follows:

1. input data are compiled by the competent departments of the Central Statistical Office on the basis of statistics on the use of materials, according to the requirements of the input–output table;

2 data relating to direct transfers (i.e., producers selling directly to consumers) are taken from the sales statistics of the producing enterprises;

3. as regards the sales effected by the turnover sphere and the distribution of imported products, there are no statistics from which the data needed for the input–output table could be taken directly;

4. there are statistics on the use of stocks.

The two difficulties mentioned under point 3 are not equally important. Data on the distribution of sales effected by the turnover sphere are necessary when compiling the table from the side of distribution, i.e., in order to check the figures obtained from inputs. At the same time, the data relating to the distribution of imported materials are necessary for the construction of both types of the input–output table, as the table of "type B" simply cannot be compiled without them.*

The most problematical point is when the value of the sales of imported goods has to be calculated from the distribution of the turnover sphere.

A great part of the turnover sphere belongs to the activities of the enterprises trading in means of production. Many of these enterprises were founded as a result of the economic reform of 1968 and they replaced the former so-called "stockpiling enterprises". As they may be considered to be typical for the whole turnover sphere, the problems of this sphere will be presented here through examples.

In Hungary, twenty-seven such enterprises were active in 1968. Their sales amounted to Ft 75,116 million, or 12 per cent of the social product. Of this, 27,418 million were imported products, representing 37 per cent of all imports.

The distribution of total sales and, within them, that of the sales of imported goods, can be calculated in a single step. For every enterprise, an input–output table is compiled, in which the denomination of the columns and the rows are the same as those in the inner square and right wing of the economy-wide input–output table. The purchasing sectors are arranged horizontally, the producing ones vertically.

* The table of "type B" shows the amount of domestic products transferred from a sector to another; the use of imported products figures globally, in a separate row.

The statistical reports supplied by these enterprises contain only two data, namely, the total of purchases and the total of sales. Thus we know only the data of the last column and the last row of the table to be compiled. Therefore, our task is to fill in the gaps.

Below the data of an enterprise trading in leather and accessories of the shoe industry will be analysed. Among the sectors only the most relevant to this field will figure separately; the others are aggregated under the heading "other sectors".

First, the equilibrium of the balance has to be established (in million forints):

	Supply	Demand
Purchase (at producer prices)	—	1,031
Sales (at sales prices)	1,127	—
Increase in stocks (at producer prices)	20	—
Balance (price margin)	—	116
Total	1,147	1,147

The increase in stocks is due to purchases made in the year in question, so it has to be taken into account in calculating the price margin.

In our table, however, similarly to the national input–output table, all the data are considered at producer prices (i.e., gross producer prices). Since the national table shows the price margin under the heading of domestic trade, as a result of the activities of this sector, we simply neglect the price margin in our first approach.

In order to eliminate the price margin from the sales receipts, we calculate the rate of producer prices to sales prices

$$\frac{1,031}{1,147} = 0.89886,$$

and multiply the sales receipts by this coefficient. In this way, both purchases and sales will figure on the same price basis, namely, at gross producer prices.

This is a preliminary table with vacant items; the last column contains the purchases of the enterprise according to sources, while the last row represents the sums of its sales according to users.

The purchases of the enterprise from the separately shown sectors amount to 96.3 per cent of all purchases, and 94.5 per cent of its sales went to these sectors. It should be mentioned here that the enterprise's original report was broken down according to the 83 sectors which figure in the national input–output table, and that the above proportions supply a typical example for the general phenomenon that the bulk of the purchases and sales of any enterprise trading in means of production is restricted to a few sectors. Consequently, the neglect of some minor items does not affect the reliability of the information obtained from the table. (In practice, we are able to reduce the share of the "other sectors" to less than one per cent; this small value is added to the data of the biggest user or supplier.)

Table 1

The turnover table of an enterprise of the shoe industry trading in leather and accessories, 1968
(million forints)

	Knitted goods	Leather and fur	Shoes	Textile clothing	Other industries	Handicraft	Domestic trade	Other sectors	Changes in stocks	Total purchases
Aluminium metallurgy	—	—	—	—	—	—	—	—	—	13
Metal mass product industry	—	—	—	—	—	—	—	—	—	78
Organic chemistry	—	—	—	—	—	—	—	—	—	—
Rubber industry	—	—	—	—	—	—	—	—	—	102
Wood processing industry (otherwise not mentioned)	—	—	—	—	—	—	—	—	—	19
Paper industry	—	—	—	—	—	—	—	—	—	18
Cotton industry	—	—	—	—	—	—	—	—	—	259
Linen, hemp and jute industry	—	—	—	—	—	—	—	—	—	19
Wool industry	—	—	—	—	—	—	—	—	—	53
Smallware industry	—	—	—	—	—	—	—	—	—	23
Knitted fabric industry	—	—	—	—	—	—	—	—	—	30
Leather and fur industries	—	—	—	—	—	—	—	—	—	223
Shoe industry	—	—	—	—	—	—	—	—	—	89
Agriculture, forestry, water management (crop growing)	—	—	—	—	—	—	—	—	—	14
Other sectors	—	—	—	—	—	—	—	—	—	39
Imports	—	—	—	—	—	—	—	—	—	52
Total (corrected)	13	110	666	25	36	59	49	55	+18	1,031
Total (including price margin)	15	122	738	28	41	66	55	62	+20	1,147

The accounts supplied by the enterprises trading in means of production contain their purchases from agriculture, forestry and water supply in an aggregated form. In the national input–output table these three branches appear separately; moreover, agriculture is further divided into crop growing and animal husbandry and, therefore, here we must resort to an estimate.

It is obvious from the data of our enterprise that it is selling its products mainly to the shoe industry, hence, its purchases must also be in accordance with the demands of this industry.

Our enterprise does not purchase directly from agriculture, as agriculture produces neither hides (a product of the meat industry) nor leather. Further, it is not likely that it purchases significant quantities of forest products. Hence, we will not make a great mistake by accounting its relatively small purchases from "agriculture, forestry and water supply" with crop growing. We can check this estimate after the summation of the data relating to all the enterprises trading in means of production, since it will then turn out whether the sum of the four items of distribution equals the sum of inputs. If there is a significant deviation, the problematic rows in the balances of these enterprises will again be revised.

The reason for "population" figuring in the heading of column "domestic trade" in Table 1 is due to the fact that the sales of the enterprises trading in leather and accessories of the shoe industry have been transferred to the sector of population (i.e., the final user).

Table 2 differs from Table 1 in treating imports. Here, imports figure under the headings of those sectors where the various imported goods are released. To calculate this, we have used foreign-trade statistics where imports are shown according to the purchasing sectors and are detailed by product groups. However, the real picture is simplified in this way, as there is no distinction between imports coming from socialist and non-socialist countries, and neither are the import values shown in terms of foreign exchange.

Table 3 gives the distribution of imported goods which could be assessed in a simple way by calculating it on the basis of the proportions observed in the total sales of the enterprise concerned. This, however, would lead to a very rough estimate, since the distribution of imported goods is quite independent of the proportions in which the home-produced goods are distributed. The distribution of the total sales performed by these enterprises may only serve for indicating the upper limits of imports that may be expected from a sector.

When estimating the distribution of imports, we also had to consider that the enterprises in question supply essentially the shoe industry; supplying other industries or the population is not their primary task.

Let us review some of the items figuring in the column of "complementary imports" (Table 2).

Metal mass products (Ft 11 million): foreign-trade statistics show that Ft 8.5 million worth of these were "accessories for fancy-leather goods". Accordingly, we divided this import between the leather and fur industries (Ft 2 million) and the hoe industry (Ft 9 million).

s

Table 2

The turnover table of an enterprise of the shoe industry trading in leather and accessories, 1968
(million forints)

	Knitted goods	Leather and fur	Shoes	Textile clothing	Other in-dustries	Handi-craft	Do-mestic trade	Other sectors	Changes in stocks	Comple-mentary imports	Do-mestic prod-ucts	Total purchases
Aluminium metallurgy	—	—	—	—	—	—	—	—	—	—	13	13
Metal mass product in-dustry	—	—	—	—	—	—	—	—	—	11	78	89
Organic chemistry	—	—	—	—	—	—	—	—	—	11	—	11
Rubber industry	—	—	—	—	—	—	—	—	—	2	102	104
Wood processing industry (otherwise not men-tioned)	—	—	—	—	—	—	—	—	—	1	19	20
Paper industry	—	—	—	—	—	—	—	—	—	1	18	19
Cotton industry	—	—	—	—	—	—	—	—	—	1	259	260
Linen, hemp and jute industry	—	—	—	—	—	—	—	—	—	—	19	19
Wool industry	—	—	—	—	—	—	—	—	—	—	53	53
Smallware industry	—	—	—	—	—	—	—	—	—	—	23	23
Knitted fabric industry	—	—	—	—	—	—	—	—	—	—	30	30
Leather and fur industries	—	—	—	—	—	—	—	—	—	13	223	236
Shoe industry	—	—	—	—	—	—	—	—	—	—	89	89
Agriculture, forestry, water management (crop growing)	—	—	—	—	—	—	—	—	—	—	—	—
Other sectors	—	—	—	—	—	—	—	—	—	—	—	—
Crop growing	—	—	—	—	—	—	—	—	—	—	14	14
Other sectors	—	—	—	—	—	—	—	—	—	12	39	51
Total	13	110	666	25	36	58	49	55	18	52	979	1,031

Table 3

The turnover table of an enterprise of the shoe industry trading in leather and accessories, 1968
(million forints)

	Knitted goods	Leather and fur	Shoes	Textile clothing	Other in-dustries	Handi-craft	Do-mestic trade	Other sectors	Changes in stocks	Total domestic purchases	Domestic purchases and imports	Comple-mentary imports
Aluminium metallurgy	—	—	—	—	—	—	—	—	—	13	13	—
Metal mass product industry		2	9	—	—	—	—	—	—	78	89	11
Organic chemistry		2	9	—	—	—	—	—	—	—	11	11
Rubber industry	—	—	2	—	—	—	—	—	—	102	104	2
Wood processing industry (otherwise not men-tioned)	—	—	1	—	—	—	—	—	—	19	20	1
Paper industry	—	—	1	—	—	—	—	—	—	18	19	1
Cotton industry	—	—	1	—	—	—	—	—	—	259	260	1
Linen, hemp and jute industry	—	—	—	—	—	—	—	—	—	19	19	—
Wool industry	—	—	—	—	—	—	—	—	—	53	53	—
Smallware industry	—	—	—	—	—	—	—	—	—	23	23	—
Knitted fabric industry	—	—	—	—	—	—	—	—	—	30	30	—
Leather and fur industries	—	5	8	—	—	—	—	—	—	223	236	13
Shoe industry	—	—	—	—	—	—	—	—	—	89	89	—
Crop growing	—	—	—	—	—	—	—	—	—	14	14	—
Other sectors	—	2	7	—	1	1	—	1	—	39	51	12
Total domestic purchases	13	99	628	25	35	58	49	54	18	979	—	—
Imports	—	11	38	—	1	1	—	1	—	52	—	52
Total purchases	13	110	666	25	36	59	49	55	18	1,031	1,031	—

Products of organic chemistry (Ft 11 million): according to foreign-trade statistics, Ft 7.5 million worth of these were adhesives; we divided this sum between the leather and fur industries (Ft 2 million) and the shoe industry (Ft 9 million).

Products of the rubber industry (Ft 2 million): import was attributed to the shoe industry(also including the manufacturing of rubber footwear).

Other wood products (Ft 1 million): due to its small value, we attributed it to the greatest user, i.e., to the shoe industry. (This procedure was confirmed by foreign-trade statistics which showed that the whole import consisted of wooden pegs, i.e., a product used exclusively by the shoe industry.)

Dividing the rest of the imports in a similar manner, we obtained the results shown in Table 3.

If we sum up the import values given in the columns, we get the sector totals of imported inputs. Since the sector totals of all inputs are known by subtracting the imported inputs from them, we obtain the sector totals of home-produced inputs.

Table 4 not only contains the distribution of imports but also that of home-produced inputs. We divided the latter on the same principle, in this case, however, no statistical information was available regarding the exact structure of these product groups. In the absence of this we have considered the following factors: type of the enterprise, the distribution of the aggregate of home-produced and imported inputs, according to product groups, experience regarding the structure of product groups and the nature of imported inputs. Our estimates may be checked subsequently by comparing them to the accounts of the enterprises trading in means of production. For each product group, the aggregated inputs of the sectors should match the aggregated sales of these enterprises. Our estimates on the use of import goods may also be checked in another way. Namely, the data regarding the use of import goods purchased from these enterprises can be added to the value of import goods directly purchased by the users. The data thus obtained on the total use of import goods are then sent to the branch departments of the Central Statistical Office which, having the information on total inputs (imported and home-produced), may suggest corrections in our estimates on the use of imported goods.

The turnover tables of the individual enterprises trading in means of production are never published or analysed separately, they simply serve as a tool for constructing the national input–output table.

The question may arise, whether or not it is possible to compile the tables of these enterprises in another way.

In view of the present availability of statistical sources, the flow of goods within the turnover sphere can be only followed by the procedure described above. These enterprises cannot draw up an input–output table on their annual turnover, since in many cases they do not know the ratio between domestically produced and imported products, or, whether an imported product has come from a socialist or a non-socialist country. Still, the question seems to be justified to some extent, as the so-called "analytical bookkeeping of materials" makes it possible to follow the flow of every item purchased or sold in an accurate way.

Table 4

The turnover table of an enterprise of the shoe industry trading in leather and accessories, 1968
(million forints)

	Knitted goods	Leather and fur		Shoes		Textile clothing	Other industries		Handicraft		Do-mestic trade	Other sectors		Changes in stocks	Domestic purchases and im-port	Comple-mentary imports
		i	*d*	*i*	*d*		*i*	*d*	*i*	*d*		*i*	*d*			
Aluminium metallurgy	—	—	3	—	10	—	—	—	—	—	—	—	—	—	13	13
Metal mass product industry	—	2	—	9	68	—	—	5	—	5	—	—	—	—	78	89
Organic chemistry	—	2	—	9	—	—	—	—	—	—	—	—	—	—	—	11
Rubber industry	—	—	—	2	102	—	—	—	—	—	—	—	—	—	102	104
Wood processing industry (otherwise not mentioned)	—	—	—	1	19	—	—	—	—	—	—	—	—	—	19	20
Paper industry	—	—	3	1	15	—	—	—	—	—	—	—	—	—	18	19
Cotton industry	5	—	30	1	144	10	—	20	—	30	—	—	20	—	259	260
Linen, hemp and jute industry	—	—	—	—	19	—	—	—	—	—	—	—	—	—	19	19
Wool industry	—	—	10	—	43	—	—	—	—	—	—	—	—	—	53	55
Smallware industry	—	—	—	—	23	—	—	—	—	—	—	—	—	—	23	23
Knitted fabric industry	—	—	5	—	25	—	—	—	—	—	—	—	—	—	30	30
Leather and fur industries	8	5	48	8	67	15	—	10	—	23	—	—	34	18	223	236
Shoe industry	—	—	—	—	40	—	—	—	—	—	49	—	—	—	89	89
Crop growing	—	—	—	—	14	—	—	—	—	—	—	—	—		14	14
Other sectors	—	2	—	7	39	—	1	—	1	—	—	1	—	—	39	51
Total domestic purchases	13	99		628		25	35		58		49	54		18	979	—
Imports	—	11		38		—	1		1		—	1		—	52	—
Total purchases	13	110		666		25	36		59		49	55		18	1,031	1,031

i = imported, d = domestic

SOME PROBLEMS OF THE INTERNATIONAL COMPARABILITY OF INPUT-OUTPUT TABLES

by

MRS. KLÁRA FILLÓ

After the first comprehensive input–output table by Professor Leontief (covering the US economy for 1919–1929) was published in 1947, the compilation of similar tables also started in Europe. Later on, these were drawn up in every socialist country and in some of them a whole set of various types was created.

Already in the early phase of this work the idea arose that, with the aid of the input–output model, diversified comparisons might be made between the economies of two or more countries. Any international comparison requires very careful preliminary work and this is especially true in the case of input–output tables of various countries where the tables must be uniform as regards both their form and content. This means working out a standard methodology to clear up countless questions ranging from the definition of basic statistical concepts to the delimitation of the statistical units to be assessed. Obviously, it is hard to imagine that all countries should compile input–output tables which have been constructed according to uniform principles, regulating even the smallest details. Comparability has to be interpreted in a relative sense. Methods must be uniform only regarding the principles which are essential from the point of view of the table itself and the object of comparison.

In the framework of the UN, and also within the EEC and CMEA, work in this line started many years ago, and some of the results are already available. The input–output tables of the EEC countries were published in 1965. In these, aggregation was uniform and the contents of the individual items were comparable, at least with respect to some important fields of activity.

A conference of experts held in Geneva (June 1971) already dealt with the question of a comparative analysis of the economic structure of ECE (Economic Commission for Europe) countries on the basis of input–output tables.

As regards the CMEA countries, the first phase of this work came to an end when in 1967 the recommendation entitled "Basic Methodological Principles and Indicators of the Statistical Input–Output Table" was approved. Here, uniform solutions were presented relating to

- the problem of aggregation,
- the prices to be applied, and
- the interpretation of foreign trade.

Later on, according to the 1970 working plan of the Standing Statistical Commission of the CMEA, the Hungarian Central Statistical Office sent questionnaires to all statistical offices of the CMEA member countries and, from the answers received, assessed the extent to which the recommendations approved by the

Standing Statistical Commission had been taken into account in these countries.

The statistical offices also agreed on compiling input–output tables in every CMEA country for about the year 1968.

In the following I shall review the essential points of the above recommendation as well as the differences in practice in the various countries, as revealed by the exchange of experiences.

THE PROBLEM OF AGGREGATION

One of the most important conditions of comparability is the uniform aggregation of items. For establishing the sectors of the table, a document approved in September 1966 ("Classification of Economic Branches in the CMEA Countries") was taken as the starting point. Among others, the following problems had to be solved: (1) delimitation of the sphere of material production, (2) establishing a uniform nomenclature, and (3) definition of the contents of items.

As regards the first problem, the guiding principle was that the "branches of national economy" figuring in the balances of both gross output and national income should have uniform denomination and contents, namely:

– industry,

– construction,

– agriculture,

– forestry,

– transport,

– communication,

– trade (including state purchases of agricultural products, and activities aimed at supplying enterprises with materials and equipment),

– other branches of material production.

In general, the CMEA countries act on the recommendation of the Standing Statistical Commission, except Bulgaria, where foreign-trade activity is classified under the non-productive sphere; Romania, where some services are recorded with material production; the Soviet Union and Mongolia, where only the transport and communication activities connected with the productive branches figure in the input–output tables. Although this latter practice is theoretically correct, the recommendation of the Standing Statistical Commission still holds it useful to include all transport and communication activities in the table for the sake of comparability.

As regards the classification of activities performed within a branch, the recommendation follows the principle of "clear profiles". Thus, e.g., when an industrial enterprise performs construction activities, these should be classified under the heading of "Construction", whereas any industrial activity performed by an enterprise of the building industry goes under the heading of "Industry". The extent of corrections made according to this principle varies widely by countries. In some countries the "alien" activities of the national economic branches (i.e., those that should be classified under another branch), supply as much as 20–25 per cent of their gross output. If not corrected, these may lead to considerable distortions in the international comparison.

An input–output table may be constructed either in a "gross" or in a "net" form. In the former case, the diagonal of the table also contains the inputs of materials, etc. produced by the branch in question itself; the "net" type does not contain these inputs. The recommendation of the Standing Statistical Commission required the construction of the table in both forms. This is done in all CMEA countries, with the exception of Mongolia where only a "net" table is compiled.

The recommendation required that the activities of the private small-scale industry should be divided and classified under the various branches, according to their nature. This recommendation is followed by every country, except Hungary and Bulgaria where private small-scale industry is treated as a separate sector.

As regards the second problem, the recommendation proposed two alternatives. The first, more aggregated form has 23 sectors and the second has 46 sectors. The 23-sector nomenclature is feasible everywhere, with some small deviations in the case of the Soviet Union, the GDR and Czechoslovakia. As regards the 46-sector nomenclature, it is not possible to ensure comparability on this basis for the time being, due to the difference in classifications applied in the individual countries. Further efforts are needed to establish a uniform nomenclature.

The recommendation considers foreign trade as a separate branch; the difference between its outputs and inputs (i.e., the price margin) is represented as intermediate input. This is followed by every country with the exception of Bulgaria where foreign trade figures as final demand, i.e., as a part of "public consumption". The recommended nomenclature for the breakdown of final demand was as follows:

- non-productive consumption,
- investments and major repairs,
- changes in the stocks of working assets (unfinished constructions excluded),
- losses and unallocated items,
- exports,
- total final use.

In Bulgaria, the public part of "Non-productive production" includes foreign trade. In Bulgaria and Hungary the column of "Losses and unallocated items" is lacking. The column "Investments and major repairs" does not include repairs in the GDR, Hungary and Romania.

The recommended nomenclature for the breakdown of primary inputs was the following:

- primary income of the population,
- primary income of the enterprises,
- depreciation,
- complementary imports.

All CMEA countries use this classification.

THE PRICES APPLIED IN THE TABLE

The table may be compiled on the basis of two kinds of prices: producer prices and prices paid by the final users.

The difference between the two kinds of price consists essentially in the costs of transport, stockpiling and trade. Depending on the kind of price applied, the economic relations of a country may be analyzed from different aspects; namely, when outputs are valued at producer prices, the analysis of direct production relations comes to the fore, when, however, the prices paid by the final users are applied, the structure of final use is primarily reflected. In accordance with the recommendation, the CMEA countries have compiled their tables at prices which best correspond to their economic structures. The tables of Bulgaria, Hungary and Romania are based on producer prices, while those of Czechoslovakia, Mongolia, Poland and the Soviet Union apply prices paid by the final users; the tables of the GDR are drawn up at both prices.

The way of accounting the turnover tax is closely related to the price problem. In view of the difference between the kinds of prices applied, the accounting of this tax is done differently. In many cases, the amount of the turnover tax also depends on to whom the products are sold. Since the deviations in practice may result in excessive distortions, the questionnaire sent to the countries contained extremely detailed questions in this respect. It turned out from the answers that in Bulgaria and in the Soviet Union the turnover tax is included in the producer prices; in Czechoslovakia, Mongolia and Poland it is included in the consumer prices, whereas in the GDR, Hungary and Romania it is partly included in the producer and partly in the consumer prices.

When actually comparing them, the extent to which the output values of the various branches contain the turnover tax also has to be assessed. (This proportion varies by countries and by years according to the prevailing fiscal rules.)

THE INTERPRETATION OF FOREIGN TRADE

An analysis of foreign-trade relations is only possible if the results of foreign-trade activity (i.e., the price margins) are separated from the values of exported and imported goods (calculated at inland prices) and are shown as intermediate inputs in the table. Exports should appear as final demand, while supplementary imports should be accounted as primary inputs.

Different variants of the table can be constructed according to whether or not the inputs of imported goods are separated from home-produced inputs. According to the procedure of this separation, there can be three types of input–output tables available.

The gross output value (i.e., the gross price margin) of foreign trade contains the inputs of materials and wages, the depreciation of fixed and working assets as well as the profits of the branch. The distribution of this value among the sectors takes place either according to the proportions at which exports and imports figure in their actual costs, or in proportion to the values of their export and import trade.

Accounting of foreign trade in the tables of the CMEA countries takes place in accordance with the recommendation, with the above-mentioned exception of Bulgaria.

Every country draws up the table in its own currency; so far there has been no possibility of converting these data to a uniform currency.

COMPARISON OF THE BULGARIAN AND HUNGARIAN ECONOMIES WITH THE AID OF THEIR INPUT–OUTPUT TABLES

Officials working in the statistical offices of the two countries have attempted to reveal how far the unconverted tables could be used for international comparison.

In the following the results of this experimental analysis will be presented.

The idea of this comparison was backed up by the fact that Bulgaria and Hungary are very similar in regard to area, population and the level of economic development. The form and content of their input–output tables do not deviate substantially; in order to make them comparable, only minor modifications and regroupings were necessary. Formally, there remained a difference due to an unallocated residium in the Bulgarian table, but its magnitude was not significant.

The methodological and accounting differences that could not be eliminated (e.g., in the accounting of transport activities and in the assessing of some fixed assets in agriculture) did not distort the comparison, since the assumed direction and magnitude of their effects were accounted for when comparing the indicators that had been affected by them.

The major limitations of comparison were caused, first, by the difference in national currencies and, second, by the time lag. The Bulgarian table used for comparison related to the year 1963, while the Hungarian one to 1965. This difference had to be taken into consideration when evaluating the indicators, for the economic growth in Bulgaria was faster than in Hungary (taking 1950 for 100, production in 1964 amounted to 370 in Bulgaria and to 220 in Hungary).

The comparison extended over the following fields:

- the major proportions of material production,
- the structure of final consumption,
- the major direct and cumulated import coefficients,
- the role of foreign trade in the national economy,
- the major relations between the productive sectors.

In view of the results obtained from the calculations, the experiment may be considered successful. It has turned out that it is possible, with some limitations, to compare certain economic fields in the two countries, on the basis of their tables computed in their own national currencies. Reliable conclusions can primarily be drawn as regards the economic structures. The analyses made on the level of the national economy or those regarding aggregated groups of industries provide more reliable results than those relating to narrower fields.

In order to eliminate the distortion caused by the differences in price proportions, "calculative prices" were applied too. These prices were intended to be proportionate to value (in the Marxian sense). They were calculated in such a way that the net social income was allocated among the branches in proportion to the sums of direct wages and other incomes arising in each branch. This method, though far from being perfect, could be used fairly well for stating the differences as regards relative prices and price levels prevailing in the two countries. With the aid of "calculative prices" it also became possible to recognize some particular features of the two price systems, and to consider their effects when evaluating the direct and the cumulated input coefficients.

Experience has shown that when values are compared with values, the distortion caused by relative prices is not as great as when values and physical quantities are compared. So far, there has been no reliable method for evaluating the indicators of this type and its elaboration requires further research.

The primary aim of this experiment was to compare Bulgarian and Hungarian economies in the field of foreign-trade relations, hence this was the most thoroughly analysed.

*

The drawing up of input–output tables in the socialist countries in a comparable form is made easier to some extent by the fact that the scope of material production is almost uniformly interpreted in these countries. In non-socialist countries, the "non-material" services (the use of residential buildings, the services of banks, health and educational organizations, etc.) are also included in the table. This excludes the possibility of a direct comparison. In order to widen the basis of comparison, the Hungarian input–output table for the year 1972 will embrace, in addition to the sphere of material production, that of non-material services too.

SECOND SESSION

STATISTICAL PROBLEMS OF THE APPLICATION OF INPUT-OUTPUT TABLES IN PLANNING

Chairman

DR. ISTVÁN HETÉNYI

THE ROLE OF INPUT-OUTPUT TABLES IN THE SYNTHESIS OF LONG-TERM PLANNING

by

MÁRIA AUGUSTINOVICS

1. Owing partly to the greater weight of socio-political considerations and partly to greater uncertainty, the possibilities of quantification are more restricted in long-term planning than in medium- and short-term plans. As regards the method of quantification, international literature and practical experience know about two kinds of approach: (a) aggregate macro-economic calculations based mainly on extrapolation, and (b) a detailed elaboration of programmes which require very long periods of implementation (e.g., road construction, protection of the environment, energetics, education, etc.), by relying on the particular indicators of the given field. In laying the methodological foundations for Hungarian long-term planning, we set out from the standpoint that neither of these approaches is satisfactory in itself, and that acceptable long-term strategic variants of economic policy can be drawn up only when they are rationally combined. Namely, in the case of centrally calculated aggregates, sufficient information is not available on the trends and requirements of social and technological progress, or on the possible strategic alternatives for the individual branches or special fields. Further, the results of such calculations could hardly be turned into socially acceptable programmes that could really influence long-term development through the short- and medium-term decisions. On the other hand, when only a few development programmes, restricted to certain fields, are taken into account, the harmony of the programmes cannot be assured, and the contradictions between these programmes and the economic fields not planned on long-term basis cannot be eliminated; neither can the commensurability of alternative variants or their combinations and their evaluation according to some general criteria of social and economic policy be ensured. Therefore, we have started out from the *necessity of relying on synthetic macro-economic calculations which are based on rationally detailed concrete information obtained from the branches.*

2. The ranking of variants for the purposes of a synthesis may take place according to various viewpoints, and also the criteria of consistency (i.e., lacking contradictions) may vary. There is hardly any viewpoint of ranking (preferences) in which either in an explicit or in an implicit form efficiency (interpreted in the broadest sense, i.e., meaning the level and pattern of per unit inputs) would have no role. Further, there can hardly be such a formulation of the consistency criteria which would allow the level of economic activities to fall lastingly and considerably below the needs of society, or rise above it. If we take into account the final consumption and its possible conversion through foreign trade, this need depends on the level and pattern of productive inputs. Thus, if we regard the

tasks of macro-economic synthesis either from the viewpoint of social preferences and efficiency or from that of consistency, it is indispensable to consider the claims of the individual activities on each other, that is, the interindustry relations.

3. From this two methodological requirements follow. The first is that two of the decisive elements of productive inputs, namely amortization and investments serving the replacement and increase of fixed assets must be taken into account within the framework of interindustry relations. The notion, the accounting and the planning of input–output relations should not be arbitrarily restricted to the current inputs of simple reproduction; they must include *the dynamic processes of extended reproduction*. The second requirement is that the *external relations* — i.e., "final" and "primary" inputs — of the productive sphere grouped by branches (including services and its inter-industry relations, i.e., its "secondary" inputs) should be examined with the same nomenclature. It is, namely, only through the mutual interrelations that the connections between "final" outputs and "primary" inputs can be recognized, that the mutual and reverberating effects can be considered, and that one of the most important questions of formulating long-term strategies can be answered, namely: "what does it cost and what does it result in?" Whatever therefore the *system of indicators* used in quantitative macro-economic synthesis be (besides the nomenclatures the other major factor of planning methods in the stricter sense), it is a fundamental requirement that every indicator should be worked out in the same breakdown by branches, according to the same uniform nomenclature*.

4. Summing up what has been said, interindustry relations play a role in the synthesis of the macro-economic quantification of long-term strategies in a double sense:

a) From the viewpoint of efficiency and dynamic equilibrium, the development variants of the individual branches can be judged economically only if we know their mutual interrelations. They cannot be evaluated independently of each other; a homogeneous conception of production policy can only be formulated within the framework of a system like this.

* The concrete nomenclature — i.e., the extent of desaggregation and the principles of classification — should be chosen in view of the practical points of view of both statistics and planning. Of course, it is always a problem which of the eventually contradicting requirements should be satisfied. The branch-nomenclature of the long-term planning now under way conforms to the 1968 input–output nomenclature of the Central Statistical Office, which contains 83 branches; of these, the branches of material production can be produced by simple aggregation (with the negligible difference that we have divided the sectors "other industries" and "private industry" among the other branches, according to expert estimates on the various industrial activities performed within them).

When we accepted the nomenclature used in the input–output table of the Central Statistical Office, we were led by the consideration that it was easier to convert some of our data (investment, labour, foreign-trade, etc.) according to its nomenclature than to transform all its data according to another nomenclature.

b) From the technical and methodological viewpoints, the mentioned branch nomenclature permits us to summarize the conceptions relating to different aspects and processes of reproduction in a uniform framework, i.e., in a system where quantification is possible.

5. As regards annual and five-year plans, the "traditional" interindustry relations consist in collating the conceptions of the supplying and purchasing sectors and then checking them against one another in terms of absolute figures. (For example, how much steel metallurgy is prepared to supply to engineering, and how much steel engineering is prepared to purchase from metallurgy.) This procedure (termed in planning jargon as "playing chess") cannot be used in long-term planning for simple technical reasons, as the three five-year periods included in a long-term plan and the several variants of the branch conceptions regarding each five-year plan would result in an almost infinite number of possible combinations, and it would be difficult to collate even two or three of them in the traditional way. However, it is even more important to consider that no branch is able independently to determine the volume of its future activities and, consequently, its inputs, as these necessarily depend on the volume of consumption and foreign trade, on the available resources and, of course, on the system of interindustry relations. Therefore, the planning activity of the branches may not simply consist in assessing their outputs and inputs; instead, alternative technological and economic variants should be worked out which can give both the upper and the lower limits of branch activities as well as the *per unit inputs* belonging to the individual variants. Accordingly, macro-economic synthesis cannot simply be done by collating the absolute figures relating to the branches. More complicated methods are needed, namely, the use of mathematical-economic models which, relying on the input coefficients and on the upper and lower limits of branch activities, automatically "determine" the absolute volume of these activities (also involving the volume of inputs). This should be done not only for a single variant, but for many and according to several possible strategies regarding living standards and foreign trade and considering several hypotheses and preferences, etc. Hence, it is not so much the input–output table itself but the per unit input *coefficients* describing interindustrial relations that are decisive in long–term planning.

6. In a given period, the value of the input coefficients is determined by the technological structure, by the price system, by organizational factors and also by the rules of accountancy. The last two cannot and need not be taken into consideration in long-term planning, whereas the planning of the changes in the price system is a separate task which cannot be undertaken at the first stage of planning. Thus, in first approximation, it is not the absolute level of future input coefficients but *merely the main tendencies of their changes as a function of technological progress that have to be planned.* This is why the knowledge of the past "behaviour" of the coefficients is of outstanding importance in long-term planning (along with the equally important international cross-section comparisons). Clearly, the past trends of such coefficients cannot be unconditionally extra-

polated; but it can only in this way be stated how sensitive they are, i.e., how the interindustry relations react to various technological and structural changes. Thus, long-term planning cannot dispense with a series of comparable input–output tables covering a long past period, nor with series of data on the main processes of reproduction (not appearing in the table, but grouped according to the same nomenclature). The role of the interindustry relations in such thesis can only be efficient in planning if it also prevails in statistics.

THE ROLE OF INPUT-OUTPUT TABLES IN NATIONAL ECONOMIC PLANNING

by

LAJOS CSERBA

The fundamental task of national economic planning consists in working out plans which reflect the economic policy of the socialist state, determine the main objectives of economic development and the most favourable proportions of the national economy, i.e., those which are able to ensure a balanced growth and provide a satisfactory basis for the coordinated application of economic regulators in order to implement the plan with success. Since the introduction of the "new" economic control and management in Hungary in 1968, provisions regarding the economic regulators have also become an organic part of planning.

Any solution of the fundamental problem of planning necessitates the simultaneous and consistent forecast of both the whole reproduction process and the individual branches and functional fields. The comprehensive analysis and the planning of the growth rate and of the major proportions of economic development, as well as the ensuring of the consistency of all reproduction processes in terms of value, are possible if national economic and financial balances are drawn up and mathematical economic models are applied.

Since its birth in the early fifties, the use of national economic accounts in planning has considerably improved in Hungary too. It has become enriched by new elements and has changed simultaneously with the methods of economic planning and control.

From the beginning, the national system of economic balances has included the balances of the global social product (gross output of material goods) and of the national income (net material product) as well as the balance of manpower. The first two, covering the starting and final points as well as the most essential aspects of the reproduction process, were complemented in the early 1960's by an input–output table and — at the end of the 1960's — by a balance of the main elements of national wealth (i.e., of fixed and of working assets). Although in value terms, these balances reflect the material aspect of the reproduction process, namely, the production of goods and the supply of services, as well as their distribution and utilization.

Another important aspect of the reproduction process relates to the income and financial processes which underly the distribution and utilization of the goods produced.* These two aspects of the reproduction process assume each other's existence, relate to each other in a specific manner and of course influence

* The study by Dr. Gy. Szakolczai in this volume discusses the role of input–output tables in financial planning.

each other. Already in the 1960's experimental calculations were made in order to work out accounts that would serve the comprehensive analysis and plannin g of the income processes; these would represent the distribution and redistribution of national income in its process of movement. The concrete methodological and quantitative solutions elaborated by the Central Statistical Office and by the National Planning Office, as well as the improved system of statistical accounts, make it possible now to apply it regularly in planning.

The main elements of the system which serves the analysis, planning and co-ordination of the financial implications of the reproduction process, are the balance of the state budget, the balance of the incomes and expenditures of the population, the balance of international payments, the credit balance, the aggregate financial balance and other related financial calculations. They have been used in planning ever since the introduction of the planned economy, but their contents and the methods applied have been continuously improving. In recent years intensive work has been done in the National Planning Office, the Central Statistical Office, the Ministry of Finance and the National Bank of Hungary in order to improve the system of financial accounts. The primary aim has been to develop a balance of financial relations which would serve both the synthesis and the checking of the individual financial accounts and would link the system of financial balances (a system based on the receipt-expenditure aspect emphasizing the circulation of money) both methodologically and quantitatively with the system of national economic accounts which express the economic proportions of the reproduction process.

Economic-mathematical model calculations started to be used in planning with the adaptation of input–output tables. Later, in the 1960's, more complicated models were also used as tools for calculating the five-year and other long-term plans; from this time on, the possibilities offered by modern computer techniques have also been made use of.

The major problems of this development process will be examined here with special regard to national accounts, mathematical models and input–output tables.

1. EXPERIENCES OF APPLYING INPUT–OUTPUT TABLES AND NATIONAL ECONOMIC ACCOUNTS IN PLANNING AND THE TRENDS OF FURTHER DEVELOPMENT

Both in economic analysis and in planning, it has become increasingly important recently to analyse the basic elements of national economic equilibrium, the conditions of proportionate economic development and the preparation of decisions on factors which affect the main proportions. These analyses serve as a starting point for the decisions to be taken, for the choice of the tools of central regulation, as well as for determining the extent of their future effects.

Plan calculations for 1969–1970

	Deadlines for performing the calculations				
	annual plan 1970		five-year plan 1971–1975		
	introductory calculations June 30th	final plan proposal Nov. 30th	basic calcula-tions Aug. 31st	coordinated plan proposal March 31st	final plan proposal May 31st
National economic balances:					
1. Sources and utilization of global social product by branches (aggregate balance)	x	x	x	x	x
2. Sources and utilization of national income	x	x	x	x	x
3. Distribution, redistribution and utilization of national income by major income recipients	—	x	—	—	xx
4. Input–output tables of the social product	x	x	xx	xx	xx
5. Aggregated balance of manpower	x	x	xx	xx	xx
6. Balance of the major elements of national wealth (fixed assets, inventories, foreign exchange)	—	x	—	xx	xx
Money circulation and credit:					
7. State budget	x	x	x	x	x
8. Credit balance	—	x	—	x	x
9. Balance of working assets	—	x	—	xx	xx
10. Aggregated financial balance	x	x	xx	x	x

Notes: x = Calculations have to be performed every year.
xx = Calculations have to be performed for 1970 and 1975.
The Economic Department of the Planning Office is responsible for calculations 1–4 and 6; the Financial Department is responsible for those under 5 and 7–10.

The investigations and the planning of the growth rate and of the main national economic proportions, as well as the techniques of national accounting are different in five-year and in annual planning, and also in the various phases of the planning process.

Problems in decisions concerning five-year plans relate mainly to development and investments. The major aim is to ensure the conditions of balanced growth and to choose the correct tools of regulation. *Annual plans* — which are mostly concerned with given production capacities — generally start from an analysis of the national economy; they disclose the equilibrium conditions, necessary for achieving the targets of the current five-year plan, and work out the tools and central measures needed for influencing the processes.

Specific tasks and methods of balance technique have also developed in the various stages of planning. In its *preparatory stage,* the main tendencies and the major proportions of the base period should be analysed, and a preliminary assessment of expected development during the plan period should be made. For this, the tendencies and interrelations detectable from the data of the national economic accounts can be used. These initial calculations serve for initiating analyses and plan-calculations covering both individual branches and partial fields, as well as for evaluating the results of such calculations. In the *stage of coordination,* the examination of the detailed analyses and calculations which have been performed in the individual economic branches clarifies the major economic proportions that can be expected. According to the preliminary principles and the balance-calculations, a central coordination of the calculations relating to the individual fields has to be performed and, depending on the conclusions arrived at, proposals have to be made regarding the further process of planning. After disclosing the effects of the proposed central measures aimed at influencing the major proportions among the individual branches, efforts should be made to coordinate these effects also in the national economic balances of various types.

The nomenclature and the scheme of an input–output table are shown below.

Nomenclature of an input–output table
of the social product (production aspect)

Rows

1. Mining
2. Electric energy
3. Metallurgy
4. Engineering
5. Building materials
6. Chemical industry
7. Light industry
8. Food industries

A) Industry, total

9. Construction industry
10. Agriculture, forestry, water management
11. Transport and communications
12. Domestic trade
13. Foreign trade
14. Balance of turnover tax and price subsidies
15. Balance of customs duties and import turnover tax

B) Material consumption
Share of material consumption

16. Depreciation

C) National income

D) Social product

17. Complementary imports

E) All distributable resources

Columns

1. Mining
2. Electric energy
3. Metallurgy
4. Engineering
5. Building materials
6. Chemical industry
7. Light industries
8. Food industries

I. Industry, total

9. Construction industry
10. Agriculture, forestry, water management
11. Transport and communications
12. Domestic trade
13. Foreign trade
14. Balance of turnover tax and price subsidies
15. Balance of customs duties and import turnover tax

II. Productive consumption

16. Personal and public consumption
17. Investment
18. Changes in stocks
19. Exports

III. Final utilization

IV. Total utilization

In order to achieve further improvement, it is important to mention our experiences and to point to certain difficulties that may emerge in national accounting in the course of drawing up the plans mentioned above.

1. Owing to the changes resulting from the introduction of the new economic mechanism, there were some transitory difficulties in connection with the analyses and forecasts of the economic processes, when they had to be expressed in terms of value, both for partial fields and for the economy as a whole. When calculating the plans for 1969, 1970 and for the five-year plan period 1971–1975, we had to apply complementary calculations and economic estimates more

frequently than usual in order to state the relations between factual and plan data precisely. Of course, such calculations will always be necessary, but their volume can be reduced by making our information system better suited to the requirements of analysis and planning.

In drawing up the plan, the assessment of the economic situation just preceding the plan period proved to be the most sensitive variable element. Therefore, it is very difficult to evaluate the direction and the extent of the major economic processes and to compare them with those of the past, and it is similarly difficult to forecast their future development. This experience emphasizes the necessity of "process analyses" (time series) and of the "process forecasts" (prognoses) especially in five-year planning.

Since the input–output tables and the national accounts were immediately related with the plan calculations of the individual fields, it was possible to coordinate them centrally by disclosing the various tendencies and disproportions in the plan calculations. Though they are very valuable in coordination, calculations on the national level cannot replace the detailed analysis and planning of each partial field relating to every major physical or financial process. Mutually complementing each other, the two types of calculation contribute to the economic foundation of the plan together.

2. Combined with other balance-type calculation, national accounts cover all major processes of expanded reproduction, and they express the most general conditions of proportionate development numerically; by this, they provide a basis for elaborating more advanced mathematical methods, including the applications of a linear programming model in five-year planning as well.

The increased requirements expected from the analysis and planning of financial and income processes have induced us to reveal and investigate the complexity of the proportions and equilibrium conditions of the distribution, redistribution and the utilization of national income, according to the three major groups (government, socialist enterprises, population). In order to establish the necessary methodological and statistical framework, experimental calculations were made and a methodology was elaborated, first on the basis of the 1968 preliminary figures and later on that of the 1971 plan data. The "insertion" of a "balance of income relations" into the planning procedure is expected to improve accounting work.

3. The analyses of national-economic accounts for annual and five-year planning also pointed out some methodological and organizational deficiencies that hindered consistent central coordination. The data of the various partial fields referred to different points or periods of time and the changes resulting from partial decisions had to be fitted continuously into the calculations; this made it difficult to complete national accounting in due time, and to feed back the changes to the branch calculations.

4. Inadequacy of information considerably hindered both the five-year and the annual planning work. The lack or the belated arrival of partial information, i.e., an inadequate flow of information, considerably impaired the efficiency of planning work.

The system of information flows is still unsatisfactory, both within the planning process proper (i.e., the flows among the central planning departments and the individual planning bodies) and between the planning organizations and the national economy (i.e., the flow of information from the Central Statistical Office, the ministries, etc. to the Planning Office).

The major deficiencies that turned out of the examination were as follows:

– the "contents" of many data were more or less different from what was needed; accordingly, they could only be used for the purposes of plan calculations with some "transformation"; in other words, in order to obtain the needed information, they had to be "processed" or converted;

– although the data were provided, they were formulated in a "language" different from the one used in planning and the knowledge necessary for their "translation" was not available;

– the conversion of these data — even if they could have been converted into a useable form — was not possible as they arrived too late.

Besides these general deficiencies, there were also some methodological problems that rendered national accounting work particularly difficult. Among these problems, the most important ones were the following:

a) Problems related to the application of "constant" and current prices. Contrary to earlier practice, under the new system of economic control and management, planning at unchanged prices was pushed to the background and planning at current prices has come to the fore. Owing to the growing role of the market and the introduction of the new price system, this is understandable and to some extent also necessary. Namely, the decisions of the enterprises, and hence their production, are considerably influenced by the system of prices, by other economic regulators established for the plan period, and by the situation of the market's supply and demand. Yet, in our opinion, greater emphasis should have been placed, especially in the five-year plan, on planning in terms of constant prices, since the new system of prices and other economic regulators got their final shape mainly in the last stage, i.e., when drawing up the 1971–1975 plan. The effect of these decisions on the volume of production and consumption could, however, be evaluated either during or in the last stage of planning.

b) The question of applying producer prices or realization (sales) prices in planning. It is necessary that the real processes of production and realization could be followed in the national accounts, in order to ensure the equilibrium of production and utilization. Hence, the exchanges among the various producers, as well as among producers and final users have to appear in the input–output table at actual sales prices, i.e., "realization prices". At present, however, calculations are carried out at "net producer prices" in both annual and five-year planning, i.e., the gross output of the individual branches does not comprise the turnover tax, whereas it includes the price subsidies granted by the state. In the national economic total, this difference disappears, since the turnover tax is included in the global social product, while price subsidy is not. In the balances of the global social product and of the national income (as well as in the input–

output table), the difference between turnover tax and price subsidy is accounted in a separate row.

In our opinion, it seems expedient to apply realization prices in the future also in the input–output tables figuring in the plan, similarly to the statistical input–output tables. However, when this is needed for the purposes of analysis, planning and price calculations, the gross output of branches less net turnover tax might also figure in the special calculations.

If an input–output table of the turnover type were compiled, it would be easier to examine the realization and the commodity exchange relations, as such a table reflects the direct relations between the producing, distributing and the user branches and fields. This would enable us to carry out various conversions, the performance of which was difficult in the past. All this, however, will only become feasible after an adequate information basis (statistical input–output tables of turnover type) has been created and some other conditions of computer processing (commodity-flow input–output tables regarding the distributive sectors, etc.) have been provided. However, the production-type input–output tables used at present will also be needed, e.g., for analysing and planning the national economic proportions and the exchanges among the individual branches.

c) The question of applying price indices in planning. For investigating national economic proportions and the growth rate, certain national economic balances must be drawn up in terms of constant prices too. When constructing the price indices and examining the effect of price changes, the belated arrival of expert calculations regarding price changes or their subsequent modifications made necessary by balance relations often caused problems. The calculation of price indices was also difficult due to the lack of information necessary for tracing the effects of organizational changes (i.e., changes in the composition of organizational sectors).

*

Starting from the experience of national accounting and the requirements of a higher quality of planning, and considering the facilities offered by up-to-date computing techniques, improvement seems to be needed along two main lines: (1) the system of national accounts must be made completely comprehensive and uniform; (2) national economic balances must be more strongly integrated and linked with mathematical models.

By making the system of national accounts to be used in planning comprehensive and uniform, we wish to reflect the complex processes of extended reproduction, its system of interrelations and major factors in a way as they actually appear in reality. To achieve this, it is necessary

– to elaborate the balances of the non-material branches,

– to connect, in the framework of balances, the development of incomes with the processes of production and utilization;

– to analyse the relationships between the accumulation of fixed and working assets, national wealth, on the one hand, and the changes in efficiency, on the other;

– to connect the national economic balances more closely with the financial and the individual product balances and with the balance of manpower.

Improvement of the system of national economic balances was made possible by the new system of national economic balances (accounts) worked out by the Hungarian Central Statistical Office. This provides a basis for constructing continuous time series to be used in the planned balances.

If national accounting is to be made more suited to the purposes of planning, the enlarged system of balances requires the application of computer techniques, of models and mathematical methods. The conditions necessary for all this must be created step by step. To achieve this, a uniform system should be created, comprising all the data needed in the national economic balances and the mathematical models. It is also possible to feed all these into the "data bank" of the Computer Centre of the National Planning Office. A continuous and regular flow of information should be ensured; the national economic balances as well as the coordination models of the various types should be fed into a computer and printed already from the elementary figures provided by the data bank. It should be also ensured that the plan variants calculated by the computer from mathematical models could be analysed and evaluated also in terms of the national economic balances. Computer programmes suitable for performing these tasks should be elaborated.

The stages, the decision system and the scheduling of planning work should be formed so that the results obtained by models and by central accounting could be fed back to the plan calculators of the partial branches and fields, in order to promote the comparison and coordination of the partial tendencies with the interests of the national economy as a whole, and of the short-term interests with the long-term ones.

Our experiences concerning linear programming models (used in drawing up the fourth five-year plan) and the models hitherto applied in long-term planning serve as a basis for the further, integrated development of the system of national accounts and of mathematical models. The creation of a computer centre within the National Planning Office provides additional help in this process.

2. POSSIBILITIES AND CONDITIONS OF USING STATISTICAL INPUT–OUTPUT TABLES AND THE SYSTEM OF NATIONAL ACCOUNTS IN PLANNING

Ever since the introduction of the planned economy, the summary balances of the social product and of national income have regularly been compiled each year by the Central Statistical Office, at both current and comparable prices, in a breakdown by economic branches according to the methodology of the Council for Mutual Economic Assistance. First in 1957, then for the years 1959, 1961, 1965 and 1968, the office compiled detailed input–output tables in a breakdown by economic activities. In addition, aggregate tables were compiled for each year from 1959 to 1968. Due to their structure and methodology, these statistical input–output tables could only be compared with those used by the National Planning Office after a laborious process of conversion. In the mid-1960's certain elements of national wealth (stock of fixed and working assets) were also assessed in the form of statistical balances.

These balances of different structure and methodology could not be linked directly to one another; moreover, some types were missing, e.g., those covering the activities of the so-called non-productive branches, the ones dealing with the incomes and the financial activities related to production and consumption, as well as those comprising the distribution and redistribution of the national income. Due to this latter deficiency, there were no direct links between the system of statistical balances and that of income and financial balances for a long time up to recent years.

Considering these deficiencies and the growing interest in economic analysis, the Central Statistical Office, in cooperation with the National Planning Office and other national bodies, elaborated proposals for improving the system of national economic balances. The essential features of the new system may be summed up as follows:

– besides material production, the performance, distribution and inputs of the non-material branches are also accounted for;

– simultaneously with the "production aspect" of economic processes, the incomes arising from economic activity, their distribution and utilization are shown as well, establishing thereby connections among the financial balances of different type within the framework of the accounting system. Within the accounting system proposed, the categories of social product and national income are shown separately (to conform to the practice in other CMEA countries). For the gross and net performance of total economic activity, which comprises the non-material branches too, the denominations of "gross and net national product" are employed.

The first comprehensive proposal of the Central Statistical Office was discussed by the Methodological Council of the National Planning Office in September 1969; there attention was drawn to the following:

1. It is desirable that the Hungarian system of national economic balances and the notions used should be closely linked to the two international systems, the MPS and the SNA. This does not preclude, however, the application of other methods in solutions of individual problems, taking domestic endowments into account. The category of national income should be used according to the principles adopted by the socialist countries.

2. It is desirable to allow a greater role for the categories and balances of social product and national income within the system, and to emphasize the particular importance of indices related to material production.

3. The Methodological Council accepts that the representatives of the Planning Office and the Statistical Office will agree on the definition of the fundamental

concepts and on the methods of assessing their contents, and on a uniform method of measuring the parameters during the whole period of the fourth five-year plan.

In view of the above remarks and the standpoint of the economic task force of the Hungarian Socialist Workers' Party, the Statistical Office worked out a detailed proposal on "The concepts and methodology of the system of national economic balances".* Having considered the remarks made by the Planning Office and other national organizations and having made the amendments, it was formulated in its final form and published in 1970.**

The new system developed by the Statistical Office has made it possible to draw up full-scope national economic balances for the purposes of planning. To achieve this, the Planning Office, the Statistical Office and other national organs (the Ministry of Finance, the banks, etc.) should actually use identical nomenclatures and accounting techniques for each economic activity (e.g., in the case of delimiting the material and non-material branches, the identity of classification relating to products, services, inputs or incomes, etc.). With these, the various groupings, summary balances and models required in economic analysis and planning can be mechanically constructed from the basic information material which covers the whole economy (this being compiled by the Central Statistical Office).

The National Planning Office and the Central Statistical Office have agreed that, on the basis of the full-scope statistical tables compiled according to the new methodology, the national economic balances of the fourth five-year plan will be recalculated in accordance with the new methods. A detailed proposal will be made, which is aimed at examining the possibilities of using the system of statistical balances in planning.

In the fourth five-year plan and in the annual plan for 1970, several mutually acceptable methodological solutions and conceptual definitions that had arisen in the course improving the statistical system of balances were already taken into consideration. In spite of this, due to the particular requirements and conditions of planning and to the deficiencies of available data, there have remained considerable differences in some fields; these, however, can be abridged in the future by unifying the methods and applying "conversion techniques".

Our experiences gained in using the new statistical accounting system and input–output tables in planning, furthermore, the problems that are awaiting solution, may be summed up as follows.

1. The methodological prescriptions of the National Planning Office relating to the annual plans and the fourth five-year plan ordered the coordination of the plan and the drawing up of national economic balances for the sphere of material production and for its branches (as aggregates of economic organization). The

* It was published in Hungarian under the title A népgazdasági mérlegrendszer továbbfejlesztése (Improvement of the system of national economic accounts) in *Statisztikai Szemle*, No. 10, pp. 1023–1053, Budapest 1970.

** A népgazdasági mérlegrendszer módszertana (Methodology of the system of national accounts). *Módszertani füzetek*, No. 9, Central Statistical Office, Budapest 1971.

social product of individual branches was planned at net producer prices (without turnover taxes). The balance of turnover taxes (i.e., the difference between turnover taxes received and price subsidies paid by the government), as well as the balances of export duties, import turnover taxes and import price subsidies were accounted in separate rows in the plan balances. Since the Statistical Office provided information on the basic figures of social product and national income without turnover taxes too, the resources figuring in the statistical and plan balances could be compared.

In the case of utilization, the two kinds of balances still showed differences in the data on the balance of trade and the changes in stocks. These were due to the different accounting of the goods in transit as they were levelled out in the totals. Thus, in respect of the aggregate balances of the social product and national income, numerical agreement can be considered ensured — if some conversions are applied. These balances provide coordinated data and they constitute a fixed framework for input–output calculations.

On the basis of our experience, it seems to be more expedient to use realization prices for the individual branches also in the input–output plan tables, since these provide a more realistic basis both for analysing the relations between suppliers and purchasers and for calculating the price indices which are needed for determining the volume. These prices include both turnover taxes and customs duties, hence, input–output tables which make it possible to analyse these within the price will be needed in the future, too.

2. The statistical input–output table for 1968 is available in two versions. In 1970 the Statistical Office published the input–output table for 1968 in a detailed breakdown according to activities. Then, taking into account the new system of national accounts, it worked out (and published in 1971) the input–output tables for 1968 and 1969 according to branches. The importance of these tables for 1968 lies in the fact that (1) they relate to the first year of the new system of economic control and management, including the regulation of prices and incomes, and (2) that beyond the usual breakdown by activities it was also prepared in a breakdown by organizational units (by which it fitted into the improved system of national economic accounts). However, in spite of the common source of data, the two 1968 tables differ in several points and this hinders their numerical comparison with each other as well as with the input–output plan tables; further, neither the statistical tables can be used as bases in planning. Experts from the Statistical and the Planning Offices concluded an agreement as to the detailed examination of these problems and to work out the necessary modifications.

3. In planning, it is an important requirement to examine the economic processes on the basis of *coordinated data* of statistics and bookkeeping; the data on activities should be deduced from the data relating to *organizational units* (enterprises, cooperatives, etc.). In this way the numerical relations between the two kinds of classification can generally be traced more reliably. In our opinion, it is advisable to satisfy this requirement not only in the case of gross and net national product, but also in that of social product and national income.

4. From the point of view of planning it is of particular importance that the statistics of branches and special fields should be directly linked to the system of national accounts and to the input–output tables. Statistics of the branches and the comprehensive balances should be harmonized so that the current (quarterly, monthly, etc.) statistics of the individual branches and fields could be numerically compared with the corresponding annual data figuring in the national economic balances.

In order that the new accounting system and the input–output tables of the Statistical Office could be used in planning satisfactory solutions should be found for the above-mentioned problems. The always changing particular requirements of economic analysis and planning should also be taken into account. Hence, the major guidelines in planning may be summed up as follows:

a) Within the framework of five-year and annual planning the classification by branches, i.e., by *organizational units,* must be used in the future too. In long-term planning, however, as well as in plans related to special themes, grouping by *activities* can also be employed.

b) As regards the full scope of economic activity, the following should still be distinguished within the system of national economic accounts:

- the economic categories corresponding to the concept of material production,
- the economic categories comprising both material and non-material activities.

The system of national economic balances should classify the economic processes in such a way that the economic and the numerical interrelations among them could be analysed and evaluated both for the economy as a whole and for the various aggregates formed within the economy.

c) National economic planning considers the system of balances published by the Central Statistical Office as basic information underlying the plans of input–output tables, national economic balances, financial balances as well as the economic branches and the functional fields. Accordingly, in grouping and accounting the material and non-material branches, efforts should be made to use uniform nomenclatures and methods. Where this is not possible, the necessary conversions should be developed to ensure that computers can process the basic information in two breakdowns (i.e., according to organizations and activities) on both national economic and branch levels. This will provide the opportunity to choose the type of balance or model which is best suited for the purpose of a given economic or mathematical analysis.

3. POSSIBILITIES AND CONDITIONS FOR COMBINING INPUT–OUTPUT TABLES, NATIONAL ECONOMIC BALANCES, MATHEMATICAL MODELS AND COMPUTER TECHNIQUES IN PLANNING

Considering the strict timetables of planning, without the extensive use of modern computer techniques it is almost impossible to satisfy such requirements as, e.g., the simultaneous elaboration of several plan variants, the perfection of the system of national economic balances or the creation of "communication bridges" among the various partial system and special calculations.

The consistency and uniformity of the basic data and, as a consequence, the supplying of national economic planning with adequate information will be promoted considerably by the creation of a "data bank" in the Computer Centre of the National Planning Office. Requiring careful preparation, this work has already been started by the Institute of Planning and the Computer Centre of the National Planning Office in close cooperation with the Central Statistical Office.

The reliability of data can be most precisely checked within a closed system of balances. Thus, the most important starting point is to elaborate a uniform system of concepts and a uniform planning method which may serve as a basis both for the accounting activities in the various bodies (Central Statistical Office, National Planning Office, Ministry of Finance, other ministries, banks and enterprises, etc.) and for the planning of the individual branches. To achieve this, the classification of data stored in the above-mentioned data bank could be based on the balances of the national economy compiled by the Central Statistical Office for 1968–1969. These balances can be considered to form a consistent central system, since before their final formulation they were thoroughly discussed by the competent bodies. The data should be stored according to national economic branches, also including the non-productive activities; furthermore, they should be broken down so that they may be grouped in various ways to satisfy the requirements arising in the course of compiling the various input–output tables.

A possible solution for linking the input–output tables and the national economic balances with mathematical models is the linear programming model; actually this was used when the fourth five-year plan was drawn up. Still needing some improvement, this model was based on the methods used by the Planning Office. With some minor differences, the main categories did have the same contents and interrelations as those used in "traditional" planning by the Planning Office.

The social product of a branch was obtained by summing up the values of its "high-priority" (i.e., separately planned) products as well as those of its "other" (non-specified) production. By building constraints into the model, the variability of the product structure could be kept between the necessary limits within the input–output table.

The experiences gained in the course of calculating this plan model can be utilized in the future when making models for both annual and five-year plans.

Besides programming models, the possibilities provided by analytical and variation calculations should also be utilized on a larger scale; these calculations on the basis of national economic balances or by using special mathematical models. Besides plan coordination, input–output tables have been used for various plan calculations, too. Based on our experiences we are going to perform the following calculations:

– in order to check the RAS-method, we determined the value of intermediate inputs for 1969 by using the 1968 coefficients, and compared the results with the actual input pattern;

– relying on an adequate time series of balances and depending on the results of the examination of autoregression, we are going to forecast some new coefficients;

– if this latter idea can be realized, the combined application of the two methods will mean a refinement of both of them. That is, the calculations based on the trend and the autoregressive schemes make the coefficients more dynamic, while the RAS method ensures adaptation to externally given limits;

– as regards the dynamic input–output model, research is being conducted, calculations are being performed at the Central Statistical Office and the possibilities of their application in planning are being examined at the Institute of Planning; the results achieved so far relate to very simplified schemes, hence their practical application is not yet feasible.

*

As the detailed elaboration of proposals to improve the system of national economic balances and to link it with mathematical models must rely on the experiences gained from the practice of national accounting, this work obviously takes a long time to be completed. The conditions for implementing the development objectives completely can only be created gradually, always starting from the given situation.

THE ROLE OF INPUT-OUTPUT TABLES IN FINANCIAL AND PRICE PLANNING

by

GYÖRGY SZAKOLCZAI

This study gives an account of the experiences gained in the use of input–output tables in financial and price planning. It examines how input–output tables could be used even more efficiently as a means of financial and price planning, and seeks to find out how the experiences of such work and its various tools can be utilized in constructing input–output tables. The first part describes the role of input–output tables in financial and price planning; the next four parts deal with the combination of the "organization" and "activity" principles, the place of financial items, the problems of the uniform price basis and of comparability over time. Finally, the last section reviews the latest mathematical methods used in constructing the input–output tables and for securing comparability over time.

1. THE ROLE OF INPUT–OUTPUT TABLES IN FINANCIAL AND PRICE PLANNING

Input–output tables were first used for the short-term planning of production processes. Today even long-term planning, as well as financial and price planning are based on input–output tables. Econometric and programming models based on input–output tables are gaining an increasing role in the planning of prices and of financial flows as well as in performing calculations aiming to determine the equilibrium or the optimum values of the incentives. Input–output tables are very suitable for modelling both finances and prices. The purpose of price planning is to forecast or to determine prices favourable to the equilibrium of economic processes and financial flows. In addition, prices should work, as far as possible, in the direction of attaining optimum efficiency on the national economic level. The aim of financial planning is to secure a smooth development of financial flows while promoting a similar development of production processes. The most important task is to adequately establish the economic incentives and taxation. Financial planning must evidently observe not only the requirements of equilibrium but also those of optimality. Moreover, efforts have to be made that the financial flows directed by the economic regulators should promote an ever stronger assertion of the efficiency requirements. Finally, it is also possible to construct a more complicated model which would simultaneously determine the correlated system of prices and other economic incentives and would solve, at the same time, all other tasks of price and financial planning.

The actual realization of this theoretically given possibility raises several practical problems. From among them, perhaps the most important is that certain variables and certain types of data can be correctly interpreted only in a table grouped according to activities, while others require a grouping by organizations. Therefore, usually some combination of activities and organizations is needed in the model. The next part is going to deal with this problem.

2. COMBINATION OF THE PRINCIPLES OF "ORGANIZATION" AND "ACTIVITY"

The most important variables of price calculations, namely prices, can only be interpreted by activities, i.e., by goods and services or their more or less "homogeneous" aggregates. Accordingly, the price index, e.g., of a mining enterprise or the whole sector of mining as an organizational unit is a weighted average of the price indices of the basic activity, furthermore, of those relating to engineering, building, etc., and even of the welfare services performed there. But such a mixed "price index" can hardly be used in economic analyses; we need a separate index for the main activity. Similarly, we must also know the individual components of final use grouped according to activities, that is, into groups of goods and services. We wish to know, e.g., how much food is available and at what price. It is but a secondary question — and frequently it cannot even be correctly answered — how much food is produced by the organizations of agriculture, by the food industry or by some other branches.

Another very important element of financial and price calculations is represented by the budgetary relations, i.e., taxes and income transfers paid or subsidies received by each individual sector. The major part of these can be interpreted only within the organizational framework. Profits, taxes and subsidies may be correctly interpreted only in relation to an organizational unit as a whole; it is only by very artificial devices that they may be divided up between the various activities of the organizational unit. The situation is similar to several other data which are available in primary form for organizational units, e.g., figures on employment, stocks of fixed assets, depreciation allowances, wages and income taxes, etc.

Finally, there are several data in respect to which the detailed figures are available according to both organizations and activities. For example, as a first approximation, the current inputs of sectors can be examined by organizational units but, within that, they can also be computed by products and services. Apart from agriculture, where for practical reasons we start from some other data, in the first approximation the work aimed at constructing input–output tables usually starts from the statistics which show the consumption of materials within the organizational units and which break down the use of materials by groups of products and services as well. The situation is similar with respect to investments and inventories. Investors are always organizational units. However, investments are shown also according to their "technical composition", that is, we know what percentages of them consist of construction equipment, and various other inputs, so that we are able to tell roughly what kinds of products and services they require. Finally, the financial items connected with the flow of commodities and services (e.g., the turnover tax) can also be included here. Although they are charged on organizational units, they may also be stated by individual groups of products and services.

Thus, a combination of the accounts resting on the principles of "organization" and "activity" seems to be a precondition of price calculation using input–output tables. The basic equation of all price-models relying on calculative methods multiplies the individual input elements with the adequate price indices, summarizes them and by starting from the requirement of financial equilibrium of each sector and observing all interrelations, determines the general index of prices. The summarization by columns can only be performed for organizational units since it is only in their framework that financial equilibrium and budget relations can be interpreted. At the same time, price indices can only be constructed for groups of products or services, i.e., for activities. Accordingly, the starting basis for the calculations must be an input–output table in the columns of which economic processes are classified according to "activities", whereas its rows show these processes according to organizations. Obviously, also the third quadrant of the table is built up on the organizational units.

It is easy to see that it would lead to grave distortions if our calculations were based on an input–output table relying exclusively either on the "organizational" or the "activity" principle. In the first case, the financial balances and interrelationships of the enterprises and the sectors consisting of organizational units could not be built into the model, or if they were, they would be seriously distorted. In the second case, we would obtain unrealistically biased and, as a matter of fact, non interpretable price indices for the organizational units which have mixed production profiles.

Also the viewpoints of financial planning require an input–output table of a similar structure. Only in this way can the model treat with satisfactory comparability the indirect taxes and subsidies relying on the flow of goods, or the direct taxes and subsidies immediately linked to organizational units. It is thus a primary requirement of financial and price planning that besides input–output tables complying either with the activity or with the organizational principle, tables combining both principles should also be constructed.

However, neither can a basic input–output table showing "activities by organizations" be the sole basis of calculations in financial and price planning. Since the number of units of activities and organizations is not necessarily the same, the internal matrix of the input–output table will, as a rule, not be quadratic. Moreover, the output value of the individual organizations is usually not identical with the output value derived from their activities performed within their main production profile. Thus, the sums of the rows and columns which belong together are frequently not equal to each other. The equalities and proportions, which are the basic condition of mathematical processing, are thus not satisfied. Therefore, other input–output tables of a different setup must be also relied upon in the analysis. In the econometric model of price planning, e.g., input–output tables of the "activity by organization" type and those based only on activity figure together. The first type is used in price analysis, the latter for finding the quantitative equilibrium necessary for price analysis.

Another precondition of financial and price calculations is a sufficiently detailed presentation of such financial items as subsidies and taxes.

3. THE PRESENTATION OF FINANCIAL ITEMS

In the sphere of financial items it is expedient to distinguish two major categories: direct and indirect taxes (or subsidies).

The accounting of direct taxes and subsidies does not involve any particular problem. These items of income distribution and redistribution are taken into account in the sectors wherefrom they originated. In an input–output table they appear in the third quadrant, i.e., among primary inputs. Nor does a breakdown or aggregation of these items according to the requirements of processing cause any difficulties.

Indirect taxes and subsidies, however, are linked to commodity flows, so their accounting is much more complicated. As a result of "financial bridges" the difference between prices paid by the purchaser and those received by the seller deviates from what is determined according to the price margin and the transportation costs. The degree of this deviation depends on the fact to whom, and by whom, the commodity is sold, i.e., on the various compositions of sales and purchases.

A full-scope discussion of the financial items related to intermediate inputs necessitates, in my opinion, the drawing up of eight matrices. These are the following:

1. the matrix of the taxes charged on production and sales, which are accounted among the costs of purchasing materials;
2. the matrix of subsidies granted depending on the purchase prices of materials;
3. the matrix of production and sales taxes which can be added to the sales prices;
4. the matrix of producer price subsidies paid depending on the sales volume;
5. the matrix of important turnover taxes charged on imports from socialist countries;
6. the matrix of import price subsidies paid on imports from socialist countries;
7. the matrix of customs duties and import turnover taxes charged on imports from non-socialist countries;
8. the matrix of import price subsidies paid on imports from non-socialist countries.

From among these matrices only the first four, that is, the items related to the domestic turnover of commodities are worth while to deal with more extensively. The distinction between turnover taxes charged on sales, on the one hand, and those that can be included in the purchase costs of materials, on the other, seems absolutely necessary because these two are linked to the input–output table and figure in the subsequent calculations in an entirely different manner. The deduction (and separate accounting) of the items connected with the purchase of materials modifies only the gross output value of the consumer branch (provided that we want to show the latter without turnover taxes), whereas the deduction of turnover taxes figuring in sales prices modifies the output of *both the producing and the consumer branches.* The accounting of the cumulated effects is possible only with the aid of complicated inverse input–output calculations. Accordingly, a separate treatment of the two types of turnover taxes (and of price subsidies) is unavoidable.

As a rule, it is much simpler to show the financial items related to final demand. The collections (turnover taxes) and the subsidies (those aimed at lowering consumer prices and various other forms of subsidies) related to personal and public consumption or to exports can be represented with vectors. It is only in the case of investments that a classification according to investing sectors is unavoidable. Some sectors, e.g., agriculture, receive large subsidies in order to lower the price of their purchases of materials serving investments. In principle, for the sake of completeness, also the financial items related to stockpiling should be treated similarly.

The compilation of the financial matrices involves much additional work compared to the practice followed so far. It would be expedient to perform this work in collaboration with all the authorities involved in financial and price planning, namely, the National Planning Office, the National Office of Prices and Materials, and the Ministry of Finance. No doubt, this work would increase the possibilities of using input–output tables not only in the planning of finances and prices but also in every other field of planning. At present, the definitions applied by these central authorities differ.

The Central Statistical Office compiles the input–output tables at sales prices. This conforms to international practice and to the present system of data collecting; any other solution could hardly be conceived of. At the same time, the National Planning Office starts from values minus turnover taxes but including price subsidies. In many cases this is justified by the requirements of analysis. A logical bridge between the two different concepts can be found exactly with the aid of the financial matrices and vectors mentioned above. Hence, the construction of the proposed matrices seems to be fully justified, since in this way the checking and the coordination of the basic data are partly made superfluous and the results received through the various calculations become unequivocally comparable.

To end this section, let us make a few practical remarks. The computation of the financial matrices and vectors is primarily aimed to put the items of domestic and foreign trade in their proper place, according to their real economic content. The basic statistical data necessary for this are mostly available. When establishing the matrices and vectors it seems expedient to start from a combined accounting of "activities" and "organizations". Namely, the financial items depending on the commodity flows can be most expediently represented, similarly to the flows themselves, by such a combined table.

The working out of financial matrices is closely related to the valuation of the items within an input–output table and thus also to its price basis. Therefore, it seems expedient to discuss this subject in greater detail.

4. THE PROBLEM OF A UNIFORM PRICE BASIS

In connection with compiling input–output tables, one of the requirements is that all elements of inputs and outputs must figure at identical prices everywhere in the table. This follows from the basic assumption relating to the homogeneity of output of the individual sectors. Furthermore, it can be easily proved that no analysis based on an input–output table is possible when the prices or the price indices differ by direction of sales.* Finally, the problem of a uniform price basis is particularly important from the viewpoint of price and financial calculations, since quite misleading results would be obtained if the price indices of the individual sectors shifted as a consequence of modifications in the direction of sales.

The input–output tables drawn up at sales prices do not satisfy the requirement of uniform prices. The prices of products sold by retail trade are modified by turnover taxes and price subsidies. The value of exports (accounted at the uniform foreign-exchange multiplier) also differs, as a rule, from domestic sales prices. As regards the domestic use of materials, deviations are caused by differences in turnover taxes and in producer price subsidies. For practical reasons, however, the basic table can only be compiled at sales prices, and only this is suitable for international comparisons. In the given situation, therefore, the most we can do is to undertake such a modification of sales prices as will render the input–output table acceptable for the purposes of financial and price calculations.

A uniform price basis can be achieved, for example, if an input–output table is compiled at prices which do not contain turnover taxes but include price subsidies. However, sometimes precisely the accounting of price subsidies leads to deviations from the uniform price basis. Therefore, it seems necessary to work out a third system of valuation for the purposes of price planning.

In our opinion, within this system, the basis of valuation would be the value of the exchanges among the productive sectors without turnover taxes but, as a rule, including price subsidies. The price level of personal and public consumption deviates from this because of the turnover taxes charged on consumption and

* See A. Csepinszky's study in this volume.

the subsidies aimed at lowering consumer prices. By deducting these, personal and public consumptions can also be reduced to the uniform price basis. The same holds, *mutatis mutandis,* for investments and stockpiling.

The case of exports is different. Here, turnover taxes are aimed to reduce excessive export returns of the enterprises to the level of domestic sales prices, whereas subsidies are aimed to raise low export returns to a level corresponding to the domestic sales prices. (In both cases, "export returns" mean the product of the foreign currency received and the uniform "foreign-trade multiplier".) Accordingly, uniform prices can be approached by adding the export subsidies to export sales returns, and deducting from them the turnover taxes. This method differs from the generally accepted principle of valuation which does not include subsidies in the sales receipts. Of course, our proposition claims neither exclusive validity, nor even the qualification that it is more correct than the traditional one. But as this system of valuation seems to be more expedient for practical reasons, the possibility of switching to this system should be secured. Simultaneously, however, the maintenance of other systems of valuation is also necessary, and optional transition from one to another should be rendered possible.

All this is essential also from the point of view of the comparability of input–output tables over time.

5. COMPARABILITY OVER TIME

The comparison of input–output tables drawn up for the Hungarian economy (1959, 1961, 1965, 1968) seems to be necessary for several reasons. In absence of comparability, the earlier tables cannot be used for the purposes of analysis and planning. The compilation of a series of tables from 1959 to 1970 made comparable over time can by no means be avoided in economic analyses.

From the viewpoint of financial and price planning, the construction of such a comparable series of tables is desirable for two reasons. First, the forecasting of prices relies mostly on assumptions regarding technological changes, and these assumptions are based on the expected future development of the technological coefficients, which in turn may be forecast from comparable input–output time series tables. On the other hand, price analysis must be coupled with an investigation of physical growth, since the assumed future prices must conform to a consistent structure of production and technology. For this purpose, the use of input–output tables corresponding to expectable future proportions and technological patterns is the most appropriate.

The solution of this problem raises, of course, many statistical questions of detail, the treatment of which would exceed the scope of the present paper. There is no doubt, however, that the comparability of the "small" input–output tables, i.e., those covering each year from 1959 to 1968, can be secured already — even if not satisfying all requirements; this shows that the problem can be solved. In the course of the calculations we could rely on mathematical methods and on computers. But even so, the securing of comparability requires such an amount of work as can only be performed — similarly to the elaboration of the financial matrices — in the framework of the planned cooperation of all central authorities involved.

In the following, I would like to sum up briefly the above-mentioned mathematical methods.

6. MATHEMATICAL METHODS APPLICABLE TO INPUT–OUTPUT CALCULATIONS

In the course of statistical work related to input–output tables, the problem regularly emerges that tables strictly conforming to given requirements of consistency have to be drawn up on the basis of limited, and often contradictory, information. When compiling an input–output table, we generally assume certain data to be exact, others to fluctuate around the most likely value, and we also assume that the exact or estimated data will satisfy the consistency conditions following from the model. In practice, however, the situation is that, e.g., in a table grouped according to organizations we know exactly — we assume so — the size of the gross output or the wage bill, but we know less reliably the composition of the current consumption of materials, which is subject to eventual modification depending on the allocation of products. At the same time, there are constraints following from the structure of the input–output table itself, e.g., that the sums of columns and rows with the same serial number in a quadratic matrix must be equal, that is, the receipts of the branches must equal the sum of their expenses and net incomes.

The most widespread method for solving such problems is the RAS method, with the aid of which it is possible to derive the inner quadrant from the sums of the columns and the rows of a matrix. It can be proved that this method is convergent, and practical experience testifies that the conditions of convergence are favourable. Thus, the procedure is suited for solving certain tasks related to the construction of input–output tables.

At the same time, the RAS method also has its disadvantages. It prescribes strict consistency only for the marginal sums (the sums of rows and columns); thus the elements of the inner quadrant may assume optional values. In spite of this, the method can be used. If we start from the value system of intermediate inputs, which approximately satisfies the consistency requirements, we need not modify it to a significant extent in the course of calculations in order to make it consistent. In spite of this, it is still true that the elements of the inner quadrant are optional.

This situation makes it difficult to use the RAS method in some cases. Quite often we know exactly a great part of the elements of intermediate inputs. In such cases we must seek a solution which satisfies the conditions of consistency with the known values of these elements. Frequently we know unequivocally which of the elements of intermediate inputs have zero value; it is evident that the solution must also yield zeros in these places. The original form of the RAS method does not satisfy this requirement. In some other cases we may exactly know various non-zero elements and therefore prescribe that the solution must yield these values. Again in other cases there may be a need for a further degree of consistency, which cannot be taken into account when the RAS method is used. Thus, it seems expedient to widen the scope of mathematical methods to be used for constructing input–output tables, beside the application of the RAS method. I would like to review here a few such methods.

a) *"Cleaning of profiles"*. Here the problem lies in the fact that from the table grouped according to organizational units the activities foreign to the main production profile of the given sector must be separated and transferred to the respective sectors. In the simplest case we may assume that the technological coefficients of these "foreign" activities are the same as those of the activity of the main profile. Since, however, there are both foreign and complementary activities in practically every sector, we actually do not know the true technological coefficients of any main production profile; almost every statistically observed technological coefficient is a weighted average of the technological coefficients characteristic of the main profile of the complementary profiles. In this case, the transformation of an input–output table can be solved with the aid of an iteration the algorithm of which mechanically imitates the traditional procedure. Obviously, the mechanical procedure can trace the consequences of the initial conditions more consistently and more exactly and it saves a lot of work, compared to the traditional manual computation. This method can also be generalized by saying that in some cases we consider the technological coefficients of the complementary activities as given.

b) *Construction of correction matrices.* These matrices modify the data of the basic table according to the methodological and structural changes. One of their characteristic features is that they modify only certain selected elements of the original table, thus most of their elements are zero. They must satisfy strict consistency requirements. Frequently, in the first quadrant there are data obtained by approximative estimates. Consistency must be secured in a way that, after correction, the zero elements should remain zero, whereas the figures should be estimated approximately. (The latter requirement may be met, e.g., by minimizing the sum of squares of the differences between the estimated and the corrected values.)

c) *Collation when the "marginal" values are fixed* is a frequent problem in connection with input–output computations. The RAS method was actually elaborated for the solution of this problem in the case when the marginal values (e.g., the gross output values of the sectors) are known, while the elements of the first quadrant, i.e., the transfers among sectors, are not known, or at least not exactly. The method proposed satisfies the consistency conditions in such a way that it minimizes the sum of squares of the deviations between the estimated values of the elements in the first quadrant and those made consistent by computation.

d) *Collation with additional constraints* can be applied if we have more exact and reliable information regarding the elements of an aggregate input–output table and wish to check, with their aid, our estimated data of a more detailed input–output table. In this case, we prescribe that not only the sums of the rows and columns with identical serial numbers should be equal but also certain aggregates of the more detailed matrix should agree with the corresponding elements of the aggregated matrix. Even here, we strive to minimize the sum of squares of the deviations between the independently estimated values and those made consistent by computation.

e) *Repricing*. This problem is a modified variant of the one reviewed under "d". In this case we are looking for a consistent matrix of price indices which exactly satisfies the constraints following from the prices of sales and the consumption of materials. Of course, when the method is actually applied, the values of the various financial variables, turnover taxes and price subsidies must also be considered. The differentiation of price indices within individual rows must rely mainly on estimates, because the prices of the different products within a sector may change to various extents and these products may play different roles in relation to buyers.

*

Above, I have dealt with the input–output tables of different structures, i.e., tables which meet different requirements. In short-term financial planning, the use of input–output tables grouped according to organizations is more expedient, while in long-term planning those grouped by activities are needed. Finally, price planning cannot be solved without an input–output table compiled in a grouping of "activities by organizations". The analysis of the transformation of the technological structure over time can be performed only with the aid of input–output tables converted to a common price basis and grouping. For planning, only a table excluding turnover taxes but including price subsidies can be used, while for price analyses that calculated on the same price basis is required. For the purposes of international comparison, tables calculated at sales prices are necessary. It seems, therefore, that instead of a single type a whole set of input–output tables is needed.

This requirement could not be met if only the traditional methods were available. However, the RAS method and the other mathematical methods listed here offer much help, and in this way the solution of the problems outlined is a realistic objective.

SOME STATISTICAL PROBLEMS OF THE INPUT-OUTPUT CALCULATIONS FOR 1972

by

ANDOR CSEPINSZKY

The next input–output table of the Central Statistical Office will be compiled for the year 1972. In its methods of statistical accounting, this table will differ somewhat from its predecessors. There will be changes in the scope of observation, in the methods of collecting, processing and presenting the data. These changes will be briefly reviewed in the following. (The methods of statistical accounting applied earlier, and remaining unchanged, are assumed to be known, and will not be dealt with.)

By way of introduction, it should be stressed that the calculations are made in a way that

a) the continuity of constructing input–output tables be maintained under all circumstances; the input–output table for 1972 belongs to a series of tables going back almost one and a half decade; the requirement of continuity is thus imperative;

b) the table should fit into the system of national economic balances, being part of this system, presenting a partial set of data interpreted within a greater, uniformly coordinated set, even if its structure is established according to its special objectives;

c) the calculations must increasingly satisfy the demand for data, permitting a better analysis and planning of the national economic processes.

1. THE ECONOMIC SPHERE COVERED BY THE TABLE (GROUPING BY SECTORS)

The 1973 calculations differ from the tables of previous years in two respects: (a) the table transgresses the "sphere of material production and services", it covers also the sectors of the non-material sphere; (b) agriculture appears here in a more detailed breakdown. Both changes have become necessary because of the claims arising on the part of input–output models.

In the financial, income and price models relying on input–output tables and interpreted for real processes, the indicators expressing the cumulated inputs have a decisive influence on the conclusions to be derived from the model. For instance, in the price models called upon to calculate "normative" prices, the so-called "transformation price indices" are calculated with the aid of these indicators. In the models treating production processes they have a fundamental importance in determining the contribution of the individual sectors. This is why it is important that the indicators represent all contributions of the sectors completely. An input–output table must present the national economy in its entirety, with all its operating sectors; in addition to the sphere of material production and services, it must also describe the inter-sector relations within the non-material sphere.

A desaggregation of the agricultural sector is justified because of the magnitude of its output on the one hand, and the very differing character and destination of its products, on the other. When agriculture is handled uniformly, items of the heterogeneous contents will appear both in the intra-sector relations and in those with other sectors. Input–output models, relying on the assumption of the constancy of these items and of the product pattern, are arbitrary and hardly tenable. Thus, the desaggregation of agricultural activities seemed to be a rational solution, permitting at the same time a more differentiated accounting of demand.

The inclusion of the non-material sphere of the national economy into the input–output calculations and the desaggregation of agricultural data do not require the discontinuation of separate investigation in the material sphere for the purposes of comparison with earlier years. A variant of the 1972 table grouped according to activities makes it possible to separate the two spheres and to interpret the table exclusively for the sphere of material production and services, i.e., in a form analogous with the input–output tables of earlier years.

The sectoral grouping of the 1972 input–output table according to organizations and activities is shown by Appendixes 1 and 2.

The discussion regarding the sectoral breakdown should be complemented with two remarks. First, the nomenclatures presented in the two appendixes show the *deepest* desaggregation made possible by the 1972 input–output table. The various investigations may, of course, require a different aggregation of economic activities. For instance, in the publications of the Central Statistical Office dealing with the balances of the national economy, a strongly aggregated (21 by 21 sector) version of the 1972 input–output table will appear. Aggregated input–output tables will also serve for measuring changes over time, e.g., in the system of technological coefficients. Variants of the input–output table differing only in the degree of aggregation can be calculated easily by using computer techniques.

The second remark is that, for the purposes of international comparison, both forms of the input–output table are necessary. In the case of comparing intra-CMEA relations, the "Material Product System" (MPS) should be used, whereas for comparisons of the CMEA countries with non-socialist ones, the System of National Accounts (SNA) is to be applied.

2. COLLECTION AND PROCESSING OF DATA

From the viewpoint of data collection, the 1972 input–output table falls into two clearly distinguishable parts. One is the sphere of material production and services, the other includes all non-material activities. In the first field, the collection of data strictly follows the usual statistical methods, i.e., it utilizes the information channels that have become organic parts of the statistical accounting system.

The situation is different with the non-material sphere. Here, we lack experience in data collection. Earlier statistical investigations of these sectors did not usually approach their subject from the economic aspect. Therefore, they failed to supply data sufficient for the construction of input–output tables. Although attempts were made to desaggregate inputs according to their origins, in the majority of cases only likely assumptions or estimates by specialists were made.

In this field an adequate system of information is still to be established. Because of the extremely heterogeneous character of the activities performed by the non-material sectors, the only practicable way of procuring the necessary data is by taking small samples. For this, the mass of available data must be classified according to a few well-chosen types of institutions. Then, within each of these strata, very detailed data should be collected (on the pattern of inputs, etc.) from a small number of selected units of observation which may be assumed to represent the population in question. The advantages of the procedure are obvious. At the price of a fraction of the costs that would be needed for a full-scope observation or for larger samples, it secures the data necessary for the compilation of the input–output table. Though these data will be less accurate, no doubt they will be better than what could be obtained by resorting to mere assumptions or experts' opinions. Moreover, the inaccuracy can be held within rather narrow limits by rationally selecting the types of institutions and by meeting the requirements of sampling with respect to probability theory.

We wish to organize the processing of the data in a way somewhat differing from earlier practice. We will work out the blocks relating to the individual national-economic branches separately. This means that for each of them an input–output table will (or can) be constructed that can, on the one hand, provide a basis for the input–output analysis of the field in question (including the drawing up of input–output models) and, on the other hand, that can facilitate a further desaggregation of the branches, and thereby the elaboration of the so-called "partial balances" (having been part of our earlier practice).

In the second stage, the separately constructed partial tables will be put together. The general-purpose input–output table will be constructed from these partial tables. Should contradictions emerge, we shall try to eliminate them through interviewing the constructors of the partial tables in question and by collating the various channels of information. Since the constructors of the individual blocks must compile their separate balances according to checked data, there is hope that the contradictions will not be solved in a formal way, and truly advantageous solutions will be arrived at.

3. THE SYSTEM OF TABLES

The system of the input–output table for 1972 conforms to the increased requirements raised against contemporary models.* The tables for earlier years were intended to meet the requirements of production analyses. The 1972 table takes a further step forward. In formulating its system of tables the requirements of the financial and price models also have a role. On the one hand, in addition to the breakdown by activities the table is constructed by organizations as well. On the other hand, the block of direct inputs, the part comprising the primary value components, is more detailed than it was in previous tables.

The system of tables is based on a table of 102 activities by 91 industries (defined by organizations) comprising both domestic and foreign resources. From this basic table is derived, by re-arranging the data of its columns, (1) the "activities by activities" type of table, and by re-arranging its rows, (2) the "organizations by organizations" type.

Depending on the way in which the basic table of "activities by organizations" is converted into the "activities by activities" and "organizations by organizations" types, i.e., depending on the assumptions used regarding the so-called industrial technologies, different coefficient matrices will be arrived at. Since the matrix of input coefficients is highly important from the viewpoint of input–output models, we are going to show the interrelations between the three types of tables starting from two basic assumptions: (1) organizations perform their activities in fixed proportions and (2) in performing a given activity, the organizations contribute to it in fixed proportions.

Of course, mixed solutions are also possible. In such cases, to some parts of the "activity by organization" table we apply Assumption 1 and to the rest Assumption 2.

Within the basic table the interrelations may be defined with the aid of the following relations:

$$X^A = S1 + Y^A \qquad (1)$$

$$X^A = T'1 \qquad (2)$$

$$X^O = T1 \qquad (3)$$

$$S\,1 = KX^O \qquad (4)$$

$$T'1 = LX^O \qquad (5)$$

$$T1 = MX^A \qquad (6)$$

* For the requirements raised by planning see the papers by L. Cserba and Gy. Szakolczai in this volume.

where:

X^A	the column vector of gross output by industries defined as *activities,*
X^O	the column vector of gross output by industries defined as *organizations,*
T	the matrix of gross national output in a breakdown of "organizations by activities", where the rows show the output of organizations in a breakdown by activities, whereas the columns present the outputs of activities in a breakdown by organizations,
Y^A	the column vector of final demand, according to activities,
S	the matrix of intermediary consumption in a breakdown of "activities by organizations",
K, L, M	coefficient matrices, of which K shows the relation between the gross output of industries as defined by organizations and intermediary consumption; L is the branch composition of activities according to the gross outputs of industries defined as organizations; and M the composition of organizations according to the gross outputs of industries defined as activities.

With the aid of equations (1) to (6), the coefficients of the two tables (i.e., "activities by activities" and "organizations by organizations") can be derived in the following manner:

$$X^A = S1 + Y^A = KX^O + Y^A \tag{7}$$

Assuming a constant composition by activities in the case of organizations we obtain

$$X^A = KL^{-1} X^A + Y^A \tag{8}$$

and

$$X^A = (I - KL^{-1})^{-1} Y^A \tag{9}$$

By analogy we may write

$$X^O = (I - L^{-1}K)^{-1} L^{-1} Y^A \tag{10}$$

This means that once the technology of activities is approved and stabilized, the coefficient matrix of the "activities by activities" table may be obtained by computing the matrix product KL^{-1} while the table "organizations by organizations" is given by the product $L^{-1} K$.

By analogy of the preceding deduction, the coefficient matrices of the "activity by activity" and "organization by organization" tables can be calculated, provided that the organizational composition of activities is fixed. In the first case, it will be equal to KM; in the latter, with MK.

However, a matrix can only be inverted if it is square, therefore, the assumption of an activity composition can only be used if the number of organizations is equal to the number of activities.

The system of input–output tables for 1972 is as follows if we set out from the basic table of activities by organizations:

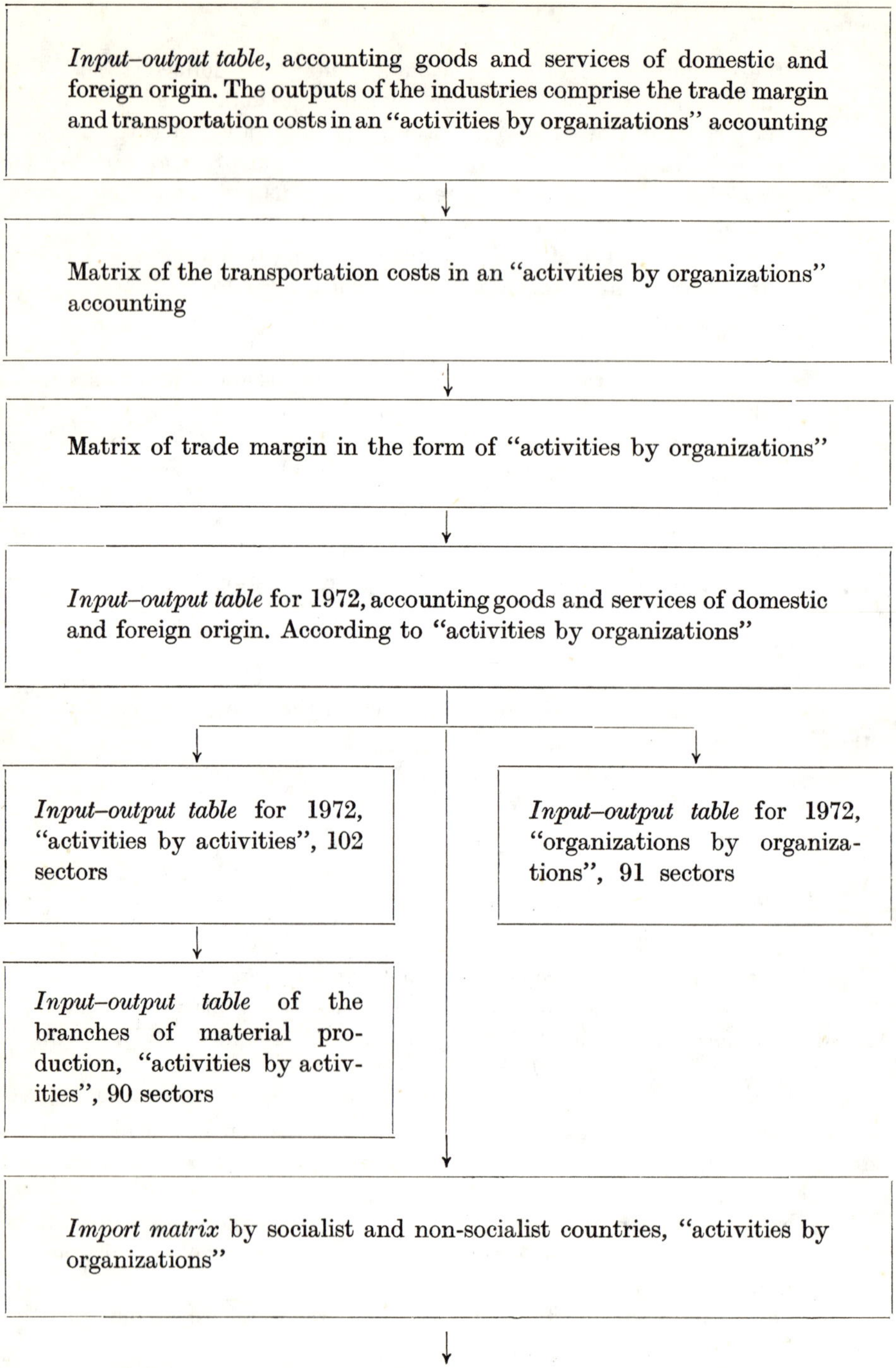
Input–output table, accounting goods and services of domestic and foreign origin. The outputs of the industries comprise the trade margin and transportation costs in an "activities by organizations" accounting
Matrix of the transportation costs in an "activities by organizations" accounting
Matrix of trade margin in the form of "activities by organizations"
Input–output table for 1972, accounting goods and services of domestic and foreign origin. According to "activities by organizations"
Input–output table for 1972, "activities by activities", 102 sectors
Input–output table for 1972, "organizations by organizations", 91 sectors
Input–output table of the branches of material production, "activities by activities", 90 sectors
Import matrix by socialist and non-socialist countries, "activities by organizations"

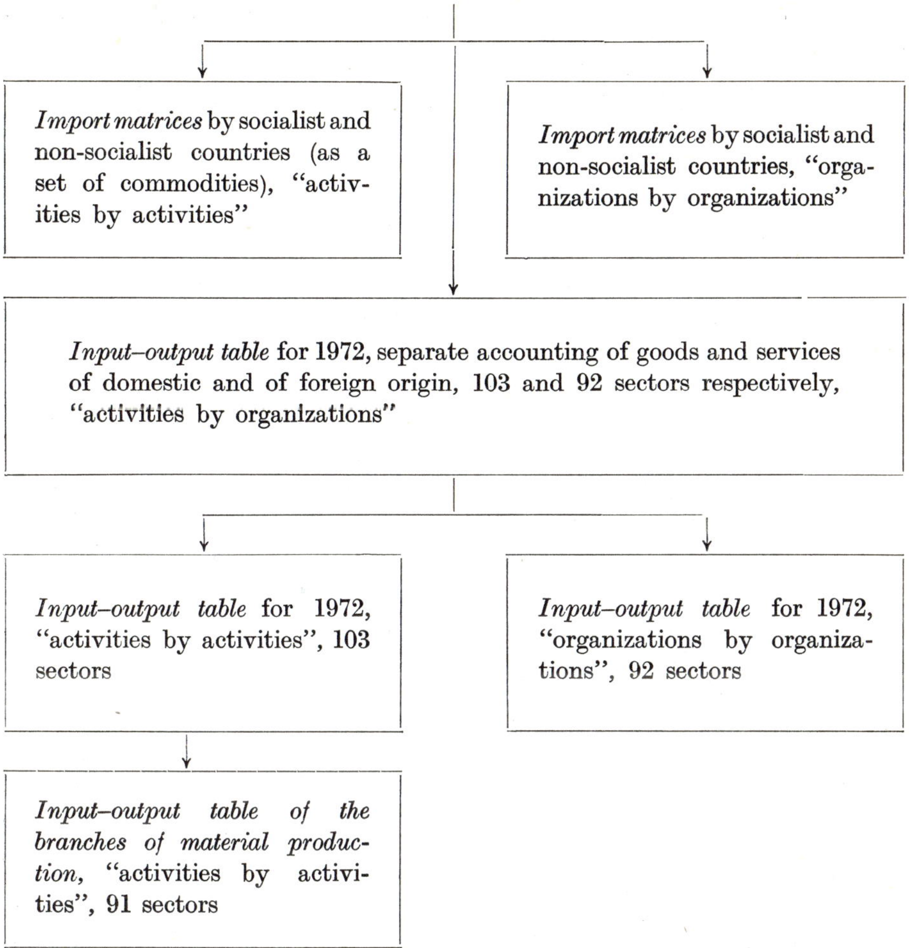

4. THE SYSTEM OF VALUATION APPLIED

Input–output models used in economic analyses and planning raise requirements against the prices to be applied in the input–output tables. The basic requirement of every input–output analysis is rather a strict one, namely, every product must have a special price. If the same product or service is valuated at different prices in different places of the input–output table, the system of equations derived from the model has no unique solution.

In order to illustrate this, let us start from gross industrial output interpreted as a sum of intermediary inputs and final use. According to our goals, we must divide the value data of the input–output table into two components: quantity and price. In this case, if more than one price exist for the same product, we should write:

$$(P_1 + \Delta P_{11})\, Q_{11} + \ldots + (P_1 + \Delta P_{1n})\, Q_{1n} + (P_1 + \Delta P_{1,n+1})\, q_{1,n+1} + \ldots$$
$$+ (P_1 + \Delta P_{1,n+m})\, q_{1,n+m} = (P_1 + \Delta P_{10})\, Q_1$$
$$(P_2 + \Delta P_{21})\, Q_{21} + \ldots + (P_2 + \Delta P_{2n})\, Q_{2n} + (P_2 + \Delta P_{2,n+1})\, q_{2,n+1} + \ldots$$
$$+ (P_2 + \Delta P_{2,n-+m})\, q_{2,n+m} = (P_2 + \Delta P_{20})\, Q_2 \qquad (11)$$
$$\ldots\ldots\ldots\ldots\ldots\ldots\ldots\ldots\ldots\ldots\ldots\ldots\ldots\ldots$$
$$(P_n + \Delta P_{n1})\, Q_{n1} + \ldots + (P_n + \Delta P_{nn})\, Q_{nn} + (P_n + \Delta P_{n,n+1})\, q_{n,n+1} + \ldots$$
$$+ (P_n + \Delta P_{n,n+m})\, q_{n,n+m} = (P + \Delta P_{no})\, Q_n$$

where:

Q_{ij}, Q_i, q_{ij} the gross, the intermediary and the final outputs of the industries, accounted in physical units of measurements; and

P_i, P_{ij}, P_{io} the prices in the industries, meaning both the unchanged and the changing parts, as well as the average level.

The above system of equations can be broken down into two parts. In the first, the outputs and uses measured in physical units are multiplied with constant prices. Let us write this in the form of a matrix equation:

$$\hat{P}AQ + \hat{P}Q^F = \hat{P}Q \qquad (12)$$

where:

$\hat{P}$ the diagonal matrix of unchanged prices

Q the column vector of gross outputs

Q^F the column vector of final uses, and

A the so-called transaction matrix, constructed by using the relation $Q_{ij} = a_{ij}Q_j$

If the system of equations is solved for the product $\hat{P}Q$, we get:

$$\hat{P}Q = (I - \hat{P}A\hat{P}^{-1})^{-1}\hat{P}Q^F \qquad (13)$$

which corresponds to the usual price formula and also meets the conditions necessary for the solution.

The situation is different as regards the second part which comprises the outputs in terms of physical units and the price differences varying according to the different fields of utilization. This system of interrelations may be written in the form of the following matrix equation:

$$\Delta\hat{P}Q = A^{\Delta}Q + \Delta\hat{P}Q^F \qquad (14)$$

Thus, the conditions required for a unique solution are, of course, not present, since the number of unknowns is greater than the number of equations.

For palpable reasons, the principle requiring the uniform valuation of a given product or service can never be fully asserted in practice. Thus, strictly speaking, the system of equations of an input–output model never has a unique solution. We only pretend that our prices are uniform in the different fields of uses, as this is necessary for a unique solution. However, it must be emphasized that the method guarantees only a formal solution. Any realistic solution of the system of equations is possible only when the price of a given product or service is the same in all uses.

When looking for the causes of price differences and for the places of their emergence, it turns out that most price differences are due to the effect of the so-called financial regulators. In other words, it is mainly due to the tax policy and to the system of financial subsidies (for reasons of economic policy or other considerations) that the price of the same product or service is different. Therefore, in order to promote a real solution of our system of equations, it is not sufficient to compile the input–output table at actual sales prices, but efforts must be made also to eliminate the effects originating from the financial regulators. It is in this way that we can best secure the assertion of the principle of uniform pricing, the condition of a unique solution.

In view of all this, we plan to work out, in compiling the 1972 input–output table, the following system of tables regarding the system of valuation:

Input–output table for 1972: inputs and outputs accounted at actual sales prices

↓

Matrix of turnover taxes and subsidies

↓

Matrix of customs duties and import turnover taxes

↓

Input–output table for 1972 (input and output values, excluding turnover tax, customs duty and import turnover tax, but including subsidies)

In this paper, an attempt was made at outlining briefly the statistical innovations comprised in the input–output table for 1972; these were made necessary by the rising needs of economic analysis and planning. Though the above discussion cannot claim completeness, it may motivate the methodological changes and show their necessity, and it may give an idea of the way along which we intend to proceed in the future.

APPENDIX 1

Sectors figuring in the input–output table for 1972, by *organizational units*

1. Coal mining and briquetting
2. Turf mining
3. Extraction of mineral oil and natural gas
4. Bauxite mining
5. Mining of other ores and non-metallic minerals
6. Electric energy production
7. Ferrous metallurgy
8. Aluminium metallurgy
9. Other non-ferrous metallurgy
10. Machine building
11. Production of vehicles
12. Production of electrical machinery and appliances
13. Production of telecommunication and vacuum-technical equipment
14. Production of precision instruments
15. Production of mass products made of metals
16. Production of bricks, tiles, and refractory material
17. Quarrying
18. Lime and cement production
19. Production of prefabricated building components
20. Production of insulating materials against heat, sound and water
21. Production of fine ceramics and grinding stones
22. Glass production
23. Production of organic and inorganic chemicals
24. Processing of mineral oil and natural gas
25. Production of municipal gas
26. Chemical processing of coal
27. Pharmaceutical industry
28. Production of dyes
29. Production of household chemicals and cosmetics
30. Rubber industry
31. Processing of synthetic materials
32. Production of sawnwood and boards
33. Production of joineries

34. Furniture industry
35. Other wood-processing industries
36. Paper industry
37. Printing industry
38. Cotton industry
39. Fibre-processing industry
40. Flax, hemp and jute industry
41. Wool industry
42. Silk industry
43. Production of smallware
44. Knitwear industry
45. Leather and fur industries
46. Shoe industry
47. Textile garment industry
48. Handicrafts and home industries
49. Other industries
50. Meat industry
51. Poultry and egg processing
52. Dairy industry
53. Canning and preserving industry
54. Flour-milling
55. Baking and pastry goods
56. Sugar industry
57. Production of sweets
58. Vegetal oil industry
59. Production of spirits and starch
60. Wine industry
61. Breweries
62. Mineral water and soft drinks
63. Tobacco industry
64. Private artisans
65. Overground construction
66. Underground construction
67. Fitting and mounting
68. Other organizations of the construction industry
69. Designing for construction
70. Private construction activities
71. Agriculture
72. Forestry
73. Water management
74. Rail transportation
75. Cross country and urban transportation
76. Other transportation
77. Telecommunications

78. Domestic trade
79. Foreign trade
80. Personal services
81. Public utilities
82. Business services
83. Housing
84. Health service
85. Social and recreation services
86. Public education
87. Arts, other cultural services, and adult education
88. Sports and physical culture
89. Science and scientific services
90. Public administration and other services
91. Financial institutions

APPENDIX 2

Sectors figuring in the input–output table for 1972, by *activities*

1. Coal mining and briquetting
2. Turf mining
3. Extraction of mineral oil and natural gas
4. Bauxite mining
5. Mining of other ores and non-metallic minerals
6. Electric energy production
7. Ferrous metallurgy
8. Aluminium metallurgy
9. Other non-ferrous metallurgy
10. Foundries
11. Machine building
12. Production of vehicles
13. Production of electrical machinery and appliances
14. Production of telecommunication and vacuum-technical equipment
15. Production of precision instruments
16. Production of mass products made of metals
17. Production of bricks, tiles and refractory material
18. Quarrying
19. Lime and cement production
20. Production of prefabricated building components
21. Asbestos-cement production
22. Production of insulating materials against heat, sound and water
23. Production of fine ceramics and grinding stones
24. Glass production

25. Production of fertilizers and inorganic chemicals
26. Production of other chemicals
27. Oil refining
28. Production of municipal gas
29. Chemical processing of coal
30. Pharmaceutical industry
31. Production of dyes
32. Production of household chemicals and cosmetics
33. Rubber industry
34. Processing of synthetic materials
35. Production of sawnwood and boards
36. Production of joineries
37. Furniture industry
38. Other wood-processing industries
39. Paper industry
40. Printing industry
41. Cotton industry
42. Fibre-processing industry
43. Flax, hemp and jute industry
44. Wool industry
45. Silk industry
46. Production of smallware
47. Knitwear industry
48. Leather and fur industries
49. Shoe industry
50. Textile garment industry
51. Handicrafts and home industries
52. Other industries
53. Meat industry
54. Poultry and egg processing
55. Dairy industry
56. Canning and preserving industry
57. Flour-milling industry
58. Baking and pastry goods
59. Sugar industry
60. Production of sweets
61. Vegetal oil industry
62. Production of spirits and starch
63. Wine industry
64. Breweries
65. Mineral water and soft drinks
66. Tobacco industry
67. Overground construction
68. Underground construction

69. Fitting and mounting
70. Designing for construction
71. Bread grain production
72. Production of fodder
73. Production of potatoes and vegetables
74. Production of fruit
75. Winegrowing and wine production
76. Production of industrial plants
77. Production of other plants
78. Cattle breeding
79. Hog breeding
80. Poultry breeding
81. Breeding of other animals
82. Other agricultural activities
83. Forestry
84. Water management
85. Railway transport
86. Cross-country and urban transportation
87. Other transport
88. Telecommunications
89. Domestic trade
90. Foreign trade
91. Personal services
92. Public utilities
93. Business services
94. Housing services
95. Health service
96. Social and recreation services
97. Education
98. Arts, other cultural services and adult education
99. Sports and physical culture
100. Science and scientific services
101. Public administration and other services
102. Financial institutions

THE UTILIZATION OF AN AGGREGATE INPUT-OUTPUT TABLE IN ECONOMIC FORECASTS

by

MIKLÓS SIMÁN

One of the problems most frequently emerging in the discussions about the utilization of input–output tables consists in their excessive aggregation. I wish to render account here on an application where, to make it easily usable, the input–output table has been aggregated in a way that its inner quadrant consisted only of six rows and columns, respectively.

The Economic Research Institute is engaged in short-term macro-economic forecasts. We prepare forecasts three times a year. We try to give reliable forecasts by simultaneously applying several methods. In some fields trends are computed, in others elasticity and stochastic analyses are performed. Experiments aiming to use econometric models are under way.

Besides the evaluation of past results and experience with the aid of mathematical methods, intuitive estimation also plays a great role in our forecasts. Only in this manner is it possible to estimate how the behaviour of consumers and economic organizations will be affected in the near future by changes in foreign and domestic market conditions, in prices, in the labour situation, as well as by centrally planned measures and "influences".

These estimates are made for partial aggregate fields, according to the availability of information, maintaining, of course, the macro-economic character of the forecast. An aggregated input–output table is generally expected to secure the consistency of the partial computations and to eliminate eventual contradictions.

It follows from our purposes that the extent of aggregation depends on how the forecasts for the economic field in question are made. In the forecasts we start, on the one hand, from *final use*, i. e., from the trends of consumption and investment. We have relatively abundant data for forecasting personal incomes and consumption, and their increase is relatively steady. For example, the figures on retail trade are available at frequent intervals in a given breakdown. In our forecasts we made efforts to adapt ourselves to this situation. The case is similar with another important item of final, use, namely, exports.

On the other hand, we endeavoured to determine the expectable production by major productive industries. Here, too, there are detailed data available at considerably frequent intervals, particularly for manufacturing. This factor, therefore, does not hinder the desaggregation of the forecast, moreover, it even becomes possible to apply the same nomenclature as was used for the data on final use.

By weighing all these factors, the aggregates figuring in the inner quadrant are the following:

- industries producing for productive consumption,
- industries producing investment goods,
- industries producing consumer goods,
- industries producing agricultural and food products,
- productive services,
- non-productive services.

The aggregation of the input–output table takes place in the same way.

In this breakdown the proportions can be better planned and can be more easily confronted with the pattern of utilization than in the case of the usual industrial classification by branches.

The industrial branches have been classified into the first three groups according to the characteristic directions of domestic sales. Where the vertical relations were unequivocal, they have naturally been taken into account. (For example, although supplying mostly for productive purposes, the building material industry has been aggregated with the construction industry to form a sector producing for investment; similarly, the textile industries producing cloth have been classified as turning out consumer goods, even though a great part of their output undergoes further processing.) The productive services include transport, communications and trade.

In order to illustrate how simple such an aggregate input–output table is, I attach the table of 1968 from which the aggregation was made. As regards annual forecasts, the 1969, 1970 and 1971 tables have also been compiled on the basis of estimated data. It is an advantage due to their small size that whenever new data or new concepts on production, consumption or foreign trade emerge, the new computations can be made very quickly.

Tables for a period to be prognosticated are compiled as follows: the specialists of each field assess the expected growth of the various items of final use: private and public consumption, investments, exports and also their pattern by commodity groups. The expected growth of the productive fields is established in a similar manner. (As regards the expected growth of productive and non-productive services, a more reliable method is just being worked out.) On the basis of the estimated growth rate of the productive fields, the changes in gross products and in the major factors can also be estimated. (Recently there were such changes in the material input ratios in this field, which had to be handled separately.) Once the second quadrant is thus compiled, the changes in inventories emerge as a residual. If the magnitude of this latter is disproportionate, this fact calls attention either to mistakes made in the forecast, or to a future imbalance of the economy. Further estimates can be obtained by determining the first quadrant with unchanged coefficients or with purposefully modified ones. The forecasting of imports takes place in a way similar to exports. In such an aggregation, the coefficients show rather high stability. If a table shows a disproportion among the partial forecasts, they should be revised.

The consideration of price changes is a problem that always emerges in connection with our forecasts. Most forecasts refer to the rate of growth, where constant (comparable) prices are used. In the first stage, also the aggregate input–output table is drawn at such prices. Since, however, income and financial data are analysed as well, a version calculated at current prices is also necessary. The table with current prices is compiled by starting from the aggregate table drawn up in the way described above, and by applying separate price index numbers for each aggregate detailed in a similar manner. (For calculating price indices mainly the data of the second quadrant are used.)

When aggregating the table, there is a recurring problem caused by those items that are difficult to interpret in the framework of the aggregate table (customs duties, value differences, etc.). Another recurring problem is how to account, in the table constructed at comparable prices, for changes in foreign prices.

With this short explanation of the purpose and usefulness of the aggregated input–output tables I do not intend to pretend to present some new scientific achievement. This is just a simple method which, according to our experience, has promoted the improvement of the reliability of forecasts. Due to its simplicity, perhaps it might be applied in planning to examine variants in an aggregated manner.

Finally, I would mention that we are now weighing the idea of utilizing a fourth quadrant of the input–output table for forecasting the redistribution of incomes. Just for the sake of curiosity, I present here the breakdown of the redistribution of net incomes in 1968 and 1970, with the assumption — not true, of course, in this strict sense — that wages serve only personal consumption while depreciation is only used for investments.

	1968	1970
	1,000 million forints	
Out of net income		
personal consumption	36	36
public consumption	26	30
investments	40	54
stockpiling	15	12
balance of foreign trade	—2	—9
Total	115	123

Within the use of net income, it is mainly the share of investments that seems to grow, usually at the expense of investments and international financial means. Of course, the method needs refinement, primarily through a detailed analysis of the credit sphere and the budget.

Aggregate input–output table for 1968, (billion F)

	Production				Services		Total	Consumption		Investments	Changes in stocks	Exports	Grand total
	means of production	investment goods	consumer goods	foodstuffs	productive	non-productive		personal	public				
Production:													
means of production	35	25	13	8	6	5	92	8	1	2	4	15	122
investment goods	6	10	3	2	3	7	31	4	—	52	5	17	109
consumer goods	5	4	13	1	4	5	32	23	1	2	3	20	81
foodstuffs	3	2	2	85	2	3	97	64	1	2	4	17	185
Services:													
productive	8	5	4	7	9	5	38	30	1	3	—	5	77
non-productive	1	2	—	1	1	1	6	31	21	—	—	—	58
Total	58	48	35	104	25	26	296	160	25	61	16	74	632
Imports	21	9	12	11	1	1	55	10	1	11	—1	—	76
Total of material consumption	79	57	47	115	26	27	351	170	26	72	15	74	708
Depreciation allowance	7	4	3	6	6	6	32	—	—	—	—	—	—
Wages, salaries and other incomes	15	23	14	45	15	22	134	—	—	—	—	—	—
Social net income	21	25	17	19	30	3	115	—	—	—	—	—	—
Grand total	122	109	81	185	77	58	632	—	—	—	—	—	—

PRICE TRANSFORMATIONS IN THE INPUT-OUTPUT TABLE — PROBLEMS OF VALUATION IN THE NEW SYSTEM OF NATIONAL ECONOMIC ACCOUNTS

by

JÓZSEF KUPCSIK

Apart from the fields of price analysis and price planning based on the traditional input–output techniques, the price problems occurring in statistical work belong to two types.

First, we must choose the pricing principles of valuation on the basis of which the "current prices" figuring in the balance of the given year should be formed. In this respect, we have to choose between alternative solutions as, e.g., producer or consumer prices, the accounting or neglecting of turnover taxes and price subsidies, the various ways of calculating agriculture's consumption in kind and the method of valuating trade and transport activities.

Second, price-statistical investigations become necessary when tables relating to different periods of time are recalculated for making them comparable and thus to show changes over time. Substantially this means obtaining value sums by multiplying quantities by "constant" or "comparable" unit prices in order to express changes in "volume". In the context of the input–output table this is a particularly difficult task. The nature of the problem is partly theoretical, partly practical. Theoretically, it is difficult to develop, from a model resting basically on value terms, a variant expressing "volume" and to give the method of price transformation used an unchallengeable, absolutely correct justification. In practice, technical problems arise mainly from the lack of data available on price changes in the necessary detail.

In Hungary, price transformations have been rather frequently adopted for input–output tables (essentially from the early sixties). Much experience was gained, several publications have dealt with the problems arising, yet it is still necessary to dwell on the problem. Beyond the fact that the procedures applied have not always yielded adequate results, price transformations usually raise specific problems.

The subject is particularly topical since already when calculating the aggregate table for 1969 we had to apply an extended notion of production, including also the service branches. Therefore, also the effects of price changes occurring in the service branches had to be registered, causing an increase in the number of methodological and practical problems to be solved.

This paper deals with the particular problems which emerged in the course of calculating the 21-sector model elaborated by the Central Statistical Office for 1969 on the basis of 1968 prices. Its statements serve only for stressing the new features of the problem.

I. GENERAL PROBLEMS OF PRICE TRANSFORMATIONS IN INPUT–OUTPUT TABLES

1. THE PROBLEMS OF THE INNER QUADRANT

In principle, the transforming of the values in the inner quadrant presents no particular difficulties. By multiplying the individual values of the block with the individual price index number characteristic of the given cell, we obtain the "volume", that is, a value calculated at comparable prices. But for doing this, we need as many price indices as there are elements in the inner quadrant. In the past, however, no such full-scope price matrix was available, nor is it at present. Safe points to start from were provided only by the output (producer) price index vectors (summarized for sectors) and by the similar price index vectors for the consumption of materials. These, however, provide only the "limiting" values, and the set of "volume" data obtained from these averages frequently seems to exceed the limits of tolerable error. The difference between the two limiting sums evidently indicates the inaccuracy of price transformations, in other words, the direction and extent of necessary corrections. In this respect, two procedures were developed, relying essentially on the same principle.

The first procedure begins by mechanically multiplying the rows with the average index number of producer prices. The values obtained are summarized by columns. The sums are then compared to the transformed value of material consumption obtained with the global price index. According to the differences, the cells presumably containing faulty or inaccurate data are identified and corrected by estimates relying on additional information. This procedure has been applied in transforming the "small" input–output tables. Its advantages lie in its simplicity and in the possibility of a flexible use of new information. Its disadvantage derives from the danger of a "built-in" bias, owing to the subjective nature of the corrections, and from its random character.

The second procedure was used for the price transformations of the "big" input–output table for 1965. (The first procedure is practically inapplicable for converting such big tables.) Its essence is that, on the basis of price indices previously established with previously determined sampling methods, "fields" are formed within the inner quadrant. Then, by taking into account the price index vectors of output and material consumption, the values found to be contradicting are corrected with the so-called RAS method.

No doubt, this second method is based on a better and more objective basis. Yet in our case it has not come up to expectations. The representation (sampling) of prices was small, some incredible values were obtained, requiring arbitrary intervention in several cases.

The experience of calculations unequivocally indicates that the average producer price indices, and indices of material prices serving essentially to check on them, do not in themselves yield satisfactory results. The average price indices of producer prices in a given sector generally show high dispersion according to the direction of sales. Evidently, this dispersion is due not only to the fact that the individual users pay different prices for the same product. Each purchaser sector buys from the same selling sector a different product-mix, and the individual prices may vary at very different ratios. Thus, e.g., in a branch of the light industry the prices of individual products changed between 1965 and 1968 at rates from a 40 per cent reduction to a 260 per cent rise. Under such conditions, the results of calculations with the aid of a "general" price index must be handled, even as a first approximation, with strong reservations. There may be, of course, exceptions. There exist branches of a more or less homogeneous nature, where the general price index may yield accurate data or at least a good approximation for each of the directions of sales.

The rough price transformations of the 1969 table was performed with "representative" price index numbers. In view of the relatively small price changes between 1968 and 1969, it seemed that only a small number of corrections would be necessary, and these could be carried out with the aid of the RAS method.

2. THE PROBLEMS OF EXPORTS AND IMPORTS

In recent years the valuation of foreign trade has been carried out in the input–output tables as well as in other national accounts with the aid of the so-called "foreign-exchange multipliers". This form of valuation is seemingly an advantage in calculations, since the multipliers remain unchanged for rather long periods. But the constancy of the foreign-exchange multipliers does not secure in itself that the values of the table calculated at current prices correctly reflect the changes in "volume". Prices may change, namely, also in terms of dollars and roubles, thereby influencing forint price levels in the same way as changes in domestic prices. In view of this, the practical problems of calculations will come to the fore.

We intend to convert the values of exports by relying on the data of sales statistics, and by formulating representative price indices.

The basis for calculating the consumption of imported materials is the input–output table of imports. The consumption of imported materials is calculated in the same form as that of the domestically produced materials. To check on the computations based on representative individual index numbers as well as the price indices of the gross consumption of materials, those of the corresponding imports have to be used, too.

3. PROBLEMS OF THE LOWER WING OF THE TABLE

One of the elements of the lower wing is *depreciation*. In working out the value at constant prices, in addition to the price changes of fixed assets, also the centrally regulated changes in the depreciation ratios must be taken into account. Price index numbers accounting for the combined effect of both these factors must be applied to each sector of the table. There is, however, hardly any practical possibility to compute such price indices. As an arbitrary solution, the valuation of depreciation at constant "prices" is based on the index number of investment prices characteristic of the given period. This involves the broad assumptions:

a) that the pattern of annual investment is the same as the composition of the already existing stock of fixed assets in the given sector;

b) that the depreciation rates remain unchanged;

c) that the price of the already existing fixed assets changes at the same rate as the price of goods figuring in current investment.

Actual experience, as a rule, generally does not justify these assumptions. It seems more expedient to weigh both labour intensity and efficiency, and, accordingly, to choose a method which best corresponds to the extent of changes taking place in the given period. For example, there are years when, by central measures the total stock of fixed assets is revalued, and also the depreciation rates are changed. In Hungary, the last such change occurred in 1968. Therefore, in all comparisons where the year 1968 is involved in the input–output table or where precisely 1968 is the basis for comparison, it is absolutely necessary to work out indices for each sector relating to the changes in the rate of depreciation. In other cases, when there occur only smaller fluctuations in the factors mentioned, it is possible to dispense with such correction.

Since between 1968 and 1969 there was no essential change in either the valuation of fixed assets or in depreciation ratios, it seems permissible to adopt, in the table calculated at comparable prices, the data according to current prices.

It needs some explanation why we do not refer here to price changes in current investments. As is known, the price level of current investments does not affect significantly the price level of the total stock of fixed assets. If we assume that the price index of investments shows a considerable rise, let us say 25 per cent, then — depending on the ratio of the investment to the total value of the already existing fixed assets in the sector, say 5, 10, or 20 per cent — the price index for the increased total of fixed assets will rise by 0.625, 1.25 and 2.5 per cent, respectively. Thus, even extreme price rises of investment do not cause serious changes in this respect. When, however, the tables compared cover a long period of time, the cumulated quantitative changes may have a stronger effect.

Finally, it must be mentioned that the conversion of the values of depreciation and of fixed assets to comparable prices must be compatible. Only in this case is it possible to draw correct economic conclusions from the changes in the indicators of depreciation and of capital-output ratios. For example, if we correct the sum of depreciation allowance with the consideration that the accounting price level of fixed assets has changed, then also the fixed assets must be converted accordingly, and *vice versa*.

A particular problem emerges in connection with converting *national income* and its constituent parts to comparable prices. Here we have to formulate "volume" sums which are not directly derived from multiplying the quantities of products by their unit prices. The characteristic feature here is that even the "volume" of the phenomenon observed is expressed in terms of value. In such cases, comparability is affected by the price change, i.e., by the changes in the purchasing power of money. Calculations must be performed even in such cases, however inconsistent it is. The sum of national income at comparable prices is obtained as the difference between the value of gross output and of the consumption of materials at constant prices. Although the volume cannot be directly assessed, the sum thus established yields a tolerable approximation of the national income.

As a quotient of the national incomes calculated at current and comparable prices, a price index number may be established, which is called — with reference to the principle of its computation — an "implicit price index".

The conversion of national income is performed in this way also in the input–output table. The real problem emerges when national income is decomposed according to its elements. The residual method is suited only for determining a single value. Thus, a direct method has to be found for converting the items of wages and net income. This is a rather difficult task since, according to our opinion, there are no objective criteria for assessing these items at comparable prices. In view of this, experiments were made where the residual value, that is, the effect of price changes has not been distributed by sectors. It was shown in a separate row of the lower wing, under the name of "price correction". But this did not prove to be an expedient solution since this separate row could not be adequately handled in the further processing and analysis of the table.

For the conversion of *wages* (and other individual incomes) into comparable prices, it seems best to start from the assumption that the growth in wages due to a rise in productivity and efficiency of labour is identical with the growth in these two factors. Hence, correction should be made only for the modification in value due to pure price effects. The question might be formulated as follows: assuming a change in the price system, what sum of wages should be paid to workers and employees in order that their value should agree with the present one. Proceeding along this line of reasoning, we arrive at the *consumer price index,* with the aid of which wages can be converted to comparable prices.

Under our economic mechanism we distinguish several kinds of *net income,* according to its way of accounting, origin, function and the form of its "with drawal" for the purposes of society. Accordingly, also the input–output table shows net income under different group headings (charges on assets, turnover tax, price subsidies, production subsidies, production taxes, other net income and enterprise profits). It is expedient to separate the part of the net income remaining with the enterprise (enterprise profits) from its other part which is centrally withdrawn from them (budget items). From the enterprise aspect, the latter can also be considered as costs, and as such, they suggest relatively simpler, more justifiable solutions for conversion.

In the budget items of net income the changes in volume and price are more clearly discernible. Thus, e.g., in the case of turnover tax a growth or decline of its sum, caused by a change in the volume of production or in its composition by products taxed at different rates, can be considered as the result of changes in volume. A change in the tax receipts caused by a new mode of levying the tax or a change in its rates can be classified as a change in prices. This approach can be uniformly followed also in respect of the other net income items collected for the budget. In 1968 there was an important change in the accounting of turnover tax (and other net income elements collected for the budget). The weight of the turnover tax decreased, and its realization was shifted in its bulk from the branches of material production to the trade. Therefore, major corrections become necessary if tables dating prior to 1968 must be converted, or comparable prices are to be starting from the price basis of a year previous to 1968.

II. PARTICULAR PROBLEMS OF PRICE TRANSFORMATION IN THE NON-MATERIAL SECTORS IN THE INPUT–OUTPUT TABLE

1. FUNDAMENTAL CHARACTERISTICS IN THE ACCOUNTING OF THE NON-MATERIAL SECTORS

We have no practical experience as yet with the price transformations of non-material production. The present study cannot thus claim to draw up a programme for the method of calculations that would be impeccable from every respect. However, it is expedient to stress first a few principles and particular features.

a) It is not only characteristic of non-material production that the result of the activity is generally a service and does not take the form of material goods, but also that in many cases the consumers are supplied with the result of the service activity without sale-and-purchase transactions. For such activities, price as an economic category can have but an indirect character. It is also disadvantageous that here the influence of the value-judgements made in the market is lacking.

b) The different nature of services also influences the accounting at current prices. The services sold as commodities (e.g., a cinema ticket) can be accounted at current "market" prices, while the non-commodity services (e.g., education) must be valued at input cost. This duplicity of valuating the services is not a "compromise" between theoretical considerations and practical possibilities; the two are in harmony. In drawing up the input–output table at current prices all this has already become a part of the practice.

c) There must be a close connection between the method of valuation and the principles applied for measuring price changes. Obviously, we would obtain a distorted value series if the actual value sums were calculated with market prices but their conversion into comparable prices would be according to the activity principle. This is, of course, an extreme example, but sometimes there are similar problems in practice (e.g., it may occur that the price indices available for calculations relate to a classification of services differing from what was used when the price sums were calculated at actual prices).

d) The question may seem justified whether it is worthwhile, or expedient, to eliminate the effect of price changes when the valuation of performances is based on the factor cost. On theoretical considerations, the question must be answered in the affirmative. Without doubt, we would create a queer and contradictory situation if we consistently converted part of the table and left another part of it untouched. It is, however, another question whether, for practical reasons, it were not advisable to neglect such very small price changes as occurred, e.g., between 1968 and 1969. In fact, price changes amounting to 1–2 per cent cannot have an essential role when we are trying to measure the changes in volume, since the differences caused by them are within the limits of error inherent to the calculation. But, in the interest of a continuous analysis of dynamics, it is recommendable to eliminate the effect of price changes regularly.

2. PRACTICAL PROBLEMS OF PRICE TRANSFORMATIONS IN THE NON-MATERIAL SECTORS

Finally, the practical problems of price transformations in the non-material sphere have to be examined. Here, we restrict ourselves to the services which are not distributed as commodities, i.e., the valuation of which takes place according to input price.

The conversion of the columns of material consumption figuring in the inner quadrant, as well as of the two complementary items showing inputs of embodied labour, i.e., the depreciation and the inputs of imported materials, raises the same requirements as do the sectors of material production. It follows that here the methods treated earlier in this context may be applied. In this field it is no doubt a disadvantage that less basic data are available, although the method of sampling can also yield results of satisfactory accuracy. As regards our concrete task, it can be considered as a propitious condition that no significant changes in prices or relative prices occurred between 1968 and 1969.

A particular solution is offered by the "row-wise" conversion of the data. It is necessary to indicate here two characteristic features. One is the concentration in the use of these services (about 90 per cent of the output of the non-material sectors belong to the sphere of final use), and the other that the price indices of the performances do not show any sizable dispersion. Thus we obtain rather high accuracy by uniformly converting the performances of the non-material sectors with the aid of the price indices established for the given sector, and by dispensing with the corrections offered by the RAS method.

As regards the conversion of *wages* in the non-material sectors, the index of consumer prices may be combined with the index for average wages. This approach may be justified by the following consideration. In material production, any change in average wages is in close stochastic relationship with the changes in the "volume of work performed". Thus, if in the course of ten years the average of real wages rises to twofold in the sphere of material production, the volume of use-values produced can be assumed to have changed at about the same rate; accordingly, it is justified to assume a similar change in the total volume of real wages. In the non-material sectors the relationship between performance and average wages is much looser. It is possible to circumvent this problem by referring to the "principle of uniform accounting", and by applying here too the consumer price index for eliminating price effects.

For repricing net income, we intend to employ the following procedure. As a first step we calculate an approximative, derived price index for the national income or the net national product. (As regards the non-material sector, this is based exclusively on wages.) With this price index we uniformly convert all elements of net income in the non-material sectors. The only argument justifying this method is that, with the aid of this price index, we can eliminate the changes in "the general purchasing power of money", and on this basis determine the value sums representing the changes in volume.

The values established at comparable prices for the non-material service sectors according to the above method show the changes in activity as measured by the inputs. This does by no means involve that, e.g., the treatment of the sick, or the educational or administrative activities really change to the extent shown. It is necessary to stress this point since, in principle, it is possible to measure the changes in such performances approximatively with the aid of a method similar to the index number computations based on "substitutive series", as applied in industry. But, owing to the nature of the input–output table conceived in value terms, it seems reasonable to perform price computations in the way proposed here.

ATTEMPTS AT SYSTEMATIZATION IN SOCIAL STATISTICS

by

RUDOLF ANDORKA and JÁNOS ILLÉS

In the field of economic science, more exact quantification and an increasing use of mathematical methods have greatly contributed to accuracy, making the application of data easier. As a result,

1. the interrelationships described are more clearly revealed;
2. the assumptions serving as a basis of a given theory, on the correctness of which the validity of this theory depends, may be expressed more unequivocally;
3. it is easier to verify a theoretical hypothesis by computing it with what in fact exists;
4. the "multiplier effects" of a process or of an economic measure may be shown numerically.

From among the social sciences, economics started the earliest and made the greatest advance in quantification and in the application of mathematics. An important step was the introduction of input–output tables. Recently, attempts have been made also in sociology at formulating the investigated processes in a mathematical form.*

1. A SYSTEM OF SOCIOLOGICAL AND DEMOGRAPHIC MODELS

One of the tendencies aimed at describing social processes by mathematical models was started by economists who were accustomed to using input–output tables in their field and recognized the practical necessity of describing and planning the interrelations between production and population (via labour force and consumption) in a similar form to what was already used with inter-industry relations. The first attempts of this kind are associated with the names of Tin-

* Coleman, J. S.: *Introduction to Mathematical Sociology*. The Free Press of Glencoe, Glencoe 1964.

Kemény, J. G.–Snell, J. L.–Thompson, G.: *Introduction into Finite Mathematics*. Vols. I–II. Prentice-Hall, Englewood Cliffs 1966.

Le vocabulaire des sciences sociales. Concepts et indices. Ed. Boudon, R. and Lazars feld, P. Mouton. Paris 1965.

L'analyse empirique de la causalité. Ed. Boudon, R. and Lazarsfeld, P. Mouton, Paris 1966.

L'analyse des processus sociaux. Ed. Chazel, F., Boudon, R. and Lazarsfeld, P. Mouton, Paris 1970.

Lazarsfeld, P.: *Philosophie des sciences sociales*. Gallimard, Paris 1970.

bergen and Correa.* Characteristically, they were aimed at forecasting the demand for general education and vocational training on the basis of the expectable future development of productive branches.

Stone** applied "socio-demographic accounts" of this type to the most diverse processes of social and demographic development. The basic idea of his accounts drawn up on the analogy of the input–output table is very simple. In the place of "inputs" figures the population (total or school age, working age, etc.) detailed according to various categories (domicile, occupation, level of education, etc.) at the beginning of the observed period, usually of a year. The distribution of the same population according to the same categories at the end of this observed period is considered as "output". The right wing of the table, where an input–output table contains the items of "final demand", shows here the number of departures from the given population (e.g., on account of deaths, emigration, retirement, etc.). The lower wing of the table, where the input–output table shows the "primary inputs", contains the increments of the given population (on account of birth, immigration, entering school or working age, etc.). Evidently, the inner matrix of the table shows the flows of population between the various categories during the period observed.

In a simplified form, the mathematical model used may be written as follows:

$$\Lambda^{\Theta}\mathbf{y} = \mathbf{A}\mathbf{y} + \mathbf{x} \tag{1}$$

where

$\mathbf{y}$ = the vector of endogenous variables;
Λ^{Θ} = a lag-operator in which Θ is the time factor. When (as it is usual) the observed period is a calendar year, then Θ is 1, and $\Lambda^{\Theta}\mathbf{y}(t) = \mathbf{y}(t + \Theta)$;
$\mathbf{x}$ = the change in the exogenous variables during the observed period;
$\mathbf{A}$ = matrix of parameters; the parameters may be either constant or variable in time; they express the intensity of flows between the various categories.

When applied to population increase, the model may take the following concrete form:

a) *change in female population*:

$$\Lambda\mathbf{n}_f = \mathbf{A}_f\mathbf{n}_f + \mathbf{B}_f\mathbf{n}_f \tag{2}$$

* Correa, H.: *The Economics of Human Resources.* North Holland, Amsterdam 1963.
Correa, H. and Tinbergen, I.: Quantitative Adaptation of Education to Accelerated Growth. *Kyklos,* No. 4, pp. 776–785, 1962.

** Stone, R.: *Mathematics in the Social Sciences and Other Essays.* Chapman and Hall, London 1966.
Stone, R.: *Educational Statistics in Relation to Systems of Socio-Demographic Accounts and Economic Accounts.* Conf. Eur. Stats/WG. 23/11, Geneva 1969.
Stone, R.: *Mathematical Models of the Economy and Other Essays.* Chapman and Hall, London 1970.
Stone, R.: Random Walks Through the Social Sciences. Lecture held at the World Congress of the Econometric Society, 1970, in Cambridge (mimeographed).

where

$\mathbf{n}_f$ = vector showing the age distribution of the female population at the beginning of the period;

$A\mathbf{n}_f$ = vector showing the age distribution of the female population at the end of the period;

$\mathbf{A}_f$ = the matrix which expresses the aging of the female population and the change in age structure, and which in the diagonal located above the main diagonal contains the survival proportions taken from the mortality table, while it contains zeroes elsewhere;

$\mathbf{B}_f$ = matrix of the age-specific fertility rates of the female population, its main diagonal showing these rates *only for female births*; thus, $\mathbf{B}_f\mathbf{n}_f$ is a column vector, by adding it we obtain the proportion of girls under one year of age for $A\mathbf{n}_f$.

b) *change in male population*:

$$A\mathbf{n}_m = \mathbf{A}_m\mathbf{n}_m + \mathbf{B}_m\mathbf{n}_f \tag{3}$$

where the lower indices m denote the male part of the population, and $\mathbf{n}_f$ stands for male births; all other notations are the same as under *a)*.

The system of analysing demographic processes by the matrix methods was elaborated even earlier by Keyfitz.* Essentially, his method was but a variant of the formula traditionally applied in population forecasts (among others, also by the Institute of Demographic Researches of the Hungarian Central Statistical Office**). The model may be refined by taking into account party the number of marriages and the fertility rates, and partly the number of children born previously, in terms of the model.

When applied to migrations, the matrix of parameters becomes more complicated. Assuming that three "regions" have to be distinguished (e.g., three geographic areas, or three different types of settlement) denoted by the subscripts p, q and r, moreover, that — contrary to the former example — we do not distinguish between male and female populations, the model may be written as follows:

$$\begin{bmatrix} A\mathbf{n}_p \\ A\mathbf{n}_q \\ A\mathbf{n}_r \end{bmatrix} = \begin{bmatrix} m_{pp} & m_{pq} & m_{pr} \\ m_{qp} & m_{qq} & m_{qr} \\ m_{rp} & m_{rq} & m_{rr} \end{bmatrix} \begin{bmatrix} \mathbf{C}_{pp} & \mathbf{0} & \mathbf{0} \\ \mathbf{0} & \mathbf{C}_{qq} & \mathbf{0} \\ \mathbf{0} & \mathbf{0} & \mathbf{C}_{rr} \end{bmatrix} \begin{bmatrix} \mathbf{n}_p \\ \mathbf{n}_q \\ \mathbf{n}_r \end{bmatrix} \tag{4}$$

* Keyfitz, H.: The Population Projection as a Matrix Operator. *Demography*, No. 1, pp. 56–73, 1964.
Keyfitz, N.: *Introduction to the Mathematics of Population*. Addison-Wesley, Reading 1968.

** Pallós, E.–Tamásy, J.–Vukovich, Gy.: *Magyarország népességének előreszámítása 1966–2001* (Forecasts for Hungary's population, 1966 to 2001), Bulletin of the Demographic Research Group of the Hungarian Central Statistical Office. No. 19, Budapest 1968.

where

$\mathbf{n}_p, \mathbf{n}_q, \mathbf{n}_r$ = vectors of population age structure by regions;

$\mathbf{C}_{pp}, \mathbf{C}_{qq}, \mathbf{C}_{rr}$ = matrix blocks expressing the survival and fertility rates of the total population living in each region; $\mathbf{C} = \mathbf{A} + \mathbf{B}$, that is, for the whole population $\Lambda\mathbf{n} = \mathbf{C}\mathbf{n}$;

m_{ij} $(i,j = p, q, r)$ = the rates of interregional migration; when $i \neq j$, they mean migration from the emitting region i towards the receiving region j as a percentage of the starting population of region i; when $i = j$, they mean the ratio of population *remaining* in the same region, in which case we obtain vectors like $m_{pp} = 1 - m_{pq} - m_{pr}$, etc.

Table 1 may serve as a basis for computing such migration coefficients.

Table 1

Migration (permanent and transitory) of population between Budapest, other towns and villages, during 1968 (in thousands)*

January 1st, 1968 \ January 1st, 1969	Budapest	Other towns	Villages	Deaths	Total
Budapest	1,826	31	109	24	1,990
Other towns	35	2,384	125	26	2,570
Villages	126	159	5,329	66	5,680
New births	23	41	91	.	.
Total	2,010	2,615	5,654	.	.

* Source: *Demográfiai évkönyv, 1968* (Demographical Yearbook of the Hungarian Central Statistical Office for 1968). Our table does not take into account the changes in administrative boundaries having taken place in 1968. Because of rounding off, the data on births and total population slightly deviate from those figuring in the source.

It is possible to work out the coefficients of migration as a percentage of the given population of each region.

In this table, the insignificant numbers of migration to and from abroad are neglected. If no births and deaths had occurred in the observed period (i.e., if the system was a closed one), the obtained matrix of migration coefficients could be conceived of as a matrix of transition probability coefficients according to a Markov chain model, and we could forecast the changes in the situation (the changed patterns of population in the three settlement types) to tell how long it would take and in what situation the patterns would stabilize as a result of opposed flows. In our case, however, such a model would be highly irrealistic.

First, the rates of natural increase in the three types of settlement strongly differ (as a matter of fact, this is the permanent motive force of migration), second, according to recent data, the migration rates are slightly decreasing, so they cannot be considered as stable transition probability coefficients.

With the aid of a similar model also the changes in the proportions between economically active and inactive population, as well as the flow of active earners from and to various branches may be analysed:

$$\begin{bmatrix} \Delta\mathbf{n}_a \\ \Delta\mathbf{n}_i \end{bmatrix} = \begin{bmatrix} \mathbf{n}_{aa} & \mathbf{n}_{ai} \\ \mathbf{n}_{ia} & \mathbf{n}_{ii} \end{bmatrix} \begin{bmatrix} \mathbf{C}_{aa} & \mathbf{0} \\ \mathbf{0} & \mathbf{C}_{ii} \end{bmatrix} \begin{bmatrix} \mathbf{n}_{aa} \\ \mathbf{n}_{ii} \end{bmatrix} \tag{5}$$

where

$\mathbf{n}_a, \mathbf{n}_i$ = vectors expressing the age structure of the active and inactive population;

$\mathbf{C}_{aa}, \mathbf{C}_{ii}$ = matrix blocks of the survival coefficients;

$\mathbf{n}_{ai}$ = active population becoming inactive during the period, as a percentage of the starting active population;

$\mathbf{n}_{ia}$ = inactive population becoming active during the period, as a percentage of the starting inactive populations;

$\mathbf{n}_{aa}, \mathbf{n}_{ii}$ = vectors showing the ratios of the active remaining active and of the inactive remaining inactive, respectively.

The value of such a model will evidently increase if it shows the "transition rates" detailed by age and sex. It seems justified to assume that proportions calculated on this basis (e.g., the percentage of people retiring from work within an age group) are fairly constant over time, or are changing at a slow and definite rate.

By the extension of this model it is also possible to describe the flows of active population between the various economic branches. In this case, the transition coefficients express the ratio of people going over from one branch to another, as a percentage of the total number of those in the first branch. At this point the system of socio-statistical balances is directly connected to the economic input–output tables.

Table 2 shows statistical data permitting us to calculate transition coefficients between activity and inactivity as well as inter-branch flows. (The table is incomplete since it does not contain data on births and deaths.)

Analogously to inter-branch flows, it is possible to describe the flows between social groups, that is intra-generational social mobility; e.g., when distinguishing three social groups (u, w, z) and considering the active population only, we may obtain the following model:

$$\begin{bmatrix} \Delta\mathbf{k}_u \\ \Delta\mathbf{k}_v \\ \Delta\mathbf{k}_w \end{bmatrix} = \begin{bmatrix} g_{uu} & g_{uv} & g_{uw} \\ g_{vu} & g_{vv} & g_{vw} \\ g_{wu} & g_{wv} & g_{ww} \end{bmatrix} \begin{bmatrix} \mathbf{D}_{uu} & \mathbf{0} & \mathbf{0} \\ \mathbf{0} & \mathbf{D}_{vv} & \mathbf{0} \\ \mathbf{0} & \mathbf{0} & \mathbf{D}_{ww} \end{bmatrix} \tag{6}$$

Table 2

Flows of population* between the employed, retired and dependent categories, and

1963 / 1960	Men					
	employed in			retired	dependent	total
	agriculture	industry and construction	other branches			
A) Numbers:						
employed in						
agriculture	661,300	51,250	36,650	100,200	10,050	859,450
industry and construction	35,500	619,850	53,600	49,400	2,600	760,950
other branches	24,100	55,550	382,400	31,150	3,300	496,500
retired	2,600	2,600	2,650	145,100	700	153,650
dependent	34,950	62,300	35,650	8,800	849,200	990,900
Total	758,450	791,550	510,950	334,850	865,850	3,261,450
B) Percentages:						
employed in						
agriculture	76.9	6.0	4.3	11.6	1.2	100.0
industry and construction	4.7	81.5	7.0	5.5	0.3	100.0
other branches	4.6	11.2	77.1	6.3	0.6	100.0
retired	1.7	1.7	1.7	94.5	0.4	100.0
dependent	3.5	6.3	3.6	0.9	85.7	100.0

* People covered by the micro-census of 1963 who lived in the same dwellings where they had been living at the general population census of 1960. Source: Bencze, B.: *A népesség foglalkozásának változása 1960–1963 között* (Changes in the occupation of the population between 1960 and 1963), pp. 28–37. Bulletin of the Demographic Research Group of the Hungarian Central Statistical Office, No. 8. Budapest 1965.

where

$\mathbf{k}_u, \mathbf{k}_v, \mathbf{k}_w$ = vectors of age structure of the economically active population belonging to each social group;

$\mathbf{D}_{uu}, \mathbf{D}_{vv}, \mathbf{D}_{ww}$ = matrix blocks expressing the survival rates of those belonging to different social groups, as well as the rates of transition from the active to the inactive population and entering into an active state;

g_{ij} $(i, j = u, v, w)$ = vectors expressing the rates of transition from one social, group to another (when $i \neq j$); the number of persons "leaving" is shown as a percentage of the starting number of the emitting social group; and when $i = j$, the number of those remaining in the same group is shown

the main branches of the national economy, 1960 to 1963

Women					
employed in			retired	dependent	total
agriculture	industry and construction	other branches			
252,450	11,300	13,700	61,050	208,200	546,700
3,150	254,050	23,550	17,550	27,850	326,150
5,300	22,300	282,600	21,950	22,800	354,950
2,300	2,000	4,350	134,850	14,250	175,750
222,300	91,350	94,250	95,350	1,901,200	2,384,450
485,500	381,000	418,450	310,750	2,174,300	3,770,000
46.2	2.1	2.5	11.1	38.1	100.0
1.0	77.9	7.2	5.4	8.5	100.0
1.5	6.3	79.6	6.2	6.4	100.0
1.5	1.3	2.8	85.4	9.0	100.0
9.3	3.8	4.0	3.2	79.7	100.0

as a percentage of the starting number of that group: $g_{uu} = 1 - g_{uv} - g_{uw}$, etc.

The picture concerning intra-generational mobility may be refined by distinguishing between the mobility of men and women and separately investigating the individual age groups.

Even more interesting than the intra-generational social mobility is inter-generational mobility. Here, however, new difficulties arise. Fathers belonging to the first generation are not regularly replaced by their sons, since the time lag between two generations differs by families. Moreover, some men have two or more sons, other only one or none. Thus, two social structures distinguished according to the average "time distance of a generation" cannot be conceived of in such a manner that the first consists of "fathers", each of whom will be replaced by one "son" in the next one. But at the cost of very strong simplifications (namely, by assuming that we may neglect the differences between the social groups in respect of the average number of children) it seems that the model may be extended to measure inter-generational mobility, too.

Some authors attempted to interpret social mobility as a Markov-type process.* But it can be shown** that the conditions of applying Markov chains to intergenerational mobility are not satisfied owing to the causes mentioned above. At the same time, the model may be used to show the correlation between differences in fertility, changes in occupational structure and social mobility.*** Moreover, for analysing intra-generational mobility an approach based on Markov chains seems to be suitable.**** Anyhow, such models can give an answer to one type of question, namely, how would the social structure develop if the mobility rates (as regards departures) observed in the past remained constant; or how would the mobility rates (as regards entrances) change merely under the effect of changes in occupational structure, if the exit rates were to remain constant.

Table 3 shows the construction of such a mobility table. It describes the flows of Hungary's adult male population among social groups from 1949 to 1963. It is imperfect in the sense that it neglects the occurrence, within the period investigated, of multiple transitions; it reflects only the initial and the final situation. Thus, the suitability of such a table for measuring social mobility and its tendencies to change depends on the time lag involved. Ideally, the situations in two subsequent years should be compared.

Of all socio-demographic models, those relating to education have been elaborated most thoroughly. After the basic works of Tinbergen and Correa, similar models were constructed by Stone and Thonstad.***** In the latter there are two kinds of parameters, interpreted by Thonstad at the analogy of the transition probability coefficients figuring in the Markov chains. These are the following:

q_{hk} = proportion within the total number of students engaged in the given year in the activity h (i.e., learning in a definite form of a definite school type), of those who in the next year will be engaged in the activity k ($h, k = 1, \ldots, S$),

r_{he} = proportion within the total number of students engaged in the given year in the activity h of those who, at the end of the given year, will leave the educational system with a qualification e ($h = 1, \ldots, S$ $e = 1, \ldots, E$).

* Prais, J.: The Formal Theory of Social Mobility. *Population Studies,* No. 1, pp. 72–81, 1955.

** Blau, P. M.–Duncan, O. D.: *The American Occupational Structure.* John Wiley and Sons, New York 1967.

*** Matras, J.: Comparison of Intergenerational Occupational Mobility Patterns: An Application of the Formal Theory of Social Mobility. *Population Studies,* No. 11, pp. 163–199, 1960.
Matras, J.: Differential Fertility, Intergenerational Mobility and Change in the Occupational Distributions: Some Elementary Interrelationships. *Population Studies,* No. 7, pp. 187–197, 1961.

**** Matras, J.: Social Mobility and Social Structure: Some Insights from the Linear Model. *American Sociological Review,* No. 4, pp. 608–614, 1967.

***** Thonstad, T.: *Education and Manpower. Theoretical Models and Empirical Applications.* Oliver and Boyd, Edinburgh 1969.

Table 3

The flow of adult male population among social groups, 1949 to 1963 (in thousands)*

1949 \ 1963	Intellectuals	Other non-physical workers	Artisans, members of industrial co-operatives	Skilled workers	Semi-skilled workers	Unskilled workers	Peasants	Departures (deaths, etc.)	Total
Intellectuals	84	12	3	8	2	2	2	7	170
Other non-physical workers	34	118	4	15	8	6	2	15	202
Artisans, members of industrial cooperatives	3	12	82	41	13	10	26	19	187
Skilled workers	11	42	26	364	16	19	15	30	493
Semiskilled workers	4	9	—	31	150	17	9	15	220
Unskilled workers	5	16	3	56	43	146	25	20	294
Peasants	12	16	9	66	95	169	792	195	1,354
Entrance of people who were dependent in 1949	48	39	10	132	44	68	60	.	.
Total	201	264	137	713	371	437	931	.	.

* Source: Klinger, A. and Szabady, E.: *A társadalmi átrétegződés és demográfiai hatásai Budapesten és a városokban* (Social restratification and its demographical effects in Budapest and other towns), Bulletin of the Demographic Research Group of the Hungarian Central Statistical Office, No. 7, Budapest 1965.

Andorka, R.: *A társadalmi átrétegződés és demográfiai hatásai Magyarországon* (Social restratification and its demographical effects in Hungary), Bulletin of the Demographic Research Group of the Hungarian Central Statistical Office, No. 30, Budapest 1970.

The table was drawn up by applying to the pattern of social groups, stated by the micro-census of 1963, the inflow coefficients obtained from our 1962–1964 investigation of social mobility; departures were estimated. The 1949 pattern of social groups shown in the table does not exactly agree with the one stated at the 1949 census. This may be due — apart from certain differences in definitions — to the fact that our investigation of 1962–1964 covered only the men who were family heads.

From these, the **Q** and **R** matrices showing the probability of transition may be constructed. Evidently, the sum of rows is always unity. (Deaths are left out of consideration.)

With the aid of the model one may obtain answers to the following types of questions:

1. What part of the students who are now engaged in activity h (i.e., studying in the fourth form of primary school) will be engaged in t years time (e.g., three years) in activity k (i.e., in the eighth form of that school)?

In order to answer this question, we must define the following rate of transition:

$q_{hk}^{(t)}$ = proportion to the total of students now engaged in the activity h, of those who will perform the activity k, t years from now.

According to this definition, $q_{hk}^{(o)}$ is 1, when $h = k$, otherwise it is zero,

$$q_{hk}^{(1)} = q_{hk}$$

$$q_{hk}^{(2)} = \sum_{s=1}^{S} q_{hs} q_{sk} \tag{7}$$

$$q_{hk}^{(3)} = \sum_{s=1}^{S} q_{hs}^{(2)} q_{sk}$$

Of course, $q_{hs}^{(2)}$ is the (h, s) element of the matrix $\mathbf{Q}^2$, and so on.

2. What is the average length of time that a student now entering into activity h (for instance, into the highest form of secondary school) is going to spend with activity k?

This period is denoted by w_{hk}. When $h = k$, one year will be spent in the first year, otherwise it will be zero. The time spent will be $q_{hk}^{(1)}$ in the second year, $q_{hk}^{(2)}$ in the third, and so on. For the whole length of time we obtain

$$w_{hk} = q_{hk}^{(0)} + q_{hk}^{(1)} + q_{hk}^{(2)} + \ldots \quad (h, k = 1, \ldots, S) \tag{8}$$

It may be shown that — with certain assumptions which are satisfied in the present case — $q_{hk}^{(t)}$ is a converging series, and that w_{hk} is the (h, k)-*th* element of the matrix $\mathbf{W} = (\mathbf{I} - \mathbf{Q})^{-1}$; thus the inverse will yield the time that will have to be spent with the activity k by those who are now entering into the activity h.

3. What part of the students now entering into the activity h will, t years from now, acquire their final diploma (for instance, a secondary school diploma)? This proportion is denoted by $r_{he}^{(t)}$.

We have to define the proportions of students who, in $t - 1$ years from now will be engaged in various activities, and to multiply these proportions with the corresponding coefficients of the certificates to be acquired.

$$r_{he}^{(t)} = \sum_{s=1}^{S} q_{hs}^{(t-1)} r_{se} \quad (t = 1, 2, \ldots; \quad h = 1, \ldots, S; \quad e = 1, \ldots, E) \tag{9}$$

Evidently, $r_{he}^{(t)}$ is the (h, e)-th element of the matrix $\mathbf{R}^{(t)} = \mathbf{Q}^{(t-1)}\mathbf{R}$.

4. What proportion of the students now entering into activity h will obtain a final certificate within x years from now?

For answering this question, we have to sum up the $r_{he}^{(t)}$ values figuring under (9):

$$\sum_{t=1}^{x} r_{he}^{(t)} \tag{10}$$

This will be the (h, e)-th element of the matrix $\sum_{t=1}^{x} \mathbf{R}^{(t)}$.

5. What proportion of the students now entering into activity h will *sooner or later* acquire the corresponding final certificate? (This proportion will be designed by r_{he}^{total}).

In order to answer, we have to add up the coefficients of (9):

$$r_{he}^{\text{total}} = \sum_{t=1}^{\infty} f_{he}^{(t)} \sum_{s=1}^{S} \left(\sum_{t=1}^{\infty} q_{hs}^{(t-1)} \right) r_{se} . \tag{11}$$

According to (8) we obtain that

$$r_{he}^{\text{total}} = \sum_{s=1}^{S} w_{hs} r_{se} . \tag{12}$$

Therefore, r_{he}^{total} is the (h, e)-th element of the following matrix:

$$\mathbf{R}^{\text{total}} = \mathbf{WR} = (\mathbf{E} - \mathbf{Q})^{-1}\mathbf{R}.$$

2. THE INTEGRATED SYSTEM OF SOCIAL STATISTICS

It was in close connection with the system of models described above that efforts were made by national statistical offices and in the framework of the Conference of European Statisticians organized by the Economic Commission for Europe of the United Nations in order to create an integrated system of social statistics, and to complete these models with internationally comparable data.*

Integration requires that the various data of social statistics be published according to a uniform system of classification, in order to ensure the possibility of linking the data describing different social processes, and of a direct transition from a given arrangement of data (e.g., according to occupational groups or residence) to another one (e.g., arranged according to income brackets or social mobility). Thus, a synopsis of the distribution under diverse social aspects may be obtained, and their changes may be observed simultaneously according to various criteria.

In the framework of such a system of social statistics the unit of observation would be in some cases the individual human being, in others the household. Any phenomenon of social and demographic statistics would be presented according to the following four basic criteria:**

- sex,
- age (by age groups),
- social grouping,
- residence (urban or rural, eventually according to regions).

* Moser, C. A.: *An Integrated System of Social and Demographic Statistics.* Conf. Eur. Stats. 273. 1969.

Bjerke, K.: An Integrated Social and Demographic Statistical System. *Statistisk Tidskrift,* No. 3, pp. 173–197, 1970.

Fastbom, L.: *On Principles for the Construction of a System of Social and Demographic Statistics.* The National Central Bureau of Statistics. Stockholm 1970.

A System of Demographic, Manpower and Social Statistics: Series, Classifications and Social Indicators. Conf. Eur. Stats/WG. 34/6. Geneva 1971.

* As a fifth criterion, nationality was also proposed. Cf. *A System of Demographic, Manpower and . . .* op. cit.

The system of social statistics would include two kinds of data:

– data relating to the stocks, i.e., the state of things at a definite point of time, e.g., at the beginning or the end of a given period (like the number of individuals belonging to the various occupations, or their distribution by branches, or the pattern of households according to the per capita incomes of their members, etc.);

– data on flows, i.e., of transition between categories defined under diverse aspects, taking place in the course of a year or a longer period of observation (e.g., changes in the occupational pattern of the population, or the number of households entering a higher or lower income bracket during the period in question).

The proposed system of social statistics would consist of eight sub-systems (see Table 4).

1. *Demographic structures and processes*. Here, the structure of the population according to the basic classification criteria and to family status would be shown at the beginning and at the end of the observed period (stock data), as well as the changes occurring in that period like births, deaths, marriages, divorces, furthermore, aging, i.e., transitions from one age group to another (flow data).

2. *Migration*. This sub-system is closely connected with the first one. Stock data show the distribution of the population by areas, the flow data its migration between the various areas.

3. *Education*. Stock data reflect the grades of formal education completed, flow data the transitions within the educational system, i.e., enrolment, continuation of studies in the same type of school entering into a higher school type, and the leaving of the educational system (in most cases equivalent to entrance into the labour force). It has been proposed* that, as an additional criterion, the income of the households to which the students belong should also be taken into account. We feel it would be similarly important to register the social group to which the head of the student's family belongs, in order to be able to follow up the continuation of studies by people belonging to different social groups, as one of the major factors determining their future social mobility.

4. *Labour force, economic activity and inactivity*. Stock data show the distribution of the population (classified according to the basic criteria) between the economically active and inactive categories, as well as by skill, economic branches of occupation and jobs held. Flow data show the number of former inactives entering into economic activity (young people joining the labour force), and former actives becoming inactive (retirement, etc.) as well as the flows of economically active people between occupations and branches. It has been proposed that, as an additional criterion of classification, the highest grade (and type) attained in general education and professional training should be applied.** This sub-system

* *A System of Demographic, Manpower and* . . . op. cit.

** *A System of Demographic, Manpower and* . . . op. cit.

Table 4

A conceivable scheme of the system of social statistics

(the connections between the sub-systems and those between them and the economic data)

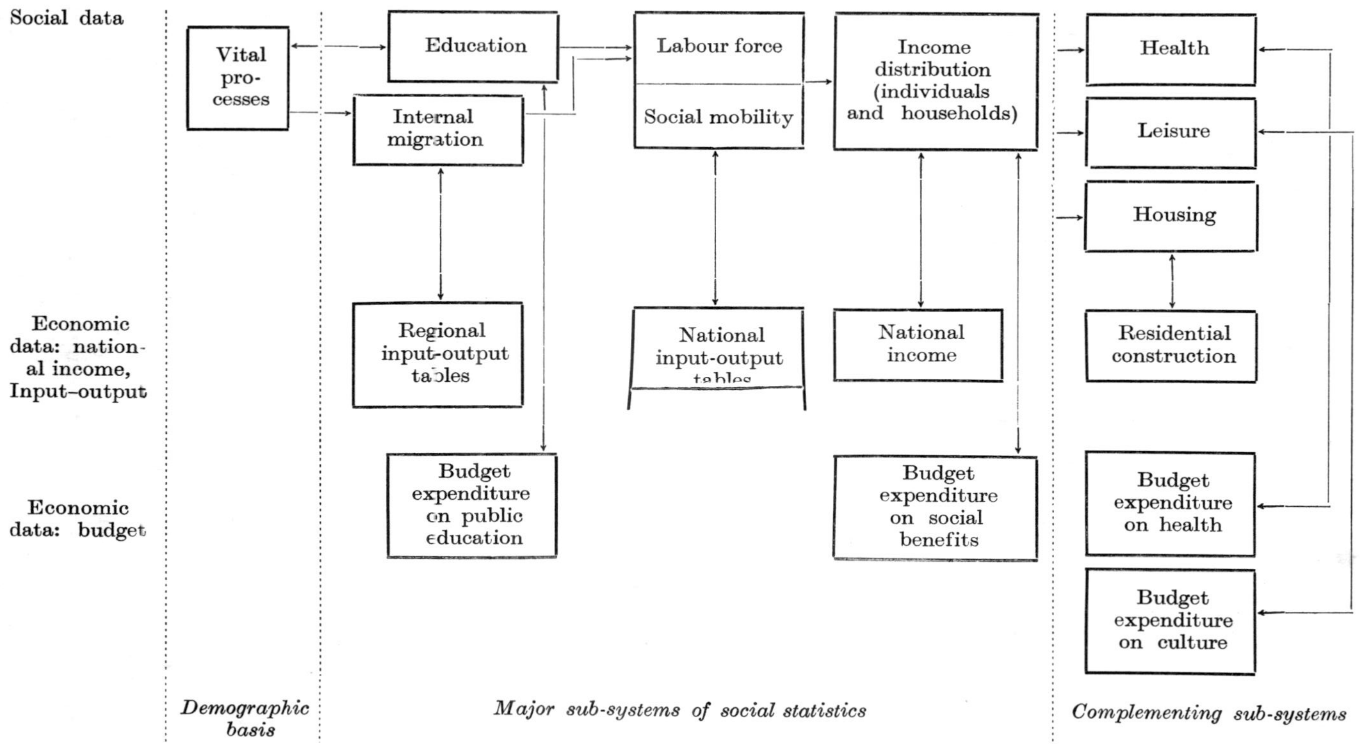

would give a picture also on social intra-generational mobility. We feel that it would be expedient to complement this picture with data relating to the social group of the subject's father, in order to follow up also the process of inter-generational mobility. In possession of all these data it would become possible to trace social mobility and to state its correlation with the grade of education, with internal migration, with changes in incomes, etc.

5. *Distribution of income and wealth; consumption.* This sub-system shows the distribution of individual earnings and household incomes according to the basic criteria in the form of stock data. Its flow data register the changes of individual and household incomes, and transitions from one income bracket to another. This sub-system enables us to follow up the development of incomes in the various social groups (averages and dispersion) as well as the factors causing them to vary, like changes in the demographic structure of households, in the proportion between economically active and inactive household members, in their occupational structure, and in the average individual incomes of the various occupational groups. Moreover, it shows household expenditures and their major elements (e.g., food, etc.), grouped according to the size and average per capita income of the households; finally, the extent to which households are equipped with various durable goods.

These five basic sub-systems are closely interrelated. For instance, the population sub-system is the basis for the educational one, where the main aspect of observation is the location of age groups within the school system. Also, the connection between demographic data (the natural increase of population) and migration is evident; the latter shows the development of population by areas. The "final output" of the educational sub-system is the "primary input" in the sub-system of the labour force. Internal migration is connected with the employment of the labour force by areas and, in many cases, with social mobility. Finally the distribution of the labour force by individual occupations, employment and branches is connected with the distribution of incomes.

In international literature, propositions can be found on the introduction of other sub-systems which, however, are less closely connected with these five well integrated sub-systems representing the main body of social statistics. Such are, e.g., the following:

6. *Health.* This sub-system shows mortality by its various causes, the occurrence of diseases causing transitory or permanent disability, the turnover in hospitals, the number of disabled or mentally underdeveloped persons, all according to the basic criteria of grouping as well as to household income.

7. *Leisure.* Here the factual extent of free time, its use according to major leisure activities and the part of incomes spent on the latter are shown.

8. *Housing.* Here the distribution of households belonging to the different social groups is shown according to the title of use and the type of buildings and flats, the number of rooms, their equipment in terms of lighting, heating, running water facilities, bathrooms, toilets, etc. Also the changes in the stock of residential buildings are registered here.

It has also been proposed* that the tables presenting the status and flows of population be complemented by accounts of the human and material resources connected with, and available to the activities covered by each sub-system. For instance, in connection with education also the number of teaching personnel, the teacher/pupil ratio, the number of classrooms and other facilities (laboratories, libraries, etc.) as well as budget expenditures on education should be registered; the health sub-system should contain accounts on health personnel and hospital facilities, and so on. All such data should be presented by types of institutions and in regional distribution. With the aid of such data, one would be able to compare the expenditures on the various kinds of social benefits and the results achieved by them (e.g., the human and material resources employed in the hospitals and departments for mental illness with the number of persons treated in them, as well as of those discharged from them in a cured state).

Since, evidently, it will take a long time to build up such an extensive system of social and demographic statistics, in the course of preparatory work performed at the Conference of European Statisticians it was suggested to begin with the implementation of a more restricted programme. According to this, certain "social indicators" should be calculated annually, in order to represent some particularly characteristic and essential elements in each field of social life and thereby to detect the tendencies of change.

This proposition started from the recognition that for characterizing the "quality" of the living conditions it does not suffice to rely on the per capita national income and, in general, on data of economic statistics; it is necessary to consider also other aspects of living conditions, e.g., the sanitary conditions (which are far from depending unequivocally on the expenditure on public health), as well as the quality of the natural environment (pollution, etc.), public security, cultural institutions, etc.**

The "social indicators" would be linked to the general system of social statistics in such a way that they would represent the most characteristic elements of each sub-system. For example, let us enumerate some indicators regarding the field of education:

1. The expected number of years to be spent at school and the expected higher level of education to be attained according to sex, social group and residence (urban and rural);

2. the proportion of pupils who, after completing primary school, are expected to continue studies in secondary school, and of those who, on completion of the

* *A System of Demographic, Manpower and . . .* op. cit.

** *Indicators of Social Change. Concepts and measurement.* Sheldon, E. B. and Moore, W. E. Russel Sage Foundation. New York 1968.

Olson, M.: New Problems for Social Policy: the Rationale of Social Indicators and Social Reporting. *International Institute for Labour Statistics Bulletin*, No. 7, pp. 18–39, 1970.

Hirsch, W. Z., Sonenblum, S. and Dennis, J. St.: Application of input–output techniques to the quality of urban life indicators. *Kyklos*, No. 3, pp. 511–533, 1971.

latter, will go to an institute of higher learning, again grouped according to sex, social group and residence;

3. average level of education attained by sex, social group, residence and regions;

4. teacher/pupil ratios by types of schools, in urban and rural districts and by regions.

3. EFFORTS MADE IN HUNGARY

Also in the Hungarian literature, proposals were made to arrange the data on social statistics into an integrated system,* and to describe certain social processes with the aid of similar models.

A system of models consisting of matrices characterizing five processes was described by Ervin Frigyes.** The processes are: (1) births (based on the fertility coefficients according to age; (2) shifts in age structure, i.e., survivals and deaths (according to the mortality tables); (3) the day-time care of children under 7 years of age (on the basis of the number of children cared for in nurseries and kindergartens); (4) the progress of pupils within the framework of formal education (according to the coefficients of continuation of studies and the number of pupils leaving the school system with various grades of qualification); (5) the changes in the number of qualified manpower.

A model of education and professional training was described by János Kovács*** on the basis of transition coefficients between the various school types. With the aid of this model, and by assuming the expectable future need for experts with various qualifications, it is possible to plan the number of pupils to be taught in the various school types.

The internal migration within Hungary was analysed by Paul Compton**** with the aid of Markov chains. He tried to establish what would happen if the migration coefficients between counties (i.e., territorial units) remained constant;

* Hungarian works of this kind were comprehensively reviewed by Dr. Lajos Bene. See his Törekvések a társadalmi és népességi statisztika egységes rendszerbe foglalására (Attempts at uniting social and demographic data in the framework of a uniform system). *Demográfia,* Nos 1–2, pp. 110–116, 1970.

** Frigyes, E.: Kísérlet egy komplex oktatási és munkaerő modellrendszer demográfiai változóinak egységes lineáris modellbe foglalására (An attempt at including the variants of educational and labour matrices into a uniform linear model). *Demográfia,* Nos 3–4, pp. 463–472, 1968.

*** Kovács, J.: Tervezési model az iskola rendszer beiskolázási előirányzataira (A plan model forecasting school enrolment) in the volume *Economic Development and Planning,* edited by the Institute of Economics, Hungarian Academy of Sciences, pp. 188–214, Budapest 1969.

**** Compton, P.: A régiók közötti vándorlás vizsgálata matrix módszerrel (Investigation of interregional migrations by matrix method). *Demográfia,* No. 4, pp. 475–496, 1966. Compton, P.: A határnépesség mint vándorlási index (Marginal population considered as an index of migration). *Demográfia,* Nos 3–4, pp. 428–441, 1968.

in other words, how would migration develop from year to year and what territorial distribution was likely to get stabilized at some future time.

A method based on principles similar to those of a socio-demographic system of models was proposed by László Cseh-Szombathy and Bálint Surányi* in order to forecast the expected amount of pensions. The number of persons receiving pensions was reduced, in each year, by the probable number of deaths and increased by the number of new retirements. In the case of the latter, the expected amount of the pension was forecast according to occupations and years spent in service.

In a study prepared for the European Seminar on Demographic Statistics (Ankara), Dr. Egon Szabady** has dealth with the present and the proposed Hungarian practice of intercensal population estimates, based on demographic statistics, population censuses, microcensuses and other sources. He described that method of estimating the formal education of the population between censuses, which was elaborated by the department of education of the Hungarian Central Statistical Office.

The importance of improving the system of social statistics and linking it to the system of economic statistics was stressed by Mrs. Margaret Mód.*** She proposed and presented two systems complementing the system of national economic balances, in close connection with the latter: (1) a system of social accounts combining, on a macro-economic level, the incomes of the population, the extent and structure of consumption, the expenditures on social benefits, public health, education and housing conditions; (2) a system of social statistics relating to the micro-economic level, e.g., the distribution of household incomes, the proportion between economically active and inactive household members, their occupations, etc. The first group of data is derived from those of the national income, the second is based on sample surveys regarding incomes and other circumstances.

Thus, — in accordance with what Mrs. Mód has expressed — it may be said that Hungary's Central Statistical Office, even in the past, instinctively followed the lines on which recently international efforts have started, as a result of the coordinating work performed by the statistical organs of the UN.

* Cseh-Szombathy, L. and Surányi, B.: *A nyugdíj összeg előreszámításához szükséges csoportosítások előzetes számbavétele* (A preliminary grouping of population needed for the purpose of forecasting the amount of pensions). MS. prepared at the initiative of the Planning Commission of Labour and Living Conditions.

** Szabady, E.: Use of Registers of Vital Events and Other Administrative Data for Intercensal Population Estimates. United Nations European Seminar on Demographic Statistics. Ankara 1971 (Mimeographed).

*** Mrs. Margaret Mód: A gazdaság és társadalomstatisztikai rendszerek összefüggései (Connections between the systems of economic and social statistics). *Statisztikai Szemle*, No. 1, pp. 15–28, 1971.

4. ATTEMPTS ABROAD AT ELABORATING PARTS OF THE SYSTEM OF SOCIAL STATISTICS

From the international literature, we know of two attempts, both of which were aimed at elaborating the *educational* sub-system belonging to the integrated system described above. Stone* described the population flows in England and Wales within the school system on the basis of comprehensive statistical data which, however, were not assessed for serving this special purpose. Since the basic data showed only the distribution of the "school-age" population by types of schools but failed to indicate the type of school where the pupils in question had studied one year before, Stone had to perform estimates based on the assumption of a "normal school career". Evidently, his estimates could cover the "net flows" only, since there was no basis for estimating flows opposed to the "normal career". For example, for pupils reaching the age of 14, he could establish only two alternatives of flows: continuation of studies or leaving the school system (either for joining the labour force or for household work). The (evidently rare) occurrence of re-entering the school system from household work or from the labour force had to be neglected. As its author had stressed, this model was only of an experimental character, serving to clear up the concepts and to determine the scope of necessary information.

The work of Thonstad,** based on a special survey on educational conditions in Norway, was based on better data and more suited for practical application. This survey stated the position occupied by each pupil *one year earlier* within the system of schooling. Therefore, accurate data could be used for calculating the transition coefficients between grades of the same school as well as between different school types, and only the leaving of the school system had to be estimated. Thonstad's matrix does not cover the grades of primary school; nevertheless, it distinguishes 54 grades in 13 different secondary and higher school types. This detailed grouping made it possible to link educational processes with the future development of manpower, by assuming that the careers of young people graduating from a distinct type of school are more or less determined. Thonstad assumed (on the analogy of Markov chains) the transition coefficients between school types as well as between school types and occupational groups to be constant. He performed hypothetical calculations regarding the structure of the future labour force resulting from the observed distribution of pupils and, inversely, regarding the educational pattern that would be needed for ensuring a given future structure of manpower. His model may afford some help in the planning of education.

* See Stone: Op. cit. (1969 and 1970).

** See Thonstad: Op. cit.

5. INFORMATION NEEDED FOR THE SYSTEM OF SOCIAL STATISTICS

In Hungary, the needed *stock data* are, as a rule, available from the recent censuses and microcensuses. Thus, for the purposes of the sub-systems dealing with population, migration, education and labour force, only a certain re-arrangement in the grouping of individual and household data according to social groups is needed. As regards income distribution, the sample surveys of household incomes may produce the necessary cross-section data.

Concerning the most important demographic statistics (the number of population and its distribution by sex, age, family status and residence) we have stock data not only for the years of censuses and microcensuses but for every year, derived from intercensal estimates.*

As regards the *flow data,* we have accurate annual returns concerning the major demographic processes like births, deaths, marriages, divorces, internal migrations (and ageing). In Table 1, an example was presented to show the construction of a "balance" based on such data. All figures in this table are based on statistical observation.

The Hungarian Statistical Office has also started the continuous observation of flows occurring within the educational system (the continuation of studies within the same school and the transition from one type of school to another) and to perform intercensal estimates regarding the formal education of the population. Accordingly, all data necessary for the sub-system of education will be available.

As yet, we have no adequate flow data to be used in the sub-systems of manpower and income. There are several conceivable ways of obtaining such information.

One of the possibilities consists in reconstruction based on retrospective data. This would mean that, in the framework of a survey, also some data from the past years might be inquired after, regarding, e.g., occupational, residential and qualificational changes, vital events, etc. The practicability of such a programme of investigation is shown by a survey of social mobility made by the Institute of Demographical Research of the Central Statistical Office.** From the questionnaires returned, it is possible to build up the mobility matrices of the investigated population for every year, and to state the correlation among mobility and internal migration, formal education, marriages and births. Table 3 was constructed from the data obtained from such a survey. It shows well the possibilities of data processing, but also the deficiencies of this type of survey. Namely, the data contained in the right wing of the table concerning "exits" (deaths and emigration) had to be estimated, since for those who were not present at the time of the survey, no accurate data on their former curriculum could be obtained.***

* See Szabady: Op. cit.

** Cf. Klinger–Szabady: Op. cit., and Andorka: Op. cit.

*** A further difficulty arises from the inaccurate recollection of the persons questioned. Such difficulties would be the greatest if past incomes had to be stated retrospectively.

Another conceivable method consists in the repeated observation of an *identical sample* of the population, and in registering the changes ("flows") occurring between two dates. This was essentially the method applied by Béla Bencze* who confronted the occupational data of the 1960 census and of the 1963 microcensus. Table 2 presented above shows the possibilities but also the basic difficulty of this kind of analysis: it contains but the data of people who were found at *both* dates to live at the same place of residence, since the coupling of data relating to people having changed residence between 1960 and 1963 would have required an enormous amount of work.

A way of obtaining comparable data (in a breakdown according to the desired patterns, e.g., residence, level of education, etc.) would be offered by a repeated survey of a sample of population between census and microcensus years, based on samples representing about one half per cent of the total of individuals or households, partly relating to identical units of observation and partly to those subject to gradual replacement.

In countries where comprehensive population records are already in practice, their data may be used for constructing the system of social statistics. Even there, however, the range of information needed for the latter is much wider than what is contained in the present population records.**

6. THE POSSIBILITIES OF UTILIZING THE SYSTEM OF SOCIAL STATISTICS

The social processes covered by the system presented here were even formerly followed up, one by one, by the Hungarian Central Statistical Office. Yet, the system as a whole would mean more than the sum of its parts, because it would integrate these parts and permit their interpretation in their mutual relations. Thus, the system would make it possible to answer questions of the following type:

– what was the age structure and formal education level of people migrating from a given area (e.g. a county) to Budapest; how did their income develop (depending on age and education) before and after the migration, what were their jobs before and after?

– what differences exist between the proportions of young people continuing their studies after primary school, according to social groups and residence (capital, other towns, rural districts and country regions)?

– what are the major characteristics of families belonging to the lowest income group (demographic structure, occupation, social group, the geographic area where they are living or where they came from)? What is the probability (frequency) of leaving the lowest income group for families showing different characteristics like occupation, educational level and demographic structure

* Cf. Bencze: Op. cit.
** Cf. Fastbom: Op. cit.

(proportion of old people and children), and to what factors may a rise in income be attributed (improved proportion between earners and dependants, rise in wages, change in occupation, migration, acquisition of higher education and vocational qualification)?

Evidently, it will take much work and time to build up an integrated system of social statistics capable of answering such sophisticated questions, and it is only possible to proceed gradually. The data obtained could be then used in three fields.

1. It would become possible to follow up from year to year the basic sociological phenomena, like the continuation of studies after primary and secondary school, changes in the proportion between economically active and inactive people, migration and social mobility. An always up-to-date statistical registration of such tendencies would signal, if and when necessary, for socio-political intervention.

2. It would supply an empirical basis for the further development of social sciences in Hungary, primarily for the analysis of changes in social structure which has high priority in the long-term and medium-term plans of scientific research. It may be particularly important that the social structure could be investigated from several aspects simultaneously (occupation, jobs, income distribution, etc.), and it would be possible directly to switch over from a pattern stated from a given aspect to another one defined according to a different aspect (for instance, from occupational structure to income structure).

3. Models constructed on the grounds of the integrated system might be used for estimating and forecasting the social conditions and expectable social effects of long-term economic plans; in other words, for planning social processes. For instance, it would be conceivable to ask and answer such questions as:

– how the school system should be developed in order to meet the future needs for manpower in respect to educational level and vocational training?

– how the change in occupational structure (planned in accordance with the expected economic growth) would influence social mobility, i.e., the rates of transition between social and income groups?

The use of the system for analysis and planning may be made easier by applying, for the grouping of economic branches, the same nomenclature on which the aggregate input–output table is based. In this case, the systems of economic and social tables would be directly linked to one another through manpower, in both cases identically grouped according to branches and qualifications. Moreover, there would exist other links between the two systems, e.g., the parts of the national income spent on education and health or on social benefits (which figure in the social sub-system of income), etc. Thus, the system of social statistics would be built upon the system of economic statistics. The first would complement the latter and would register the social conditions and the way in which they would be affected by economic processes and decisions.

THE INPUT-OUTPUT TABLE GROUPED BY LINES OF MANUFACTURING AS A TOOL FOR ECONOMIC PLANNING

by

FERENC KISS

I. INTRODUCTION

Input–output tables have enabled us to investigate the national economy as an aggregate of economic branches, of industrial groups or of individual industries. They revealed the interrelationships of the production and utilization of goods and services in much greater detail than the balances of the social product and the national income.

After elaborating the more aggregated input–output models dealing with large sectors, the necessity of obtaining information on their components and elements was felt. Those at the head of ministries, economic branches and large enterprises, before making decisions aimed at increasing economic efficiency, must know what factors are likely to enhance improvement or act counterproductively.

The leaders of every economic field wanted to disaggregate the "central" input–output table (elaborated in Hungary by the Central Statistical Office) according to different points of view, and to draw up partial tables.

The Ministry of Heavy Industry was the first to initiate the construction of a special input–output table on the activities performed by industries belonging to its sphere, broken down according to product groups as homogeneous as possible but covering, at the same time, also the rest of the national economy. The Ministry wanted a model suitable mainly for deciding on the allocation of materials, for calculating export efficiency, for drawing up a table on incoming and outgoing foreign exchange, and for determining the economy-wide efficiency of the major activities.

Recently, similar combined input–output models covering the national economy as a whole but dealing in detail with certain parts of it were also elaborated by various research institutes, e.g., for the Ministry of Metallurgy and Engineering, for the Ministry of Construction and Urban Development, and for the Ministry of Food and Agriculture.

II. PRELIMINARIES

1. EXPERIENCE OBTAINED FROM CONSTRUCTING FACTUAL TABLES

The Institute for Industrial Economics and Business Organization of the Ministry of Heavy Industry was commissioned to construct an economy-wide table which was to show the activities supervised by this Ministry in a "magnified" form, i.e., shown according to individual products or homogeneous product groups.

When our work started, the experiences of elaborating the "central" input–output models relating to 1961 and 1965 were already available, and also work on the combined, more detailed model relating to 1968 was going on. In the course of several years spent on this work we obtained information on the structure of the national economy, on the activities of the enterprises supervised by our Ministry, on the diverse possibilities of analysis offered by an input–output table, as well as on the problems and difficulties involved in the collecting, checking and processing of the necessary data, in other words, on everything concerning the construction, completion, computing, and evaluation of the model.

In the meantime, a team of economic and technical experts was formed by recruiting some experts from the Ministry and from the enterprises concerned. This team became increasingly able to exploit the possibilities of analysis offered by the model. At present, every major proposition concerning the economic policy of our Ministry takes into account the interrelationships derived from our input–output model. With the aid of this model, all major activities supervised by the Ministry as well as the output of every important product or product group may be analysed in the same way as it is done with the "sectors" of the central input–output model.

This model has enabled us, among other things, to clear up problems involved in the development of the chemical industry, in particular its effects on the balance of foreign exchange. In these investigations, it was important to show, apart from the allocation of materials, how the products of the chemical and energy-producing industries were "built into" the activities of other sectors and which are the latent, indirect effects influencing economic interrelationships.

The enterprises supervised by our Ministry use very large quantities of imported materials. The model shows, e.g., which sectors of the national economy require imported chemicals used in home-made materials. This kind of information is crucial for decisions on development, since it shows how the balance of foreign exchange — and even the average efficiency of our national economy — is influenced by indirect effects.

Our model was also used for establishing the long-term plans of the Ministry and of the individual sectors supervised by it. By analysing inputs and outputs of individual manufacturing processes, i.e., by also taking into consideration the aspects of technology and the expectable changes in technology and in technological coefficients, we were able to estimate the demand for chemical products in 1975, 1980 and 1985, as well as the resources available for meeting it. In the course of analysis the following factors seemed decisive: the increasing role of chemicals in industrial and agricultural production; the growing possibilities of substituting chemical products for others (e.g., synthetic materials for metals, wood, rubber, etc.); the expectable changes in the product pattern; the development of production techniques; and the trends of development obtained by the investigation itself.

The variations of the expectable demand for chemicals obtained by assuming different technological coefficients revealed a new approach to planning the production of the chemical industry, which seemed suitable for checking the production plans drawn up by the enterprises.

2. THE VARIOUS POSSIBILITIES OF DRAWING UP A COMBINED PLAN TABLE, AND THE TYPES OF COMBINED MODELS

A combined model enables us to analyse in detail the activities supervised by a ministry within the framework of the national economy as a whole. For this purpose, the data on the activities to be analysed in detail are arranged, as it were, in an "enlarged" form.

The activities of the Ministry may be grouped according to (a) enterprises, (b) products, (c) lines of manufacturing

Thus, three major types of combined tables may be drawn up. The main features of these are the following:

a) A table reflecting the relationships among producing enterprises, inclusive of their indirect connections taking place through trade. The interaction of trade blurs part of the interenterprise connections; the factual exchange of goods between producing enterprises may be revealed by disregarding the intermediary role of trade, i.e., by assuming that the transactions were taking place directly between two enterprises. The results obtained in this way are, however, not fully satisfactory from the point of view of economic analysis. Essentially, it is more important for us to know what kinds and what quantities of materials and products are used in the production processes of the individual enterprises than to know which enterprise has produced these materials and products.

b) The use of a model grouped according to *products* seems expedient when the bulk of the production in the field under analysis consists of a few homogeneous products, each of which is important for the national economy as a whole; in other words, when the totality of the activities of an industrial branch may be adequately represented by some outstanding individual products and the residuum of "other products" (figuring as a lump sum in the balance) is relatively small. Since in most cases it is possible to determine which enterprise turns out a major product, it is more practical for the experts using data derived from this type of model to classify inputs and distribution by products than by enterprises. In addition, data regarding homogeneous products may be assessed also in terms of physical units, so that the major technological coefficients prevailing in the field investigated may be built into the model. This, in turn, means that the eventual re-pricing of the model and its use for the purpose of planning becomes much easier. In our combined balances elaborated for the Ministry of Heavy Industry regarding 1965 and 1968, the data of products are available also in terms of physical units, so the models relating to these two years can be made comparable by processing and evaluating them by mathematical methods.

c) The grouping of activities according to production lines means that the products are grouped according to the similarity of technologies applied in production or to that of their consumption. A combined table based on this principle may, apart from its perspicuousness, offer a possibility of analysis not only for economists but also for technical experts, since in this model the technological situation may be more correctly presented.

When establishing *factual (statistical) tables* on the activities supervised by the Ministry of Heavy Industry, we applied a model grouped by *products*. From this, the enterprises were able to obtain some information on the efficiency of their past production (as represented by their major products), whereas the Ministry was able to get a picture on the results and the shortcomings of the past period.

In the case of drawing up *plan balances*, the model based on *manufacturing lines* was preferred. The economic and technical experts and planners more readily perceive changes in the economic and technological factors within the framework of a manufacturing line. For ensuring comparability, also the data of former years and of the factual table are available in a form representing manufacturing lines.

The grouping of activities by manufacturing lines took place in accordance with the technological experts of the Ministry, in such a way that it satisfied the requirements of analysis, on the one hand, and, on the other, it enabled the comparison of figures with those derived from the grouping applied by the Central Statistical Office. Also certain development concepts were taken into account, e.g., the production of synthetic rubber figures as a separate group.

Planning within the Ministry of Heavy Industry switched over to development concepts formulated according to manufacturing lines, and analyses are now being made within this framework. In order to ensure comparability in spite of changes in prices and in organization, the data for the years 1960, 1965 and 1968 had to be recalculated accordingly.

This type of model has the further advantage of being relatively simple. For instance, the 1968 model grouped by enterprises contains about 120 "sectors", whereas in the model for the same year, there are 83 sectors grouped by products. The combination of the two models results, even after some simplification, in at least 350–400 units of observation. Our model based on manufacturing lines contains only 38–40 items (as regards the activities supervised by the Ministry). Thus, in addition to its being easier to evaluate from the point of view of technology, it is also preferable on account of its clarity.

III. THE APPLICATION OF OUR COMBINED PLAN MODEL BASED ON MANUFACTURING LINES

1. RELATIONSHIPS BETWEEN THE CENTRAL AND OUR COMBINED PLAN MODEL

Essentially, our model can be completely fitted into the central model, since its figures regarding the other sectors of the national economy were taken from the latter, and only the activities supervised by the Ministry are presented in a more desaggregated form. But even these detailed figures, after adequate aggregation, fully correspond to those contained in the central model. This is due to the character of the models themselves; at the same time it reflects the close connection between the law on the national economic plan and the more detailed plan conceptions.

Thus, the basic data and direct indicators included in the central and the combined models differ only in their degree of aggregation. Not only are the main data identical (as the social product, primary inputs and final uses of the national economy), but also the aggregated values figuring within the inner square. For the purposes of analysing the plan tables of 1975, we performed the mathematical elaboration not only with respect to the combined but also to the central model.

The inverse coefficients derived from the direct ones are, evidently, not identical in the two models, due to the different levels of the aggregation.

Table 1 compares the cumulated values of the two inverse matrices.

Table 1

The values (in per cent) along the main diagonals of the inverse matrix (1968)

	Central model (12 sectors)	Our model (45 sectors)
Metallurgy	118.050	116.101
Engineering	115.575	114.862
Building materials	106.256	106.219
Light industry	135.751	135.695
Food industry	116.171	116.073
Construction	101.093	101.097
Agriculture	134.525	134.263
Transport and communications	101.296	101.326

Thus, the values obtained from the two models do not differ considerably, with the exception of metallurgy and engineering. In these two fields the main cause of the deviation was that our model shows separately aluminium metallurgy and engineering belonging to the Ministry of Heavy Industry.

The allocation of primary resources according to final use may be determined by matrix-multiplication.

$$(\mathbf{KR})\mathbf{Y}$$

where

$\mathbf{K}$ = the matrix of primary resources,
$\mathbf{R}$ = the inverse matrix,
$\mathbf{Y}$ = the matrix of final use.

Table 2

Shares of primary resources employed in non-productive consumption and investment, respectively (in per cent of the total required by final use)

	Central model (12 sectors)	Our model (45 sectors)
a) The share of nonproductive consumption:		
Depreciation	50.20	50.29
Wages and incomes	52.46	52.71
Net social income	46.85	46.59
b) The share of investments:		
Depreciation	21.76	21.91
Wages and incomes	21.53	21.27
Net social income	25.77	25.68

Our model, though containing nearly four times as many sectors as the central one, deviates only by fractions of one per cent from the central model as regards the main values and even this deviation may be explained.

Thus, the main indicators serving for an economy-wide evaluation of the efficiency of exports and investments are almost identical in the two plan models, in spite of the differences in the extent of their aggregation. Accordingly, our model is an organic part of the central model, and the economy-wide figures obtained from the two types are comparable. This is particularly important from the point of view of analysis, because it enables us to compare the figures relating to the lines of manufacturing obtained from our model with those of the central model relating to industrial branches, and to reveal the causes of the differences.

Table 3

The cumulated imports and depreciation needed for exports and investments (the corresponding values of the central model equal 100)

	Exports destined to		Investments
	socialist	non-socialist	
	countries		
Imports measured in foreign exchange forints:			
of socialist origin	99.12	98.40	100.93
of non-socialist origin	99.78	99.79	101.37
Depreciation (Ft):	98.43	98.73	100.06

2. SOME EXAMPLES OF ANALYSES

Our model is suitable for performing every kind of analysis usually applied to input–output tables, from the structural analyses based on direct values to the economy-wide evaluations based on complete indicators.

The analysis of cumulated wages. The evaluation of the cumulated wages is important in decisions concerning development. A variant of cumulated accounting (so-called complete accounts) includes all inputs of live and embodied labour, by taking into account the use of home-produced and imported materials, as well as the employment of fixed assets on the grounds of their depreciation. Thus, one of the most comprehensive indicators figuring in our model is this variant (see Table 4).

As regards cumulated wages the chemical industry is the second least labour-intensive one after the production of electric energy. Nevertheless, analysis has to show in what lines of production and by what measures the cumulated wages could be further reduced. Of all our production lines, the cumulated wages are highest in the processing of synthetic materials. This is due in part to the high direct input of imported materials, and in part also to the fact that about 30 per cent of inputs serving the domestic production of basic synthetic materials is also derived from imports. Along with the development of the domestic basis of petrolchemicals, the cumulated wages of the processing of synthetic materials may be expected to decrease. This is likely because the indicators of some related production lines (e.g., the processing of organic chemicals and of mineral oil) are already favourable.

Table 4

Two variants of cumulated wages in the output of the major manufacturing lines belonging to the chemical industry (in per cent)

Lines of manufacturing	Variant 1	Variant 2
	(complete accounting)	
Chemical fertilizers	14.915	36.454
Basic synthetic materials	16.144	41.036
Processing of synthetic materials	21.450	43.261
Synthetic fibres	14.607	32.109
Inorganic basic materials	23.840	40.192
Organic basic materials	21.346	38.121
Household chemicals and cosmetics	24.627	40.030
Dyes and lacquers	18.785	36.675
Pesticides	14.545	30.238
Pharmaceutics	18.745	31.224
Rubber industry	21.078	42.060
Photochemical industry	21.326	41.309
Processing of crude oil	8.746	32.061
Average for the chemical industries	19.590	38.631

The *cumulated imported materials:* the chemical industry uses imported materials in a very high proportion (coresponding to almost 25 per cent of the total value of its activities). It is necessary to find out which branches require imports in an indirect form. Traditional calculations show the difference between "direct" and "cumulated" import requirements of a sector only in a global way. Our model, however, makes it possible to show this difference in detail, by multiplying the matrices

$$\mathbf{C^*R}$$

where $\mathbf{C^*}$ is the matrix of direct inputs of imported materials detailed by lines of manufacturing and by sectors of provenience, and $\mathbf{R}$ is the inverse matrix.

From the resulting matrix it may be read which sectors are the final users of an imported material processed within a given manufacturing line.

The food industry, the building industry and agriculture, e.g., do not use directly crude oil or natural gas but, according to the cumulated indicators, their indirect demand for these materials is very high, mainly because they are very transport-intensive and therefore big consumers of the products of oil and gas processing (to which, in the case of agriculture, also the consumption by tractors and other machines is added). In the sector of transports and communication, the products of oil and gas processing make up 55–60 per cent of all inputs. Moreover, the high indicators are partly connected with other indirect inputs, e.g., of natural gas used in the fertilizer industry or in the manufacturing of building materials, and partly with further interrelationships expressed in the inverse matrix. Thus, for instance, when the building industry contributes to increasing the capacity of oil and gas processing, at the same time it adds to the demand for imported oil and gas.

The balance of foreign exchange: the high share of imports in the inputs of the chemical industry is a major factor in the country's balance of foreign exchange. As it was seen above, the high demand of the chemical industry on foreign exchange is mainly due to the indirect demands of other branches. It is evidently necessary to reveal which branches are the final users of the chemical products requiring imports and how the final user of each product would have to be charged with the foreign-exchange costs of imports. For this purpose, a matrix can be obtained by multiplying

$$(\mathbf{C^*R})\hat{\mathbf{Y}}$$

where $\hat{\mathbf{Y}}$ is the diagonal matrix of the y vector expressing the total of home-produced inputs needed for the given final use.

When adding the data of the resulting matrix by *rows,* we obtain what the individual producing sectors have used from the imported materials belonging to each sectoral range. Thus, this matrix shows the import needs of the national economy re-arranged according to the directions of final use. The results obtained indicate that the bulk of materials imported on account of the chemical industry goes into the engineering industry, the light industry, the food industry, the building industry and agriculture, so that these sectors may turn out products for final use. In order to develop these branches, it seems expedient also to reveal its indirect demand for imported materials.

When adding the data of the table by *columns* we obtain the amounts of imported materials used by the various sectors in order to turn out products for final use. When drawing up an economy-wide balance of foreign exchange by branches, the figures obtained in this way have to be used.

According to the factual and plan balances analysed so far, the chemical industry's foreign-exchange balance shows an annual deficit of about Ft 700 million, when only the direct relationships are taken into account. It is, however, highly positive (ranging from —700 versus 7,500 million forints annually), when drawn up according to final use.

*

From the diverse possibilities of analysis offered by the input–output table only a few were mentioned here. Our future programme includes also a type of investigation which, instead of restricting the analysis to a single year, should reveal the changes over time, too, relying on a series of tables for 1965, 1968, 1970 and 1975, all of which are comparable both in construction and content.

THIRD SESSION

SOME METHODOLOGICAL PROBLEMS OF THE APPLICATION OF INPUT-OUTPUT TABLES IN ECONOMIC ANALYSES

Chairman

DR. SÁNDOR GANCZER

THE ROLE OF INPUT-OUTPUT TABLES IN ANALYSING INDUSTRIAL EFFICIENCY

by

MRS. VERA NYITRAI

A highly important field of using input–output tables is economic analysis. In our practical analytical work performed in the last ten years, particularly as regards the situation and development of industry, we have frequently applied this method. In this field, analysis of efficiency occupies an important place. In this paper, I wish to concentrate on this problem by trying to show the role of input–output tables in the past and what role they are expected to have in the future in the analysis of industrial efficiency, with a view to the particular features of the use, advantages and limitations of such tables.

THE CONCEPT OF INDUSTRIAL EFFICIENCY

Before determining the role of input–output techniques in the analysis of efficiency, first of all the concept of efficiency itself, and the possibilities of measuring it, have to be clarified.

In Hungarian economic literature efficiency is defined in different ways. Some economists interpret it in a very wide sense, while others restrict it to a narrower scope. In my opinion, a definition suitable for *every* situation is hardly conceivable; the interpretation of industrial efficiency may change depending on several objective and subjective factors.

Among the objective factors, the concrete objectives of economic policy serve evidently as a starting point for the interpretation of efficiency, together with the actually prevailing economic mechanism as a tool available for implementing these objectives. By way of example, the comparison between the 1950's and the present time offers itself. In the 1950's when one of the objectives of economic policy consisted in a quantitative satisfaction of the consumer demand, and the system of economic management was of a strictly centralized nature, an enterprise or industrial branch was considered to be operating efficiently when it was able to turn out maximum quantities of the product prescribed in its plan and to fulfil maximally its other plan commitments (e.g., range, quality and cost level or products) by the required deadlines.

Clearly, with the present economic policy and economic mechanism it is much more difficult to state directly whether an enterprise or an industry is operating efficiently or not. The objective of our present economic policy consists in building a higher level of socialism, and our present economic mechanism offers many different tools serving this objective. The so-called "efficient operation" may be

interpreted differently, depending on our point of view. An enterprise may be considered as very efficient from the point of view of its workers and managers because it yields high profits and thus, there is a high material incentive for them, but it is not certain that it will qualify as being efficient from the viewpoint of the national economy as a whole. In judging efficiency, beyond the objective factors, a series of *subjective* elements may also assert themselves, depending on what features are considered important. Some research workers interpret economic efficiency, and within that, the efficiency of industry, in an extremely broad sense. Though this study cannot go into this problem in detail, I would like to refer, among others, to the definition given by J. Wilcsek in his study prepared for the Industrial Committee for Long-Term Planning,* to the formulation of K. Szabó** and to the definitions of B. Csikós-Nagy.*** Also the related investigations of the Institute of Economic Sciences are known, where the economic efficiency of the industrial branches was analysed with the aid of an aggregated system of indicators: the net income per unit of the combined input of wages and productive assets; i.e. in this analysis the concept was characterized by a single group of indicators.****

Obviously, all these interpretations seem suitable, although they approach the concept of industrial efficiency from different aspects. In my opinion, however, both the rather broad definition and the narrow interpretation restricted to a single indicator have their drawbacks. If industrial efficiency is interpreted too widely and its changes are expressed by a whole set of indicators of varying types, it will be rather difficult to obtain a relatively unambiguous picture of its development. It is conceivable — and also occurs in practice rather frequently — that some of the indicators show an improvement and others a deterioration, and it is rather difficult to establish the weight of the individual indicators within *global* efficiency. An interpretation relying on a single type of indicator, however — as the other extreme — invokes the danger that the problem will be all too much simplified: factors will be neglected that may exert considerable influence on the development of efficiency.

In my opinion, industrial efficiency and its development should be characterized unequivocally with relatively few indicators. By industrial efficiency I mean the following:

- the level of labour productivity,
- capital-output ratio,
- material intensity, with particular respect to imported materials,

* Jenő Wilcsek: A gazdasági hatékonyság elemzése (Analysis of economic efficiency). Manuscript, Budapest 1970.

** Kálmán Szabó: *A szocialista termelés alapvonásai* (Basic features of socialist production) Kossuth Könyvkiadó, p. 409, Budapest 1970.

*** A gazdasági hatékonyságról (On economic efficiency). An interview with B. Csikós-Nagy. *Valóság,* No. 2, pp. 14–18, 1971.

**** We speak of a *group* of indicators because the net income originating in industry has been calculated at different prices.

– the product pattern of saleable output, with a particular view to the ratio of up-to-date products in production and sales.

This interpretation is acceptable, in my opinion, both on macro- and micro-economic levels. There is no doubt, however, that we cannot work with the same types of indicators on the different levels.

Therefore, when discussing the methods of analysing industrial efficiency, it must also be specified on what level efficiency is intended to be examined. In this respect, three levels can be fairly well delimited:

– enterprise level,
– branch level, and
– national economic level efficiency.

In investigating *enterprise level* efficiency, the analysis can be based mainly on the traditional system of statistical indicators. Though it is conceivable that some large enterprises which represent whole branches of the industry have statistical and accounting data enabling them to perform even more complicated computations, it is possible also in such cases to apply the input–output method.

Branch level and *national economic level* efficiency can be best analysed by using the input–output method. In my view, this type of analytical method is particularly important in the analysis made on the national level.

When analysing the "branch efficiency", we generally wish to obtain a picture on the functioning of a branch or group of industries in the phase of production characteristically covered by them. If, e.g., we investigate the branch efficiency of engineering or, within it, that of the production of telecommunication equipment, we leave out of account the phases of metal extraction and processing that *precede* the activities of engineering proper, or the production of telecommunication equipment, respectively. When analysing efficiency on a national economic level, this can be performed either for individual industrial branches (groups), or for the industry as a whole. Thus, we may speak about the "national-level efficiency" of, e.g., the engineering industries, or of the industry producing telecommunication equipment. In these cases, we mean the *combined* efficiency of *all* inputs made throughout the national economy in order to produce the final output released by the industry or group in question.

THE ROLE OF INPUT–OUTPUT TABLES IN ANALYSING THE NATIONAL ECONOMY LEVEL EFFICIENCY OF INDUSTRY

In addition to precisely defining the type of efficiency we are going to investigate, we must unambiguously select the system of indicators to be used. In previous practice the following types of indicators were used for an approximate measuring of efficiency:

1. The indicators of *labour productivity* or, frequently, their inverses, i.e., the indicators of labour intensity. In this field, three kinds of indicators were regularly

l, relating output (a) to the number of employees, (b) to the number of , and (c) to the total of man-hours performed by workers.

nbined analysis of the three subtypes of indicators enables a more detailed nent of changes in labour intensity. The *cumulated labour* of production ds, namely, on several factors. The cumulated labour can be best computed on the basis of man-hours. A reliable picture on how the different branches are supplied with manpower can be obtained by analysing the number of workers (or all employees) per unit of production. In practice this indicator is calculated in both forms, since the ratio of workers to other employees varies considerably by branches as well as by stages of industrialization. As a rule, the proportion of white-collar employees tends to grow with industrial development.

2. *Capital-intensity* (the inverse of capital–output ratio) is examined by accounting for both the fixed and the working assets. Here, too, the stock value per unit of output is computed.

The proper examination of capital intensity on national level requires a more detailed breakdown, particularly in respect to fixed assets. One of the most important problems in a fast developing industry is the amount of capital needed for the development of its production. In this respect, in the first place the engagement of productive fixed assets per unit of output has to be investigated. Namely, the volume of non-productive fixed assets is not primarily a function of production, but of a set of other factors (e.g., measures of social and cultural policy, etc.). In many cases, it also becomes necessary to examine separately, within the engagement of productive fixed assets, that of vehicles, buildings, and machinery and equipment.

3. Though we mention it in the third place, from the viewpoint of input–output techniques the analysis of *material intensity* ranks first. It is the table that sums up the values of materials required by the individual branches both directly and in a cumulated form, including the materials needed by their suppliers.

Within the analysis of material intensity, also a detailed investigation of import needs can be performed. Maybe the earliest use of input–output methods for analytical purposes in Hungarian economic literature was connected with calculations regarding "import intensity". This was so not only because — as in every open economy — the import problem was important for our country, but also because the various tables offered a possibility of analysing import intensity to a depth inaccessible with the traditional tools. Within material intensity, it is energy intensity and the analysis of the pattern of energy utilization that we are mostly concerned with.

4. The input–output method gained an important role in analysing profitability. Here, in the first place the ratio of "net social income" turned out by individual branches to their "social product" is investigated. Of course, also the changes in the individual elements of the net social income, e.g., taxes, subsidies, gains and losses, etc. may be analysed separately.

Moreover, the input–output tables also provide the opportunity to assess the "cumulated" wages and incomes of a unit of final use, as well as its cumulated net social income. In other words, with the aid of input–output tables we can trace all domestic inputs of materials to wages, net income, depreciation allowance, or to the use of imported material. The "cumulated profitability" taken in this sense shows, for each individual branch, the size and composition of net income included in the value turned out for final use; it also shows the distribution of this net income between profits (or losses), and payments to the state (turnover tax, wage tax, charge on assets, etc.). The use of the input–output table also enables us to convert the cumulated imports and depreciation of the individual branches into wages and net incomes. This procedure rests on the assumption that imports are the counter-value of exports, so their cumulated wages can be approximated with the aid of the average cumulated wages of exports of the same value in the given year.

In this way, we can obtain a picture on the *cumulated wages and net incomes* per unit of net output in the individual branches. Working with the assumption that imports worth Ft 100 are equal to exports worth Ft 100, our calculations more or less serve our purposes; i.e., they can be used for comparing the indicators of branch and national-level efficiency of the individual branches.

5. Finally, when analysing industrial efficiency, the so-called *indicator of input efficiency* is also used. For this purpose, e.g., the amount of electric energy used for driving motors and the depreciation allowance of the latter are reduced, with the aid of the input–output table, to man-hours or to the number of employees. The purpose of the conversion is only to obtain data reduced to the same unit of measurement, and in this way to summarize them in a single indicator. This aggregate indicator is intended to approximate the *combined efficiency of live and embodied labour.*

Another remark is necessary on the kinds of indicators listed. In practice, namely, when analysing national-level efficiency, the concept of "production" is interpreted in different ways. When the phase efficiency of the branch is examined, generally the indicator of *gross output* is used. When, however, we intend to characterize the national-economic efficiency, the "cumulated inputs" (a concept widely used in the terminology of the last ten years) are confronted with the *output released for final use.* Finally, when the so-called "total input indicators" are used, they are compared to the *net output.* Thus, the indicators investigated are calculated both for the unit of final use of the branches and for the unit of their net output.

For analysing national-level efficiency the input–output tables can be used in investigations of different types. In general, three main fields of use are known:

1. Comparison between branches: in such cases the efficiencies of different branches, groups of industry, or different sectors are compared to each other. Of course, these comparisons have an interpretable economic meaning only when prices correctly reflect the value relations prevailing in the branches, that is the producer prices (or the prices used in valuation in the input–output tables) are suited for obtaining a realistic picture about the actual efficiency of each branch. If, on the grounds of considerations of economic policy or for other reasons,

prices are deflected from the input– or value–proportionate prices, some of the comparisons will lose their foundations. Of course, even in such cases there is a way of comparing the efficiency of various branches, but this necessitates new computations made at calculated prices. In our statistical practice such computations were made by the Economic and the Industrial Departments of the Central Statistical Office; also the research workers of the Institute of Planning have performed such calculations. The calculated prices may be either input-proportionate or value-proportionate, according to the character and type of the question to which an answer is needed.

In comparing branch efficiencies, the question emerges from what type of input–output tables it is expedient or necessary to set out; we shall return to the discussion of this problem.

2. Input–output tables can also be used for comparing efficiency in various geographic areas. In the case of Hungary such comparisons within the country itself have but a secondary importance, particularly in industrial analyses, since a substantial part of industry is concentrated in and around Budapest. Much more important are the international comparisons. In this field, we can point to some rather successful Hungarian experiments. Practice has proved that a basic condition for international comparisons of efficiency is that the countries to be considered should have input–output tables of the same structure and of approximately identical contents. Even under such conditions, the indicators in which value data were related to value data could be better interpreted than when the efficiency coefficients are the ratio of a value and a quantity (e.g. man-hours, number of workers, etc.). In the interest of a realistic evaluation, also in international comparisons we may apply calculated prices, provided they were formed according to identical principles in both countries as, e.g., in the case of the Bulgarian–Hungarian comparison.

3. Finally, and perhaps to the greatest extent, the input–output indicators can be used for investigating efficiency over time, within a country. In this respect, we have considerable experience in Hungary. In investigating the changes of efficiency in the function of time, either for industry as a whole or for its various branches, the input–output tables have been used regularly, inclusive of almost all indicators available with their aid. In the following I should like to survey the applicability of the indicators reviewed, but without claiming to exhaust all possibilities.

The input–output tables for 1968 provide the possibility for interindustry efficiency comparisons. No doubt, the comparison of labour- and capital-productivities among branches is influenced by a series of particular characteristics, and in many cases the effect of the latter cannot be eliminated. Yet attention should be drawn to a few interesting phenomena. In Table 1 we listed the branches in which the relative value of machinery and equipment engaged in production (on the branch level) were the highest or the lowest, i.e., the first four and the last four from among the 67 industrial branches figuring in the 1968 input–output table.

Table 1

Range of branches as regards the relative value of machinery and equipment engaged in 1968*

Branch	Value of machinery and equipment engaged in producing a value of one million forints (million Ft)		
	directly in the last production phase	cumulated	on the national economic level
Electric energy	1.39 (1)	1.76 (1)	4.31 (20)
Production of fertilizers and inorganic basic chemicals	1.02 (2)	1.47 (2)	5.83 (2)
Sugar industry	0.94 (3)	1.21 (6)	3.22 (46)
Production of gas (from coal)	0.92 (4)	1.24 (4)	5.39 (6)
Poultry and egg processing industry	0.08 (64)	0.43 (57)	2.86 (54)
Textile garment industry	0.06 (65)	0.56 (45)	3.30 (43)
Handicrafts and home industries	0.05 (66)	0.42 (58)	2.25 (62)
Meat industry	0.05 (67)	0.34 (65)	2.42 (61)

* Calculated from the nationali nput–output table of Hungary (1968); the figures in parentheses indicate a serial order, 1 fo the highest and 67 for the lowest value.

The data clearly show that the relative value of equipment engaged in the last production phase does not coincide by far with the values engaged on the national economic level. The value of equipment necessary in the preceding phases of production considerably modifies the size and order of the requirements raised against the national economy. Investigations of this type, similar to those presented in the table, are important not only for the analysis of past periods, but also for offering significant help to the computations preliminary to development plans of individual branches.

I would like to mention another example in this field, namely the interindustry comparison of profitability. Of course, we must not lose sight of the fact that every indicator of profitability is closely connected with the given price system and thus the ranking of branches depends on the extent to which the prices express the real value relations among their products. The data computed from the 1968 table show, e.g., that from among the engineering branches the highest ratio of net social income (in the last phase of production) was produced by the precision engineering enterprise (26.7 per cent of the value of gross output). The rate of social net income was lowest in the enterprises producing vehicles (13.3 per cent). The picture, however, becomes quite different if we examine, instead of the net income produced in the final phase, the cumulated net income as a percentage of the value of final output, or the total net income as a percentage of net output. The farther we follow back the inputs of materials (domestic or imported), and of depreciation, i.e., the greater the extent to which we convert them into wages and net income, the smaller will be the differences among the branches.

The ratios of cumulated net social income of the engineering branches diffe much less, the two extremes being 43.5 and 35.5 per cent (the two extreme branches are the same as in the former case). If, however, we calculate the ratio of net income on the national level, the two extreme values get still closer to each other, the highest being 58.8 per cent and the lowest 53.3. Here, the lower limit is still represented by vehicle production, but the highest place is taken by electrical engineering. From the example the conclusion can be drawn that the ratio of the net income produced in the last phase of production is far from being conclusive as regards the ratio on national level. This is particularly true for such branches (e.g., engineering) the inputs of which contain relatively much embodied labour. The example allows us to conclude that among branches which are closely interrelated with the work of others, the great differences shown by the net income ratios on the phase level tend to diminish with cumulation and on the national economic level the dispersions become still smaller.

The two examples offer only partial information about the possibilities of branch comparisons in this field. Practical application can be much more diversified and its exploitation is not nearly exhausted by our analyses made so far. The more we get to know the available possibilities, the more and newer viewpoints we get for practical application.

As regards regional comparisons, we can list mainly international ones. Our Bulgarian–Hungarian comparison was considered as an experiment, its purpose was to illustrate the applicability of input–output tables for international comparisons. Possibilities in this respect were to a certain extent limited by the fact that in the past relatively few comparable input–output tables could be found in different countries. The near future promises greater possibilities, since efforts in the Council of Mutual Economic Aid member countries aimed at constructing comparable input–output tables have succeeded, and today many countries compile tables having fairly similar accounting systems. In addition, the computations and analyses performed in the Institute of Economic Sciences of the Hungarian Academy of Sciences have shown that a set of relevant conclusions may be drawn even from international comparisons based on not quite comparable tables, having rather different structures. I believe that even broader possibilities for further work are provided since a department of the UN Economic Commission for Europe also deals with the problems relating to the comparability of data derived from the input–output tables of European countries.

It is regarding comparisons over time that we have the widest experience and, in my opinion, this is the field where we will have the greatest possibilities even in the future for the application of the input–output methods. It would like to survey a few examples also in this field from our latest table.

From the index numbers relating to the efficiency of inputs interesting conclusions can be drawn on the development of input efficiency in the socialist industry and in the major industrial branches; this can be seen in Table 2.

From the values of the indicators we may conclude that the changes in the combined efficiency of all inputs (fourth and eighth columns) were practically

Table 2

Efficiency of inputs in the socialist industry of Hungary

Branch	Output in 1967				Output in 1969			
	(1) per employee	(2) per unit of electric energy used in motors	(3) per unit of depreciation	(4) per unit of total inputs	(5) per employee	(6) per unit of electric energy used in motors	(7) per unit of depreciation	(8) per unit of total inputs
	1960 = 100				1967 = 100			
Mining	132.9	82.8	107.0	124.2	103.6	105.2	101.5	103.3
Electric energy	168.3	106.9	138.0	152.0	113.0	129.6	124.1	118.2
Metallurgy	135.3	107.1	134.1	133.0	103.1	92.5	103.8	102.4
Engineering	148.1	107.9	167.5	149.1	101.6	103.2	85.4	100.4
Building materials industry	148.9	86.0	199.0	150.7	92.3	90.9	70.5	89.5
Chemical industry	165.4	93.9	141.9	153.0	103.8	99.9	89.6	100.1
Heavy industry	148.5	99.2	144.6	145.7	101.7	99.5	96.6	100.8
Light industry	131.0	88.7	177.6	132.6	95.2	98.7	63.5	93.6
Food industry	183.3	90.2	118.7	134.7	95.0	98.7	73.3	92.6
Socialist industry total	141.9	95.1	142.3	140.3	100.3	98.8	89.8	99.0

determined by the changes in productivity of live labour (first and fifth columns). The combined indicator has been less affected by changes in the efficiency of the use of electric energy for driving motors, and of depreciation. While the efficiency of live labour has considerably increased between 1960–1967 and was stable between 1967–1969, the efficiency of electric energy deteriorated in both periods, and that of depreciation, after having improved between 1960–1967, fell back between 1967–1969.

As a result, the efficiency of total inputs improved in the first period at about the same rate as that of live labour, whereas in the second it slightly fell back not only in the whole of the socialist industry, but also in the majority of the branches examined.

The situation is somewhat different if the efficiency of inputs is examined in the longer run, i.e., in the ten-year period between 1960 and 1969. In this, the efficiency of labour increased in every branch and so did the efficiency computed on the basis of depreciation allowance; but in many branches the efficiency of the use of electric energy in motors changed unfavourably even in this period. It is a particular advantage of this kind of indicator that it enables us to show the changes in efficiency of live and embodied labour both separately and in a summarized form. The data presented in the table, besides showing changes over time also facilitate interindustry comparison. I should like to call attention to

Table 3

Value of assets engaged per unit of net output in the

Branch	Average gross value of assets engaged			
	real estate		machinery and equipment	
	1965	1968	1965	1968
Oil refining	1.64	1.92	6.79	5.82
Production of gas from coal	3.67	3.22	8.30	5.39
Coal processing	2.54	2.67	6.70	4.63
Pharmaceutical industry	1.49	1.45	4.71	3.15
Paints and dyes	1.76	1.57	6.50	4.98
Household chemicals and cosmetics	1.45	1.44	6.30	4.02
Rubber processing	1.40	1.44	6.31	4.62
Plastic industry	1.24	1.35	5.20	3.96
Fertilizers and inorganic basic chemicals	2.50	2.42	8.33	5.83
Production of other chemicals	1.69	1.81	5.88	4.55

two branches: in the last decade our chemical industry increased dynamically and here both the efficiency of live labour and that of live and embodied labour combined show a favourable change. Mining, on the other hand, presents the relatively least favourable development in this respect. In connection with the chemical industry, I wish to show another example of efficiency analysis; the various kinds of capital engaged per unit of production in 1965 and 1968 are compared in this capital-intensive branch (see Table 3).

In view of the considerable investments made in the chemical industry, it would seem justified to expect the capital intensity to increase, at least transitorily, when the new projects are put to use. But the data in Table 3 indicate that the new investments made between 1965 and 1968 were of a higher efficiency than the existing stock of capital, so the total capital intensity of production not only did not increase, but it even decreased in several branches of the chemical industry (e.g., the production of gas from coal, fertilizers, etc.). It is particularly noteworthy that also the value of machinery and equipment engaged per unit of production has decreased, indicating the higher efficiency of new equipment.

Similar analyses over time can be made with any of the indicators listed. The input–output tables enable a comparison over ten years.

INPUT–OUTPUT TABLE VARIANTS UTILIZABLE IN EFFICIENCY ANALYSES

A realistic examination of industrial efficiency raises rather serious requirements against the input–output techniques to be employed. It seems, however, that it is possible to meet them. The kinds and details of the tables available secure the basic conditions for analysing efficiency.

chemical industry (million forints)

in producing 1 million forints of net output

vehicles		other fixed assets		all productive fixed assets		working assets	
1965	1968	1965	1968	1965	1968	1965	1968
1.79	1.67	0.11	0.09	10.34	9.49	0.74	0.44
1.99	1.54	0.17	0.11	14.12	10.26	0.88	0.64
1.64	1.31	0.19	0.18	11.07	8.78	0.80	0.58
1.21	0.98	0.07	0.04	7.36	5.63	0.81	0.63
1.80	1.70	0.09	0.05	10.14	8.30	0.95	0.55
1.76	1.33	0.08	0.05	9.59	6.83	0.99	0.79
1.66	1.45	0.07	0.04	9.43	7.55	0.81	0.53
1.40	1.29	0.06	0.04	7.90	6.64	0.74	0.56
2.05	1.63	0.13	0.09	13.01	9.97	0.93	0.72
1.55	1.40	0.11	0.08	9.22	7.85	0.84	0.71

In our present practice of economic analyses mainly the type "B" of the input–output tables is used, that is, the kind which shows the distribution of domestically produced products by branches while imports are shown in an aggregate form, in a single row. A relatively smaller role was given in our analyses to the variants "A" and "C". As regards the variant "A", I believe that neither in the future will it have as great a role as the other two. Here, namely, the distribution of imports is shown together with that of the domestically produced goods. This involves that in the case of cumulated calculations we proceed as if imports required the same inputs of wages, materials and depreciation as the domestically manufactured ones. This assumption is, however, rather forced and unrealistic in a country having an open economy.

The situation is quite different with the input–output tables of type "C". We should accord a greater role in our analyses to this type. It can be of particular importance in the analysis of cumulated inputs when the imports have to be distinguished not only according to their character but also according their provenience from socialist or non-socialist countries. This type of table, however, has a greater role in economic analysis than in planning. Imports may change considerably from year to year both in volume and in pattern, being perhaps the most unstable element of the input–output table, so table "C" can be used in planning only with strong reservations.

If the input–output tables are to be used for analysing efficiency, the prices at which they are compiled deserve particular attention. In Hungarian practice computations are performed at current factual sales prices but, in the interest of comparison, tables of several consecutive years are compiled at comparable prices as well. Other variants based on practical considerations also occur, e.g., the Economic Research Institute computed tables at rouble and dollar prices.

In the introduction I mentioned our practical experiences gained with "calculated prices". All these show that, from the viewpoint of efficiency analysis, it is both expedient and advisable to apply different kinds of prices and price systems for evaluating the tables; but I believe that the computations performed at factual realization prices are the most important, since for judging the given situation and for analysing interbranch relations these are the prices actually prevailing that may serve as a basis.

Another — seemingly technical — problem is whether the main diagonal of the model should contain data, or should we operate with a so-called "net" model. The data in the main diagonal show the volume of purchases and sales *within the branch,* under the prevailing organization pattern of industry and of the other economic branches. Obviously, this holds only for input–output tables compiled according to *organizational units.* If, however, we have a table built up according to *activities,* the data in the main diagonal show the purchases and sales occurring within the same activity. This viewpoint is worth attention in dynamic comparisons made within a country. Therefore, our tables are generally drawn up in a variant in which there are data in the main diagonal. In international comparisons, however, a distorting factor may arise — with tables compiled according to organizations — when the organizational pattern of industry significantly differs in the countries covered by the comparison. In the first place, when in a given industry of a country there are but a few big enterprises, the volume of purchases and sales within the industry will be substantially smaller than in another country where the same industry consists of many medium-size or small enterprises cooperating with each other. This problem is particularly important for international comparisons regarding the engineering industry, where enterprises greatly rely on each other and where the extent and diversity of specialization and cooperation are characteristic of the development level of the industry in question, of the degree to which the advantages stemming from internal division of labour are utilized. Therefore, in international comparisons the tables containing the "net" values along the main diagonal have at least the same importance as those containing the "gross" values.

As regards the model to be used, the problem of desaggregation is highly important both in terms of international comparisons and those made over time. The advantages of the so-called "small input–output tables" in respect to the stability of technological coefficients and of the homogeneity problem are well known. The analysis of efficiency requires a rather high degree of homogeneity, and this can only be assured by desaggregation. The efficiency of strongly aggregated industrial groups depends to a great extent on the internal pattern of inputs and outputs, therefore, the changes (both improvement and deterioration) are highly dependent on structural changes.

Finally, I would like to stress the importance of comparability. I have already mentioned earlier that the problem of comparability as one of the criteria of exactness in analysing efficiency comes to the fore particularly in the case of international comparisons. But the problem may emerge also in the form that the efficiency analyses based on the input–output table do not have an independent existence, being but an element, however important, in the complex analysis of industrial efficiency. In this case, it can only be a really important element if comparability is maintained also between the input–output tables and the traditional statistical methods. I hold this viewpoint to be important because if we carry out too many "profile cleanings"* in the interest of securing homogeneity, we risk destroying the comparability of our data with those of traditional statistics which are grouped according to organizational units, and this may have an unfavourable effect on the reliability of efficiency analyses.

* For "profile cleaning", see the study by Éva Koós in this volume.

INPUT-OUTPUT TABLES CALCULATED AT WORLD-MARKET PRICES AS A TOOL FOR ECONOMIC ANALYSIS

by

ALADÁR SZABÓ

The problems related to economic structures and mechanisms occupy a central place in economic research. From among mathematical models covering the whole of material production and revealing its direct and indirect relationships, at present input–output tables are the most expedient tool for solving such problems.

Data and indicators derived from an input–output table *worked out at inland prices are valid only for that given price system.* The Hungarian system of inland prices is serving particular objectives of our economic policy, which are not quite free from autarkistic concepts. True, one of the requirements set against our price system consists in that it has to take into account also the valuations of the market; however, in view of the country's particular circumstances, this requirement can be satisfied only to a limited extent. It is also known that our foreign trade must adapt itself to the prices of two (socialist and non-socialist) world markets, where both relative prices and their dynamics are different.

The foreign prices are connected with the inland prices through the so-called "foreign-trade price multiplier", but also certain financial regulators (import duties, turnover taxes on imported goods, export subsidies, etc.) have a certain role. It is through these channels that prices prevailing in foreign markets influence the internal price system, the smooth functioning of which, being an objective of economic policy, requires consistency, relative price stability and the maintenance of equilibrium between supply and demand.

In view of all this, it may be said that — together with the home market which is primary and decisive from our point of view — there are three markets that have to be considered.

A comprehensive economic analysis postulates the revealing of the roles and effects of every major factor. Without doubt, when analysing Hungary's "open economy" it is particularly important to state *the efficiency of our foreign-trade relations.* (In 1969, Hungary imported goods to the value of 21,000 million "foreign-exchange forints" and exported goods worth more than 23,000 million.*) For the purposes of such analyses *an input-output table constructed at world market prices* may be very useful, and some role might be given also to a closed "product model" elaborated for the more important products.

* "Foreign-exchange forints" mean the sum of forints obtained by multiplying the sums of roubles or dollars, acquired through exports or spent on imports, by the official medium rates of exchange.

Models based on world-market prices are "constructed models". When building such a model, one assumes that the prices of the foreign market in question assert themselves in all productive branches of the national economy (directly in the competitive branches and indirectly in the non-competitive ones), and that they may be compared with the domestic physical inputs. Thus, one valuates all domestic inputs and outputs either in roubles or in dollars in order to obtain a picture, on the basis of foreign value estimates, regarding our economic structure, the profitability and efficiency of the individual branches, the differences between domestic and foreign price proportions and the relation between prices prevailing in the socialist and the non-socialist world markets.

We must not forget, however, that our internal price system expresses factual economic relations and is adapted to our particular conditions and objectives. At the same time, foreign-trade prices have but a limited validity and are not able to exert an economic pressure comparable to that of domestic factors on the system of prevailing domestic prices. Therefore, indicators derived from models based on world-market prices are but of an orientating character. The main advantage of such a model consists in its completeness and its complexity.

By world-market prices we mean, in the first place, prices realized (or realizable) for the Hungarian economy through its foreign-trade relations, i.e., export and import prices at frontier parity (exports FOB, imports CIF). It is also possible, however, to construct a model based on prices actually quoted in the leading foreign markets of the products in question. In this case neither the transport costs arising between the leading markets and the Hungarian frontier, nor the effects of the greater or poorer efficiency of our foreign-trade organs will have a bearing on the prices. It is also conceivable to choose, for special purposes, some other foreign-price basis (e.g., the inland price system of another country).

By selecting, from a complete model computed in foreign exchange, only the competitive branches, i.e., those directly taking part in foreign trade, the realistic nature of the calculation may be increased. It is also possible to examine certain fields of foreign trade turnover separately (e.g., in order to state the relation between the domestic costs of earning a rouble and a dollar more accurately, or to analyse the profitability and efficiency of our foreign trade). Anyhow, *it is always necessary to elaborate a complete model* covering the whole of the national economy. This is also necessary for being able to construct a "product model", since the wages and depreciation costs can only be converted to foreign exchange on the basis of the forint/foreign-exchange rate derived from the complete model.

In Hungary the elaboration of economy-wide and product models at world-market prices and their use in theoretical analyses and economic policy started about ten years ago. Their application coincided with the recognition that the former conceptions regarding both the central economic control exercised through rigid directives and the former autarkistic tendencies had to be revised, hence, the categories of the market had to be utilized as tools of indirect control. With this, the importance of analyses dealing with foreign-trade relationships and with the possibilities of better utilizing the advantages offered by the international division of labour came to the fore.

Models based on world-market prices were elaborated in the following research institutes:

a) The Institute for Industrial Economics and Business Organization of the Ministry of Heavy Industry has been commissioned by this ministry and the National Office of Materials and Prices to regularly construct such models since 1963. One of the initiators of constructing models at foreign prices was T. Liska, who has led the work of converting the input–output tables of 1959 and 1961 to foreign-exchange prices.

The methodology of conversion was developed in the course of experimental research. Drawing on the experience gained therefrom, the method was improved and subsequently used for building economy-wide models for the years 1961, 1965 and 1968 at rouble and dollar prices, according to several variants. Also a product model for the year 1961 was constructed. More than a hundred experts took part in the work of valuating branch activities at foreign-exchange prices, under the supervision of the economists F. Cságoly, Gy. Simon, L. Rácz, A. Szabó, Mrs. Stefánia Koczka, L. Gerencsér and Katalin Kovács.

b) The Institute of Economic Sciences of the Hungarian Academy of Sciences has performed comparative calculations based on foreign-exchange prices — in a more aggregated form — regarding three socialist countries.

c) In the Institute of Economic Research of the Central Statistical Office a model based on capitalist world-market prices (using rates of conversion derived from samples) was constructed; the results obtained were analysed in two papers by comparing them with indicators based on inland prices. (This research was performed, among others, by T. Liska, M. Simon and A. Fáy.) Recently, also the elaboration of a combined foreign-exchange balance aimed at analysing the situation of Hungarian agriculture has been started (led by M. Fecske).

d) The Economic Department of the Ministry of Metallurgy and Engineering (E. Longa, M. Gede and their colleagues) constructed an experimental foreign-price-based product model for the metallurgical and engineering industries with 1964–1965 data.

The sector breakdown of the input–output tables mentioned under a) (1961, 1965, 1968) was identical with that applied in the domestic-price-based tables of the Central Statistical Office. Generally, the conversion of forint values to roubles and dollars took place at conversion rates established separately for each individual product or product group. In principle, we had to state for each individual element of the calculation, either a factual unit price (in terms of foreign exchange) or a characteristic forint/foreign-exchange rate. By having such a detailed conversion, major distortions on the branch level could be prevented.

The first quadrant and the second quadrant of the table were thus calculated by converting outputs and complementary imports to a common denominator, and by dividing up their aggregate between individual users. As regards the third quadrant, the value of depreciation was converted at the same forint/foreign-exchange ratio as was obtained for investment; wages were converted at the rate obtained for consumer goods. The value of the various kinds of fixed assets engaged was converted according to the conversion rates of investment inputs; the value of working assets was obtained by using the average conversion rates of the material inputs in the various branches.

The main difficulty of constructing and calculating such a model (apart from its being very labour-intensive) is connected with the problems of valuating the activities of noncompetitive branches, like building industry, trade, services, etc.

Both the structural changes in the material branches of domestic production and the dynamics of foreign-exchange prices require the drawing up of this balance for every second or third year, in order to assess changes and tendencies over time. A set of such models may be utilized in forecasts regarding the expectable effects of certain planned price changes (e.g., in the inland prices or in those to be fixed in the trade contracts between socialist countries). They may also prove helpful when a modification of foreign-exchange rates is intended.

Models based on world-market prices supply useful information for various economic analyses. Therefore it seems worthwhile to deal with their contents and to define the possibilities of their utilization.

The two essential factors to be considered are the quantities and the prices. Both can be interpreted from an economic point of view: the relations between the physical quantities express the conditions of production, the foreign-exchange prices reflect the value-judgements of foreign markets relating to our production.

An input–output table computed in terms of foreign-exchange prices is built upon the physical quantities of the resources used (live and embodied labour). But foreign-exchange prices tend to change in relation to the relatively constant inland prices. Accordingly, the table calculated in terms of foreign-exchange prices will deviate from that calculated at inland prices, as regards the values of outputs, inputs, net income, etc.

The data of physical quantities reflect the conditions of domestic production. These conditions may be up-to-date or backward, but in any case they are factors that, on an economy-wide level, tend to change rather slowly. Generally speaking, within a given plan period their changes will result only in minor structural modifications although, in the case of certain branches, enterprises or lines of production, even substantial changes may occur.

As regards prices, the situation is different. Models may be constructed on the basis of various systems and types of prices, permitting a comparison with the actual price system. *When relative prices change, the shares of branches in the total output, their indicators of relative profitability and efficiency are also bound to change.*

Since one of the most important possibilities of utilizing our model is in the field of structural analyses, the foreign value-judgements reflected by it may induce our economic policy to revise and to modify the proportions of physical quantities, i.e., to change the product pattern, to introduce more up-to-date products, etc.

The introduction of new technologies is a continuous but rather slow process. Foreign prices (in particular, those of the capitalist world market) fluctuate continually. There is a mutual effect between technological progress and prices. But prices are affected, particularly in the short run, by many other influences which, in view of various economic and political considerations, may divert them from their long-term trends. Thus, from a static model based on foreign-exchange prices, relevant conclusions can only be drawn when the foreign-exchange prices figuring in it do not deviate substantially from their long-term price trends. Accordingly, in the course of conversion we must eliminate the incidental price fluctuations reflected in individual transactions.

To sum up: *models based on world-market prices* make it possible to assess which products are produced at relatively higher or at relatively lower costs in our national economy, when compared with international value proportions expressed in the prices produced by international competition. Since, however, the "world-market price" reflects international valuations only with certain restrictions and limitations, it is both possible and necessary to examine the "realizable" prices from various aspects. Thus, for instance, the differences between import and export prices, the alternatives of choosing the "relevant" capitalist market of a given product, the concentration on a certain part of the capitalist world market (e.g., the EEC), the necessity of eliminating the price effects of obvious monopoly situations or of political influences, etc., have all to be considered if we want to "clean" the "world-market price" from incidental distorting influences and to use it as a basis of comparison with inland inputs.

By starting from the commodity pattern of either our domestic production or our foreign trade, i.e., *viewed explicitly from the point of view of our own national economy,* we can state the value relations between the rouble and the dollar, the forint and the rouble or the forint and the dollar. We may also compare the relative prices existing within the three price systems. The results thus obtained are independent of technology, but are influenced by the commodity pattern.

As regards the possible uses of the model, we shall restrict ourselves to a few examples.*

PRICE ANALYSIS

The correct shaping and maintenance of our inland price system requires continuous work aimed at comparing inland and foreign-exchange relative prices, at revealing the causes of their deviations and at comparing the absolute magnitudes of inland and foreign prices.

* For a more detailed review of the purposes, structure and computation results of the model, see F. Cságoly and A. Szabó: Az első világpiaci árakkal képzett népgazdasági model (The first economy-wide model based on world-market prices). *Közgazdasági Szemle,* No. 5, 1969.

Indeed, our National Office of Materials and Prices utilizes models based on foreign-exchange prices as a tool for solving theoretical and practical problems of pricing. When an economy-wide model is built, the deviations of relative prices by branches are also subject to analysis.

The deviation of "rouble" and "dollar" price levels in the main product groups from the corresponding Hungarian inland price levels are shown by the following figure:

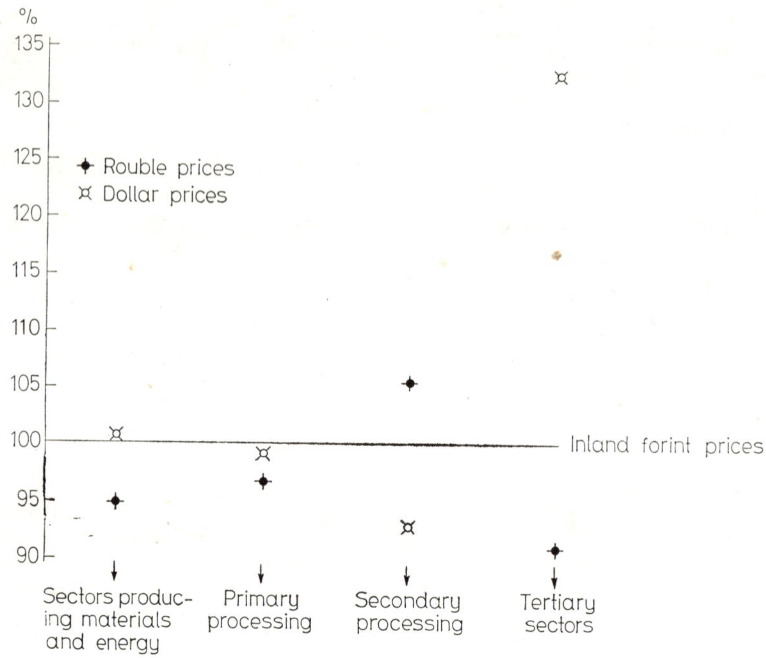

Rouble and dollar price levels in the major groups of commodities, as a percentage of the Hungarian domestic price level

In theoretical research, not only actual but "constructed" or "ideal" prices (value-type and production-type prices) can also be used. These can be calculated on the basis of both inland and foreign-exchange prices, and their deviations may be examined.*

The comparison between rouble and dollar prices is important as the contractual prices governing a considerable part of the trade among socialist countries are subject to revision from time to time. When established, these prices generally conform to the prices of the capitalist world market. However, as a result of changes in the latter, substantial deviations may take place in a few years. In order to

* See P. Glattfelder and P. Mátéffy: Ártipusszámítások tapasztalatai és irányai (Experiences and directions of calculating prices of various types). *Közgazdasági Szemle,* No. 11, 1970.

perform the necessary corrections of the socialist contractual prices, we must know the extent of such deviations, and must be able to forecast the expectable effects of any planned correction.

STRUCTURAL ANALYSES

Analyses regarding the relative shares of individual branches in the material production of the national economy, their contribution to national income and to the net income of society, as well as the ranking of branches according to their profitability and efficiency, serve, in the first place, as a basis for planning further development. As a matter of fact, the methods of such comparisons are not yet fully developed since the experience gathered in this field is still insufficient.

Patterns of gross output and national income
of the socialist (state-owned and cooperative) industry
of Hungary, 1965 and 1968 (percentages)

Branches	1965			1968		
	rouble	dollar	inland forint	rouble	dollar	inland forint
	price			price		
A) *Gross output*						
Mining	5.8	5.8	5.6	4.8	6.3	5.5
Electric energy	3.5	4.0	3.8	3.7	4.2	3.0
Metallurgy	10.0	9.1	11.5	9.1	10.5	10.0
Engineering	26.8	26.9	23.6	30.1	26.6	28.1
Building materials	3.9	3.8	3.5	3.9	3.8	3.7
Chemical industries	9.5	8.8	9.9	10.6	10.2	9.7
Light industry	20.7	18.3	21.0	20.2	18.6	20.0
Food industries	19.8	23.3	20.2	17.6	19.8	20.0
Total	100.0	100.0	100.0	100.0	100.0	100.0
B) *National income*						
Mining	9.7	12.6	8.1	6.8	13.4	8.5
Electric energy	2.8	4.2	3.6	4.6	8.1	4.0
Metallurgy	5.8	9.8	8.7	7.8	11.6	7.7
Engineering	36.3	29.5	23.1	35.9	23.6	31.4
Building materials	5.9	6.2	4.2	7.8	9.6	5.6
Chemical industries	9.5	6.3	10.1	12.8	9.6	8.9
Light industry	23.7	19.2	27.3	19.4	18.5	23.6
Food industries	6.3	12.2	14.9	4.9	5.6	10.3
Total	100.0	100.0	100.0	100.0	100.0	100.0

In the preceding table the shares of the main groups of industries in production as well as their contribution to the national income are presented on the basis of the models calculated for 1965 and 1968. The table shows the differences in proportions calculated at rouble, dollar and domestic prices, as well as the change in differences between 1965 and 1968 (here, obviously, the effects of changes in volume, structure and prices appear simultaneously).

In connection with the ranking of branches according to efficiency, it should be emphasized that such a calculation may be based on different conceptions and will lead, accordingly, to different results. (Thus, e.g., various types of calculations may be used depending on how the differential rents, the changes in world-market prices, the system of preferences, etc., are taken into consideration.)

Analyses regarding the efficiency of the utilization of resources — including, in this case, both embodied and live labour — made by the Institute for Industrial Economics and Business Organization of the Ministry of Heavy Industry, have shown

– that the efficiency of utilizing resources in the various branches will differ widely even when calculated on the basis of foreign-exchange prices;

– that the average efficiency of the resource-intensive branches (i.e., of those using relatively great amounts of both live and embodied labour) is generally lower than that of less resource-intensive branches;

– that Hungary's trade with the socialist and non-socialist countries is characterized by two opposed tendencies; its exports to the socialist countries generally consist of products of the relatively more efficient branches, whereas the imports coming from these countries generally contain products of the relatively less efficient branches. In the trade with non-socialist countries the situation is inverted. Thus, as regards the period investigated, trade with the socialist countries is more advantageous for Hungary.

Foreign-trade share of branches
with above-average production efficiency
(per cent)

	Trade with	
	socialist countries	non-socialist countries
Export	75	25
Import	60	40

COMPUTATIONS OF FOREIGN-EXCHANGE PARITIES

In connection with the planned development of the economic integration of the socialist countries, the requirement arises for a common unit of accounting and for realistic exchange rates of the national currencies. For the solution of this problem the models based on foreign-exchange rates may provide rich and usefu- material. With their aid we may state the exchange rates rouble-to-dollar, roublef to-*forint* and dollar-to-*forint,* weighted according to the product structure either oɽ Hungary's total output or of its foreign-trade turnover. These rates may then be compared with those obtained by other methods (e.g., on the basis of the structure of the final output of all socialist countries, or according to the structure of their aggregated foreign trade). Anyhow, the exchange rates thus calculated should be considered as marginal, because the exchange rates between the national currencies are influenced by other factors, too, e.g., the proportions of supply and demand, the different economic potentials of the countries, the internal purchasing power of the currencies, etc.

*

The possibilities of using the input–output tables based on world-market prices have been outlined here only very briefly. The examples cited illuminate only the most important fields; besides these, many other possibilities of analysis are open for workers dealing with economic problems. The importance of the model lies partly in that it lays emphasis on "market-consciousness", and partly in the possibility of comprehensive investigation. Its use is made necessary, among other things, by the efforts aimed at widening international cooperation, an effort very much justified from the angle of problems awaiting solution in the socialist economies, like the approaching of socialist and non-socialist world-market prices, the shaping of more realistic exchange rates, etc.

The task of research in this field consists in elaborating several variants of the model and improving its methodology, in order to offer a useful tool for economic practice.

THE APPLICATION OF INPUT–OUTPUT TABLES CALCULATED AT FOREIGN-TRADE DOLLAR AND ROUBLE PRICES IN ANALYSING THE EFFICIENCY OF FOREIGN TRADE

by

JÓZSEF FÁY

One of the decisive efficiency problems of the reproduction process and of economic growth consists in the degree of efficiency of a country's participation in the international division of labour. This consideration has induced theoretical and practical experts

– to elaborate calculation methods for measuring the realization of comparative advantages,

– to create, in the framework of the reform of the economic mechanism, an economic atmosphere in which enterprises are made interested in the better utilization of such advantages.

The characteristics and conditions of a mechanism of this type may be summed up theoretically in the following:

– existence of uniform exchange rates (or foreign-trade price multipliers);

– complete absence (or a very limited application) of special economic regulators modifying the exchange rate (export subsidies, customs duties and the like);

– a minimum use of preferential systems affecting domestic production processes and trade;

– in connection with the above mentioned requirements, a strong influence of world-market price relations on the domestic price system, primarily on the prices of "competitive" products.

The principles of the new economic mechanism introduced in 1968 have reckoned with the above-mentioned requirements of utilizing comparative advantages. However, in the course of their practical implementation — partly in order to avoid transitional disturbances, and partly because perhaps some political and economic considerations contra-indicating the application of the principle of comparative advantages had been given too much weight — a wide system of preferences affecting almost every field of the reproduction process was created, with the result that both the survey of the utilization of comparative advantages and the development of central control methods aimed at improving it were made difficult or even impossible. Under such circumstances, the question again arises how the existing comparative advantages could be reliably assessed and how, on this basis, the central control regarding the country's participation in the international division of labour should be implemented.

As regards the microsphere, i.e., on the level of enterprises or individual products, there would be no point, in my opinion, in undertaking calculations that take directly into account national economic interest in connection with foreign-trade efficiency, adapted, however, to the individual enterprise. In this field, the channelling of enterprise activities has to be effected as fully as possible with the indirect tools of the economic mechanism, i.e., by means of an adequate price policy and other, mainly financial, incentives available for the purpose.

The situation is different at the top level where economic policy is formulated. Here it is absolutely necessary that decision-makers know the requirements of improving economic efficiency in general and the efficiency of an international division of labour in particular, and be able to recognize the tendencies the utilization of which may lead in this direction. Only in the knowledge of all this will it become possible to formulate economic policy adequately, and to serve the attainment of correctly chosen targets by all means available in the field of prices, finances, and with all other tools of economic control.

Under such circumstances the necessity of efficiency calculations continues to prevail, in order to orientate top-level economic control. Accordingly, calculations must furnish answers to questions regarding the macro-economic level, that is, they must produce aggregate results specifying at most a branch of industry. It is known that the input–output table describes the interindustry relationships of the reproduction process in such an aggregate form, and hence it represents an adequate starting point for calculations regarding foreign-trade efficiency. Besides its convenient aggregations, another property of the input–output table makes it highly useful for the purposes of efficiency calculations, namely, that its essential method consists in the comparison of inputs and outputs. It shows the inputs of materials, wages and depreciation on the one hand, and the resulting net income of society, on the other.

If one wishes to characterize numerically the foreign-trade efficiency of individual branches — in other words, to measure their comparative advantages or disadvantages against those of other branches — the input–output table calculated on the basis of domestic prices has to be converted into another table calculated at world-market (dollar or rouble) prices. Obviously, a table calculated at world-market prices expressed in dollars or roubles will show the net income — in terms of the foreign exchange in question — of the activity investigated. This "specific" net income will show the comparative situation of the branch. For the purpose of comparing the net income levels of individual branches, various income-indicators may be calculated. The branches showing the highest income-indicators are those the productive activities of which are recognized as most efficient on both the socialist and the capitalist world markets. Thus, in the first approach, available labour and means of production should be concentrated into the expansion of these branches. This is how — through international exchange — the largest amount of distributable national income, i. e., the highest efficiency of the national economy may be attained. Obviously, such an additional increase of the national income — since it presupposes a participation in international exchange — can be associated only with the so-called competitive branches, with their internal and interindustry proportions. In the non-competitive sphere of the economy, including mainly infrastructural branches, efficiency may be increased in the first place by reducing their inputs. Namely, their products and services cannot be imported and in their case the average of the national economic efficiency cannot be improved by buying from abroad, against the exports of other branches recognized more efficient on the world market. Of course, the input level and thus the efficiency even of the non-competitive branches are not independent of international exchange. Also these branches are using smaller or greater quantities of products belonging to the competitive sphere. For this part of their inputs, the choice between purchases at home or abroad has to be considered.

Before describing the indicators that may be derived from input–output tables calculated at rouble or dollar prices, it seems expedient to return once again to the leading idea that the net income in roubles or dollars, i.e., the difference between the values of outputs and inputs calculated at foreign-trade prices, serves as a criterion for judging the comparative situation of a branch.

As regards the value of output as the first element of the calculation, it is obvious that, with a given amount of inputs, the efficiency situation of the branch in question is the more advantageous, the higher the internationally recognized value of its product. Thus, in this respect there can be no doubt that the value of the product must enter into the calculation at the world-market price which reflects the international valuation of the product.

The question is somewhat more complicated in the case of evaluating inputs. When a branch uses in its production the product of another home branch, the latter may be either more expensive or cheaper than the corresponding importable product. In the first case, the profitability interests of the user branch would lead it to choose the imported product. Of course, in reality an enterprise will be permitted to do so only when, first, the prevailing domestic price system reflects correctly the cost difference between the two sources of purchase (that is, according to costs calculated on an economy-wide level), and, second, if the scarcity of foreign exchange does not counter-indicate a purchase from abroad. In the case of macro-economic calculations, however, when we want to know how the production structure should be changed in order to utilize *every* possibility of advantageous substitution offered by international exchange, it is always necessary to take into account all possibilities promising a reduction of the national economic average of the relative level of inputs. (It is another question that, when the further steps of formulating economic policy are being made, one has to consider to an increasing extent the economic, social and political factors that may hinder the practical implementation of changes which, in principle, would seem desirable.)

Thus, when an input of domestic make proves more expensive than the imported one, it seems justified to evaluate it at its foreign-trade (rouble or dollar) price. Here, the national economic interest of reducing the average level of input and thereby improving average efficiency coincides with the profit interest of the user branch.

As regards the second case, when according to the prevailing domestic price the home-produced input is cheaper than the imported one, it turns out that here, again, it is justified to evaluate this input at foreign-trade prices. Namely, efficiency considerations require in this case that the supplier branch should sell the product in question to foreign purchasers offering a higher price, rather than to the domestic users. And even when this is not the case in reality, it is justified to debit, in the efficiency calculation, the domestic user with the (higher) foreign-trade price which the supplier could have received in case he exported this product.

Thus, as regards both the output values and all inputs of domestic origin, it is justified to account them at foreign-trade prices. Obviously, all other items of productive inputs — imported materials, depreciation and wages — also have to be calculated at foreign-trade prices, if we want to judge correctly, on the grounds of our calculations, the comparative advantages realizable through foreign trade and the relative efficiencies of the various branches. The justification of this statement follows essentially from what has been said above in connection with the output values and the materials used; therefore it does not seem necessary to expound it in detail.

By converting the whole input–output table to rouble or dollar prices we obtain an answer to the question how much (in absolute sums) the net income of the various branches would be according to the evaluation of the socialist or the capitalist world market. Taken in itself, however, this does not suffice for appraising the *efficiency* of individual branches. For this, it is necessary to compare their *relative* net incomes. Here, however, we have reached the point beyond which the application of foreign-price based input–output tables for calculating efficiency indicators does not differ in any way from that of input–output tables based on domestic prices, as regards the (much discussed) principles and calculation procedures of efficiency indicators. Therefore, we may restrict ourselves to presenting some possible variants of indicators which, in our opinion, correctly reflect the relative levels of profitability. Essentially, all indicators of relative net income show the proportion of the latter, either to the sum of productive inputs, or to the labour and means of production (fixed and working assets) engaged in production.

As an example of the indicators belonging to the first group let us take the following:

$$\frac{\text{Net income}}{\text{Value added — Net income}}$$

From among productive inputs, this indicator neglects the inputs purchased from other branches or from abroad; it compares only the inputs coming from the given branch with the "net" income of the same given branch. Thus, this is a "net" variant of the "input-type" indicators. It serves for judging comparatively the activities performed within the branch itself, rather than its cumulated total output. Since the appraisal of the structure, the shaping of economic policy and central planning take place mostly at the branch level, in our opinion the "net" indicators are more suitable for such purposes than the "gross" ones.

On the other hand, the efficiency indicators belonging to the second type, which may be called "indicators of yield" (or return) and which compare net income with the amount of labour, fixed and working assets engaged in production, are better suited for judging the optimum allocation of labour and means of production than the indicators of the input type. In principle, the indicators of yield offer an even wider scope for choice than the input-type indicators do. There are opinions according to which one cannot rely on any single indicator; one should separately calculate the proportion of net income to the amount of live labour and to the means of production engaged in production, respectively, and conclusions regarding the efficiency of branch activity should be drawn from the weighted average of the two indicators. According to this opinion, the weights attributed to each of the two indicators should be chosen according to whether labour or investment represents the "bottleneck" in the process of extended economic reproduction.

The indeterminate character of such a calculation (depending on the choice of weights) may be eliminated by introducing the so-called "indicators of normative yield". In the case of foreign-trade efficiency, such an indicator might take the following form:

$$\frac{\text{Net income}}{\text{Normative net income}}$$

where "normative net income" reflects the amount of net income expected from a branch engaging a given amount of fixed and working assets and of labour (e.g., 8–10 per cent of the value of fixed and working assets *plus* 100 per cent of the wages).

ANALYSIS OF FOREIGN TRADE BASED ON THE INPUT–OUTPUT TABLE OF THE METALLURGICAL AND ENGINEERING INDUSTRIES

by

TAMÁS SZABÓ

The Institute for Industrial Economy Organization and Computation of the Ministry of Metallurgy and Engineering has elaborated its first combined input-output table of the metallurgical and engineering industries broken down by product groups for the year 1968. It contains 81 engineering and 14 metallurgical product groups; the rest of the national economy is represented by further 18 sectors of the table.

Having finished drawing up the table and the mathematical calculations, various economic analyses were performed. Their aim was to find out what conclusions might be drawn from an input–output table at this level of elaboration (containing relatively homogeneous product groups), for control and management on the ministry level. (In Hungary, the Ministry of Metallurgy and Engineering supervises the industries figuring in this input–output table.)

Among the various analyses, a separate study dealt with the foreign-trade relations of these industries.

Intensive and efficient participation in the international division of labour is of particular importance for open economies with a relatively small area and population. In the case of the so-called "small countries", intensive foreign trade is partly a condition and partly a consequence of the growth of productive forces.

In such countries, the relatively advanced production levels mean that the absorptive capacity of the home market (for products of a high technological level) is less than what an economically lucrative scale of production dictates. At the same time, natural and economic endowments do not permit any small country to develop its economy in an all-round way; primarily those branches have to be developed for which the resources are the most advantageous. In this way, the growth of productive forces can be accelerated.

Metallurgy and engineering have a particularly important role in the foreign trade of the Hungarian economy; hence the significance of input–output analyses relating to this field.

For investigations into the foreign trade of these product groups, the following basic data were available:

– the input–output table of imports in terms of current forints, obtained with the aid of the foreign-exchange multiplier;

– the input–output table of imports elaborated separately for socialist and non-socialist countries, in terms of foreign-exchange forints;

– the export vector, partly in terms of current forints and partly of foreign-exchange forints elaborated separately for socialist and non-socialist countries.

Of course, the mathematical work also included the calculation of various economy-wide indicators that could be derived from the data with the aid of an inverse matrix.

The study on foreign-trade relations dealt separately with imports and exports in its first part.

Imports have been dealt with from two aspects: partly as "complementary" imports and partly as consumption of imported materials.

From the first aspect, essentially the commodity pattern of imports has to be examined. An input–output table is not absolutely necessary for this purpose but its availability proved to be helpful for two reasons.

First, with the aid of the basic data included in it, one may examine the pattern of imports by branches, as well as the relative shares of raw materials and of the metallurgical and engineering products. The analysis of imports by products was able to show the relative weight of equipment, semi-finished products, etc. in the complementary imports of these two industries.

Second, complementary imports could be grouped according to their make from socialist or non-socialist countries.

Imports of a given period may also be grouped according to whether they were destined for use in the productive or the non-productive sectors. In this case, imports appear as "inputs of imported products" and are shown in the form of a separate row vector in the third quadrant of the table. The input of imported products taken in this sense is an indicator characteristic of a given phase of production, whether it is shown in absolute figures or as the share of imported inputs in the total value of output. The share of inputs of goods imported directly for the production purposes of a sector is characteristic of the "import sensitivity" of that branch.

When analyses and/or decisions on the micro-economic level are performed, it is sufficient to take into account the indicators relating to the given phase of production, since generally the indirect (multiplier) effects lie beyond the sphere of observation accessible to individual producing units.

For the purposes of macro-economic analysis and decision, however, it is necessary to calculate indicators showing the inputs of imported goods on an economy-wide level, i.e., summing up such inputs made at every stage of production. Accordingly, most attention was given to the "cumulated" imports in our study as well.

We calculated this according to the traditional input–output techniques, by multiplying the row vector of "direct" imported inputs with the inverse matrix:

$$\mathbf{i}'^* = \mathbf{i}^*(\mathbf{R} - \mathbf{A})^{-1}$$

where

$\mathbf{i}^*$ = row vector of direct share of imported inputs,

$\mathbf{i}'^*$ = row vector of share of imported inputs in the unit net output of the sectors, on an economy-wide level.

The mathematical processing of the table produced not only the inverse of the combined table of all producing sectors of the national economy but also that of a partial table showing (in the first quadrant) only the metallurgical and engineering products.

The inverse of this partial table shows only the multiplier effects with the sphere of these two industries, leaving out of account inputs from the rest of the national economy.

The calculation of the share of this "cumulated imports of metallurgy and engineering" took place as follows:

$$\mathbf{i}'^{*}_{m} = \mathbf{i}^{*}_{m}(\mathbf{R} - \mathbf{A}_{m})^{-1},$$

where

$\mathbf{i}^{*}_{m}$ = row vector of the share of imported inputs for the metallurgical and engineering product groups,

$\mathbf{A}_{m}$ = the matrix of technological coefficients calculated from the first quadrant containing the product groups mentioned above,

$\mathbf{i}'^{*}_{m}$ = row vector of the cumulated imported inputs, restricted to the sphere of the two industries.

By calculating the two kinds of cumulated imports, it is possible to divide the "indirect" part of such inputs between those appearing within and without the sphere of these two industries.

It follows from the definition of our indicators that the difference vector

$$\mathbf{i}'^{*} - \mathbf{i}'^{*}_{m}$$

expresses the indirect import requirements raised by our industries against the other sectors of the national economy.

Since economic policy regarding foreign trade with socialist and non-socialist countries may differ, we calculated the indicators of cumulated import requirements for both directions of foreign trade separately.

The disadvantage of the indicator of "cumulated imported inputs" projected to a unit of net output consists in that it does not take into account the effects of changes occurring in the volume of gross output, that is, it does not reflect the import requirement on the economy-wide level according to the actual outputs of the sectors.

This disadvantage may be eliminated by multiplying the indicators of cumulated imported inputs with the actual output of the sectors:

$$\mathbf{i}'^{*}\hat{\mathbf{Y}} = \mathbf{i}'^{*(y)}$$

where

$\hat{\mathbf{Y}}$ = the diagonal matrix constructed from the actual net outputs of the sectors.

The row vector $\mathbf{i}'^{(y)}$ expresses the import requirements (on an economy-wide level) for the actual outputs of the sectors. The sum of these import requirements

$$\mathbf{i}^{*(y)} \cdot \mathbf{1}$$

equals the actual sum of imports during the given period. In this way we may construct a pattern of cumulated inputs of imported goods, grouped according to the sectors the final output of which they served, independently of the intermediate phases.

A comparison of the direct and cumulated import structures has enabled us to draw some interesting conclusions. Generally, the shares of branches producing mainly final products (e.g., engineering, food industry, construction) are much greater in the total of imported inputs measured on an economy-wide level than their shares in the direct inputs of imported goods. At the same time, the share of branches producing mainly means of production (as e.g., metallurgy, the chemical industry, building material production) becomes smaller when measured on an economy-wide level. The reason for this is that most of their direct inputs of imported goods do not serve their own purposes but those of the branches releasing the final product.

The analysis of exports took place in a similar manner, i.e., partly according to the direct indicators and partly to those of "cumulated" production serving exports; both in terms of current forints calculated with the uniform foreign exchange multiplier, and separately for exports destined to socialist and non-socialist countries in terms of foreign exchange forints.

The direct figures show the commodity pattern of total exports and of those destined to the two blocks.

The data of cumulated production serving exports were calculated by multiplying the inverse matrix by the export vector, that is $(\mathbf{I} - \mathbf{A})^{-1}\,\mathbf{e}$, where $\mathbf{e}$ is the column vector of exports.

Figures of cumulated production serving export show what part of the production of each branch has served directly or indirectly (in the form of productive inputs made by other branches) the purposes of exports. This calculation also reflects the differences between the production volumes of the branches.

Since the sphere of products belonging to the various sectors differs widely, as do the production volumes accordingly, it seemed expedient to measure the share of production destined for exports also as a percentage of the gross output. This was expressed by the vector

$$[(\mathbf{I} - \mathbf{A})^{-1} \cdot \mathbf{e}] \cdot \left\langle \frac{1}{\mathbf{x}} \right\rangle,$$

the elements of which show the share of gross output required for the purposes of direct and indirect exports.

It also seemed expedient to analyse the output required by exports by the various elements figuring in the product of multiplication.

When substituting $\mathbf{R} = [r_{ij}]$ for $(\mathbf{I} - \mathbf{A})^{-1}$ the product $\mathbf{Re}$ consists of the following elements:

$$\mathbf{Re} = \begin{bmatrix} r_{11}e_1 + r_{12}e_2 + \ldots + r_{1n}e_n \\ r_{21}e_1 + r_{22}e_2 + \ldots + r_{2n}e_n \\ \vdots \\ r_{n1}e_1 + r_{n2}e_2 + \ldots + r_{nn}e_n \end{bmatrix}$$

The members of the sum

$$r_{i1}e_1 + r_{i2}e_2 + \ldots + r_{in}e_n$$

show how much from the products of the i-th sector is required by each sector (on the economy-wide level) in order to produce its actual exports; in other words, how the cumulated output destined for exports of the i-th sector is distributed among the exporting branches.

The sum of multiplication products may be analysed from a different aspect as well.

It is possible to construct the sum of

$$r_{1j}e_j + r_{2j}e_j + \ldots + r_{nj}e_j$$

showing the amount of output (of each sector and of the national economy as a whole) required for the direct exports of the j-th sector, taking into account also the multiplier effects.

Accordingly, the product $r_{ij}e_j$ expresses the contribution of the i-th sector to the exports of the j-th sector.

The share of the production of the j-th sector in its exports was calculated according to the following formula:

$$\frac{r_{jj}}{r_{1j}e_j + r_{2j}e_j + \ldots + r_{nj}e_j}$$

An important part of the analysis consists in the combined examination of export and import figures.

Namely, the export figures show — either in terms of current forints converted on the basis of the foreign-trade price multiplier, or in terms of foreign-exchange forints — the gross amount of foreign exchange yielded by the various sectors, but they do not express the variations caused by the differences in the need for imported inputs.

The difference between the direct exports and the direct use of imported commodities expresses the net yield of foreign exchange attained at the final production stage of the sector in question. It is important to examine the conversion performed through foreign trade separately for the groups of socialist and non-socialist countries, because of the non-convertibility between the two groups of foreign exchange.

As regards the metallurgical and engineering products, it has been proved that — as regards orders of magnitude — differences in imported inputs do not change significantly the relations obtained from the export data of the various products.

Namely, direct exports consist mainly of the products of a few sectors. The overwhelming part of the exports by the engineering industry is supplied by not more than 8–10 sectors. The use of imported inputs shows a much greater dispersion.

The picture is somewhat different when outputs destined for exports and cumulated imports are being compared on an economy-wide level, particularly in the case of materials and components, on the one hand, and of final products, on the other.

As regards the first group of goods (most conspicuously in the case of metallurgy) a comparison of the figures of direct exports and direct imports shows a great import surplus, because of the small export volume of metallurgical products. When examined on an economy-wide level, this balance is reversed because the indirect contribution of most metallurgical products to the exports of other branches is considerable. At the same time, when evaluated on an economy-wide level, the active balance of direct exports and imports diminishes in the case of products obtained through several stages of production, since here the multiplier effect tends to influence the amount of imported inputs much more strongly.

Our analysis also included the calculation of indicators of export efficiency concerning the various products. In its general form, the indicator of export efficiency compares the inputs needed for producing an exported commodity with the amount of foreign exchange acquired through its export. The great advantage of calculating export efficiency with the aid of an input–output table on an economy-wide level consists in that it is possible to accurately calculate the inputs of the national economy as a whole. Obviously, the indicators obtained in this way are subject to the limitations generally characteristic of an input–output table (e.g., that the figures used relate to an earlier period, linearity is assumed, etc.).

An important limitation of the export efficiency indicators consists in that, first, the figures of the input–output table are available in terms of value only, second, export and import figures in terms of current forints are values obtained with the foreign-trade price multiplier, rather than actual inland forint values.

Thus, the efficiency of exports going to socialist and non-socialist countries could not be calculated separately, so the efficiency indicators were worked out independently of export destination.

We have calculated "gross" and "net" export efficiencies, but the "net" indicators were considered decisive.

The net efficiency indicators were calculated in the following way:

$$G_j = \frac{v_j'' + \beta a_j''}{100 - i_j''}$$

where

G_j = the net export efficiency indicator of the j-th sector,
v''_j = wage inputs (on an economy-wide level) of 100 forints of final product in the j-th sector,
a''_j = cumulated depreciation per 100 forints worth of final product in the j-th sector,
β = cumulated wages per 100 forints of depreciation,
i''_j = cumulated imports per 100 forints of final product in the j-th sector.

The G_j thus calculated for individual product groups expresses the real costs (on economy-wide level) of the exported product (per 100 forints value).

Since the G indicators were calculated for all product groups of metallurgy and engineering, the average efficiency of the industries can also be calculated, separately for exports going to socialist and non-socialist countries.

The average G indicator of an industry is obtained by weighing the individual G indicators by the actual exports of the products or product groups concerned, that is:

$$\bar{G}_s = \hat{\mathbf{G}}\mathbf{e}_s$$

and

$$\bar{G}_c = \hat{\mathbf{G}}\mathbf{e}_c$$

where

$\bar{\mathbf{G}}_s, \bar{\mathbf{G}}_c$ = average efficiency of exports going to socialist and non-socialist countries, respectively,
$\mathbf{e}_s, \mathbf{e}_c$ = vector of the actual exports (in the period investigated) towards the two blocks,
$\hat{\mathbf{G}}$ = diagonal matrix constructed from the indicators of the products (product groups).

The indicators $\bar{\mathbf{G}}_s$ and $\bar{\mathbf{G}}_c$ show the real costs at which the exports of metallurgy and engineering produce socialist and non-socialist foreign exchange. Thus, they reflect the effect of the commodity pattern of exports going to each block of nations.

THE METHOD OF NATIONAL ACCOUNTING AND INPUT–OUTPUT ANALYSIS — A THEORETICAL APPROACH

by

RÓBERT HORVÁTH

In the course of the development of statistical methodology, the theory of index numbers and the methods of analysing time series had been elaborated directly for the use of economic statistics, and were introduced into demographic and social statistics only later, not to mention other fields where they are less frequently applied.

However, in his university lectures on general statistics, the present author has expressed for a long time the view that the method of input–output tables, this most important achievement of economic statistics in the last half century, has developed lately in a direction enabling it to be applied also in other fields of statistics; this is indicated, e.g., by such applications as drawing up tables on the population and so on. As a logical follow-up, I have included the balance method in my lectures on general statistical methodology, as a last chapter.* Since, however, I have not as yet expounded this concept theoretically, I wish to use the opportunity of this conference for presenting my views.

As a first approach to the question raised in the present study, let us sketch here the historical development of economic-statistical analyses and of the general theorems that may be derived from them; in other words, apply the Marxian method of using historical materialism as a tool of general epistemology.

When, in 1758, Francois Quesnay, the father of economism or the physiocratic school, published his first essay on economic circulation in his famous *Tableau Économique*, even the theoretical economists capable of analytical reasoning were hardly aware of the fact that he had tried to make an approach to economic processes on the basis of the balance method.**

* Horváth, R.: A mérlegmódszer és a társadalmi termék mérésének problémái (The input–output method and the problems of measuring the social product). Chapter XVI of the University Textbook for the Faculties of Law and Political Science. Budapest, 1967.

** Horváth, R.: "Quesnay, a Tableau Économique és a mai statisztikai tudomány" (Quesnay, the "Tableau Économique" and the statistical science of today). *Statisztikai Szemle*, No. 12, 1970. From the point of view mentioned, Marx is to be considered as the first exception. See also Horváth, R.: Die Beiträge von Marx zur Grundlegung der statistischen Wissenschaft. *Wirtschaftswissenschaft*, No. 1, p. 61, Berlin 1955.

The first application of the method of economic balances is, however, much older; in fact it may be traced back to 1494 and associated with the name of Fra Luca Pacciolo. The method of double-entry bookkeeping was applied only in the sphere of private capitalist enterprises for a long time. It was only much later that, under the influence of mercantilism, the governments of the capitalist states also showed interest in such macro-economic balances as the balance of trade or of international payments. This tendency, mainly characteristic of Western Europe, was somewhat belatedly followed by a similar one in the monarchies of Central and Eastern Europe that had gradually switched over to the capitalist mode of production, above all in the three hundred and odd states that mushroomed, after the Thirty Years' War, in the Holy Roman Empire. It was mainly here that the school of "cameralism" developed. The existence of all these states depended on the government having a regular income, and the concept of cameralism was accordingly centered around the state budget, being the first and most important basis of national accounting.

In the nineteenth century, however, the official statistical services (including also the fiscal statistics) made good progress, yet still tended to lag behind the theoretical descriptions of macro-economic processes and interrelationships. This fact may be best shown by the example of the Marxian analysis of economic processes. Although the Marxian schemes of simple and extended reproduction analysed the macro-economic processes and their interrelations essentially in the spirit of Quesnay, i. e., according to the balance method, the contemporary state of official statistics (including the narrower field of economic statistics) did not make it possible to complement the Marxian schemes with concrete economic statistics.* This is why the verification of the Marxian economic theory, as well as its practical application in economic policy, was so difficult for a long time, although theoretically the Marxian approach was correct.

The verification of the Marxian approach became possible only after the first socialist state, the Soviet Union, had developed its own statistical apparatus and started to work out a comprehensive accounting of the national economy in the early 1920's. Thus, the institutional basis was created, first for the planning of industrial activities on an economy-wide level by the end of the 1920's, and later on for the introduction of central planning embracing the whole of the national economy. All this proved Marx's statement that an objectively true macro-economic presentation of the economic system of a modern country — i.e., one relying on economic statistical data — would be possible only within socialism.**

* Horváth, R.: *Die Beiträge von Marx,* etc. where attention is drawn to the fact that Marx analysed the evolution of industrial capitalism according to the example of England and that of agricultural capitalism on the basis of Russia because statistical surveys were relatively most developed in England as regards industry, and in Russia as regards agriculture.

** A short epistemological review of this question may be found in the book by O. Lange entitled "Essays in Economic Planning". *Indian Statistical Series,* No. 4. Calcutta 1960, especially in Part I and its Appendix.

As regards the capitalist countries, the application of similar methods of approach started only several decades later, and even then in a less comprehensive way. The process cannot yet be considered as closed and it is still going on at present. The first incentive was given by J. M. Keynes during the interwar world economic crisis and by the economic strain of World War II. Thus, in spite of the serious efforts of bourgeois statistical science after the 1860's, when Quetelet convoked the International Congress of Statistics, to assess national wealth, and in spite of the methodological formulations made within the framework of the International Statistical Institute since the beginning of our century regarding the national income, the theorem expounded by Keynes in 1935 was the first to create some rudimentary macro-economic basis for such an accounting in bourgeois economic science.

Keynes's *General Theory of Employment, Interest and Money* has, on the one hand, made possible an approach to the national income and enabled bourgeois theory to develop the category of social product; on the other hand — and this is even more important from our point of view — it has contributed to conceiving output, distribution and consumption as parts of the macro-economic balance.* His method proved particularly helpful under the conditions of the wartime economy of Britain during World War II, in the form of the "National Budget" elaborated in 1944.** The statistical basis of the latter was provided, in the framework ot the official British statistical service, by Stone. This system was further developed in both Britain and the USA in the form of the so-called "Social Accounting". However, the theoretical foundations of this system cannot yet be considered as fully clear, and its statistical sources are also deficient.***

Later on, elements were built into the contemporary bourgeois macro-economic methods, which had already been available before the war. Among these, Leontief's "input–output method" proved to be the most important one.**** Its inclusion was, indeed, the transplantation of an earlier method of official Soviet economic statistics and its further methodological development, in accordance with contemporary capitalist conditions.

* The first elaboration and systematization of these problems — from the point of view of contemporary bourgeois statistics — was given by Kuznets, S.: *National Income, a Summary of Findings.* National Bureau of Economic Research, New York, 1946.

** *White Paper on National Income and Expenditure of the United Kingdom.* Cmd. 6623. HMSO, London, 1945, and Stone, J. R. N.: The National Income, A Statistical Account of the British Economy. *The Times,* May 27, 1946.

*** Stone, J. R. N.: Social Accounting. I. National Income Before and Since the War; II. Consumption and the Course of Prices. *The Times,* August 29 and 30, 1947. For a more recent review on the development of this method, see Stone, R. and Croft-Murray, C.: *Social Accounting and Economic Models.* London 1959.

**** Leontief, W. W.: *The Structure of American Economy 1919–1929.* Cambridge, Mass., 1941. More recent publications by the same author: *Input–Output Analysis* (1965) and *Input–Output Economics* (1966).

In the context of this development, from the point of view of our argument, it seems necessary to emphasize that, besides "Social Accounting", the input–output method came into the fore, as an alternative macro-level accounting covering the whole of the economic system. True, the possibilities of filling out its framework completely with statistical data obtained by observation are by no means better than in the case of any other accounting system mentioned so far. There are gaps to be filled in with estimates, the reliability of which varies widely. Because of all this, the social accountings based on the input–output method have the same characteristics of "conjectural statistics" as any of the calculations regarding national income attempted between the turn of the century and World War II. Nevertheless, they undoubtedly show a higher degree of reliability, both in detail and in general. By adequately choosing the criteria of homogeneity and confidence interval, the reliability of the calculations can be greatly improved.

From the point of view of the completeness of statistical documentation or — what amounts to the same thing — of a realistic approach to the object of cognition, the macro-economic systems elaborated by modern bourgeois economics and economic statistics are undoubtedly at a disadvantage when compared with the apparatus of economic planning developed in the socialist countries. This difference has serious consequences, mainly in the field of economic policy.

If we wish to draw adequate conclusions from this short historic review, it seems expedient to start from the differences that may be stated to exist theoretically between balances based on bookkeeping and statistics, respectively.

Accountings are characterized, in the first place, by the formal strictness of the principles guiding their construction and registration. The principles of bookkeeping are "cogent rules" (in terms of juristic language), not only in so far as they require the detailed and continuous registration of all items in terms of money, but also as regards the structure of the balance and the methods of its valuation. The strictness of this approach is expressed, among other things, also by the accurate identity of the sums on both sides of the balance. This requirement is in full accordance with the fundamental objective of bookkeeping by double-entry under capitalist conditions, namely to calculate the exact sum of profits. The strict rules governing double-entry bookkeeping exclude from the methodological viewpoint any regrouping of the elements figuring in the balance (or, according to the statistical term, of the statistical units) deviating from the grouping prescribed by the rules of commercial law. It is impossible to make any changes in the structure of the population or in its constituent parts, in other words, a grouping from various points of view which is the very essence of every statistical operation.

Thus, in connection with the drawing up of a balance-sheet we cannot speak of statistical operations in the true sense of the word, and the information obtained from such a balance is not primarily of a statistical character, although it is a numerical one. The neglect of this fundamental difference has caused much confusion during the past development of economic statistics, and it cannot be claimed that such epistemological confusions have been eliminated once and for all.

The main characteristic of statistical balances, in contrast to what has been said above, is their diversity, that is, a property of every methodological apparatus which is able to approach its objectives by several ways and means. Let us investigate this property somewhat more closely.

1. The elements of the economic system, either as statistical units or their aggregates may be, from the point of view of statistical techniques, grouped and regrouped "optionally" according to the interrelationships shown by the balance — provided that the groups are interpretable in the categories of economic science, and that they have adequate counterparts on the other side of the balance, in the form of equally interpretable quantities. In principle, it is even possible for a balance to have more than two sides. Statistically it is conceivable that the same population has several interpretable counterparts. Thus, e.g., the interrelationships between production, distribution, redistribution (eventually several times) and consumption represent the "sides" of the same balance.

2. Although in principle the concordance of the two or several sides is required even in the case of statistical balances, this requirement is interpreted statistically rather than in the mathematical or commercial law sense. One cannot eliminate the occurrence, during the whole operation, of smaller or greater statistical errors and omissions. In other words (even when all information necessary for drawing up a balance is available), strict accuracy and concordance in the sense of bookkeeping can never be reached, because of errors and inaccuracies of statistical observation, and perhaps because of certain incongruencies existing between the various observations. The latter type of error will obviously occur when, although the general conception of the balance is homogeneous, its various elements are taken from heterogeneous sources. From the neglect of small errors, in themselves insignificant from the statistical point of view, a total difference of a considerable magnitude may arise as a consequence of cumulation. Therefore, insertion of a "balancing" item (of the opposed sign) becomes necessary, even when the drawing up of the balance has taken place under the most favourable condition, that is, when the statistical documentation is complete.

From the point of view of statistical methodology and of information theory, we must make a sharp distinction between this well-known difficulty and the case when information regarding certain partial populations belonging to the balance is lacking or more or less incomplete. Nevertheless, to draw up an economic-statistical balance from incomplete data with conjectural methods may still prove expedient, considering that in spite of its considerable margin of error, even a balance thus obtained might offer more information about, and a better approach to, the structure of the total population or about the interrelationship between its parts, than what would be available if we did not carry out its construction. In our opinion an interesting marginal case of such an approach in the English literature was the input–output table of A. Gosh* who considered as "lacking" all insignificant or indetermined economic relationships of which the magnitudes (or changes in relation to the base period) were small. Thus, he attempted to determine the decisive relationships only, and this became possible with much less statistical information. Such a method may produce, by estimating certain relationships or by adapting earlier information, quick results, hence it is worth the attention of economic statisticians.

3. Certain items or aggregates figuring in a statistical balance cannot only be measured in terms of money at current prices (or at some other unit values legally declared admissible for accounting purposes). It is also possible to construct balances in physical units of measurement or, in some "converted" physical unit of measurement — provided that the macro-economic interrelationships permit the use of the latter (as, e.g., in the case of the "energy balance"). This possibility is, however, restricted to certain sectors of the economy. As regards accounting in terms of money, even for this there are wider possibilities in a statistical balance. Beside calculations made at current prices or at legally determined "constant prices", the use of statistically interpretable average values and even of fictitious accounting prices is also permissible; these latter being used mainly in the difficult cases when balance relationships must be compared internationally. The sphere of available methodological alternatives is not a closed one, even when pursuing the same statistical objective. All this ensures a high degree of elasticity for the statistical application of the balance method but, at the same time, it may result in a good deal of arbitrariness.

4. Finally, also as regards continuity in time, statistical accounting shows considerable differences from that of bookkeeping. From the methodological point of view, balances of bookkeeping represent typically continuous time series, in the sense that when broken at any point of time, the sides of the balance may be summed up, the obtained result showing the structural state of the population at that point of time. By way of contrast, conventional economic statistics operate partly with time series based on continuous observation and partly with the results of surveys reflecting the condition existing at a certain point of time. Such data may be aggregated only in a form assessing some final (e.g., end-of-year) status. Even if, according to its original objective, statistics also attempts to sum up the results of processes that took place within certain periods of time, its balances may be considered at best as parts of a time series reflecting the state of things discontinuously, relating to certain points of time, rather than as a truly continuous time series. Thus, we have to work always with status surveys expressing typically macro-economic interrelationships.

* Gosh, A.: Input–Output Analysis with Substantially Independent Groups of Industries. *Econometrica*, 1960, No. 1, p. 88. Professor Leontief himself has also hinted at the possibility of such a simplified method, if only regarding the inner matrix. See Rácz, A.: Konzultáció W. W. Leontief professzorral az input–output módszerről (A discussion with Prof. Leontief on the input–output method). *Statisztikai Szemle*, No. 5, 1964.

What has been said so far should make it clear that conventional economic statistics has elaborated, in the form of the balance method, a tool with the aid of which is has become possible to reveal causal relationships over time within the framework of the economy. The methodological importance of revealing these relationships or, if we care to use the more sophisticated terminology of Lucien March,* "covariances" became obvious only after the first input–output tables as a specific form of economic-statistical balances had been elaborated. By the inclusion of the methods of mathematical statistics, new ways were opened in this field also for the economic statistics of the socialist countries. This resulted not only in the possibility of relying on the achievements of new scientific disciplines like cybernetics, vector analysis, operation research, decision theory, etc., but also in the considerably improved exactness of investigations.

In the following we wish to mention, from the methodological point of view, that when the input–output table contains in its rows the output equations one below the other, and in its columns the input equations one beside the other, according to Walras, in fact it combines the methods of mathematical economics with the conventional method of economic statistics. This combination becomes complete with the extension of the so-called first quadrant towards the second quadrant and the third quadrant.

If, according to Marxian terminology, we describe the creation of the social product within a certain period of time with the "$c + v + s$" scheme, only the elements of the c type, that is those of the current production costs, are represented within the so-called "inner matrix" of the input–output table. Beyond this, the strict identity of the double grouping, characteristic of the input–output table, ceases: the accounting of the v and s elements as inputs and outputs does not show any identical or parallel grouping. Here, the balance can only be utilized with the economic-statistical groups taken over from the conventional balance method.

From the point of view of economic theory, it is easy to distinguish the different characters of the elements contained in the second and the third quadrants by the criterion that, essentially, the elements of input represent "purchases", whereas the elements of output stand for "sales". Accordingly, by adding the wages and other incomes to net social income, in the third quadrant we obtain the national income (that is, "$v + s$"). When adding to this the value of depreciation, we obtain the "value added", a familiar category to economic statisticians. As regards the second quadrant, here, again, the sum of the elements v and s is obtained, but according to entirely different economic considerations. Here, national income appears as the sum of "consumption" and "capital formation", completed by a balancing item representing the increase or decrease of stocks.

In other words, we have here a combination of a mathematically treatable matrix and of a traditional balance of economic statistics. The result is a model

* March, L.: *Les principles de la méthode statistique.* Paris 1930.

showing "mixed" structural characteristics, appearing in a form that follows the grouping of the traditional balance.

For the sake of simplicity, so far we have neglected the foreign-trade transactions. These, however, do not raise any theoretical difficulties since imports figure in the third quadrant and exports in the second one.

From the statistical point of view, an input–output table represents the combination of the first, second and third quadrants, or of "blocks" **A**, **B** and **C**. There are two ways of combining them:

1. one may consider as given the structure of inputs **A** + **C**, which then determine the numerical structure of **B**;
2. one may consider as given the structure of utilization **A** + **B**, which then determines the numerical structure of **C**.

From the methodological point of view, the validity of the above will not be affected even if we conceive the input–output table as a dynamic (rather than a static) model, that is, if we wish to account for the effect of investments on output with the aid of difference equations. Recently, according to a study by Mrs. Éva Koós,* the Central Statistical Office of Hungary has also elaborated models of this type. However, it seems necessary to call attention to the circumstance that technically (in the first place from the point of view of statistical operations) a dynamic input–output analysis does not make it easier to fill out the complete input–output table with data obtained by statistical observations; on the contrary, it makes it even more difficult.

Finally, as an example of the deliberate combination of the mathematical and traditional elements of input—output analysis along the lines described above, let us briefly report on an experiment made in 1962–1963 by the present author (in the capacity of theoretical adviser) and J. Felvidéki, of the National Bank of Hungary. This experimental calculation started from the first alternative mentioned above, that is, the structure of final consumption when block **B** was assumed to be determined by the planned structure of national income (blocks **A** + **C**).

In fact, the problem to be solved arose in the context of planning the credits to be granted. Namely, it seemed necessary to elaborate methods for determining the "adequate" magnitude of working stocks, i.e., a magnitude that would be consistent (or at least compatible) with the actual state and structure of the national economy. Namely, in the context of Hungarian economic development in 1961–1962 it could be stated that an ever growing part of accumulation was

* Koós, Mrs. Éva: Kísérlet a statikus típusú ágazati kapcsolatok mérlegének dinamizálására (An attempt at making the input–output table dynamic). *Statisztikai Szemle*, No. 7, 1971.

used for increasing the working stocks, although this tendency could not be justified on the grounds of purely economic considerations.*

As the increase of stocks in the industry and in trade, especially in wholesale trade, greatly exceeded the rates of earlier years without any greater change in the overall pattern of capital formation, it seemed obvious that an economically unjustified increase was taking place. This assumption seemed to be corroborated by some other indicators of conventional economic statistics. It was also obvious that the development of fixed assets and of working stocks showed a very wide dispersion by branches, according to the role each branch was playing in the process of extended reproduction, as well as to the variation in certain natural endowments and factors of productivity. The effect of all these is reflected by the so-called technological coefficients and their changes over time.**

It seemed expedient to estimate the increase in stocks theoretically required by a given structure of output on the grounds of a model derived from the input–output table, more exactly according to technological coefficients calculated for the groups figuring in the system of economic planning and in the credit plans. Therefore, the inner matrix of the input–output table of the National Planning Office was used. It was assumed that in the short run — from one year to the next — relatively minor changes were taking place in the technological structure. Thus, the data of outputs and inputs figuring in the credit plan could be considered as operative values. For this, it was only necessary to convert the figures of the credit plan (calculated on a net basis) to "gross" figures, and to estimate, on a similar basis, the relatively small output and use of materials by the private sector. Starting from the technological coefficients of earlier years and knowing the plan objectives regarding output and commodity turnover, it was not difficult to calculate the productive inputs with the aid of the inner matrix. Thus, the intermediate consumption, representing the amount of materials needed by the economy, could be determined with the aid of the customary input–output equation as a balance relationship:

$$\sum_{i=1}^{n} x_i^{op} \cdot a_{ij} = \sum_{i=1}^{n} \sum_{j=1}^{n} x_{ij}^{op}$$

The values were calculated as follows:

for $\sum_{i=1}^{n} x_i^{op}$ according to the figures of the annual plan,

for a_{ij} (technological coefficients of production) according to input proportions in earlier years;

* Felvidéki, J.: Forgóeszközök tervezése és finanszírozása (The planning and financing of working assets). Budapest 1965, Part II, p. 28. The author deals with the problem on the basis of statistical data on stocks between 1959 and 1962. See also Horváth, R.: Development and Present Status of Input–Output Methods in Hungary, in *Economics of Planning*, No. 3, 1963.

** Felvidéki, J.: Op. cit., Part III, p. 64.

for $\sum_{i=1}^{n}\sum_{j=1}^{n} x_{ij}^{op}$ (intermediate consumption in the plan year) according to the figures of the annual plan.

The calculation of distribution, i.e., in the case of our experiment the structure of the stock volume, could also be solved by converting the operative values of the credit plan to "gross" values, and by considering conventional balance interrelationships as well as the relationships within the right wing. Namely, for calculating the volume of stocks required by a given economic structure it is sufficient to apply (to fill in with data) the following simple equation of production:

$$\sum_{i=1}^{n} x_i \left[\sum_{i=1}^{n}\sum_{j=1}^{n} x_{ij} + \sum_{i=1}^{n} x_i^1 + \ldots + \sum_{i=1}^{n} x_i^5\right] = \sum_{i=1}^{n} x_i^6$$

which may be interpreted according to the customary terminology as follows:

$\sum_{i=1}^{n} x_i$ = social product,

$\sum_{i=1}^{n}\sum_{j=1}^{n} x_{ij}$ = the amount of materials necessary for its production;

$\sum_{i=1}^{n} x_i^{1\ldots5}$ = its final use;

$\sum_{i=1}^{n} x_i^6$ = the value of stocks.

Perhaps it is interesting to mention in the context of this experiment that after the elaboration of our concept and during the time of its implementation a collective study was published by three Soviet authors, Berri, Klocvóg and Satalin.* This study expounded the application of input–output tables for the purposes of macroeconomic planning on a more general level but much in the same spirit as we tried to use them in our experimental calculation serving more restricted objectives.**

* (Berri, L., Klocvog, F. and Satalin, S.) Берри, Л. — Клоквот Ф. — Шаталин, С.: Опытрасчета Экспериментального планового межотраслевого баланса на 1962 год (Experiences obtained from calculating an experimental input–output table for 1962). *Плановое хозяйство*, No. 9, Moscow 1962.
For a more recent and more general review of the problem see also (Nemtchinov, V.) Немчинов, В.: Развитые мажотраслевого баланса в модельнароднохозяйственного плана (The input–output balance in the model of the national economic plan). *Плановое хозяйство*, No. 1, Moscow 1963.

** Felvidéki, J.: Op. cit., p. 73.

In connection with our experiment, it is necessary to add that in a following stage, in accordance with its special purpose, a second approach was also attempted, aimed at utilizing the balance interrelations outlined not only in annual planning but also in the plans drawn up for quarters. The results obtained in this second stage of the experiment were by no means poorer than those of the first, in spite of the fact that in this case the operative values had to be estimated by various methods for many branches, considering seasonal fluctuation in some fields and the presence of production periods exceeding one year in others.

INDICATORS FOR EXAMINING THE EXTENT AND DIRECTION OF STRUCTURAL CHANGES

by

ERVIN FRIGYES and MRS. NÓRA SIMON

The necessity of analysing structural changes and deviations emerges in the case of problems with several variables, that is, when the units investigated can be characterized with more than one figure, i.e., they are represented by vectors.

The general practice is that in such cases the data are simply presented, or verbally evaluated. This, however, does not always provide sufficient opportunity for evaluation and the drawing of adequate conclusions, particularly if the purpose is not to get deeply involved in the data but rather to gain a comprehensive orientation.

There is a need for such aggregate indicators which make is possible to compare different structures, and which unequivocally express the extent and the tendency of the differences existing between them.

The indicators and analytical methods suggested in this paper have been designed for this orientation.

1. GENERAL PROBLEMS OF MEASURING STRUCTURAL DIFFERENCES

Measuring structural differences is only possible if the given structures can be numerically characterized. Let us introduce the concept of *measurable structure*.

The structure of an "A" unit to be examined is considered measurable if it

$$\mathbf{a} = \begin{bmatrix} a_1 \\ \vdots \\ a_n \end{bmatrix} = \text{structural vector}$$

can be assigned to it.

The structures of the investigated units "A" and "B" can be considered as commensurable if it holds true for the structural vectors a and b that the components a_i and b_i are *of the same contents* for every i, and the dimensions of the two vectors are equal. We must also distinguish structures characterized by *additive, quasi-additive and non-additive vectors.*

A given structural vector $\mathbf{a}$ is *additive* if it is possible to interpret the scalar product $\mathbf{1}^*\mathbf{a}$. In this case the individual values of a_i $(i = 1, \ldots, n)$ are homogeneous and can be summarized in their given form, and their sum can be also interpreted in terms of the economy. This is the situation, e.g., when the structures are characterized by vectors with components given in value terms, number of people, etc., or with the distribution ratios of components like these.

In the case of a *quasi-additive* structure, for the vector characterizing a given structure "A" the equation $\mathbf{a} = \langle \mathbf{k} \rangle^{-1} \mathbf{g}$ holds, and the sums $\mathbf{1}^*\mathbf{k}$ and $\mathbf{1}^*\mathbf{g}$ can be interpreted. In this case the components of vector a are quotients of the type $\mathbf{g}/\mathbf{k}$, that is, $a_i = g_i/k_i$, where $\mathbf{g}$ and $\mathbf{k}$ are additive vectors.

The structures characterized by vectors consisting of these types of relatives are considered quasi-additive because — although the sum of the elements cannot be given an interpretation — the elements are homogeneous and problems due to an arbitrary choice of the unit of measurement do not arise.

We have a *non-additive structure* when the structural vector $\mathbf{a}$ is neither additive nor quasi-additive. Thus, the structural vectors consisting of elements expressed in different units of measurement are non-additive.

Before introducing a measure for structural deviations, first the concept of *identical structure* must be defined.

The structures characterized by vectors $\mathbf{a}$ and $\mathbf{b}$ can be considered identical if and only if

$$\mathbf{b} = \alpha \mathbf{a} \qquad \text{where } \alpha > 0$$

In our opinion the following requirements should be made of an indicator of structural differences:

1. Based on the definition of "identical structure" — conforming to the economic concept of structural differences — it should not indicate any structural difference when the compared structures are characterized by the vectors $\mathbf{a}$ and $\alpha\mathbf{a}$; in other words, for some z indicator of structural differences the following equation must hold:

$$z(\mathbf{a}, \mathbf{b}) = z(\alpha\mathbf{a}, \mathbf{b}), \qquad (\alpha > 0)$$

2. In the interest of unequivocal measurement, the indicator should satisfy the requirements of metrics, that is:

a) the value of z should be zero if, and only if, $\mathbf{a} = \alpha\mathbf{b}$, $(\alpha > 0)$ else $z(\mathbf{a}, \mathbf{b})$ should not be zero;

b) the indicator should be symmetrical, i.e., should satisfy the equation $z(\mathbf{a}, \mathbf{b}) = z(\mathbf{b}, \mathbf{a})$;

c) the so-called triangular inequality should be met: $z(\mathbf{a}, \mathbf{b}) + z(\mathbf{b}, \mathbf{c}) \geq$ $\geq z(\mathbf{a}, \mathbf{c})$.

In view of these requirements, the following two indicators can be proposed:

1. the angle of inclination between the two structural vectors,

2. the distance between two structural vectors normalized to unit length.

By the angle of inclination of two given vectors $\mathbf{a} \neq \mathbf{0}$ and $\mathbf{b} \neq \mathbf{0}$ we mean an angle φ which satisfies the following equation:

$$\cos \varphi = \frac{\mathbf{a}^*\mathbf{b}}{|\mathbf{a}| \cdot |\mathbf{b}|}$$

where

$\mathbf{a}^*\mathbf{b}$	is the scalar product of the two vectors.
$\|\mathbf{a}\|$ and $\|\mathbf{b}\|$	are the lengths of the vectors **a** and **b**.

The distance between the structural vectors **a** and **b** normalized to unit length could be determined as follows:

$$d'(a, b) = \left| \frac{1}{|\mathbf{a}|}\mathbf{a} - \frac{1}{|\mathbf{b}|}\mathbf{b} \right|$$

In this case it is easy to see that

$$d'(a, b) = d'(\mathbf{a}, \alpha\mathbf{b})$$

For both indicators (the angle of inclination and the distance between vectors) it is an important restriction* that $\mathbf{a} \geq \mathbf{0}$, $\mathbf{b} \geq \mathbf{0}$. For the inclination it is also necessary to stipulate that $\mathbf{a} \neq \mathbf{0}$, $\mathbf{b} \neq \mathbf{0}$.

The requirements of metrics also hold for both indicators. These two indicators can be mutually and unequivocally transformed into each other. Thus, from the theoretical point of view, no distinction can be made between them.

For φ and d' it holds true that:

in the case of φ: $\left[0, \frac{\pi}{2}\right]$ if $\mathbf{a} \geq \mathbf{0}$, $\mathbf{b} \geq \mathbf{0}$ and $\Sigma a_i \neq 0$, $\Sigma b_i = 0$;

in the case of d': $[0, \sqrt{2}\,]$ if $\mathbf{a} \geq \mathbf{0}$, $\mathbf{b} \geq \mathbf{0}$.

In the case of additive and quasi-additive structural vectors, these indicators unequivocally characterize the extent of structural differences.

In the case of non-additive structures, however, the problem of different units of measurement arises.

Since there does not exist and, in our opinion, a system of units of measurement which would eliminate the problem cannot be conceived of, it seems expedient to introduce some convention that is independent of the unit of measurement.

This convention can be a substitution of the original components by distribution ratios (i.e., dimensionless data), in order that the difference between the structural vectors should be determined exclusively by the proportions between the corresponding vector components.

The basis of such ratios can be:

a) the structural vector of some chosen unit of investigation (*selection convention*);

b) the average data of the units investigated (*averaging convention*).

* This stipulation is possible because in the case of economic applications it can be generally assumed that the elements of the vectors are non-negative.

In connection with the second convention it must be noted that it unavoidably involves the calculation of a *new* average for the basis, whenever a new unit is drawn into the scope of analysis. Namely, in the case of non-additive structures, the unit of measurement is always linked up with the given system of units to be examined.

It must also be noted that the indicators of structural differences are very sensitive to aggregation, or to any change in the number of components.

Aggregation and any changes reducing the dimension modify both the angle φ and the distance d'. Since φ and d' mutually and unequivocally determine each other, it will suffice for us to show the modification for the case of $\cos\varphi$.

As regards *aggregation*, let us add two elements of both vectors **a** and **b**, namely, the i-th and the j-th. The relation between the inclination of $\varphi_{\text{aggr}}(\mathbf{a}, \mathbf{b})$ and that of the original vectors a and b will be the following:*

$$\text{arc}\cos_{\text{aggr}}(\mathbf{a}, \mathbf{b}) = \varrho \; \text{arc}\cos(\mathbf{a}, \mathbf{b})$$

where

$$\varrho = \frac{1 + \dfrac{a_i b_j + a_j b_i}{\mathbf{a}^*\mathbf{b}}}{[(1 + 2a_i a_j)(1 + 2b_i b_j)]^{\frac{1}{2}}}$$

If the compatibility of data relating to the investigated units "A", "B" and "C" can be achieved only by omitting some component, say the n-th, that is, by reducing the number of components without aggregation, the equation must be modified as follows:

$$\cos(\mathbf{a}_{n-1}, \mathbf{b}_{n-1}) = \eta \cos(\mathbf{a}, \mathbf{b})$$

where $\mathbf{a}_{n-1}, \mathbf{b}_{n-1}$ are the vectors obtained by omitting the n-th element, and

$$\eta = \frac{1 - \dfrac{a_n \cdot b_n}{\mathbf{a}^*\mathbf{b}}}{[(1 - a_n^2)(1 - b_n^2)]}$$

Thus the values $\cos\varphi$ and, consequently, also d' must change when the number of components is reduced, either by aggregation or otherwise. These consequences should be taken into account already in the preparatory stage of the analysis.

* For the sake of simplicity, the relation is shown here only for the vectors normalized to unit length.

2. EXAMINATION OF THE DIRECTIONS OF STRUCTURAL CHANGES

It is a frequent occurrence in structural analyses that the grouping criteria serving to distinguish the individual units to be investigated are members of a quantitative or a time series.*

In order to shorten the present discussion, we will restrict ourselves to the case of time series, as the analogies relating to the quantitative series are evident.

In the case of units forming a time series, the following problems should be examined:

First: to what extent do the structural deviations (in comparison to the initial situation) represent an approximation of the final structure, or of some "normative" structure; that is, *to what extent can the structural deviations be considered as acting in the main direction?*

This problem can, in the final analysis, be approached from two aspects:

a) If the structural vectors of the time series form the series $s_1, \ldots, s_t$, we may examine the proportions within the two series

$$\varphi(s_1, s_2),\ \varphi(s_1, s_3), \ldots,\ \varphi(s_1, s_t),$$

or

$$d'(s_1, s_2), d'(s_1, s_3), \ldots, d'(s_1, s_t)$$

in order to state whether the extent of structural change increases, diminishes' remains constant or is fluctuating as a function of time.

b) But also the two series

$$\varphi(s_1, s_2),\ \varphi(s_2, s_3), \ldots,\ \varphi(s_{t-1}, s_t),$$

or

$$d'(s_1, s_2), d'(s_2, s_3), \ldots, d'(s_{t-1}, s_t),$$

that is, the rates of structural changes between adjacent points of time may be examined.

The analysis of these two series informs us, however, *only about the extent* of the structural differences, and does not provide information about their *direction*.

Second: another problem related to the structural analysis of time series, involved in the examination and measurement of structural deviations *working in the main direction* might become very interesting.

By *main direction* we mean here the direction of *structural changes* where they are tending to lead, or where they have actually led. For establishing the "main direction", there seem to exist two possibilities:

a) we may accept the direction pointing to some normative (planned) structure; and/or

b) we may consider the changes leading towards the last *actual* structure as representing the main direction.

* By time series we do not mean here a special stochastic process, but a series of structural vectors arranged by time sequence.

In the following we shall consider as the "main direction" of structural development that which leads towards the structure of the final period.

The methods presented here can, however, be easily applied also to "normative" investigations.

Therefore *"main direction" is represented by that vector which,* together with the vector of the structure observed, *results in the "final" structure.*

If we note the main direction of change by $\mathbf{d}'$ then

$$\mathbf{s}_1 + \mathbf{d}' = \mathbf{s}_t, \text{ that is, } \mathbf{d}' = \mathbf{s}_t - \mathbf{s}_1$$

where $\mathbf{s}_i (i = 1, \ldots, t)$ are normalized vectors.

By a change acting in the main direction we mean the orthogonal projection (length) of any deviation vector $(\mathbf{s}_j - \mathbf{s}_1)$, $(j = 2, \ldots, t)$ falling in the direction of vector $\mathbf{d}'$.

If this orthogonal projection is denoted by Δ_j, we obtain

$$\Delta_j = \cos(\mathbf{d}', \mathbf{s}_j - \mathbf{s}_1)\, d'(\mathbf{s}_j, \mathbf{s}_1); \quad j = 2, \ldots, t$$

Of course, the values of Δ_j must be accounted according to their proper signs.

The Δ_j values denote the distance between the initial and the j-th point of time, falling in the main direction. In order to measure the distances belonging to the individual points of time (and falling into the main direction) we may introduce the following measure:

$$\Delta'_j = \Delta_j - \Delta_{j-1}; \qquad j = 2, \ldots, t.$$

It is easy to see that

$$\sum_{j=2}^{t} \Delta'_j = |\mathbf{d}'| = d'(\mathbf{s}_1, \mathbf{s}_t)$$

When examining the changes acting in the main direction, we wish to answer two questions:

a) what series is composed by the individual Δ'_j values, that is, *at what rate* have the structural changes occurring in the course of the time series approached the structure of the final period?

b) if we sum up the development over the entire period, to what extent can it be considered as *"consistent"*, that is, *as a gradual approximation* of the final structure?

The answer to question a) can be given by analysing the series Δ_j $(j = 2, \ldots, t)$. For answering the second one, further indicators can be established.

Such indicator may be either

$$K_1 = \frac{d'}{\sum_{j=2}^{t} |\Delta'_j|},$$

or

$$K_2 = \frac{\varphi(\mathbf{s}_1, \mathbf{s}_t)}{\sum_{j=2}^{t} \varphi(\mathbf{s}_j, \mathbf{s}_{j-1})}$$

It is characteristic of both indicators that their values appear, in the case of

$$\sum_{j=2}^{t} |\Delta'_j| \neq 0; \qquad \sum_{j=2}^{t} \varphi(\mathbf{s}_j, \mathbf{s}_{j-1}) \neq 0$$

(that is, when the necessity of such analysis emerges at all) in the interval of [0, 1].

In connection with these two indicators it must be noted that they are not interchangeable, but their information contents are complementary.

$K_1 = 1$ means that in the period investigated no retrograde structural change occurred opposed to the main direction represented by the vector $\mathbf{d}'$.

$K_2 = 1$ implies that all changes have taken place in the main direction and that all $\mathbf{s}_j$ structural vectors (and also $\mathbf{d}'$) are situated on the same two-dimensional subspace. It must be noted that in the case of $K_2 = 1$, the equation $K_1 = 1$ must also hold.

Both K_1 and K_2 have zero value when $\mathbf{d}' = \mathbf{0}$, that is, when the structure does not change during the period examined, i.e., when the consecutive changes in several directions result in the restitution of structure $\mathbf{s}_1$.

3. DECOMPOSITION OF DYNAMIC CHANGES INTO COMPONENTS

So far we have dealt with the method of examining the extent and meaning of structural changes.

When investigating dynamic changes, however, other problems also could occur. Here we wish to define two components of inter-temporal changes: The inertial component tending to maintain the structure of the initial period (this will be called "non-structural effect"), and the trend pointing in the direction of structural deviations (henceforth, "structural effect"). In analysing these two components we start from the assumption that both the structural and the non-structural effect emerge evenly over time.

Let us write

$$\mathbf{d} = \mathbf{s}_t - \mathbf{s}_j$$

where

$\mathbf{s}_j$ is the (non-normalized) structural vector of the initial period and
$\mathbf{s}_t$ is the (non-normalized) structural vector of the final period.

According to our assumption

$$\mathbf{d} = \mathbf{v} + \mathbf{w},$$

where

$\mathbf{v}$ is the vector of non-structural effects,
$\mathbf{w}$ is the vector of structural effects.

The vectors $\mathbf{v}$ and $\mathbf{w}$ can be unequivocally determined between any two periods since the directions of the two vectors are given. Namely, the direction of $\mathbf{v}$, by definition, necessarily agrees with (or is opposed to) the direction of the structural vector of the initial period $\mathbf{s}_j$, while the direction of $\mathbf{w}$ may only depend on the structural changes between the j-th and the t-th periods; it therefore agrees with the direction of the vector expressing the structural change, defined earlier as

$$\mathbf{d}' = \frac{\mathbf{s}_t}{|\mathbf{s}_t|} - \frac{\mathbf{s}_j}{|\mathbf{s}_j|}$$

Relying on the well-known parallelogram rule, the coordinate form of vectors $\mathbf{v}$ and $\mathbf{w}$ can also be produced

$$\mathbf{v} = \alpha \mathbf{s}_j, \qquad \text{where} \qquad \alpha = \frac{|\mathbf{s}_t|}{|\mathbf{s}_j|} - 1$$

$$\mathbf{w} = \beta \mathbf{d}', \qquad \text{where} \qquad \beta = |\mathbf{s}_t|.$$

The correctness of this decomposition can also be proven as follows:

$$\mathbf{w} + \mathbf{v} = |\mathbf{s}_t| \mathbf{d}' + \left(\frac{|\mathbf{s}_t|}{|\mathbf{s}_j|} - 1 \right) \mathbf{s}_j = \mathbf{s}_t - \mathbf{s}_j = \mathbf{d}$$

As a matter of fact, with the vectors $\mathbf{v}$ and $\mathbf{w}$ we have determined — by an analogy taken from physics — the *two forces* that have brought about the *total resultant* characterized by vector **d**. It also seems necessary to break down into its factors the actual change coming about *in the direction of vector* **d** separately under the effect of each factor. This is equal to the orthogonal projection of vectors $\mathbf{v}$ and $\mathbf{w}$ falling in the direction of vector **d**.

Denoting these orthogonal projections by $\mathbf{d}_v$ and $\mathbf{d}_w$:

$$\mathbf{d}_v + \mathbf{d}_w = \mathbf{d}$$

where $\mathbf{d}_w$ is the vector of actual changes coming about under structural effects, and $\mathbf{d}_v$ is the vector of actual changes coming about due to non-structural (inertial) effects.

The length of these projections

$$|\mathbf{d}_v| = \cos(\mathbf{d}, \mathbf{v})\,|\mathbf{v}|$$

$$|\mathbf{d}_w| = \cos(\mathbf{d}, \mathbf{w})\,|\mathbf{w}|$$

and, naturally

$$|\mathbf{d}_v| + |\mathbf{d}_w| = |\mathbf{d}|.$$

Thus, we have decomposed the total change occurring between the two periods represented by vector **d** into two parallel components.

The intensity of the effect of structural and non-structural changes on the total effect can be expressed in the case of $d \neq 0$ with the quotients

$$q_w = \frac{|\mathbf{d}_w|}{|\mathbf{d}|} \quad \text{and} \quad q_v = \frac{|\mathbf{d}_v|}{|\mathbf{d}|}.$$

Up to now we have expressed only the change between the initial and final periods as a resultant of the vectors of structural and non-structural effects. But the decomposition can also be made in respect to several intermediate periods, thus offering the possibility of a more detailed analysis.

ANALYSIS OF THE SHARE OF ECONOMIC SECTORS IN PRODUCTION AND DISTRIBUTION ON A NATIONAL ECONOMIC LEVEL

by

LÁSZLÓ SZABÓ

Input–output tables can be directly used for analysing the pattern of shares of individual sectors in output and distribution, since, owing to the structure of the table, the columns of the first quandrant mean the productive inputs (of each sector) and the rows the distribution of outputs by sectors. Distribution serves partly for productive consumption and partly for final use.* Yet the distribution ratios directly obtained from the elements of the table by summing them up horizontally and vertically, though important in structural analyses, cannot be considered as exclusive indicators characterizing the proportions of inputs and distribution. This is understandable, since the gross output of the sectors in the basic table, together with the related inputs, as well as its distribution serve not only the net output of the sector in question, but — in the form of productive inputs — the needs of some other sectors as well. It follows that the indicators mentioned also reflect a pattern of inputs and distribution that serves the interests of several sectors.

The requirement may be made to construct such indicators of input and distribution which will separately show what should be needed for the net output of individual sectors (or part of it) on an *economy-wide level* in both absolute and relative terms. In this way answers may be obtained to such questions as, e.g., what amount of gross production is directly or indirectly needed for the unit of exports performed by a given sector, or to what extent the gross production of the various sectors should be increased in order to attain a given increment of exports or investment in a given sector. It can be calculated how the gross output of a sector is distributed in the interest of a given amount of present or future net output of any individual sector. A fundamental condition of solving such and similar problems is that we should be able to measure numerically the rate of net output to gross output. This requirement can be met by the mathematical processing of the input–output table.

The purpose of the present paper is to suggest a few indicators that may serve these objectives and to review their application in practical analysis.

* The major elements of final use are: personal and public consumption, gross investment and exports. These items appearing in the second quadrant of the table represent the *economy-wide net output of the sectors*. In the following, whenever net output is mentioned, always the economy-wide output is meant.

1. BASIC DEFINITIONS

The *complete share** of a sector means the aggregate of the products and services it requires from the various other individual sectors, or from all sectors combined for productive purposes when it must produce a given amount and pattern of net output (i.e., "net" from the point of view of the national economy as a whole). The *complete distribution* of a sector means the aggregate of its products and services by which it contributes to the productive inputs of another sector, or of all other sectors. Both the shares and allocations will be assigned to the net output of the sectors taken in the above-mentioned sense. The basis for their measurement is constituted by the matrix **A** of direct per-unit inputs, with the aid of which the inverse matrix $\mathbf{R} = (\mathbf{I} - \mathbf{A})^{-1}$ can be computed. The column vectors of this show the *productive requirement* (or share) necessary for producing, in the given sector, a unit of net output. This share can also be shown in relation to the other sectors. The row vectors of the inverse matrix show the contribution (or distribution) expected from each sector to the productive inputs of all other sectors (divided up by purchasing sectors) required by the latter for releasing a unit of their net outputs. Let us call these requirements and constributions the "complete share" and "complete distribution" belonging to a unit of net output in the given sector. If we wish to determine the complete share and distribution belonging to the actual aggregate of net output rather than to the unit of the net output, the matrix series

$$\mathbf{R}\hat{\mathbf{Y}} \tag{1}$$

must be formulated. (The elements of the diagonal matrix $\hat{\mathbf{Y}}$ are the net outputs of the 1, 2, . . . , n-th sector.) The j-th column of the resulting matrix, the vector

$$\mathbf{Y}_j^* \mathbf{r}_j \tag{2}$$

expresses the complete share belonging to the j-th sector when its actual net output is y_j. The i-th *row* of the resulting matrix, that is, the row-vector

$$\mathbf{r}_i^* \mathbf{Y} \tag{3}$$

means the complete distribution (contribution from the output of the i-th sector needed for the actual net output of all other sectors).

As mentioned, the complete share and the complete distribution of the sectors are assigned to their "net" output (i.e., "net" from the point of view of the national economy). Accordingly, also the computation of the indicators is based on these concepts. Thus, in this respect we *deviate from the method hitherto followed* in practice, which started from the gross output or production of the sectors.

* Henceforth "complete" refers to the combined accounting of direct and indirect productive requirements or contributions.

According to the traditional method, the complete actual share of the j-th sector is denoted by the elements of the vector

$$\mathbf{x}_j^* \mathbf{r}_j \tag{4}$$

A somewhat better, but also debatable variant is conceivable, based on the formula

$$\frac{\mathbf{r}_j^*}{\mathbf{r}_{jj}} \cdot \mathbf{x}_j \tag{5}$$

where the vector of complete share relating to the unit of gross output of the j-th sector is multiplied by the actual $\mathbf{x}_j$ gross output of the sector.

A failure common to both latter methods is that they do not satisfy the "proof of sums". This proof requires, namely, that the sum of the complete shares of all sectors in the gross output of the i-th sector, in other words, the sum of complete distribution made by this sector should be precisely equal to its gross output $\mathbf{x}_i$. In cases (4) and (5) the "proof of sums" is not satisfied, since the vector of complete shares computed with the actual gross output of the sectors is greater than the gross output vector $\mathbf{x}$ of the sectors. That is

$$\mathbf{Rx} > \mathbf{x}, \quad \text{and} \quad \mathbf{R}\langle \mathbf{r}_{jj}\mathbf{x}\rangle^{-1} > \mathbf{x}, \tag{6}$$

where the vector $\mathbf{r}_{jj}$ is composed of the elements of the inverse matrix $\mathbf{R}$ along the main diagonal.

Both inequalities can be easily proved.

To illustrate what has been said, and to show the order of magnitude of the impermissible "overlapping" let us present here the complete distribution of the Hungarian chemical industry, computed according to formulae (4), (5) and (3), respectively.*

The actual net output of the chemical industry in 1968 $\mathbf{x}_i$ was Ft 31.969 million. As can be seen, the aggregated claim for shares of the sectors calculated according to formulae (4) and (5), that is, based on their gross output (Ft 72.041 and 60.638 million), considerably exceed the available resource, the gross output of the chemical industry.

On the basis of what has been said, undoubtedly the method based on net output is more consistent. Its basic formula is but a version of the generally known relation

$$\mathbf{Ry} = \mathbf{x} \tag{7}$$

written in matrix form. Its application thus does not require the acceptance of any new conception.

* The source for the basic data and the inverse coefficients was the publication "A magyar népgazdaság ágazati kapcsolatainak mérlege, 1965–1968, 14 termelő szektorra" (Input–output tables of the Hungarian economy by 14 productive sectors for 1965–1968). Central Statistical Office of Hungary, *Statisztikai Időszaki Közlemények*, Vol. 180.

Table 1

The complete distribution of the production of the Hungarian chemical industry and the complete share of sectors in this production in 1968

Sharing sector (j)	The sharing sectors'						
	own gross output	complete share in the output of the chemical industry	gross	net	complete share according to		
			output		gross output		net output
	per forint of net output				on the basis of formula		
	r_{jj}	r_{ij}	x_j	y_j	(4)	(5)	(3)
	forint		million forint				
1. Mining	1.0866	0.0724	17,971	6,560	1,301	1,197	475
2. Electric energy	1.0366	0.1001	10,043	2,761	1,005	970	276
3. Metallurgy	1.4302	0.0873	35,183	5,223	3,071	2,148	456
4. Engineering	1.3253	0.0742	88,926	48,759	6,598	4,979	3,618
5. Building materials	1.0673	0.0653	12,273	2,018	779	730	128
6. Chemical industry	1.1426	1.1426	31,969	12,068	36,528	31,969	13,790
7. Light industry	1.3799	0.0715	67,470	36,864	4,824	3,496	2,636
8. Food industry	1.1940	0.0648	67,199	50,953	4,354	3,647	3,302
9. Private industry	1.0087	0.0823	3,481	2,932	286	284	241
10. Construction	1.0112	0.0534	55,801	52,321	2,980	2,947	2,794
11. Agriculture	1.4299	0.0644	102,057	36,651	6,572	4,596	2,360
12. Transport	1.0233	0.0811	27,624	10,617	2,240	2,189	861
13. Domestic trade	1.0129	0.0309	38,481	28,845	1,189	1,174	891
14. Foreign trade	1.0042	0.0281	11,158	5,010	314	312	141
1–14. All sectors	—	—	569,636	301,582	72,041	60,638	31,969

2. THE INPUT–OUTPUT TABLE OF COMPLETE SHARE AND COMPLETE DISTRIBUTION

Essentially, the analysis of complete shares starts by dividing up the gross output values of the sectors according to the economy-wide inputs needed for the given net sector outputs. In order to present this in a tabulated and general form, the operations given in Table 2 have to be performed.

Thus, the elements of the table can be computed with the aid of the matrix equation (1), namely $\mathbf{R}\hat{\mathbf{y}} = \mathbf{X}$. In general, the complete share of the j-th sector in the output of the i-th sector is equal to r_{ij} which means at the same time that the complete distribution from the output of the i-th sector going into the j-th sector must be the same.

Table 2

Input–output table of the complete share and distribution of individual sectors

Releasing sector	Complete share of the 1st	2nd	...	n-th	Complete distribution (gross output)
	sector from the production of the releasing sector				
1st	$r_{11}y_1$	$r_{12}y_2$	...	$r_{1n}y_n$	$\mathbf{r}_1^*\mathbf{y} = x_1$
2nd	$r_{21}y_1$	$r_{22}y_2$	...	$r_{2n}y_n$	$\mathbf{r}_2^*\mathbf{y} = x_2$
...	...	...	...	...	$\ldots = \ldots$
n-th	$r_{n1}y_1$	$r_{n2}y_2$	...	$r_{nn}y_n$	$\mathbf{r}_n^*\mathbf{y} = x_n$
Complete shares	$\mathbf{1}^*\mathbf{r}_1y_1$	$\mathbf{1}^*\mathbf{r}_2y_2$	...	$\mathbf{1}^*\mathbf{r}_ny_n$	$\mathbf{1}^*\mathbf{R}\mathbf{y} = \Sigma x_i$

The above table, therefore, corresponds to an input–output table the rows and columns of which may be interpreted in the same manner as those of the basic input–output table. In the horizontal direction the complete sector distribution, in the vertical direction the complete sector share can be read. The characteristic features of this table are that

a) it is a quadratic table, that is, it has no side wing since the net output of the sectors is included into the $r_{jj}y_j$ elements along the main diagonal;

b) the sum of the complete distribution of a sector always equals its gross output;

c) the sum of the complete share of a sector ($\mathbf{1}^*\mathbf{r}_jy_j$) includes only the complete inputs related to its own net output, and the value of this net output.

It is important to stress this latter property, since when we neglect it we may arrive at erroneous conclusions. It may occur — mainly in the case of industries producing basic materials — that the complete share of the sector less its net output (that is, the complete sum of inputs) is smaller than the sum of its direct consumption of materials as shown in the basic input–output table. The cause of this paradox is obvious.

The complete divided-up distribution may be further differentiated according to the demands of the various components of net output. It is possible to show how much of the gross output of a sector is necessary for fulfilling the demands of consumption, gross investment and exports. By computing these proportions for all sectors, we can assess the absolute and relative sizes, as well as the patterns, of the complete share assigned to these components, and of the distribution needed. This, however, is nothing else but the distribution of the social product according to the demands of final use. The general scheme of the table necessary for such analyses is the following:

Table 3

General scheme representing the shares of gross production needed for final use

Releasing sector	Shares of gross production needed for			Total of distributed gross production
	consumption	capital formation	exports	
1st	$\mathbf{r}_1^*\mathbf{y}_a$	$\mathbf{r}_1^*\mathbf{y}_b$	$\mathbf{r}_1^*\mathbf{y}_c$	x_1
2nd	$\mathbf{r}_2^*\mathbf{y}_a$	$\mathbf{r}_2^*\mathbf{y}_b$	$\mathbf{r}_2^*\mathbf{y}_c$	x_2
...	...	...	...	...
n-th	$\mathbf{r}_n^*\mathbf{y}_a$	$\mathbf{r}_n^*\mathbf{y}_b$	$\mathbf{r}_n^*\mathbf{y}_c$	x_n
Complete share altogether	$\mathbf{1}^*\mathbf{R}\mathbf{y}_a$	$\mathbf{1}^*\mathbf{R}\mathbf{y}_b$	$\mathbf{1}^*\mathbf{R}\mathbf{y}_c$	$\sum x$

In this table, $\mathbf{y}_a$ is the vector of consumption, $\mathbf{y}_b$ that of gross investment, $\mathbf{y}_c$ that of exports and $\mathbf{1}^*$ is the summarizing vector. The economic interpretation of the indicators is obvious and their computation presents no new problems, so we may dispense with their discussion.

If we know the complete share and distribution, we may make comparisons by ranking the sectors according to these indicators, and by computing the differences between each pair of indicators of share and distribution. In this way we obtain indicators which show more exactly a sector's real dependence and effect on other sectors than do the indicators of complete share and complete distribution. These "net" indicators may be arranged in a table, the elements of which show the difference between complete share and complete distribution in respect to pairs of sectors. A positive balance indicates in the individual columns the excess share of the sector named in the heading of the column against the releasing sector, while a negative one means excess distribution (see Table 4).

3. INDICATORS OF PROPORTION

In statistical analyses usually the proportions of magnitudes characterizing the processes taking place in time and space are examined, as well as the changes in these proportions. This is why the indicators showing the proportions of complete share and distribution have also acquired particular importance, although their content is somewhat different. According to what has been explained above, the index of the complete share of sector j in the production of sector i will be defined by dividing j's complete share from i's production by the total production of i.

Table 4

Balance of complete shares and distribution between sectors in 1968 (million forints)

Distributing sectors	Excess sharing (+) of, or excess distribution (—) by the						
	chemical industry	food industry	construction	agriculture	transport	other productive sectors	Row total
Chemical industry		+ 2,941	+ 2,565	+ 1,766	+ 320	+ 3,351	+10,943
Food industry	— 2,941		— 258	—38,551	— 2,224	—10,900	—54,874
Construction	— 2,565	+ 258		— 739	— 5,075	—31,920	—40,041
Agriculture	— 1,766	+38,551	+ 739		— 622	— 1,000	+35,902
Transport	— 320	+ 2,224	+ 5,075	+ 622		+ 3,787	+11,388
Other productive sectors	— 3,351	+10,900	+31,920	+ 1,000	— 3,787		+36,682
Column total	—10,943	+54,874	+40,041	—35,902	—11,388	—36,682	—

Denoting this index with h_{ij}, we get

$$h_{ij} = \frac{r_{ij}\, y_j}{x_i} \tag{8}$$

Technically, when calculating the indices of the complete share of a receiving sector from the production of all releasing sectors, we must fix the index of j. If the value of i runs from 1 to n, the h_{ij} indices obtained yield the vector of complete share. This vector is

$$\mathbf{h}_j = \hat{\mathbf{X}}^{-1}\mathbf{r}_j y_j \tag{9}$$

where the first factor on the right side is a diagonal matrix, the elements of which are the reciprocals of the gross output values of the individual sectors. The $\mathbf{h}_j$ vectors calculated for all sectors can be built into an $\mathbf{H}$ matrix, which can be represented with the formula

$$\mathbf{H} = \hat{\mathbf{X}}^{-1}\,\mathbf{R}\mathbf{Y} \tag{10}$$

In formulating the distribution indices h_{ij} we can also fix i and let run j from 1 to n. In this case the indices show the part of the production of a given releasing sector handed over to a user sector. The indicators thus obtained are identical with the $\mathbf{h}_i^*$ row vectors of the former $\mathbf{H}$ matrix and have the particular property that the sum of their elements is always equal to unity, that is:

$$\mathbf{h}_i^*\mathbf{1} = 1 \tag{11}$$

Namely,

$$\mathbf{h}_i^* = \frac{1}{x_i}\,\mathbf{r}_i^*\hat{\mathbf{Y}} \tag{12}$$

and

$$\mathbf{h}_i^*\,\mathbf{1} = \frac{1}{x_i}\mathbf{r}_i^*\,\mathbf{y}\,\mathbf{1} = \frac{\mathbf{r}_i^*\,\mathbf{y}}{x_i} = \frac{x_i}{x_i} = 1 \tag{13}$$

In practice it may occur that it is not necessary to work out all distribution proportions for all sectors. Perhaps a triple division is sufficient, saying what percentage of a sector's gross output is used for its own net output, what percentage is used for purchasing its inputs originating from without, and what percentage is used for contributing to the production of other sectors. In view of relation (11) it is sufficient to compute the first two percentages and then subtract them from one hundred.

A comparison over time of the structures of complete share and distribution requires the identity of contents in all indicators relating to different periods of time, regarding both sectoral structure and valuation. It is therefore necessary that already the basic tables used for computing the indices should be comparable, that is, the extent of aggregation of the sectors and the comparable prices used for valuation must be identical.

Table 5 shows the structure of the complete distribution of the Hungarian chemical industry in the two years for which the above requirements could be met.

Table 5

Distribution of the production of the Hungarian chemical industry

Year	Complete shares (%) of								Complete distribution of the chemical industry
	engineering	chemical industry	light industry	food industry	construction	agriculture	transport	other sectors	
		from the production of the chemical industry							
1965	11.6	40.2	8.9	12.5	8.0	7.1	2.8	8.9	100.0
1968	11.3	43.1	8.2	10.3	8.7	7.4	2.7	8.3	100.0

In structural analysis the changes in all such factors [cf. formula (8)] must be taken into account, as they have a role in shaping the structure (changes in the net output of the sharing sectors, in the gross output and the inverse elements of the releasing sector). It must be remembered that the indices change proportionally with the net output of the sharing sector in question as well as with the change in the inverse coefficient used, but in inverse proportion to the gross output of the releasing sector. In the final result only the effect of the factors changing at a higher rate is asserted.

As is shown by Table 6, the complete share of the food industry in the gross production of the chemical industry declined between 1965 and 1968 (from 12.5 to 10.3 per cent) because the net output of the food industry increased at a lower rate than the gross output of the chemical industry. The diminishing of the inverse

Table 6

Factors affecting the changes in the total share of the food industry in the gross production of the chemical industry

	1965	1968	Index 1968/1965
Net output of the food industry (million Ft)	44,375	50,953	114.8
its total share in the chemical industry:			
a) computed per one forint net output (Ft)	0.0688	0.0648	94.2
b) computed for total net output (million Ft)	3,053	3,302	108.2
Gross production of the chemical industry (million Ft)	24,328	31,969	131.4
Complete share of the food industry (per cent)	12.5	10.3	82.4

coefficient also had an unfavourable effect on the development of the distribution index.

The effect of individual factors on the result may also be examined. Assuming the constancy of the other two factors, in this case we investigate how the sharing claim would have changed under the effect of the third factor.

4. LIMITS TO APPLICATION

The indices of complete share and distribution of the individual sectors may provide useful information about the actual role of the various products serving final use, of the sectors actually releasing them, and about the actual contribution of each sector to the production of others. Since the level of these indices is influenced by many factors, their use requires particular circumspection, especially in forecasting and planning. The limits to their application exist at least to the same extent as in the case of the indices of direct material inputs calculated from the basic tables. In this context particular attention should be paid to the case of fast growth rates usually occurring along with technological changes. Moreover, computations relying on value data are never free from the effects of the price system, whose characteristics are contained in the basic table, and thus also affect our indices. In this respect some importance should be attached to the so-called price model computations which aim at eliminating the distortions due to the price system.

Even apart from the above, we cannot claim that in possession of the indicators discussed in this paper we already have all objective conditions for analyses of this kind. For a fuller analysis and better knowledge of the economic processes, indicators defined and constructed in many other ways are also conceivable.

INVESTIGATION OF THE DYNAMICS AND THE EFFICIENCY OF PRIMARY PRODUCTION FACTORS WITH THE AID OF AN UNCHANGED INVERSE MATRIX

by

TAMÁS IVÁNYI

The investigation of the dynamics of primary production factors with the aid of input–output tables is limited by the fact that these tables are compiled only at rather long intervals. So-called small tables having but a few sectors can be calculated for every year which, however, make only rather superficial analysis possible, owing to their high aggregation. The purpose of the experiment to be reviewed here was to work out a method using the available statistical data and the inverse matrix of a year, enabling us to calculate with a minimum of cost and time, the indicators of cumulated wages, labour and fixed assets for several years.

Before reviewing the data necessary for the computations and the method applied, two problems should be mentioned which influence the accuracy of the results available with the aid of this experimental method and of the conclusions drawn. The first problem is whether the inverse matrix of some arbitrarily chosen year can be used for all the years investigated. This question is all the more topical since the annual changes in the indicators of "cumulated labour" are influenced by changes in the total input of labour (i.e., both live and embodied labour). In our experiment, however, we assume that embodied labour inputs ("per unit material consumption") do not vary through some longer period. We cannot review here the great number of Hungarian and foreign studies dealing with the changes or the stability of the "technological coefficients" and the arguments both for and against their usefulness. In our opinion, for attaining certain special objective the matrix of technological coefficients of a given year, or its inverse, can be used for a period of three to five years. Later on, I shall return to the verification of this assumption.

The other problem is that, in order to simplify computations, we do not "clean" the data taken from common statistics to achieve the usual homogeneity which is theoretically required for the input–output tables.

The data used and the method of computation will be presented here only for the case of calculating "cumulated labour", since the computation regarding cumulated wages and fixed assets is analogous. The computations have been performed for the years 1959 through 1967, using the inverse matrix of the 83-sector input–output table for 1965 and the row vectors for the same year of the cumulated imports and depreciation allowances, as well as the scalars for each investigated year, relating to per-unit cumulated labour and fixed assets in the unit value of imports coming from socialist and non-socialist countries and in that of the depreciation allowance.

These indicators, as well as the vector of direct labour inputs, were calculated first for the year 1965. For this we needed, in a breakdown corresponding to the sectors of the inverse matrix of 1965, the number of workers and employees, and the value of gross output. The indicator of "direct labour" inputs was, according to the well-known formula

$$l_i = \frac{T_i}{X_i}$$

where

l_i = labour per unit of output in branch i,
T_i = total employment in branch i (number),
X_i = gross output in branch i (million forints).

To calculate the vector of direct labour inputs of the socialist sector for the years 1959 to 1967, two methods can be employed. (For direct labour inputs outside the socialist sector and for direct inputs of fixed assets and wages the second method — see below — was employed in all the 83 branches.)

For applying Method 1, there were available in a breakdown by industries:

a) the index numbers of production based on product series on a 1950 = 100 basis,

b) the index numbers of employment, on the same basis.

By dividing series *a* by series *b*, the 1950-based index numbers of "productivity", i.e., production per employed person may be obtained. Since, however, in our computations 1965 was chosen as the base year, the above series was changed over to the 1965 base. Then, starting from the indicator of direct labour inputs worked out for 1965, we computed, with the aid of the index series of productivity, the direct labour input indicators for each individual year. For example, from 1964 to 1965 the computation was as follows:

$$l_i^{64} = l_i^{65} : \left(\frac{\sum_{i=1}^{n} X_i^{64}}{\sum_{i=1}^{n} X_i^{65}} : \frac{\sum_{i=1}^{n} T_i^{64}}{\sum_{i=1}^{n} T_i^{65}} \right)$$

where l_i^{64} and l_i^{65} are the direct labour inputs of branch i in 1964 and 1965 and the formula in parentheses characterizes the ratio of productivity in 1964 to that of 1965.

As mentioned, with this method the direct labour inputs are obtained in a sector-breakdown of the input–output table, but only for the socialist sector.

The indicators of direct labour input for the non-socialist sector and for the non-industrial branches were calculated by dividing the total employment in individual branches with the value of gross output (performance) at unchanged prices in each year. (The determination of cumulated *wages* and *fixed assets* took place for all 83 branches according to this second method; here, of course, we had, in the numerator, the wage-bill and the gross value of productive fixed assets, respectively.)

For example, the computation of cumulated labour inputs for 1967 was made in the following manner:

$$L_i^{67} = l_i^{67}(\mathbf{I} - \mathbf{A})_{65}^{-1} + \mathbf{b}_{sh}^{65}\alpha^{67} + \mathbf{b}_{ch}^{65}\beta^{67} + \mathbf{k}_h^{65}\gamma^{67},$$

where

L_i^{67} = the cumulated labour of the i-th branch in 1967,
l_i^{67} = direct labour inputs of the i-th branch in 1967,
$(\mathbf{I} - \mathbf{A})_{65}^{-1}$ = the inverse matrix of the input–output table for 1965,
$\mathbf{b}_{sh}^{65}$, $\mathbf{b}_{ch}^{65}$, $\mathbf{k}_h^{65}$ = the row vectors of cumulated imports from socialist and non-socialist countries, as well as of depreciation,
α^{67}, β^{67}, γ^{67} = per-unit cumulated labour in 1967, of imports from socialist and non-socialist countries as well as of depreciation.

The computation of cumulated wages and fixed assets is analogous, only the corresponding vectors are different.

From the indicators of cumulated labour, national-level productivity indices were also computed for the years 1959 through 1967. By applying the 1965 matrix of technological coefficients, we also computed one of the important factors influencing national-level productivity, namely, the effect of productivity changes *outside* the branch investigated. This was computed in the following manner (the formula presented here refers to the ratio of the change from 1964 to 1965*):

$$K_j = \frac{\sum_{i=1}^{n} a_{ij}^{65} L_i^{64} + l_j^{65}}{\sum_{i=1}^{n} a_{ij}^{65} L_i^{65} + l_j^{65}}$$

where

K_j = change in productivity outside the j-th branch,
a_{ij} = technological coefficients of embodied labour inputs (domestic and imported materials, depreciation of the j-th branch bought from the i-th branch,
L_i = cumulated labour of the i-th branch in 1964 and 1965, respectively,
l_j = direct labour inputs in the i-th branch in 1965.

With the aid of the available data, it is possible to desaggregate the index number of the national-level productivity (of live and embodied labour). The effect

* The formulae used for computing the indices were derived from a study by Rácz, A. and Újlaki, Zs.: A költségszint és termelékenység elemzése (Analysis of the cost level and productivity). *Statisztikai Szemle,* No. 6, 1962.

of changes in the productivity of live labour alone on branch productivity was also computed. For 1965 (taking into account the 1964 data) the calculation was the following:

$$E_j = \frac{L_j^{65} - l_j^{65} + l_j^{64}}{L_j^{65}}$$

where

E_j = the ratio of change in the productivity of live labour in the j-th branch,

L_j^{65} = cumulated labour of the j-th branch in 1965,

$l_j^{65,64}$ = direct labour inputs of the j-th branch in 1965 and 1964, respectively.

From among the factors influencing the index number of national productivity, the effect of changes in branch productivity and in the input of embodied labour were computed according to the ratios existing between the multiplication products relating to the factors concerned.

THE RESULTS

By using our method, a large amount of data was obtained. The accuracy of the results and the method itself had to be checked. This may be done in two ways. First, the general indicators computed with our method may be compared with the corresponding indicators obtained for the same branches from the input–output tables regarding 1959, 1961 and 1965. The results of this checking are shown by Table 1. Another method of checking consists of repeating computations with the inverse matrices of 1968 and 1965 (after having converted the 1965 inverse matrix according to the 1968 conditions).

Owing to the restricted scope of the present paper, it is impossible to present the data obtained from this computation. Instead, we shall present a few examples.

The engineering industries appearing in Table 1 figure in the individual tables identically, at least as regards the denomination. But the sector nomenclature, methodology and homogeneity of the tables compiled in 1959–1961 and 1965 are different, and the prices cannot be compared either.

Table 2 shows the indicators of only three branches out of the 83. The direct input indicators are also available in the same breakdown.

Table 3 presents the indicators of national-level productivity only for two years and in a highly aggregated form.

The factors investigated necessarily affect the comparability of the tables and are well known to experts applying the input–output method. We therefore feel that the errors due to our method of computing long time-series (the greatest of which seems to occur in the precision engineering industry), hardly interfere with the analysis of efficiency. Yet, the correctness of the method requires further proof, to be obtained by future computations.

Table 1

Checking cumulated labour

Branches	Data		Deviation of (2) from (1)	
	according to the original input–output table	obtained with our method	absolute	per cent
	(1)	(2)	(3)	(4)
1959:				
Electrical machinery and equipment	22.7578	25.2853	2.5275	11.1
Telecommunication and vacuum technology	26.6492	30.3882	3.7390	14.0
Precision engineering	24.1274	32.4519	8.3245	34.5
Production of metal mass products	23.5240	26.8627	3.3387	14.2
1961:				
Electrical machinery and equipment	19.9307	22.1837	2.2530	11.3
Telecommunication and vacuum technology	22.6285	26.4840	3.8555	17.0
Precision engineering	20.0301	26.6014	6.5713	32.8
Production of metal mass products	20.5506	22.6073	2.0569	10.0
1965:				
Electrical machinery and equipment	18.6834	19.0264	0.3430	1.8
Telecommunication and vacuum technology	21.8648	21.9969	0.1321	0.6
Precision engineering	21.9370	21.9935	0.0565	0.2
Production of metal mass products	18.7815	19.1386	0.3571	1.9

Table 2

Original and trend values of full-scope indicators

Year	Wages		Employment		Total fixed assets		Immovables		Equipment	
	original	trend value	original	trend value	original	trend value	original	trend value	original	trend value
1. *Coal mining*										
1959	62.108384	60.503782	26.233431	25.726549	2.738866	2.717817	1.924155	1.927176	1.645199	1.614060
1960	59.954166	50.441153	24.792378	25.021069	2.802671	2.811875	1.961771	1.958143	1.683647	1.701318
1961	58.757284	60.378589	24.134344	24.334935	2.892253	2.903398	2.008458	1.997547	1.741331	1.772439
1962	59.503846	60.316089	23.634909	23.667616	2.970627	2.992384	2.040320	2.045390	1.817428	1.827424
1963	60.879213	60.253655	22.910802	23.018597	3.036766	3.078835	2.069448	2.101670	1.838578	1.866272
1964	60.827689	60.191284	22.163978	22.387275	3.226964	3.162749	2.193394	2.166390	1.955757	1.888984
1965	59.689965	60.128979	21.927770	21.773462	3.292533	3.244128	2.247311	2.239547	1.930169	1.895559
1966	61.287733	60.066738	21.165811	21.176385	3.273476	3.322971	2.312148	2.321142	1.840445	1.885998
1967	59.351127	60.004561	20.750544	20.505680	.	.	.	.	.	.
2. *Briquetting*										
1959	48.482578	47.524141	21.155687	20.734000	2.766766	2.739789	1.857355	1.859993	1.707439	1.671334
1960	46.966761	47.313274	19.950393	20.149375	2.799859	2.814182	1.872251	1.870100	1.740371	1.760694
1961	45.922371	47.103343	19.373901	19.579291	2.849067	2.881176	1.889918	1.887390	1.786403	1.830022
1962	46.522956	46.894344	18.989283	19.026280	2.937375	2.940770	1.919466	1 911837	1.873080	1.879315
1963	47.287356	46.686271	18.448377	18.488889	2.973350	2.992966	1.922598	1.943450	1.894875	1.908574
1964	47.169563	46.479122	17.836383	17.966676	2.086425	3.037762	1.997000	1.982228	1.979130	1.917800
1965	45.678103	46.272892	17.585999	17.459213	3.107916	3.075159	2.023643	2.028172	1.937667	1.906992
1966	46.730790	46.067577	16.918580	16.966083	3.066205	3.105157	2.082231	2.081282	1.831916	1.876150
1967	45.490082	45.863173	16.607227	16.486881	.	.	.	.	.	.
3. *Turf mining*										
1959	76.414412	81.821937	33.898835	38.423542	4.284598	4.260225	2.887592	2.887600	2.446691	2.412405
1960	82.031793	79.574732	38.291327	37.279192	4.233404	4.288290	2.769912	2.912173	2.493622	2.542345
1961	75.796179	77.389244	35.527934	36.168924	4.341713	4.290042	2.784604	2.743277	2.634044	2.634130
1962	78.129243	75.263781	37.240417	35.091723	4.269840	4.265481	2.676553	2.680914	2.711605	2.687761
1963	78.324493	73.196692	35.116374	34.046603	4.101640	4.214608	2.552019	2.625083	2.630632	2.703237
1964	72.359840	71.186375	39.326769	33.032610	4.244920	4.137420	2.636987	2.575784	2.766999	2.680558
1965	67.945726	69.231270	31.569598	32.048816	4.040736	4.033920	2.532249	2.533017	2.622044	2.619725
1966	66.639213	67.329862	31.346954	31.094322	3.877240	3.904106	2.487718	2.496783	2.495260	2.520737
1967	63.316583	65.480675	26.189794	30.168255	.	.	.	.	.	.

Table 3

Economy-wide productivity indicators and their components

Branches	Indices of national productivity	Of this: changes		Of the latter: change in	
		outside	within	live	embodied
		the branch		labour	
	(1)	(2)	(3)	(4)	(5)
1. Mining	102.1	101.2	100.9	100.9	100.0
2. Electric energy	102.8	101.8	101.0	101.3	99.7
3. Metallurgy	102.4	102.0	100.4	100.8	99.6
4. Engineering	102.5	101.4	101.1	101.2	99.9
5. Building materials	103.1	101.2	101.9	101.9	100.0
6. Chemical industries	103.2	102.1	101.1	101.6	99.5
7. Light industries	104.1	101.5	102.6	102.7	99.9
8. Food industries	103.7	103.0	100.7	100.8	99.9
9. Other industries	107.0	101.1	105.8	105.7	100.1
10. Socialist sector (1–9)	103.4	101.7	101.7	101.8	99.9
11. Private industry	101.9	101.0	100.9	100.2	100.7
12. Construction	106.4	101.5	104.8	104.5	100.3
13. Private construction	104.5	101.8	102.7	102.7	100.0
14. Agriculture	103.9	101.2	102.7	102.2	100.5
15. Transport and communication	102.3	100.7	101.6	101.5	100.1
16. Domestic trade	102.7	100.9	101.8	101.7	100.1
17. Foreign trade	102.4	102.1	100.4	100.4	100.0
18. Total (1–17)	103.4	101.5	101.9	101.9	100.0

DESCRIPTION OF INTERREGIONAL TRANSPORTATION THROUGH AN INPUT–OUTPUT TABLE

by

TAMÁS BIHALY

The table of interregional transportations proposed here does not constitute a "regular" input–output scheme. It has no wings, and does not contain data on output values. Nonetheless, it may serve as a means of linking the "genuine" input–output table and regional planning.

I have not yet constructed the model as a set of equations (at least not in an explicit form). Instead, I have tried to draw up a system of notation and a closed system of matrices suitable for minimizing transport costs with the aid of linear programming. Even this system is similar to Dr. Csepinszky's regional input–output schemes, although differing in purpose, content and approach. Whereas Csepinszky looked for a regional variant of the input–output table, my objective is to find some basis from which the forecast (or normative planning) of transport activities serving the purposes of regional planning could start. Thus, there are two alternatives of approaching the problem.

The scheme presented in the Appendix contains, in the matrix shown on the lower right of the table, nothing else than the inner square of the economy-wide input–output table, expressed in terms of transport performance (weights or costs). Namely, as a result of summarizing, it does not contain interregional relationships any more, whereas the interindustry aspects are maintained. This summarizing matrix is essential for the whole scheme, being the connecting link to the "genuine" input–output table.

SOME PROBLEMS OF BUILDING UP AN OBJECTIVE FUNCTION

The purpose of the model is to *minimize the necessary transport performances*, which can be measured in terms of transport distances, transport hours or costs. This is how it may — in the capacity of an interregional model — complement interindustry models.

What is the exact meaning of the minimizing of transport performances (distances, etc.) under circumstances where the development of the social division of labour among branches involves also a growing social division of labour among regions, and thereby an increase in average transport distances? The problem can only be solved correctly in the course of development.

Social development, and the level of interindustry division of labour determined by it, involve a defined number of relations, that is, a defined volume of transport performance. More exactly:

– the *number of people gainfully employed* determines the transport performance connected with travel between homes and places of work,

– the *level of supplies and services* determines the volume of travel *between homes and suppliers* taken in the broadest sense (retail shops, servicing and recreational units, etc.),

– the prevailing *division of productive labour* determines the volume of transports between productive units.

If these performances depended exclusively on the *interindustry* division of labour, they could be considered as being determined up to 80 or 90 per cent. This is not true, however, because of the *interregional* division of labour, where the situation is different. Not only because the location of production and settlements are influenced by a host of natural (geological, soil, climatic, hydrological, etc.), and human (political, economic, etc.) factors, however important all these may be, but also because, as a result of the inertness of the network of productive plants, the interindustry relations themselves are pre-determined by earlier decisions regarding location, taken at a time when the branch structure widely differed from the present one. As a rule, plants may be reconstructed but they usually remain where they are. That is, we are able to modernize interindustry relations, but interregional relations cannot be freed from the above-mentioned decisions.

The task of regional planning consists in assessing the regional consequences and requirements involved in the development of productive branches, and in looking for optimum solutions. It has to make decisions regarding the location of new plants, the division of production among the various enterprises of an industrial branch and the relative extent of their development. In some cases it has to decide whether an existing plant should be reconstructed or a new one built elsewhere. Moreover, it must make decisions regarding the location of new settlements, the reconstruction of existing ones, etc., and other investments serving the needs of the population.

In all these decisions, the objective of minimizing the costs of transporting goods and people cannot be considered absolute; it is always combined with the objective of minimizing investment and operation costs. In the final analysis, a common optimum has to be sought. (Generally, one is able to tell even without a detailed calculation that the transfer of a large plant somewhere else would cost more than what it could save in transport costs; but there are extreme cases when the opposite may be true.)

Thus, the requirement of minimizing transport costs is always related to a certain determined state of the division of labour, under the conditions of an ever growing total of necessary transport commitments. Namely, economic growth necessarily involves an increase in the total of transport volume (in terms of costs, distance, number of persons, and volume of goods transported); our efforts should be directed at minimizing the *growth rate* of transport distance.

Apart from communications (which are left out of consideration here), passenger and freight transports are the two large areas to be covered. Under the regional aspect, the two behave rather differently. Whereas the bulk of passenger transport extends over relatively small distances of commuting and its individual districts may be treated as homogeneous units (even if they are frequently overlapping), the distances at which the transport of goods takes place are increasing. In the following, I shall deal only with the transport of goods, in close connection with the economy-wide input-output table. Thus the model expresses the interregional flow of goods.

This flow of goods cannot be followed up consistently because they are also subject to changes in the shape, stage of processing, specific weight and value, etc., of each commodity. However, for the purposes of description and planning, it is sufficient to assess the flows taking place between each pair of "generating points". Such generating points are, in Hungary:

- industrial plants (5–6,000)
- large agricultural farms (3–4,000)
- trading units (5–6,000)
- servicing units (15–20,000).

The numbers of units figuring in brackets were obtained either by selection (e.g., in industry, the omission of plants where employment was less than a certain minimum), or by aggregation (e.g., instead of the total number of retail shops, only the number of "district trade enterprises" operating all of the shops of a whole district was considered).

For describing traffic among these generating points, a 30,000 by 30,000 matrix would be needed. Each cell of this matrix would express an interindustry relation and a transport relation, although not by the same figure. (Namely, a model using only a single set of data would be insufficient since, clearly, the distribution of traffic in terms of tonnage greatly differs from its distribution in terms of value.) Obviously, an aggregation according to both sectoral and geographic criteria would be unavoidable. But in any case, such a matrix would only be suitable, either in the original or the aggregated form, for descriptive purposes. No planning could be based on it, even if it were desaggregated again according to kinds of goods or transport means used, because it would not supply information in respect to our problem.

Planners want to know the changes in the volume and direction of transport induced by a given change in production. In other words, they want to forecast the effects of the planned changes of interindustry relations on transports. The answer obviously presupposes consistency, or at least some organic link, between interindustry and interregional models.

The economy-wide input–output models now generally applied in the Western world — as distinguished from the micro-economic enterprise models — reflect an approach pointing beyond the original capitalist way of thinking. This approach

›cial efficiency as an objective phenomenon, and wants to define the ⁞ growth rate and product structure from the point of view of society And we share the opinion of Dr. Csepinszky that our socialist condi- .t (and require) us to utilize economy-wide indicators — as distinguished ɘ reflecting the situation and objectives of individual enterprises — in order to optimize growth rates and structural changes. This is true even in our case, where technological and "transport" coefficients are concerned.

THE AGGREGATION OF THE MODEL

Essentially, technological coefficients express the extent to which the growth of a given industry necessarily depends on that of another. Each cell of our assumed 30,000 by 30,000 matrix would reflect such a technological coefficient, except that, in lack of aggregation, they would express relations between two *plants* rather than between two *industries*. Thus, our matrix would consist of technological coefficients. Since, however, each of its elements reflects an objective transaction between two plants, it reflects not only interindustry relations but also interregional, i.e., transport relations. For instance, when aluminium plant A located in town X orders 1,000 tons of coal from mine C situated near the village Y, this reflects not only a relation between the aluminium industry and coal mining but also another one, that 1,000 tons of coal must be transported from the railway station at Y to a station in X.

As regards the *aggregation of industries* we must apply the nomenclature of the latter, in order to maintain the link with the economy-wide input–output table. At the same time, regional (transport) considerations must be also taken into account. Namely, in order to reduce the matrix to a manageable size, we must aggregate the relations involving identical or similar transport distances, that is, some territorial aggregation is also necessary.

The first possible step of this *territorial aggregation* is the aggregation of the "transport–generating" units in the same settlement (town, community, etc.). Thereby we could — from the territorial point of view — reduce our matrix to a size of about 3,000 by 3,000, assuming that, on the average, 16 industries are distinguished within a settlement. Thus, transport relations between settlements would be expressed by partial submatrices of industries. By this, the picture becomes more systematized and easier to survey. The scheme presented in the Appendix denotes the territorial units (towns or communes) by Arabic numerals (1, 2, 3, ... , 50, . . . , 3,000), the industrial branches by capital letters ($A, \ldots, K, \ldots, P$). The volume of transport activity, i.e., the physical quantity of products to be transported, is designated by Q. Thus, when, e.g., A means coal mining and B stands for aluminium metallurgy, 1 = a community, where a coal mine is operated and 2 = a town where an aluminium plant is working, then Q_{AB}^{12} means the necessity of transporting Q tons of coal from railway station 1 to station 2.

The general expression of a matrix cell is, accordingly, Q^{ij}_{IJ}. By summarizing such data we obtain the partial matrices showing the transports that must take place between each pair of geographic points.

A further aggregation might be achieved, from the geographic aspect, by adding up the data of places belonging to the same "district" or — what would practically amount to the same thing — of places belonging to the "sphere of attraction" of a given transport junction. (It has to be stressed that, in both cases, the *aggregation of all data* must be performed, rather than a "representation" of a given area by sample data regarding selected towns, communities or transport junctions.) The extent of aggregation depends on the nature of the task to be solved. For solving economy-wide tasks, a division according to large regions (counties) may be sufficient, while for analyses related only to a part of the country, that part has to be divided into smaller units.

A matrix reflecting present conditions permits us to follow up directly the extent of transport performance brought about by the interindustry relations; namely, we may read from the matrix which interindustry relations, and to what extent, would cause changes in the volume of transports taking place between each pair of transport junctions.

Let us illustrate this by the transport matrix presented in the Appendix. (Roman numerals designate the partial submatrices within the table given in the Appendix.)

I. The contents of the general form of a partial submatrix regarding the relations between pairs of geographic points (settlements) was already explained in the foregoing. The data figuring in the last *column* (the sums of the rows) of such a matrix express how much of the products of the settlement i (distinguished according to the rows of the matrix) was supplied to settlement j (without distinction by branches). The data figuring in the last *row* (the sums of the columns) express how much of the products of settlement i (regardless of their origin by branches) was supplied to the various branches (distinguished according to the columns of the matrix) of settlement j. Finally, the last square of the last row ($\Sigma\Sigma Q$) in the submatrix expresses the total quantity of goods transported from settlement i to settlement j, disregarding their origin or destination by branches.

II. The partial submatrix summarizing the rows shows separately the sums of the general cells and that of the sub-totals. Therefore, its general cells represent the transports taking place between the individual branches of settlement i (divided according to branches as shown by the rows), and the branches of all settlements (divided according to branches as shown by the columns). Accordingly, the last column of this partial submatrix (the sum of the rows) expresses the transports from settlement i (divided according to branches shown by the rows) into all branches of all settlements. The last row of the submatrix (the sum of columns) shows all transports from settlement i to the branches of all settlements as shown by the columns.

Finally, the far-right square of the lowest row ($\Sigma\Sigma\Sigma Q$) contains the total amount of transports from all branches of settlement i to all branches of all settlements.

III. This partial submatrix, summing up the columns of I, summarizes the transports directed to settlement j in the same way as the transports from settlement i were summarized under II.

IV. This submatrix summarizes all the data of the model. As has been mentioned earlier, this matrix no longer contains any territorial elements, since these have been eliminated in the course of the summing up. Accordingly, its general cell shows only the transport relations arising between pairs of branches. Its far-right column (the sum of rows) expresses the volume of transports from each branch (i.e., the "output" of branches taken in this sense), whereas its lowest row (the sum of columns) shows the total transports directed to individual branches (i.e., their "inputs"). The far-right square of the lowest row ($\Sigma\Sigma\Sigma\Sigma Q$) expresses the total volume of necessary transport performances in the national economy as a whole.

Thus, the interregional (transport) balance of interindustry relations is able to express the volume of transports taking place between any pairs of settlements or of branches, and even among the various branches of any pair of settlements. The table makes it also possible to calculate diverse combinations of these elements.

It is to be noted that the term "all settlements" also includes the settlement in question. Therefore, the partial submatrices located in the main diagonal contain also the transactions taking place *within* the same settlement.

By confronting the matrix of technological coefficients (in terms of values) obtained from the interindustry relations, on the one hand, and the matrix of "transport coefficients" (expressed in units of transport performance) on the other, we obtain — provided that both sets of data are arranged according to the same nomenclature — parameters for the two types of interindustry relations.

Knowing these parameters (or their variants that may be forecast for the future) and the long-term input–output table, it becomes possible to make decisions regarding the optimum location of any new investment project in view of transport costs, and, inversely, one can assess how the various options regarding location may affect the volume of transports.

The data needed for the proposed calculations may be collected from the bills of freight; as regards long-range development, we have to rely on the forecasts contained in the economy-wide input–output table. From what has been expounded here, it follows that this calculation does not use any element contained in the second and third quadrants of the economy-wide input–output table.

APPENDIX

The regional (transport) balance of interindustry relations (transport matrix)

		1				2				3				50				3000				Σ			
		A	K	P	Σ	A	K	P	Σ	A	K	P	Σ	A	K	P	Σ	A	K	P	Σ	A	K	P	Σ
1	A																								
	K																								
	P																								
	Σ																								
2	A									Q^{23}_{AA}	Q^{23}_{AK}	Q^{23}_{AP}	$\sum_{J=A}^{P} Q^{23}_{AJ}$									$\sum_{j=1}^{3000} Q^{2j}_{AA}$	$\sum_{j=1}^{3000} Q^{2j}_{AK}$	$\sum_{j=1}^{3000} Q^{2j}_{AP}$	$\sum_{j=1}^{3000}\sum_{J=A}^{P} Q^{2j}_{AJ}$
	K									Q^{23}_{KA}	Q^{23}_{KK} I.	Q^{23}_{KP}	$\sum_{J=A}^{P} Q^{23}_{KJ}$									$\sum_{j=1}^{3000} Q^{2j}_{KA}$	$\sum_{j=1}^{3000} Q^{2j}_{KK}$ II.	$\sum_{j=1}^{3000} Q^{2j}_{KP}$	$\sum_{j=1}^{3000}\sum_{J=A}^{P} Q^{2j}_{KJ}$
	P									Q^{23}_{PA}	Q^{23}_{PK}	Q^{23}_{PP}	$\sum_{J=A}^{P} Q^{23}_{PJ}$									$\sum_{i=1}^{3000} Q^{2j}_{PA}$	$\sum_{j=1}^{3000} Q^{2j}_{PK}$	$\sum_{j=1}^{3000} Q^{2j}_{PP}$	$\sum_{j=1}^{3000}\sum_{J=A}^{P} Q^{2j}_{PJ}$
	Σ									$\sum_{I=A}^{P} Q^{23}_{IA}$	$\sum_{I=A}^{P} Q^{23}_{IK}$	$\sum_{I=A}^{P} Q^{23}_{IP}$	$\sum_{I=A}^{P}\sum_{J=A}^{P} Q^{23}_{IJ}$									$\sum_{j=1}^{3000}\sum_{I=A}^{P} Q^{2j}_{IA}$	$\sum_{j=1}^{3000}\sum_{I=A}^{P} Q^{2j}_{IK}$	$\sum_{j=1}^{3000}\sum_{I=A}^{P} Q^{2j}_{IP}$	$\sum_{j=1}^{3000}\sum_{I=A}^{P}\sum_{J=A}^{P} Q^{2j}_{IJ}$
3	A																								
	K																								
	P																								
	Σ																								
50	A																								
	K																								
	P																								
	Σ																								
3000	A																								
	K																								
	P																								
	Σ																								
Σ	A									$\sum_{i=1}^{3000} Q^{i3}_{AA}$	$\sum_{i=1}^{3000} Q^{i3}_{AK}$	$\sum_{i=1}^{3000} Q^{i3}_{AP}$	$\sum_{i=1}^{3000}\sum_{J=A}^{P} Q^{i3}_{AJ}$									$\sum_{i=1}^{3000}\sum_{j=1}^{3000} Q^{ij}_{AA}$	$\sum_{i=1}^{3000}\sum_{j=1}^{3000} Q^{ij}_{AK}$	$\sum_{i=1}^{3000}\sum_{j=1}^{3000} Q^{ij}_{AP}$	$\sum_{i=1}^{3000}\sum_{j=1}^{3000}\sum_{J=A}^{P} Q^{ij}_{AJ}$
	K									$\sum_{i=1}^{3000} Q^{i3}_{KA}$	$\sum_{i=1}^{3000} Q^{i3}_{KK}$ III.	$\sum_{i=1}^{3000} Q^{i3}_{KP}$	$\sum_{i=1}^{3000}\sum_{J=A}^{P} Q^{i3}_{KJ}$									$\sum_{i=1}^{3000}\sum_{j=1}^{3000} Q^{ij}_{KA}$	$\sum_{i=1}^{3000}\sum_{j=1}^{3000} Q^{ij}_{KK}$ IV.	$\sum_{i=1}^{3000}\sum_{j=1}^{3000} Q^{ij}_{KP}$	$\sum_{i=1}^{3000}\sum_{j=1}^{3000}\sum_{J=A}^{P} Q^{ij}_{KJ}$
	P									$\sum_{i=1}^{3000} Q^{i3}_{PA}$	$\sum_{i=1}^{3000} Q^{i3}_{PK}$	$\sum_{i=1}^{3000} Q^{i3}_{PP}$	$\sum_{i=1}^{3000}\sum_{J=A}^{P} Q^{i3}_{PJ}$									$\sum_{i=1}^{3000}\sum_{j=1}^{3000} Q^{ij}_{PA}$	$\sum_{i=1}^{3000}\sum_{j=1}^{3000} Q^{ij}_{PK}$	$\sum_{i=1}^{3000}\sum_{j=1}^{3000} Q^{ij}_{PP}$	$\sum_{i=1}^{3000}\sum_{j=1}^{3000}\sum_{J=A}^{P} Q^{ij}_{PJ}$
	Σ									$\sum_{i=1}^{3000}\sum_{I=A}^{P} Q^{i3}_{IA}$	$\sum_{i=1}^{3000}\sum_{I=A}^{P} Q^{i3}_{IK}$	$\sum_{i=1}^{3000}\sum_{I=A}^{P} Q^{i3}_{IP}$	$\sum_{i=1}^{3000}\sum_{I=A}^{P}\sum_{J=A}^{P} Q^{i3}_{IJ}$									$\sum_{i=1}^{3000}\sum_{j=1}^{3000}\sum_{I=A}^{P} Q^{ij}_{IA}$	$\sum_{i=1}^{3000}\sum_{j=1}^{3000}\sum_{I=A}^{P} Q^{ij}_{IK}$	$\sum_{i=1}^{3000}\sum_{j=1}^{3000}\sum_{I=A}^{P} Q^{ij}_{IP}$	$\sum_{i=1}^{3000}\sum_{j=1}^{3000}\sum_{I=A}^{P}\sum_{J=A}^{P} Q^{ij}_{IJ}$

AN INPUT-OUTPUT MODEL FOR THE INDUSTRIAL AREA OF KAZINCBARCIKA FOR THE YEAR 1965*

by

FERENC KISS

Recently, a new requirement has arisen to elaborate and analyse input–output models relating to a geographic area. After investigating and weighing various possibilities for a solution, a partial model was built covering the industrial area of Kazincbarcika. Its construction has made it possible to clear up not only the theoretical and practical problems of such a model but also the ways and means for its analytical application.

THE STRUCTURE AND ELABORATION OF THE MODEL

The structure of interindustry relations of the area was built into the model in accordance with the general scheme of input–output tables, adapted to the special requirements of a table covering a geographic area.

Essentially, there are two basic solutions: the partial regional table and the regional combined table.

In the *partial table of a geographical area* the first quadrant refers only to activities performed within the area examined (district, county, economic region, etc.). The third quadrant also contains, in addition to the usual items of primary resources and summarizations, the values of goods and services purchased from without the area. They may be grouped either according to the sectors (industries) or to the geographic areas (counties, etc.) from where they have been purchased. In the second quadrant, in addition to the components of final use within the area, the external sectors to which goods and services produced within the area have been sold, are also represented. As regards the grouping of the latter, again the alternatives mentioned above are possible.

The *combined table of a geographic area* contains, within the first, second and third quadrants described above, also the mutual interrelations among the external productive sectors. Such a table enables us to undertake analyses on a national economic level. A relatively simple way of constructing such a model is possible when the classification of the external sectors is identical with the sectors appearing in the national economic input–output table constructed by the Hungarian Central Statistical Office. Another conceivable construction would consist in grouping the external sectors by geographical units (e.g., counties). This, however, would require the re-grouping of the national economic model,

* This area is in the North-Eastern part of Hungary.

i.e., an amount of work exceeding the resources available for elaborating a territorial model. It is evident that in the future, mainly for investigating questions concerning regional development, such models will be elaborated, but they will also have to contain, in addition to the regional groups, the interrelations of the national economic branches. For this, however, the construction of a complete system of regional tables would be necessary.

The row and column vectors of the second and third quadrants are in accordance with the national economic model.

Our model of Kazincbarcika was constructed according to the principles of the *partial table.* External purchases and sales were grouped by counties, i.e., the location of the supplier or user. Those supplying the data were able to tell accurately from where they had purchased goods and services, and to where their own products had gone. In the cases of sales or purchases to or from commercial enterprises trading in means of production, the places where these goods had been produced or where they were going to be used were established with the aid of estimates based on the general lists of suppliers and purchasers of the trading enterprises. The supplier and consumer counties were ranked in the model according to their distances from Kazincbarcika.

Our table reflects the activities of the three large plants located in the town of Kazincbarcika (the power plant, the chemical combine and the prefabricated housing plant) as well as the four mines located 10–12 km away. These seven producing units constitute an industrial centre, relying on a common energy basis and having a close technological interdependence. All these activities could be described in eighteen sectors. The major items, the production and sale of which entered into the table, were coal mining, production of electric energy, steam, nitrogenous fertilizers, sodium hydroxide, hydrochloric acid and pulverized polyvinyl chloride, as well as the maintenance of mining equipment.

The enterprises supplied their data not on the basis of total output, (i.e., including their own consumptions), but — in accordance with the rules of industrial statistics — on the basis of commodity production (gross output). Although this method facilitated the comparison of our data with the economy-wide input-output table and that of the Ministry of Heavy Industry, it made the supplying of data by the enterprises more difficult. The elimination of double accounting was especially difficult in the case of the Borsod Chemical Combine, since the twin products of electrolysis serve partly the production of caustic soda and partly that of hydrochloric acid, whereas the remaining chlorine is used in the production of polyvinyl chloride. A so-called "proto-calculation" was made for the purpose of showing the amounts of basic materials needed for the output of the final (marketed) products, by tracing back, through the intermediate stages of production, the cumulated inputs of materials, wages and other costs.

THE CONSTRUCTION OF THE MODEL AND THE EVALUATION OF THE RESULTS

Our model was elaborated in the form of two typical variants.

The model *Type A* contained the technological coefficients existing *within* the area investigated. In addition to the calculation made in terms of money, another variant was elaborated in which all the data that could be expressed in physical units of measurement were shown in tons. Accordingly, also the most important technological coefficients could be expressed in terms of physical units. Out of the total value of materials used within the area, 98.8 per cent could be expressed in physical units. This variant made it also possible for technical experts to utilize our model and to appraise the production processes described by it. The inclusion of technological coefficients has also opened the way for utilizing the model for purposes of planning.

The *Type B* model, together with its sub-matrices of material inputs and sales, grouped in both cases by counties, makes it also possible to analyse, in addition to the flows of goods and services within the area investigated, the tasks of the transporting apparatus. On the basis of the average distance of the various counties from Kazincbarcika, it is possible to estimate the transport capacities required by the work performed. Imported materials were grouped partly according to whether they were purchased from a socialist or from a non-socialist country, and partly also according to the direction of transports.

As regards the first quadrant of our model, it may be stated that the flow of materials within the area is generally one-way (coal to power plant to chemical industry, or to the production of prefabricated building components), but there also some minor feedbacks (e.g., use of sodium hydroxide in the power plant). Of the total value of materials used in the area, 27 per cent are locally produced. The strongest external relations of the area are with the rest of the county of Borsod (of which it is a part), more exactly with the industrial region of the Sajó Valley. This means that about 85 per cent of all materials used in the area investigated are purchased from either within it or its direct neighbourhood. Among the supplies coming from a greater distance, those purchased from Budapest and the counties of Hajdu and Komárom are substantial.

As regards external sales, the area supplies, in smaller or greater quantities, all areas of the country. The most important buyers are Borsod county and Budapest (40 and 13 per cent of all external sales, respectively).

The industry of the area investigated may be considered, from the point of view of both the supply of materials and the marketing of products, as a fortunate choice for an industrial location. There is a combination of industries centered around a single energy source.

With the aid of our table as a mathematical model, it is possible to calculate the cumulated output values, the value of output by counties and by the components of the final use. For this, it is necessary to examine what external uses are served by the internal inputs, the internal consumption by the area. This can be worked out with the inverse matrix of the first quadrant, which shows the cumulated inputs necessary for outputs sold outside the area. By multiplying the inverse matrix with these "external outputs" we could state, e. g., that whereas the direct share of Budapest of the final products of the area amounted to Ft 271 million, the cumulated value of its products used by the capital (inclusive of indirect input made) was Ft 316 million. Most of the Ft 45 million of indirect use consisted of coal and electric energy; essentially, both went into the production of pulverized and granulated polyvinyl chloride.

Thus, for example, two coal mines of the area (Berente and Tervtáró) do not sell any coal outside of the area; all of their output goes to a central coal-separating plant. But the calculation described above showed that more than 16 per cent of the coal produced by the two mines was indirectly used in the capital.

The analysis of the relationships obtained through multiplying the inverse matrix by the external output may be utilized in planning. If, e.g., additional requirements arose against supplies from our area, it would be possible to allocate the tasks among the enterprises located there in order to meet those requirements.

According to the above example, with requirements growing in the capital for pulverized or granulated polyvinyl chloride, a greater portion of the coal produced in our area would be needed for this purpose. If, at the same time, the other counties also increased their indirect requirements of the coal mines of our area, at a certain point the aggregate demand would exceed their capacity, and either the expansion of their capacity or supplementary purchases of coal from elsewhere would become necessary. If Budapest demanded an increased supply of polyvinyl chloride, this might cause a reduction in the direct supplies of coal from our area to the capital.

The system of inverse coefficients makes it possible to determine the materials purchased from outside (grouped by counties of origin) according to the various external outputs they were used for. This can be done by the matrix multiplication

$$\mathbf{M}^* = (\mathbf{R} \cdot \mathbf{Y}),$$

where

$\mathbf{M}^*$ = the coefficient matrix of the input of materials purchased from without (by counties),

$\mathbf{R}$ = the inverse matrix of the internal relations within the area investigated,

$\mathbf{Y}$ = a matrix expressing the value of external sales of the area, by counties of destination and by kinds of final use.

The rows and columns of the resulting matrix show the counties as suppliers and purchasers. Thus, it becomes possible to state what relations are created between them *through the intermediary of our area.*

It is also possible to state how, and to what extent, the materials imported from abroad and used within our area satisfied the needs of the various counties, as well as to state how the materials purchased from other counties or from abroad were allocated among the various items of final use.

To continue with the Budapest example: the Ft 271 million worth of products directly supplied to the capital from our area have necessitated Ft 242 million of external purchases, with the decisive majority (Ft 186 million) from the county of Borsod. Most of the latter sum consisted of coal purchased from Borsod county by the coal-separating plant operating in our area. As regards the final use of this coal, most of it was directly sold to Budapest; a smaller portion was used for producing pulverized or granulated polyvinyl chloride and certain other chemical or other products.

But the Budapest enterprises also contributed to the production of such goods in our area that were to be sold to Budapest. The capital supplied materials worth nearly Ft 95 million and of these, goods worth more than Ft 10 million had been supplied by Budapest for the purpose of producing other goods which were then sold to Budapest. A more detailed investigation is likely to make it evident that the volume of such "round trips" might be reduced, not to mention the even longer round trips where basic materials produced in Budapest are transported to Kazincbarcika and, after further processing, sent to Western Hungary (i.e., via Budapest).

Another example: materials purchased by our area (mostly calcium carbide used in the production of polyvinyl chloride) from Dorog (in the county of Komárom located west of Budapest) play a considerable role in the production of goods finally destined for Budapest. This round trip will be eliminated when the raw material basis of polyvinyl chloride production will switch over to natural gas.

A third example: most of the imported materials used in our area for producing goods to be sold to Budapest (Ft 18 million out of Ft 20 million) arrive via Budapest.

The summing up of all the data shows that more than 20 per cent of the materials purchased by our area in order to ensure supplies going to Budapest arrives there via Budapest.

INTERRELATIONS BETWEEN OUR MODEL AND THE "CENTRAL" AND "COMBINED" INPUT–OUTPUT TABLES

The "central" input–output table covering the national economy as a whole is closely related to the data of individual enterprises, in fact, its elaboration is built upon the enterprise balance-sheets. The classification of their data by industrial branches and groups as well as their mutual checking make it possible to build up a national economic model.

The "combined model" shows the interrelations within a group of industries (or those supervised by the same ministry), or within a whole branch of the national economy. Similarly to the "central model", this "combined model" also relies on the figures supplied by the enterprises, so comparisons between the two types of models are possible. Besides the identical basic data, the principles of constructing the two models are also identical, and their grouping by sectors ensures comparability.

A table covering a given geographic area is always a partial model since it examines a specially determined part of the production process and its interrelationships. Accordingly, the data used in it, as well as the principles governing its elaboration, may considerably differ from those applied in drawing up the "central" or "combined" tables. When constructing our model of Kazincbarcika, we did not fully utilize this possibility. Another consideration was weighed according to which an improvement of the model should be attempted, consisting of a combination of input–output data regarding several geographic units and even the extension of this type of analysis to the national economy as a whole; at least, we wanted to suggest a practical solution to such an improvement. It was in view of these plans that we did not want to deviate considerably from the principles of the tables on a national economic level.

The breakdown of our model by sectors is essentially in accordance with the input–output tables elaborated for the industries supervised by the Ministry of Heavy Industry. In fact, the input–output table of the Ministry considers the production of nitrogenous fertilizers and pulverized polyvinyl chloride in the Borsod Chemical Combine as independent "sectors". From this point of view, our model may be seen as a part of the "combined" model of the Ministry. By starting from the interrelations existing between these two models, it becomes possible to compare the economic efficiency and capital intensity of production in our area and elsewhere.

In addition to the possibility of comparing direct indicators, we may appraise the economic activities performed in the area investigated, partly in the framework of the input–output table of the Ministry of Heavy Industry (in the case of the output of nitrogenous fertilizers and of pulverized polyvinyl chloride) and partly with the aid of the inverse matrices of the "central" or the "combined" models. Thus, for instance, when a row vector of a known structure, showing the cumulated wages is available, we may multiply it with the sufficiently detailed column vector of material inputs regarding the product or activity to be examined. The scalar value obtained will show the value of cumulated wages within the material inputs in production. By adding to this the direct wages, we obtain, on a national economic level, the indicator of the cumulated wages of the activities pursued in the area examined.

The following table shows some of the results of the calculation.

The complete indicators in the two columns are identical for nitrogenous fertilizers and pulverized polyvinyl chloride, i.e., the two products which figure as separate sectors in the input–output table of the Ministry of Heavy Industry. This proves the correctness of our method.

In the case of nitrogenous fertilizers, it may be stated that the production in the Borsod Chemical Combine which uses natural gas is, on a national economic level, much more advantageous (less labour intensive) than the coal-based production of the Nitrogen Works of Pét, where cumulated wages amount to 89.02 per cent against the 57.47 per cent shown above. It also follows that production in Borsod is more capital intensive than in Pét. The lower live labour requirements and the

Cumulated wages of some activities in the Kazincbarcika area
(per cent)

	Cumulated wages	
	calculated with the inverse matrix of the Ministry's input–output table	figuring in the Ministry's input–output table
Borsod Power Plant:		
Electric energy	50.17	47.88
Steam	62.07	58.15
Borsod Chemical Combine:		
Sodium hydroxide	70.45	56.46
Hydrochloric acid	93.03	69.41
Nitrogenous fertilizers	57.47	57.47
Polyvinyl chloride, pulverized	94.24	94.24

up-to-date technology of Borsod, however, contribute to reducing both direct costs and total inputs.

The cumulated wages of the production of sodium hydroxide and hydrochloric acid by the Borsod Chemical Combine exceeds the average level shown by the three hydrolysis plants existing in Hungary (one of which is the Borsod Combine). The Budapest Chemical Works, the chief producer of these two items (supplying almost half of the Hungarian output), has two plants. In the older one the value of fixed capital is very small. Although this plant operates with relatively high material inputs, this disadvantage is counterbalanced by the very low level of depreciation allowance and therefore it seems justified to continue its operation. (The calculations show, namely, that the value of cumulated wages in depreciation is very important; it represents about one fifth of the value of cumulated wages in output.)

Our results seem to prove that it is necessary to evaluate the efficiency of the activities performed within various geographic areas, in various enterprises, in order to clear up the causes of efficiency differences. For instance, it is very important for planners to know the extent of dispersion behind the national economic averages. If, e.g., a new electrolysis plant were to be established in Hungary, planners would have to start from the indicators of the Borsod Chemical Combine.

Partial models relating to a geographic area may help us investigate an actual location problem comprehensively, according to uniform points of view. These models also contribute to forecasting the effects of a development project on the national economy.

AN EXPERIMENTAL INPUT-OUTPUT TABLE FOR VAS COUNTY (1968)

by

TIBOR KOVÁCS, ANDOR CSEPINSZKY and ZOLTÁN NOVÁK

The construction of input–output models and their utilization of analysis have a relatively long history in our country. Besides economy-wide tables including statistics and plan figures, a few tables have been drawn up for some industries, or for industry groups supervised by a ministry. Recently, a growing interest in regional problems has laid some emphasis on the necessity of attempting to draw up a table (at first with limited requirements) for a county.* It is well known that the regional distribution of productive forces over Hungary, far from being even, is considerably disproportionate. Accordingly each of the various regions has a "specific" character as regards the branches of their economic activity. It is necessary and important for regional research to concentrate on the question how and to what extent the various parts of the country are taking part in the social division of labour, especially from the regional aspect, to what extent their economic resources are activized, what movements of goods and other economic relationships result therefrom and, finally, what effects are exercised by all these on social differentiation, in the first place on the distribution of income, and on the related living conditions and demographical behaviour.

The advantage of regional input–output tables consists in that with their aid one may analyse the efficiency of productive activities, the product pattern and productive capacity, the directions of desirable development of a region, as well as the interrelation between and mutual effects on each other of the economic activities pursued within the region and outside of it — all these in such a complex way for which there has been no possibility so far. Regional tables are also valuable because they make it possible to observe not only the movements of goods within, from and to the region, but also the technological coefficients of, as well as the interrelations between, the individual branches or activities.

In consideration of all this, it has seemed desirable to start the elaboration of a system of regional tables primarily under the sponsorship of the Statistical Section of the Hungarian Economic Association, with the experimental drawing-up of an input–output table relating to a county. Let us, however, emphasize here: we do not believe that the county is necessarily the ideal unit for which such a table should be constructed. A regional division of the country according to economic criteria would perhaps be more suitable for the purpose. But since it was relatively easier to obtain the necessary data in a breakdown by counties and since,

* Apart from the five biggest towns, Hungary's territory is divided into 19 "counties". One of these is Vas, the fourth smallest in area, located on the Western confines of the country. Its area amounts to 3,340 sq.km (about 4 per cent of the total area of Hungary, its population in 1970 was 281,000 (3 per cent of the total population of the country).

in our present system of economic control and management, central and local leaderships are more interested in regional information which is grouped by counties, we have chosen this solution.

On the grounds of several considerations, we believed that Vas county afforded a suitable basis for elaborating an experimental table. They were the following:

1. It seemed expedient to choose a county with a "mixed structure" where experience may be gathered in the fields of both industry and agriculture. Vas county is excellently suited for this purpose, since here both industrial and agricultural production has an important role in economic life.

2. The industry of the county — in spite of the lack of mining and of industries producing basic materials — is relatively diversified, and several industrial branches are represented.

3. There are diversified economic connections between the various activities pursued within the country (as between agriculture and the food industry; forestry and the wood industry; the textile an the clothing industry), thus also the contents of the inner matrix of the input–output table is fairly "full".

4. The enterprises in the county are of a medium size; thus their data give sufficient opportunity for gathering experience, without the difficulties of collecting information through the administrative channels of large enterprises.

5. Finally, all types of industrial organizations can be found here (independent enterprises, plants belonging to enterprises located elsewhere, and even enterprises operating some plants elsewhere); hence, all kinds of problems connected with data collection were to turn up but — and this is also important for an experiment — they were not over-complicated. (Thus, for instance, most of the industrial plants were economic units with independent bookkeeping.)

The table has been elaborated only recently; thus, at present, we are able to report only on the general principles and methods applied, and on the experience gained in the course of its elaboration. At the end of this paper we publish the table itself, including the proportions calculated on its basis. Our next task will be to perform all the economic analyses allowed by the table. Some potential directions of such analyses will be mentioned briefly, without any claim to completeness.

In the input–output table for Vas county, the "gross" output of 1968 was shown for all productive branches ("gross output" means the value of outputs including turnover tax). In this table the first quadrant contains only the inputs of goods or services produced within the county; the county's inputs of goods and services produced elsewhere in Hungary or imported from abroad are shown in a single row (in the third quadrant of the table). In view of the experimental character of our table, we have found it expedient to consider all goods and services purchased both from elsewhere in Hungary or from abroad as "import" and, similarly, to consider as "exports" all goods and services sold anywhere outside of the county, independently of their origin and destination, and of whether they were imports or exports when considered on an economy-wide level. (Of course, when input–output tables for several or all counties are drawn up, this simplification will cease to be practicable, and the principles of grouping will have to be changed.)

In constructing the balance, both the "organizational" and the "regional" principles were applied. Data were collected according to the organizational principle, i.e., the units of observation were the units of economic activity like state-owned enterprises and farms, industrial and farming cooperatives, since in this way the collecting of data was the easiest. The table itself, however, follows the regional principle, containing the net inputs and outputs that took place within the county, independently of the organizational structure.

Much concern was given to the question of classifying the various economic activities. Considering the experimental character of the table, we believed that a simplification (in comparison to the economy-wide input–output tables) was justified even at the price that, in some cases, estimates had to be used based on the best economic information available. As regards the actual data used, they were collected by the Vas county section of the Hungarian Statistical Office.

Considering the local situation, it seemed expedient to apply the following breakdown:

Production

1. Engineering
2. Wood industry
3. Textile industry
4. Leather, fur and shoe industries
5. Textile clothing
6. Food industry
7. Other industries
8. Industry, total
9. Construction
10. Agriculture, forestry, water management
11. Transport and communications
12. Trade
13. Services (excluding banking and insurance)
14. Total of inputs produced within the county
15. Inputs of goods and services purchased from elsewhere (domestic or imported)
16. Total of material inputs

Primary inputs

Costs of live labour (wages, wage tax and social insurance contribution)
Depreciation allowance
Gain or loss
Turnover tax, charges on fixed and working assets
Complementary "imports" from the rest of Hungary or from abroad

Final demand

Non-productive consumption
Investment
"Exports" to the rest of Hungary and abroad

Our table covers the whole economy (both the socialist and the private sector) with the exception that "services" do not contain the "financial services". Later on, a way will have to be found for including banking and insurance services in the table. The "output value" of financial institutions might be obtained, e.g., by summing up their expenditures on materials and the wage bill. Subsequently, their incomes from interests, etc. would have to be stated and their "output value" divided between the various branches as users according to the proportions in which they contribute to the income of the banks.

The data needed for the scheme described above could be finally collected — although with difficulty and considerable amount of work — primarily from the balance sheets of the enterprises or cooperatives and — regarding investments and consumption — from the data supplied by the County section of the Statistical Office. The figures of the first quadrant were obtained, in the case of the socialist sector of industry and the building industry as well as of the state-owned farms, by a comprehensive collection of data. As regards farming cooperatives, we relied on samplings. Namely, as regards the farming cooperatives, in about 10 per cent of them we performed a systematic data collection regarding inputs and outputs. We generalized these representative findings, believing that the extent and direction of the relationships within cooperatives working under similar conditions and having a similar production structure are not likely to differ considerably. Of course, when generalizing our representative findings, the different production structures of the cooperatives were duly observed. The figures of all other sectors were obtained by estimates based in part on economy-wide proportions and partly on local information.

It already seems possible to draw some conclusions from the table constructed in this way. Of the total output values of the productive branches working in the county, more than one half comes from industry and about 30 per cent from agriculture. The industrial output of the county amounts to about 1.9 per cent of the Hungarian total, whereas the county's share in industrial employment is 2.4 per cent. This indicates unequivocally that the productivity of industrial labour is lower in the county than the national average. This is due partly to technological inferiority and partly to the product pattern of the county, which is more labour intensive than the national average.

The structure of production by economic branches is shown by Table 1.

We compared the aggregated sums of the third quadrant of the 1965 input–output table relating to Vas county with those of the economy-wide table of the same year. This comparison — made on the basis of "gross output", i.e., of output values including turnover tax — shows that the output of Vas county (characterized by the absence of any heavy industry of consequence, and by the relatively old age of the productive equipment) has to cover a relatively low rate of depreciation but, at the same time, it shows (with the exception of agriculture) an above-average rate of material inputs. Accordingly, the relatively high proportion of wages indicates that production in this county is relatively labour intensive.

Table 1

Production structure by branches of the national economy, 1968

Branches of the national economy	Value of gross output	
	million forints	per cent
Industry	6,536	51.4
Construction	934	7.3
Agriculture	3,812	30.0
Transport and communications	773	6.1
Trade	628	4.9
Services*	41	0.3
Total	12,724	100.0

* Without banking and insurance.

It follows from the particular condition of Vas county that its productive branches have to purchase more than one half of the goods needed for their production from the rest of Hungary or from abroad. There are some materials (e.g., fuel, with the exception of firewood, and certain industrial raw materials), all of which are "imported", and also some other inputs (e.g., components and spare parts) are mostly purchased from the rest of Hungary or from abroad. At the same time, the county "exports" (to the rest of Hungary and abroad) considerable quantities of general equipment for agriculture and the food industry, as well as certain

Table 2

Pattern of inputs as a percentage of output, 1968

Branches of the national economy	Material consumption		Depreciation allowance		Wages, other incomes and accumulation	
	as a percentage of gross output					
	Hungary	Vas county	Hungary	Vas county	Hungary	Vas county
Industry	67.0	68.1	4.1	2.6	28.9	29.3
Construction	48.8	56.3	3.1	1.2	48.1	42.5
Agriculture	47.7	45.2	4.7	3.7	47.6	51.1
Transport and communications	33.9	32.6	17.3	19.7	48.8	47.7
Trade	23.2*	10.9	2.2*	2.5	74.6*	86.6
Services**	.	36.0	.	1.6	.	62.4

* Domestic trade only.
** Excluding financial services (banking and insurance).

Table 3

Allocation of output, 1968

Branches of the national economy	Intermediate consumption		Final consumption		Investment	
	as a percentage of gross output					
	Hungary	Vas county	Hungary	Vas county	Hungary	Vas county
Industry	50.4	11.3	23.2	15.5	3.0	0.7
Construction	7.0	5.6	15.2	10.0	77.7	78.1
Agriculture	64.1	60.5	26.3	26.0	1.6	0.7
Transport and communications	61.6	43.4	27.0	21.0	2.4	2.0
Trade	25.0*	12.5	72.2*	86.5	1.3*	1.0
Services**	.	6.0	.	94.0	.	0.0

* Domestic trade only.
** Excluding banking and insurance.

products of the textile, shoemaking and food industries, and even some agricultural products. As regards the internal relationships between the branches working within the county, the most important of these exist between agriculture and the food industry, but also the amount of goods going from the textile to the clothing industry is significant.

Of the goods and services produced within the county, about 28 per cent are used for productive inputs and 72 per cent serve final consumption. As regards allocation, the proportions prevailing in Vas county differ widely from the national economic average.

Our work with the input–output table of Vas county must not be considered finished. Our primary aim was to reveal what problems of methodology and of data collecting one has to reckon with when constructing an input–output table for a county, arising from the diversity of the organizations supplying the data, and in what way, with how much work it is possible to solve these problems. Our experience has shown that, in spite of several problems, there is a possibility for drawing up county (or regional) tables of this type.

The next phase of our work will include the mathematical processing and evaluation of the table. By drawing on the experience gained with economy-wide input–output tables, we shall attempt to characterize the economy of Vas county, the mutual relations existing between the economic organizations active there and the extent of their dependence on activities taking place beyond its boundaries, in a way that has not been accessible so far, that is, with a new approach to regional problems.

FOURTH SESSION

MATHEMATICAL PROBLEMS IN THE CONSTRUCTION AND APPLICATION OF INPUT-OUTPUT TABLES

Chairman

DR. GYÖRGY SZAKOLCZAI

THE DEVELOPMENT OF THE INPUT–OUTPUT MODEL FOR THE PURPOSES OF NATIONAL ECONOMIC PLANNING

by

EDE THEISS

Input–output models characterize the relations between the various productive sectors and comprise a certain part of the system of interdependent relations existing within the national economy. This explains their particular importance for economic planning. When making decisions affecting the economy as a whole, we must know the whole system of quantitative economic relations prevailing in the national economy. This is possible only when we use a mathematical model covering the whole national economy, of which the input–output model constitutes but a part. Thus, the insertion of the input–output model into a comprehensive model of the whole national economy is a prime requirement both for elaborating a national economic plan and for the success of the economic policy.

It will be expedient to divide the economy-wide models into two groups. To the first belong the so-called mathematical models as, e.g., the input–output model, and the models of linear programming. To the second belong the so-called *econometric models,* consisting of simultaneous, stochastic systems of equations. These models enable us to measure uncertainty, this being an indispensable condition for the efficiency of economic policy decisions. At the same time, these models can be statistically verified. Insofar as we succeed in developing the input–output system with the aid of an econometric model, it will also become empirically verifiable, in contrast to the models of linear programming which cannot be verified statistically.

Any detailed treatment of developing the input–output model would require, in view of the vast international literature involved, an entire monograph. Therefore, with the given limitations, I will restrict myself to outlining the principles of development, discussing mainly such models as are instructive from the viewpoint of a socialist planned economy. A special aspect will be given to our investigations by the circumstance that we intend to discuss mainly the models allowing an econometric interpretation and, thus, statistical verification. Of course, the models will be discussed in a strongly simplified form, with emphasis laid on the major features.

To start with, let us briefly review the basic equations of the static input–output model. The first of these is:

$$\mathbf{x} = \mathbf{A}\mathbf{x} + \mathbf{y} \tag{1}$$

where $\mathbf{x}$ is the column vector of the output of the productive sectors (dimension: $n \times 1$), $\mathbf{A}$ is the matrix of technological coefficients ($n \times n$), and $\mathbf{y}$ is the column vector of final demand ($n \times 1$).

The equation of the primary factors of production is

$$\mathbf{z} = \mathbf{Cx} + \mathbf{h} \tag{2}$$

where $\mathbf{z}$ is the column vector of the primary factors $(m \times 1)$, $\mathbf{C}$ is an $(m \times n)$ matrix and $\mathbf{h}$ means the primary factors immediately used for final demand.

So far, we have expressed in the equations the amounts of inputs with the aid of such units on the basis of which their market price was equal to unity. If prices change, a $\mathbf{p}$ vector must be introduced for prices, for which the following equation will hold:

$$\mathbf{p}'^* = \mathbf{p}'^*\mathbf{A} + \mathbf{r}'^*\mathbf{C} + \mathbf{p}'^*_s \tag{3}$$

where $\mathbf{p}'^*$ is the price vector of the productive primary factors and $\mathbf{p}'_s$ is the vector of indirect taxes, various margins, and of price changes due to changes in profits.

As has been mentioned, the input–output model comprises but a fraction of economy-wide relations and thus it has to be complemented to obtain a comprehensive and verifiable model. This can be achieved in different ways: thus, e.g., we may introduce relations regarding final demand, primary productive factors, exports, etc. In this way, the model will comprise the relations of the economy that are important for planning decisions; thus it will become an effective tool for elaborating the plan. It must be emphasized that this objective can be attained only with the aid of a model consisting of a system of interdependent equations rather than with *ad hoc* analyses of the input–output system, because the consistency and verification of the latter are uncertain.

The above-outlined complementing of the static input–output model may be illustrated with the practical model serving to plan the annual budget in Norway.* It is based on a 130-sector input–output model. In a simplified form, the major equations of this model are the following:

a) $\mathbf{x} = \mathbf{A}_x\mathbf{x} + \mathbf{y}_c + \mathbf{y}_n$, where $\mathbf{x}$ is the column vector $(n \times 1)$ of sector outputs, $\mathbf{y}_c$ is that of household consumption and $\mathbf{y}_n$ that of non-consumption final demand;

b) $\mathbf{b} = \mathbf{A}_b\mathbf{x} + \mathbf{b}_c + \mathbf{b}_n$, where $\mathbf{b}$ is the column vector $(n \times 1)$ of imported products, $\mathbf{b}_c$ imports for household consumption, $\mathbf{b}_n$ imports serving other purposes;

c) $\mathbf{r} = \hat{\mathbf{p}}_w\mathbf{Wx}$, where $\mathbf{r}$ is the vector of various income categories (wages, entrepreneurial incomes, incomes of public bodies, indirect taxes, etc.) calculated at current prices, $\hat{\mathbf{p}}_w$ is the price index diagonal matrix for incomes, $\mathbf{W}$ is the matrix of income coefficients;

d) $\mathbf{c} = \mathbf{c}_0 + \mathbf{D}\left(\frac{1}{\pi}\mathbf{r} - \mathbf{r}_0\right) + \mathbf{N}\left(\frac{1}{\pi}\mathbf{p} - \mathbf{i}_c\right)$, where $\mathbf{c} = \begin{bmatrix}\mathbf{y}_c\\ \mathbf{b}_c\end{bmatrix}$ the vector of household consumption, π is the price index for consumption goods, $\mathbf{i}_c$ is a unit column vector, $\mathbf{D}$ means the marginal propensities to consume, and $\mathbf{N}$ is the matrix of the consumer price coefficients;

* *Macroeconomic Models for Planning and Policy Making*, pp. 161–171. United Nations, Geneva 1967.

e) $\mathbf{p}'^*_x = \mathbf{p}'^*_x\mathbf{A}_x + \mathbf{p}'^*_b\mathbf{A}_b + \mathbf{p}'^*_w\mathbf{W}$ where $\mathbf{p}'^*_x$ is the price index vector of all productive sectors and $\mathbf{p}'^*_b$ is the price index vector of imports.

In this model, investments, consumption other than private, import prices, and the data of wages and entrepreneurial profits are exogenous variables. The endogenous variables are: the output of the sectors, household consumption and imports (all detailed by products), the changes in the incomes of workers and entrepreneurs, and the various prices.

The making of the static input–output model dynamic is based on accounting for investments in an explicit way. Namely, investment is both a part of production and a factor of its expansion. This dual role has been elaborately cleared up by the aggregate model developed by Harrod and Domar (in the following: H–D). This may be considered as a one-sector input–output model. Thus, in several respects the dynamic input–output model can be traced back to the basic relations of the H–D model. These are summed up in the following equations.

The H–D model assumes a constant linear relationship between the K_t stocks of capital and the x_t production

$$K_t = \varkappa x_t$$

On the above basis, investments can be described as follows:

$$i_t = K_{t+1} - K_t = \varkappa(x_{t+1} - x_t) \tag{4}$$

Here $\varkappa$ is the ratio of capital and output. The equation connects the volume of investment directly with the growth of production. But in reality investment serves in the first place to increase productive capacity, k_t, expressed in the following equation: $i_t = \varkappa(k_{t+1} - k_t)$. Yet even this equation simplifies the economic background of investments too rigidly. Namely, the building up to full capacity takes place in more than one step. Entrepreneurial behaviour is better approximated in this respect, according to the "flexible" acceleration principle by the following equation:*

$$i_t = \alpha\varkappa(x_{t-1} + \beta - k_t) \tag{5}$$

This equation is based on the consideration that the investment decision of the entrepreneur regarding a given year must have been made about the end of the preceding year, when only the volume of production of that year is known. Let us assume that the entrepreneur decides to increase capacity by β. This growth of capacity, however, is intended to cover only a certain α part of the additional demand arising for the product in the year in question, in view of the uncertainty factor. This is why we have inserted a factor $\alpha(\alpha < 1)$ into equation (5). On the basis of equations (4) and (5) we may write:

$$i_t = \alpha\varkappa(x_{t-1} - x_{t-2}) + (1 - \alpha)i_{t-1}$$

* Chenery, H. G.: Overcapacity and Acceleration Principle. *Econometrica*, Vol. XX, pp. 1—28, 1958.

According to the H–D model, in a closed economy the following equation will hold:

$$x_t = c_t + i_t\,; \quad c_t = (1-\pi)x_t\,; \quad i_t = \pi x_t$$

Utilizing the above equations, we obtain:

$$i_t - \left(1 - \alpha - \frac{\alpha\varkappa}{\pi}\right) i_{t-1} + \frac{\alpha\varkappa}{\pi}\, i_{t-2} = 0$$

The characteristic equation of the dynamic process expressed by the preceding equation is:

$$\lambda^2 - \left(1 - \alpha - \frac{\alpha\varkappa}{\pi}\right) \lambda + \frac{\alpha\varkappa}{\pi} = 0$$

If we now break down the H–D model into sectors, the dynamic input–output model is obtained, the basic equation of which is

$$\mathbf{x}_t = \mathbf{A}\mathbf{x}_t + \mathbf{i}_t + \mathbf{c}_t + \mathbf{g}_t + \mathbf{e}_t \tag{6}$$

where $\mathbf{i}_t$ is the vector of investments by sectors, $\mathbf{c}_t$ that of household consumption, $\mathbf{g}_t$ of public consumption and $\mathbf{e}_t$ of exports. According to (4) we can write

$$\mathbf{i}_t = \mathbf{B}(\mathbf{k}_{t+1} - \mathbf{k}_t) \tag{7}$$

B is here a matrix of $(n \times n)$ dimension, consisting of the ratios of investment to output, and $\mathbf{k}_t$ is the column vector of capacities by sectors. This investment matrix strongly simplifies reality: as regards the relation of investment to production, it considers volume variables only. It neglects the time lags due to the implementation of investments, as well as the effects of prices, of technological progress and of financial factors.

Based on the preceding exposition, let us now briefly outline the *model of balanced economic growth,* which is a form of the improved dynamic input–output model most frequently applied in economic planning. We assume that proper decisions of economic policy secure an economic growth *free of fluctuations.* This can be attained with a *short-term input–output* model, for the discussion of which we have no space here. For the sake of simplicity, we assume that economic growth is a linear function of time. In this case, if we denote the years of the plan period by $t = 0, 1, \ldots, t, \ldots, f$, then the vector of investments in year t will be:

$$\mathbf{i}_t = \mathbf{i}_0 + \frac{t}{f}(\mathbf{i}_f - \mathbf{i}_0) \tag{8}$$

Here $\mathbf{i}_0$ and $\mathbf{i}_f$ are the vectors of investments in the initial year and in the final year, respectively. Since in the case of linear economic growth the investments following upon each other constitute an arithmetic series, we may write:

$$\sum_{t=0}^{f-1} \mathbf{i}_t = \frac{1}{2}(\mathbf{i}_0 + \mathbf{i}_{t-1}) = \frac{1}{2}(f+1)\,\mathbf{i}_0 + \frac{1}{2}(f-1)\,\mathbf{i}_f \tag{9}$$

In the case of a balanced growth we may assume that — *at least in the last plan year* — capacity is equal to output. Thus we can write:*

$$\sum_{t=0}^{f-1} \mathbf{i}_t = \mathbf{B}(\mathbf{k}_f - \mathbf{k}_0) = \mathbf{B}(\mathbf{x}_f - \mathbf{x}_0)$$

From this, and by using equations (6) and (9), we may obtain the production vector of the last plan year:

$$\mathbf{x}_f = \left(\mathbf{A} + \frac{2}{f-1}\mathbf{B}\right)\mathbf{x}_f + \mathbf{c}_f + \mathbf{g}_f + \mathbf{e}_f - \frac{2}{f-1}\mathbf{B}\mathbf{x}_0 - \frac{f+1}{f-1}\mathbf{i}_0 \qquad (10)$$

where $\left(\mathbf{A} + \frac{2}{f-1}\mathbf{B}\right)$ is the matrix of balanced growth.

This strongly simplified dynamic model can be used for constructing an optimum economic plan where the optimum criterion consists in maximizing the value of $\mathbf{c}_f$. The maximum must be determined under the constraint of equation (10). At the same time, other constraints must also be taken into account in the context of economic growth. Such as, e.g., the balance of foreign trade

$$\gamma_t^* \mathbf{x}_t = \mathbf{s}_n^* \mathbf{e}_f + \varepsilon$$

where the left side means total imports and the right side total exports, $\mathbf{s}_n^*$ being a summarizing vector and ε some equalizing exogenous constant, e.g., the size of capital imports. Additional constraints relate to the utilization of manpower, to financing investments, etc., which cannot be discussed here in greater detail. It must be emphasized that *an economy-wide plan based on such — essentially linear — relationships cannot claim giving an optimum.* First, important *non-linear relationships* are missing from the model. Second, the preference function determining the criterion of maximum is all too primitive. Nevertheless, dynamic models, similar to the one here outlined, have served — with proper complementing — as a starting base of *medium-term* planning in several countries.

So far we could review only some of the major possibilities of improving the dynamic input–output model, as applied in practice. A continuous improvement of such a model was carried on by the Central Planning Office of the Netherlands, where two variants were elaborated. The first is the so-called *short-term stabilization model,* improved in the form of several versions ever since 1955, which was proved highly suitable in preparing short-term economic policy measures. Similar models have been applied also in other countries, the largest being the *Brookings model* in the USA. Another variant of improving the dynamic input–output model serves for *long-term planning and prognosis.* This model is much more aggregated in structure than the short-term variant. A combination of the two variants has also proved to be useful in practice. The parameters and endogenous variables deter-

* Heesterman, A. R. G.: *Forecasting Models for National Economic Planning.* Dordrecht 1970.

mined with the aid of the long-term model are mostly average values which can be desaggregated into their components with the aid of the short-term model, and their consistency can be checked. Thus, it also becomes possible to establish what effects the measures elaborated by the aid of the aggregated model exert on the various economic sectors. Finally, it should also be noted that an economic policy project determined on the basis of a long-term aggregated model may be compatible with several short-term model variants. Considering the latter, one may establish different partial measures and select the most suitable one.

To illustrate how dynamic input–output models can be further developed in the framework of a socialist planned economy, we shall briefly review the latest model of the Soviet Union of this character.* The main equations of the model are as follows:

a) $$X_{it} = \sum_j a_{ijt} X_{jt} + \sum_j b_{ijt} X_{jt} + P_{it}$$

where X_{it} is the total output of sector i in year t, X_{jt} is that of sector j, when $i, j = 1, 2, \ldots, n$; and $t = 1, 2, \ldots, N$; P_{it} is the final output of sector i excluding the production of new fixed capital; a_{ijt} are the technological coefficients in the input–output system, and b_{ijt} is the part of the output of sector i used in sector j for the production of new fixed capital.

b) $$P_{it} = Y_{it} + S_{it}(Y_t - Y_{t-1}) + G_{it} X_{it} + D_{it}$$

where Y_{it} is the consumption by households from the output of sector i, and Y_t is the total consumption by the population; S_{it} is the part of the output of sector i to be turned into fixed capital used in order to increase the total consumption of population; G_{it} is the part of the final output of sector i proportionate with the volume of X_{it}, and D_{it} is the component of the output of sector i determined by exogenous factors.

c) $$Y_{it} = Y_{i(t-1)} + C_{it}(Y - Y_{t-1})$$

where C_{it} is the proportion of planned growth in total consumption to be covered by sector i;

$$\left(\sum_i C_{it} = 1, \ Y_t = \sum_i Y_{it}\right)$$

d) $$K_{jt} = (1 + \psi_{jt})[(\Phi_{j(t+1} - \Phi_{jt}) + W_{jt}\Phi_{jt}]$$

where K_{jt} is the stock of new fixed assets in sector j, ψ_{jt} is the ratio of the new increment of the volume of unfinished investments to the volume of finished new stock, W_{jt} is the coefficient of depreciation, Φ_{jt} is the stock of fixed capital in sector j.

e) $$f_{jt}(X_{jt} - X_{j(t-1)}) = Q_j(\Phi_{j(t+1)} - \Phi_{jt}) + (1 - Q_j)(\Phi_{jt} - \Phi_{j(t-1)}),$$

* *Long-Term Planning.* United Nations, New York, 1971.

where f_{jt} is the intensity coefficient of applying the new fixed capital in sector j, Q_j is the ratio of the mean annual increase to the annual increase of the stock of fixed capital in sector j.

f) $$T_t = \sum_i \tau_{it} X_{it}$$

where T_t is the total volume of labour employed and τ_{it} is the productivity of labour in sector i.

In one alternative of the above system of equations the variables $Y_1, Y_2, \ldots, Y_N$ are exogenous; in another alternative it is the variables $T_1, T_2, \ldots, T_N$ that are exogenous.

In this context we mention the dynamic model of Lange* with the aid of which the optimum allocation of investments among sectors can be determined. In connection with this model, the volume of investments in sector j can be expressed as follows:

$$i_j = \sum_{i=1}^{n} b_{ij} \Delta x_j, \quad \text{or} \quad \left(\sum_i b_{ij}\right)^{-1} = \Delta x_j / i_j = \beta_j$$

This latter β_j quotient is Lange's sectoral output–investment ratio. If the total volume of investments in the economy is indicated by i, the quotient $\lambda_j = i_j/i$ characterizes the distribution of investments by sectors. The optimum is obtained, according to Lange, by determining the maximum of the national-economic investment ratio

$$\beta = \sum_{j=1}^{n} \lambda_j \beta_j$$

for the case when in every sector a certain minimum remains for non-productive consumption.

In the model developments reviewed so far prices did not figure explicitly. In a realistic dynamic model, of course, the interrelations due to price developments must be also given a proper place. To illustrate this, we will briefly outline the basic equation of Johansen** which has been used with good results, among others, for drawing up long-term prognoses in Norway. The model comprises 22 sectors. From these sectors 1–19 comprise household and productive consumption and exports. In sector 20 construction, in sector 21 the production of other investment goods and in sector 22 the production of non-specified goods are included. The equations of the model are as follows:

a) $$X_i = A_i L_i^{\gamma_i} K_i^{\beta_i} e^{\varepsilon_{it}}, \qquad (i = 1, 2, \ldots, 20)$$

* Lange, O.: Output–Investment Ratio and Input–Output Analysis. *Econometrica*, Vol. XXVIII, pp. 319–324, 1960.

** Johansen, L. in *Long-Term Planning*, pp. 48–50. United Nations, New York 1971.

where X_i is total production, L_i is labour employed, K_i is the stock of productive capital in sector i. The equation corresponds to a Cobb–Douglas type production function with the technological progress involved. $A_i, \gamma_i, \beta_i, \varepsilon_i$ are constant parameters.

b) $$X_{ij} = a_{ij}X_j, \qquad (i, j = 1, 2, \ldots, 22)$$

These equations determine the input coefficients.

c) $$M_i = \mu_i X_i, \qquad (i = 1, 2, \ldots, 22)$$

Here non-competitive imports are related to the volume of production.

d) $$X_i = \sum_{i=1}^{22} X_{ij} + C_i + Z_i \, (i = 1, 2, \ldots, 19)$$

This equation gives the distribution of the production of sector i among the productive sectors; C_i corresponds to household consumption and Z_i to exports. Household consumption:

$$C_i = C(P_1, \ldots, P_{19}, P_0 y)$$

is a function of domestic prices, of the non-competitive import price level P_0 and of the per capita average of total consumption y.

e) $$X_{20} = \sum_{j=1}^{20} D_{B_j} + \sum_{i=1}^{20} \frac{dK_{B_i}}{dt} + Z_{20}$$

where D_{B_j} is the depreciation coefficient of buildings, $K_{B_i} = H_i K_i$ is the stock of buildings, K_i being the total stock of capital goods in sector i and H_i a constant parameter.

f) $$X_{21} = \sum_{j=1}^{20} D_{M_j} + \sum_{i=1}^{20} \frac{dK_{M_i}}{dt} + Z_{21}$$

This is analogous to the equation under e), but relating to the capital goods other than buildings; D_{M_j} is the depreciation coefficient, $K_{M_i} = (1 - H_i)K_i$ is the stock of these goods.

g) $$X_{22} = \sum_{j=1}^{20} X_{22j} + Z_{22}$$

This equation determines the distribution of non-specified production.

When economic equilibrium prevails, marginal return of each factor of production equals the costs of these factors. This is expressed by the following equations:

h) $$\gamma_i P_i^* X_i = W_i L_i, \quad \text{and} \quad \beta_i P_i^* X_i = Q_i K_i$$

where P_i^* is the price of products less the inputs of materials and taxes, W_i is the wage level and Q_i the charge for using assets in sector i.

Exogenous variables of the model are: the total capital stock, total number of those employed, number of population, exogenous demand, and the price level of the non-competitive import goods.

Endogenous variables are: the distribution of capital and labour by sectors; employment, prices and production in the individual sectors, the size of capital rent, the volume of household consumption and its distribution by products, and the quantities of imported goods.

It will be obvious from the above that in a planned economy short-, medium- and long-term models are all applied in various ways. In each of them the input–output systems play an important role as sub-models constructed according to several variants. The planning models are going to constitute foundations for economic-policy decisions. Therefore, in constructing them the principles of statistics based on decision theory should be employed, in order to account for the influence of uncertainties in making decisions; otherwise the decisions cannot yield wholly satisfactory results. This is why the use of econometric models or of stochastic macro-economic models is particularly important. Here the medium-term models have a central role. In constructing them, the aggregation of the model is a problem closely related to the input–output sub-model. The solution of this problem as well as the determination of the parameters are provided by the principles of decision theory.

Relying on these, in solving the problem of aggregation the requirement of successive approximation should be observed. It is therefore expedient to work out a whole series of stochastic macro-models, the disaggregation of which gradually increases, starting from a basic model with relatively few sectors. A further requirement is that every member of such a series of models should comprise all essential interrelations of the economy, in a breakdown corresponding to the disaggregation applied. It must be pointed out that it is not expedient to increase disaggregation beyond a certain degree. After having reached a certain degree of disaggregation, it will be a better procedure for obtaining further details to work out sub-models comprising only one sector or just a few, and subordinate them to the global model. With the aid of such sub-models, the quantitative conditions of economic optimum can be much more realistically determined than by disaggregation of the increased model. Originally, the economic optimum computations based on linear programming started from micro-economic enterprise models. Later on, however, it became more and more obvious that optimal decisions based on micro-models are — owing to the deficient quantitative knowledge of preferences and relations underlying them — not always sufficiently realistic. Therefore, large enterprises made efforts to find, instead of the optimum, so-called "satisfying" solutions; in this case, extreme conditions have no place in the economic model, so the solutions of the model equations are more realistic.* Obviously, this procedure can be also frequently used for planning in the case of sub-models.

* Simon, H. A.: *Models of Man*. New York 1957.

Finally, in order to illustrate how the considerations reviewed here are realized in practice, let us briefly review the econometric model of the French medium-term planning. In the preparation of the fifth French national economic plan covering the period 1965–1970, the details of the economic equilibrium were established in physical, i. e., volume terms, calculated with the aid of a series of models gradually desaggregated and based on a dynamized input–output scheme. Subsequently, an equilibrium of valuation and finances was also established, accounting for price changes but lacking a strict mathematical formulation. The experiences gained in the course of implementing the fifth French plan have shown that it is necessary to determine the equilibrium in physical and value terms *simultaneously*, and this can be done only on the basis of a *completely formalized mathematical model*, which, in its turn, determines also the financial conditions of investments. This has led to the construction of the so-called *physical-financial (FIFI) model*,* as a basis for the sixth plan of 1971–1975. This model comprises about 1,500 equations, in a completely formalized manner, so that solutions may be obtained in a very short time with up-to-date computers. In connection with the construction of the physical equilibrium, the model has an input–output table broken down into 65 sectors. For the establishment of the financial equilibrium, prices as a system of endogenous variables broken down to seven economic sectors are calculated by iterative procedure. In accordance with the various subsequent phases of this procedure, the input–output table must be recalculated several times which, with computers, can be quickly performed. Moreover, the model makes possible the computation of several variants of economic policy, which is of prime importance for the appraisal of economic policy decisions.

In France, parallel with medium-term models, also *long-term modelling* is elaborated. In its framework an input–output table is constructed which comprises the technological coefficients of new products and new production technologies expected to be used widely in the next plan period (i.e., following the sixth one). Though these innovations are now but in the experimental stage, some partial experiences permit the evaluation of their future roles. It seems that this most up-to-date type of dynamization of input–output tables reflects not only the existing technology and its expected development in the near future, but also *structural transformations in the longer run, as a result of technological progress.*

* Courbis, R.: *The Physico-Financial Medium-Term Economic Projection Model (FIFI)*. United Nations ECE, First Seminar on Mathematical Methods and Computer Techniques, Varna 1970.

SOME REMARKS ON THE THEORY OF THE RAS METHOD

by

PÉTER GLATTFELDER and PÁL VÁCZI

The RAS method is one of the possible tools of forecasting input–output schemes. Both its Cambridge authors* and its Hungarian practitioners** have used it for several purposes in theoretical and practical research. The method has become widely used the world over. The algorithm does not originate with Stones and his colleagues but with W. E. Deming,*** and its logical structure, simplicity and the diverse possibilities of its application seem to have contributed to its popularity. Several suggestions have been made for its further development. Among such contributions, most attention has been drawn by the one investigating the development, as a function of time, of certain important, "crucial" coefficients individually, then extending the RAS algorithm to the other, "less relevant" coefficients and, finally, combining the results of the two sets of forecasts.

In the present paper we are attempting a generalization of the RAS method. Our thesis is the following: the method, as a tool of forecasting, assumes, by implication, an exponential time-function of the technological coefficients. In view of the fact that in practice there is nothing to prove the correctness of this assumption (indeed some research, e.g., by Gy. Szakolczai and colleagues**** decidedly contradict it), it seems expedient to extend the RAS method, or other

* The primary sources are Stone, R. and Brown, A.: A Long-Term Growth Model for the British Economy. In the volume *Europe's Future in Figures*, ed. by R. C. Geary, North Holland Publishing Co., Amsterdam 1966; and Stone, R., Bates, J. and Bacharach, M.: *A Programme for Growth. Input–Output Relationships 1954–1966.* University of Cambridge, 1963.

** For example, see Glattfelder, P.: A Nehézipari Minisztérium ágazati kapcsolati modelljének előrebecslése (A forecast relating to the input–output model of the Ministry of Heavy Industry). *Statisztikai Szemle*, Vol. 47, No. 3, pp. 282–297, 1969; Kupcsik, J. and Rácz, A.: Az ágazati kapcsolati mérlegek dinamikai összeha- sonlítása (Dynamic comparison of input–output tables). *Statisztikai Szemle*, Vol. 47, No. 4, pp. 335–368, 1969; Lipták, T.: A RAS módszer kiterjesztése hármas bontású áramlásokra (An extension of the RAS method to tripartite flows). A working paper prepared for the Hungarian Institute of Economic and Market Research, 1966; Németh, S. and Pór, A.: Az ÁKM koefficiensszámításainak egyik módszeréről (On one of the methods of calculating input–output coefficients). A working paper of the Hungarian National Planning Office, Budapest 1968.

*** Deming, W. E.: *Statistical Adjustment of Data.* Wiley, New York 1943.

**** Az ártervezés ökonometriai modellje (The econometric model of price planning). The publications of the National Price Office and "INFELOR" (Enterprise for Systems Engineering), Budapest 1968–1971.

solutions relying on its basic idea, to cases where the coefficients to be forecast show a linear change through time, or at least some trend approaching it.

Our research work has resulted in the devising of a procedure that applies a non-iterative, direct algorithm as distinct from the original Stone–Brown variant. Experimental calculations have proved that the results obtained by this procedure are not inferior to those obtained with the original RAS method.

In the first part of this paper we are defining a general mathematical problem consisting in forecasting (under certain conditions) the A_{ij} technological coefficients of an input–output table. These conditions, although inspired by those assumed in the original RAS method, are more general.

The second part deals with two special cases within the general system. We shall try to prove that, whereas by assuming an exponential time-function of the technological coefficients one is led automatically to the RAS method, the assumption of a linear function supplies a direct, non-iterative algorithm of forecasting.

In the third part we report on a procedure which approximates the iterative algorithm of the RAS method by a direct one.

1. THE MATHEMATICAL FORMULATION OF THE PROBLEM

Let us apply the following system of symbols: italics denote a vector or a vector-scalar function, while bold-face types denote a matrix, or a tensor-scalar function with double subscript. The sign $\hat{T}$ means a diagonal matrix, **1** means the summarizing vector. In this paper, the dimension of the quantities qualified by indices is n. When they are functions of time, this is expressed by a superscript when the point of time is fixed, e.g., $\mathbf{A}(t_0) = \mathbf{A}^0$.

Let us determine $\mathbf{A}(t)$ when:

I. $\mathbf{A}^0$, $\mathbf{a}(t)$ and $\mathbf{b}(t)$ are known,

II. the equations

$$\mathbf{A}(t)\mathbf{1} = \mathbf{a}(t) \tag{1.1}$$

$$\mathbf{A}^{\mathrm{T}}(t)\mathbf{1} = \mathbf{b}(t) \tag{1.2}$$

$$\mathbf{a}^*(t)\mathbf{1} = \mathbf{b}^*(t)\mathbf{1} \tag{1.3}$$

are true and

III. the relations

$$\mathbf{A}(t) \geq \mathbf{0} \tag{1.4}$$

$$\mathbf{a}(t),\ \mathbf{b}(t) > \mathbf{0} \tag{1.5}$$

are fulfilled (for each component).

In general, Conditions I, II and III do not determine $\mathbf{A}(t)$ unequivocally. In order to reduce the number of the feasible $\mathbf{A}(t)$-s, we introduce additional restrictions which — as will be seen — do not exclude economically interpretable solutions.

Condition II makes it possible to determine a $2n$ number of scalar-scalar (in the following "scalar") functions; from among these only $(2n - 1)$ are independent (because of 1.3). $\mathbf{A}(t)$ has n lines and n columns. Therefore, from among the $2n$ functions, we assign n functions to the columns of $\mathbf{A}(t)$, since nothing justifies preferring any row(s) or column(s). We want, therefore, that a fourth condition should be also satisfied namely that

IV. the form of any component of $\mathbf{A}(t)$ be only

$$A_{ij}(t) = A_{ij}\left(A_{ij}^0, x_i(t), y_j(t)\right), \tag{1.6}$$

where $x_i(t)$ and $y_j(t)$ are the functions assigned to the i-th or j-th column, respectively.

Obviously, $\mathbf{A}(t)$ cannot depend on t_0, only on $t - t_0$ and on $\mathbf{A}^0$; else, when starting from $t_1 \neq t_0$, we could obtain a different, and uninterpretable, $\mathbf{A}(t)$. At the same time, $\mathbf{A}(t)$ can be obtained also by determining $\mathbf{A}^1$ from $\mathbf{A}^0$ and $t_1 - t_0$ and afterwards determining $\mathbf{A}(t)$ from $\mathbf{A}^1$, $t - t_1$ where $t_1 = t_0 + \lambda(t - t_0)$; $0 \leq \lambda \leq 1$. Mathematically, this can be formulated as a functional equation:

$$\mathbf{A}(t) = \mathbf{A}(\mathbf{A}^0, t - t_0) = \mathbf{A}\left(\mathbf{A}(\mathbf{A}^0, \lambda(t - t_0)), (1 - \lambda)(t - t_0)\right). \tag{1.7}$$

Since t_0 may be chosen optionally, let us choose the starting point of time $t_0 = 0$.

Considering Condition IV, we must establish a further constraint:

V. Any component of $\mathbf{A}(t)$ must satisfy the functional equation

$$A_{ij}(A_{ij}^0, g_{ij}(t)) = A_{ij}(A_{ij}(A^0, g_{ij}(\lambda t)), g_{ij}((1 - \lambda)t)), \tag{1.8}$$

where

$$g_{ij}(t) = f(x_i(t), y_j(t)). \tag{1.9}$$

Thus, the problem consists in determining under Conditions I–V.

2. THE CASE OF LINEARITY AND THAT OF EXPONENTIALITY (RAS)

In this section we are dealing with two types of solutions to our problem, namely:

a) $$A_{ij}\left(A_{ij}^0, g_{ij}(t)\right) = A_{ij}\left(A_{ij}^0 + g_{ij}(t)\right) \tag{2.1}$$

b) $$A_{ij}\left(A_{ij}^0, g_{ij}(t)\right) = A_{ij}\left(A_{ij}^0\, g_{ij}(t)\right) \tag{2.2}$$

As will be seen, the time function of $A_{ij}(t)$ is linear in Case (2.1), and exponential in Case (2.2).

a. The linear case

The form of the functional equation (1.8) established as Condition V is now

$$A_{ij}(A_{ij}^0 + g_{ij}(t)) = A_{ij}(A_{ij}(A_{ij}^0 + g_{ij}(\lambda t)) + g_{ij}((1-\lambda)t)). \tag{2.3}$$

The solution of (2.3) is, on the assumption of the first lemma in the Appendix,

$$A_{ij}(t) = A_{ij}^0 + \gamma_{ij} t, \tag{2.4}$$

where γ_{ij} is constant. Since $A_{ij}(t)$ is computed according to (2.4), the relations (1.1) and (1.2) can be fulfilled only when $a_i(t)$ and $b_j(t)$ are linear functions, that is, when

$$a_i(t) = a_i^0 + u_i t \tag{2.5}$$

$$b_j(t) = b_j^0 + v_j t. \tag{2.6}$$

In the following, let us assume that the relations (2.5) and (2.6) are fulfilled. Because of Condition IV,

$$\gamma_{ij} = x_i + y_j \tag{2.7}$$

where x_i, y_j are constant. In order to determine them, let us substitute (2.7) into (2.4):

$$A_{ij}(t) = A_{ij}^0 + (x_i + y_j)t, \tag{2.8}$$

then substitute (2.5), (2.6) and (2.8) into (1.1) and (1.2)

$$\sum_{j=1}^{n} (A_{ij}^0 + (x_i + y_j)t) = a_i^0 + u_i t \tag{2.9}$$

$$\sum_{i=1}^{n} (A_{ij}^0 + (x_i + y_j)t) = b_j^0 + v_j t. \tag{2.10}$$

Since $\sum_{=1}^{n} A_{ij}^0 = a_i^0$ and $\sum_{j=1}^{n} A_{ij}^0 = b_j^0$, we obtain that

$$nx_i + \sum_{j=1}^{n} y_j = u_i, \tag{2.11}$$

$$\sum_{i=1}^{n} x_i + my_j = v_j. \tag{2.12}$$

When $\mathbf{A}^0$ contains zero elements as well and we want them to remain unchanged, we write, instead of (2.11) and (2.12), the following:

$$n_i x_i + \sum_{\substack{j=1 \\ A_{ij} \neq 0}}^{n} y_j = u_i \tag{2.11/a}$$

$$\sum_{\substack{i=1 \\ A_{ij} \neq 0}}^{n} x_i + m_j y_j = v_j \tag{2.12/a}$$

where

$$n_i = \sum_{\substack{j=1 \\ A_{ij} \neq 0}}^{n} 1, \qquad m_j = \sum_{\substack{i=1 \\ A_{ij} \neq 0}}^{n} 1.$$

The linear equation system (2.11), (2.12) is of the rank $(n - 1)$, thus we are free to choose one of the x_i-s and y_j-s. The problem is solved by substituting the constants x_i, y_j (into (2.8)

b. The exponential, or RAS case

The functional equation (1.8) now has the form of

$$A_{ij}\big(A_{ij}^0 g_{ij}(t)\big) = A_{ij}\big(A_{ij}(A_{ij}^0 g_{ij}(\lambda t))\, g((1-\lambda)\,t)\big)\,. \tag{2.13}$$

The solution of (2.13) is, according to the second lemma of the Appendix, the following:

$$A_{ij}(t) = A_{ij}^0 e^{\gamma_{ij} t}, \tag{2.14}$$

where $\gamma_{ij} t$ is constant. It can be directly seen from (2.14) that (1.1) and (1.2) may be fulfilled only when $a_i(t)$, $b_j(t)$ are linear combinations of exponential functions having a defined exponent, that is,

$$a_i(t) = \sum_{j=1}^{n} \alpha_{ij} e^{\beta_{ij} t}, \tag{2.15}$$

$$b_j(t) = \sum_{i=1}^{n} \alpha_{ij} e^{\beta_{ij} t}. \tag{2.16}$$

In view of (1.1) and (1.2) this can be fulfilled only when

$$\alpha_{ij} = A_{ij}^0 \tag{2.17}$$

$$\beta_{ij} = \gamma_{ij} \tag{2.18}$$

that is, when $A_{ij}(t)$ is produced in an ordinary manner.

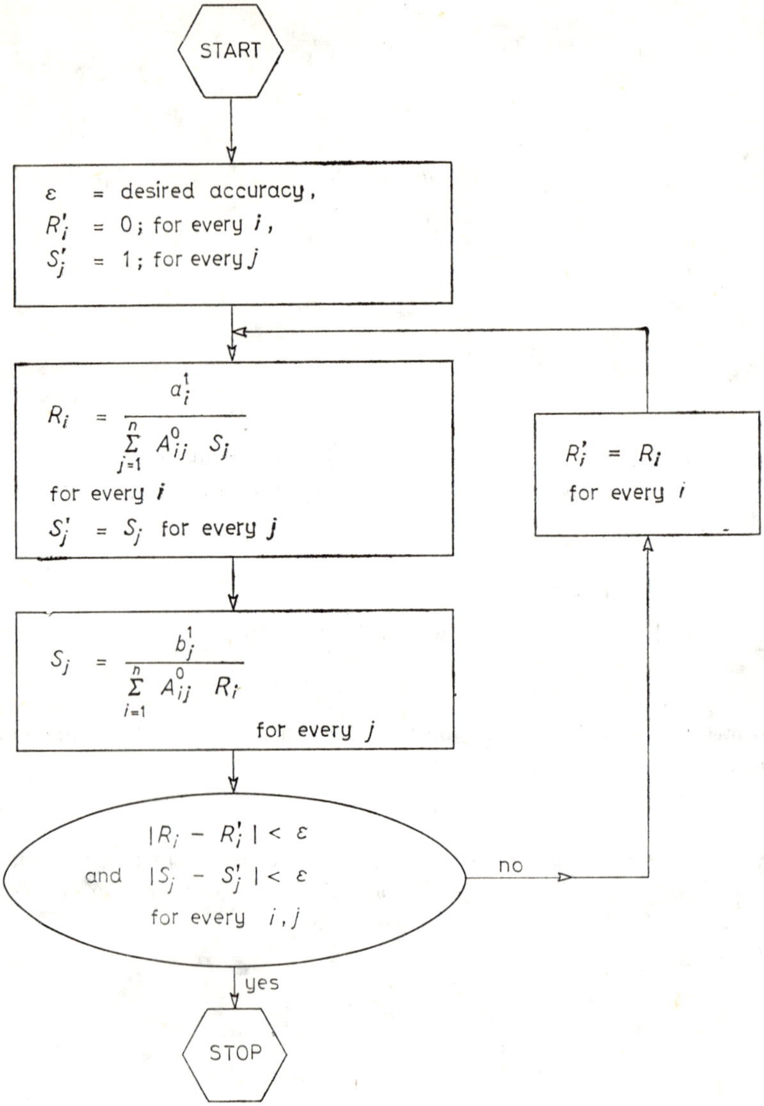
START
ε = desired accuracy,
R'_i = 0; for every i,
S'_j = 1; for every j
R_i = a_i^1 / Σ_{j=1}^n A_ij^0 S_j
for every i
S'_j = S_j for every j
S_j = b_j^1 / Σ_{i=1}^n A_ij^0 R_i
for every j
|R_i − R'_i| < ε
and |S_j − S'_j| < ε
for every i, j
no
R'_i = R_i
for every i
yes
STOP

Fig. 1

It occurs very frequently that the values of $a_i(t)$ and $b_j(t)$ are known only in relation to the points $t = 0$ and $t = t_1$, that is, we know only a_i^0, a_i^1, b_j^0 and b_j^1. Even in this case it is possible to determine $A_{ij}(t)$. Namely, because of Condition IV, the

$$\gamma_{ij} = x_i + y_j \tag{2.19}$$

prevails even in this case.

Substituting (2.19) for (2.14) we obtain

$$A_{ij}(t) = A_{ij}^0 e^{(x_i+y_j)t}, \tag{2.20}$$

where x_i and y_j are constants. Substituting (2.20) for (1.1) and (1.2) we obtain for $t = t_1$

$$\sum_{j=1}^{n} A_{ij}^0 e^{(x_i+y_j)t_1} = a_i^1 \tag{2.21}$$

$$\sum_{i=1}^{n} A_{ij}^0 e^{(x_i+y_j)t_1} = b_j^1 . \tag{2.22}$$

By introducing the notation

$$R_i = e^{x_i t_1} \tag{2.23}$$

$$S_j = e^{y_j t_1} \tag{2.24}$$

from (2.21) and (2.22) we obtain the well-known RAS equations:*

$$\sum_{j=1}^{n} R_i A_{ij}^0 S_j = a_i^1 \tag{2.25}$$

$$\sum_{i=1}^{n} R_i A_{ij}^0 S_j = b_j^1 . \tag{2.26}$$

The solution of the RAS equation may be determined with the aid of an iterative algorithm called the "RAS" method. The logical structure of this method is presented in the flow chart of Fig. 1.

In the knowledge of R_i and S_j it is now easy to obtain x_i, y_j and $A_{ij}(t)$ with the aid of (2.23), (2.24) and (2.20):

$$x_i = \ln (R_i)/t_1 \tag{2.27}$$

$$y_i = \ln (S_j)/t_1 \tag{2.28}$$

$$A_{ij}(t) = A_{ij}^0 e^{\ln (R_i S_j) t/t_1} = A_{ij}^0 (R_i S_j)^{t/t_1} . \tag{2.29}$$

According to our results, the application of the RAS method does not produce correct results in all cases of $\mathbf{a}(t)$ and $\mathbf{b}(t)$. A necessary condition for correctness is that $A_{ij}(t)$ should be an exponential function of time in the form of (2.20).

* See Johansen: Op. cit.

When, however, the conditions of applying the RAS method are fulfilled, there must exist a direct procedure that fairly well approximates the RAS results. In the following, we present such a method.

3. A LINEAR APPROXIMATION OF THE RAS METHOD

Let us assume that for $t = t_1$ the Conditions I–IV are met, and the RAS method can be applied. Let us apply the following notations:

$$r_i = e^{x_i t_1} - 1 \tag{3.1}$$

$$s_j = e^{y_j t_1} - 1 \tag{3.2}$$

and substitute these for (2.20), when $t = t_1$:

$$A_{ij}^1 = A_{ij}^0(r_i + 1)(S_j + 1) = A_{ij}^0(1 + r_i + s_j) + r_i A_{ij}^0 s_j\,, \tag{3.3}$$

where r_i and s_j mean the relative changes in A_{ij}^0 under the "row" and "column" effects, respectively. When these changes are not too strong (according to empirical experience gained from practical examples, they do not exceed the average order of magnitude of 10^{-2}), $r_i s_j$ can be neglected on account of its smallness in comparison to $r_i + s_j$. This finding is the basis of the direct method, also setting the limit to its application.

Let us determine A_{ij}^1 in the form of

$$A_{ij}^1 = A_{ij}^0(1 + \varrho_i + \sigma_j) \tag{3.4}$$

when writing (3.4) in a matrix form:

$$\mathbf{A}^1 = \mathbf{A}^0 + \mathbf{A}^0\hat{\sigma} + \hat{\varrho}A^0 \tag{3.5}$$

and considering (1.1) and (1.2) ϱ and σ may be obtained from the following equations:

$$\mathbf{a}^0 + \mathbf{A}^0\hat{\sigma} + \hat{\varrho}\mathbf{a}^0 = \mathbf{a}^1 \tag{3.6}$$

$$\mathbf{b}^0 + \hat{\sigma}\mathbf{b}^0 + \mathbf{A}^{0T}\boldsymbol{\varrho} = \mathbf{b}^1. \tag{3.7}$$

Since $\hat{\varrho}$ and $\hat{\sigma}$ are diagonal matrices, whereas ϱ and σ are column vectors derivable from these, (3.6) and (3.7) can be transcribed as follows:

$$\mathbf{A}^0\sigma + \hat{\mathbf{a}}^0\varrho = \mathbf{a}^1 - \mathbf{a}^0 \tag{3.8}$$

$$\hat{\mathbf{b}}^0\boldsymbol{\sigma} + \mathbf{A}^{0T}\boldsymbol{\varrho} = \mathbf{b}^1 - \mathbf{b}. \tag{3.9}$$

$\boldsymbol{\varrho}$ and $\boldsymbol{\sigma}$ can be determined from the inhomogeneous system of linear equations

$$\begin{bmatrix} \mathbf{A}^0 & \hat{\mathbf{a}}^0 \\ \hat{\mathbf{b}}^0 & \mathbf{A}^{0T} \end{bmatrix} \begin{bmatrix} \sigma \\ \varrho \end{bmatrix} = \begin{bmatrix} \mathbf{a}^1 - \mathbf{a}^0 \\ \mathbf{b}^1 - \mathbf{b}^0 \end{bmatrix}. \tag{3.10}$$

The rank of the matrix of this system of equations is lower than n. Therefore, we are free to choose at least one ϱ_i or σ_j component.

The advantage of the method suggested consists in its being a direct procedure while, similarly to the RAS method, it leaves the zero elements of $\mathbf{A}^0$ unaffected.

APPENDIX

Let us assume that $f(\alpha, x)$; $g(x)$ are continuous, monotonic functions while $0 \leq \lambda \leq 1$ and α are parameters chosen optionally, then

Lemma (I)

The functional equation

$$f(\alpha, x) = f(\alpha, g(x)) = f(f(\alpha + g(\lambda x)) + g((1 - \lambda) x)) \tag{I.1}$$

can be satisfied only by the type of functions

$$g(x) \quad = mx + b \tag{I.2}$$

$$f(\alpha, x) = \alpha + g(x) - b = \alpha + mx \tag{I.3}$$

where m, b are constants chosen optionally.

Proof:

Since $f(\alpha, x)$ is monotonic, it follows from (I.1) that

$$\alpha + g(x) = f(\alpha + g(\lambda x)) + g((1 - \lambda) x). \tag{I.4}$$

By substituting $\lambda = 1$ into (1.4) we obtain

$$f(\alpha + g(x)) = \alpha + g(x) - g(0). \tag{I.5}$$

Let us determine $f(\alpha + g(\lambda x))$ from (I.5) and write it into (I.4):

$$g(x) = g(\lambda x + (1 - \lambda) x) = g(\lambda x) + g((1 - \lambda) x) - g(0). \tag{I.6}$$

The functional equation (I.6) can be satisfied only with a unique type of function,* namely:

$$g(x) = mx + b, \tag{I.7}$$

where m, b are constants chosen optionally. By substituting (I.7) into (I.4) with $\lambda = 1$ we obtain

$$f(\alpha, x) = \alpha + mx. \tag{I.8}$$

The functions of the (I.8) type are, indeed, solutions of (I.1.)

* Szász, P.: *A differenciál és integrálszámítás elemei* (Elements of differential and integral calculations). Közoktatásügyi Kiadó, Budapest 1951.

Lemma (II)

The functional equation

$$f(\alpha, x) = f(\alpha \cdot g(x)) = f(f(\alpha g \cdot (\lambda x)) \cdot ((1 - \lambda) x)) \tag{II.1}$$

can be satisfied (when $\alpha \neq 0$ only by functions of the type

$$g(x) = be^{mx} \tag{II.2}$$

$$f(\alpha, x) = \frac{\alpha}{b} g(x) = \alpha e^{mx} \tag{II.3}$$

where m, b are constants, and $b \neq 0$.

Proof:

Since $f(\alpha, x)$ is monotonic, it follows from (II.1) that

$$\alpha \cdot g(x) = f(\alpha \cdot g(\lambda x) \cdot g((1 - \lambda) x)) \,. \tag{II.4}$$

By substituting $\lambda = 1$ into (II.4) we obtain

$$f(\alpha \cdot g(x)) = \alpha \frac{g(x)}{g(0)} \,. \tag{II.5}$$

Let us determine $f(\alpha \cdot g(\lambda x))$ from (II.5) and substitute it into (II.4);

$$g(x) = g((\lambda x + (1 - \lambda) x) = \frac{g(\lambda x) \cdot g((1 - \lambda) x)}{g(0)} \,. \tag{II.6}$$

The unique type of solution of the function equation (II.6) is:*

$$g(x) = be^{mx} \tag{II.7}$$

where $b \neq 0$ and m are constants chosen optionally. By substituting (II.4) with $\lambda = 1$ we obtain

$$f(\alpha, x) = \alpha e^{mx} \,. \tag{II.8}$$

The functions of the (II.8) type are, indeed, solutions of (II.1).

* See Szász: Op. cit.

THE PLAN OF AN ECONOMETRIC MODEL BASED ON INPUT–OUTPUT TABLES

by

KATALIN HULYÁK

The draft model to be discussed here is the fourth experiment of the Econometric Laboratory of the Central Statistical Office (Model M-4), which is new in comparison with the earlier ones insofar as it connects the stochastic econometric model with an aggregated input–output model. This connection contains on the one hand an entire series of new possibilities for analysis, in that the econometric model is complemented with the sphere of current productive consumption, and the input–output model is complemented with stochastic relations. At the same time, many methodological difficulties emerge as regards the linking of two models of a different type. The endeavour to take into consideration the alternative possibilities for solving the latter difficulties and the availability of statistical information justify the small size of the experimental model.

1. *Background.* For years now the Econometric Laboratory of the Hungarian Central Statistical Office has been engaged in constructing econometric models consisting of simultaneous equation systems. The first one, the model M-1, was intended to be a methodological experiment.* The goal of model M-2 was, first of all, economic analysis, and this was also served by the larger size of the model, as well as a more circumspect application of the technique of model construction.** In the course of forecasts completed with model M-2*** an experiment was made to utilize the information contents of the model. Simultaneously with the forecasting experiments we again worked out an aggregate model in cooperation with the Computing Research Centre U.N.D.P. of Bratislava (model M-3), the purpose of which was to make use of the possibilities for comparison stemming

* Halabuk, L., Kenessey, Z., Theiss, E., Mrs. Kotász, Gy. and Nyáry, Zs.: A magyar népgazdaság M-1 statisztikai makromodellje (The M-1 statistical macromodel of the Hungarian national economy). *Nemzetközi Módszertani Füzetek*, No. 7, Statisztikai Kiadó, Budapest 1965.

** Halabuk, L.: Specifikációs elgondolások az M-II/A modellel kapcsolatban (Specification concepts with regard to model M-II/A). *Laboratóriumi munkaanyagok*, No. 5, Statisztikai Kiadó, Budapest 1967; and
Halabuk, L., Hulyák, K., Nyáry, Zs. and Vithalm, Z.: Az M-2 modell: Becslés és struktúra (The M-2 model: estimation and structure). *Laboratóriumi munkaanyagok*, No. 10, Statisztikai Kiadó, Budapest 1970.

*** Halabuk, L. and Mrs. Kotász, Gy.: Előrebecslés az M-2 modellel (Forecasting with the M-2 model). *Laboratóriumi munkaanyagok*, No. 15, Statisztikai Kiadó, Budapest 1972.

from the quantification of existing economic relations in the Hungarian and Czechoslovak national economies.*

2. *The purpose of our modelling experiment.* The M-models elaborated so far were systems of equations explaining the creation of the net production value, its use, exports, imports, employment, etc. Since the formation of the net production value and the economic phenomena related to it, as well as their circulation, only provide a narrow picture of the economic sphere, it is unquestionably useful to investigate the phenomena contained in it in a more comprehensive manner, including the turnover among the sectors of production, and in this way, the formation of gross production value as well. The large number of input–output models worked out to different degrees of detail can prove very useful in solving this question, on the one hand, through putting the information contents of the tables to use, and, on the other, by including the input–output interrelations directly in the model. If we accept the possibilities offered by the input–output model (and the constraints as well, of course) in explaining the sphere of current productive consumption, there is no need for the econometric model to describe the sphere of production in a way different from the input–output model (with interrelations specified in another way). In this way our task is limited to building a suitable input–output model into the econometric model as a (special) part of the econometric model conforming to the breakdown of the econometric model. Therefore, our model explains net production and total final use within the framework of a system in accordance with the practice of econometric models, but, as an organic part of the model, it also contains the interidustry production relations, and the pattern by branches of final use, taken from the input–output tables.

The variables of our former model were taken into consideration at unchanged 1959 prices. Since then the transition to the 1968 price level has been completed (as was made necessary by the new system of economic control and management introduced in 1968). The new model calculations have been completed at unchanged 1968 price levels.

3. *Statistical possibilities and limits.* According to the above, the starting basis from the point of view of the model are the length of the comparable time series of the variables to be studied, and the input–output tables worked out so far. The time series of the accounting categories of the new type are available at the 1968 price level for the years 1960–1970.** This eleven-year period puts a sharp limit on our possibilities since the reliability of the conclusions drawn from the model depend to a great extent on the proportions between the length of the time series (sample size) and the size of the model (number of variables and equations). We have to state well in advance that we could specify only a small-sized, strongly aggregated model (at least small with regard to the stochastic part of the model).

* Hulyák, K. and Nyáry, Zs.: "Magyar–csehszlovák ökonometriai modell" (A Hungarian–Czechoslovak econometric model). *Statisztikai Szemle,* March 1971.

** *Népgazdasági mérlegek 1960–1970* (National economic balances 1960–1970). Statisztikai Kiadó, Budapest 1971.

Regarding the second question, the input–output tables worked out, the situation is highly favourable because small tables which can be taken into consideration are available for each year from 1959 on.* These tables are not available, however, at unchanged 1968 prices nor do they include the non-material branches. Since the model is not at present intended to explain interindustrial relations in a stochastic way, there is no need for an entire table series, for we can begin on the basis of a single annual table. This table, which is most suited for our purposes, is the aggregate input–output table for 1968.

4. *The structure of the model.* Within the framework of a uniform system, the planned model contains stochastic equations, identities (definition equations) and balance equations. Its structure can be divided into two major blocks, the stochastic and non-stochastic ones. The former contains the stochastic equations, the latter the balance equations, while identities are included in both blocks.

The model contains national economic (material and non-material) production in a breakdown of seven branches (by organizations). These seven branches are as follows: industry; the building industry; agriculture; forestry and water management; transport and communications; commerce; non-material activities.

This pattern can be derived by further aggregation from the input–output table.

The *stochastic block* of the model investigates the formation of value added by branches, and the various uses of the total value added. Causal relationships are described by the stochastic equations, while the interrelations existing by definition by identities. In essence, the stochastic block is not different from the structural form of earlier models, in which the interrelations between the endogenous and predetermined variants of the model are described mainly in the form of direct relation between "explanatory variable and result variable". For this reason, the model contains the customary functional relations (production functions, consumption functions, etc.). The category of value added (the value of net production plus depreciation) complemented by imports constitutes the source of total final use. Since current productive consumption is explained by the interrelations of the input–output table, in the stochastic production functions of the branches only the creation of the value added is examined as a function of the primary factors of production (fixed assets and labour). The model comprises six production functions (the production function cannot be interpreted for the "other branch"). The explanatory variables of these functions are

* *A Magyar népgazdaság ágazati kapcsolatainak mérlegei, 1959–1964 (13 termelő szektorra)* (Input–output tables of the Hungarian national economy, 1959–1964 [for 13 productive sectors]). Statisztikai Kiadó, Budapest 1966.

A Magyar népgazdaság ágazati kapcsolatainak mérlegei, 1964–1966 (16 termelő szektorra) (Input–output tables of the Hungarian national economy, 1964–1966 [for 16 productive sectors]). Statisztikai Kiadó, Budapest 1968.

A magyar népgazdaság ágazati kapcsolatainak mérlegei, 1965–1968 (14 termelő szektorra) (Input–output tables for the Hungarian national economy, 1965–1968 [for 14 productive sectors]). Statisztikai Kiadó, Budapest 1970.

employment in the branch and the gross value of fixed assets per person employed. In the agricultural function other special variables, the indicators of weather and of the use of fertilizers may also be added. An identity combines the value formed in the branches into total value added. Furthermore, stochastic equations explain the development of final use according to major directions. (Final use by branches will be taken into consideration on the basis of the input–output interrelations only.) With regard to domestic use, total consumption by the population (broken down into two parts, material and non-material consumption) and national economic investments have been considered. In this way we have established two functions relating to consumption by the population and one for investments. The explanatory variables of the consumption functions are total employment, real wages and the ratio of earners to dependents. The investments have been explained with the variables of total value added and the stock of investments in process carried over from the previous year, in which the former variable would explain trends in national economic investments from the aspect of the source, and the latter from the aspect of necessary investments brought over from the previous year. In the identity summarizing the major items of total domestic use we find two other variables which are considered exogenous, those of public consumption and inventory accumulation (stockpiling). The identity expressing the sum of exports and total domestic use defines the final use.

The model uses stochastic equations to explain the export and inport data series, the former as a function of total available resources less current productive consumption, and the latter as a function of two variables, i.e., of total value added and exports.

Aside from what we have stated, the stochastic block contains two further identities, one defining the value of net production and the other expressing the agreement between the productive side and the uses, according to which total domestic use is equal to total value added and the balance of foreign trade.

Therefore, the stochastic block of the model contains a total of sixteen equations (of which 11 are stochastic and 5 are identities), with sixteen endogenous variables. This block is identified even when separated from the model, thus making parameter estimation possible.

The *non-stochastic block* contains equations derived from the 1968 aggregate input–output table. These equations determine the gross output values of the branches from the value added data of the branches using the technological coefficient matrix, and then, the sum of these values, i.e., the gross national product is defined by an identity. The technological coefficient matrix is also used to express total final use by origin starting from the gross output by branches and applying the well known input–output interrelationships.

The question is how these interrelations, taken from the input–output tables, can form a part of an econometric and, in the final analysis, stochastic model. The estimates of the parameters of the stochastic block are arrived at by using a time series and applying some method of parameter estimation, and the parameter values of the non-stochastic block (the input–output coefficients) are brought into the model from outside, knowing that their estimation was not made in a stochastic manner. Since according to sufficiently well founded assumptions the important technological coefficients only change to a slight extent in a model of this sort — which is projected for a comparatively short period of time, and the goal of which is not to analyse the structure of current productive consumption — they can be assumed to be unchanged, and their value can be included in the model as external information.

Therefore, the balance equations appearing in the non-stochastic block of the model should be considered as equations which exist only in 1968 in the form of identity from among the years of the period observed. For the other years of the period of observation they are met only approximately, and the differences are caused by the deviation of the concrete table structure of the year in question from that of 1968. The value of gross output and final use relating to the seven branches, and the gross national product according to the qualification of the variables are another fifteen endogenous variables of the model, to which the above-mentioned fifteen equations refer.

Due to the linking of the two types of blocks, the structure of the model is special in nature. The stochastic block is in itself interdependent, but the relationship between the stochastic block and the non-stochastic block is unidirectional and, therefore, the model can be treated as a block-recursive one. The block-recursive character of the model is advantageous for performing the planned forecasting and simulation experiments.

To sum up the data of the two types of blocks, the model has thirty-one endogenous variables and thirty-one equations which are solved partly (in the stochastic equations) on the basis of time series by the usual econometric estimation techniques, and partly on the basis of the technological coefficient matrix of the aggregate 1968 input–output table.

5. *The equations and variables of the model.*

A. *Stochastic block:*

$$v^i = \alpha_0^i + \alpha_1^i \frac{a^i}{l^i} + \alpha_2^i l^i + u$$

$$v^c = \alpha_0^c + \alpha_1^c \frac{a^c}{l^c} + \alpha_2^c l^c + u$$

$$v^a = \alpha_0^a + \alpha_1^a \frac{a^a}{l^a} + \alpha_2^a l^a + \alpha_3^a w + \alpha_4^a f + u$$

$$v^t = \alpha_0^t + \alpha_1^t \frac{a^t}{l^t} + \alpha_2^t l^t + u$$

$$v^d = \alpha_0^d + \alpha_1^d \frac{a^d}{l^d} + \alpha_2^d l^d + u$$

$$v^{nm} = \alpha_0^{nm} + \alpha_1^{nm} \frac{a^{nm}}{l^{nm}} + \alpha_2^{nm} l^{nm} + n$$

$$v^i + v^c + v^a + v^t + v^d + v^{nm} + v^0 = V$$

- -

$$c^m = \beta_0^m + \beta_1^m r + \beta_2^m L + \beta_3^m p + u$$

$$c^{nm} = \beta_0^{nm} + \beta_1^{nm} r + \beta_2^{nm} L + \beta_3^{nm} p + u$$

$$I = \gamma_0 + \gamma_1 V + \gamma_2 i^i + u$$

$$U = c^m + c^{nm} + I + c^P + i^s$$

- - - - - - - - - - - - - - - - -

$$e = \delta_0 + \delta_1 (V + i) + u$$

$$i = \omega_0 + \omega_1 V + \omega_2 e + u$$

- - - - - - - - - - - - - - - - -

$$Y = U + e$$

$$N = V - a^f$$

$$U = V + i - e$$

B. *Non-stochastic block:*

$$\mathbf{x} = \begin{bmatrix} x^i \\ x^c \\ x^a \\ x^t \\ x^d \\ x^{nm} \\ x^0 \end{bmatrix} = \begin{bmatrix} \dfrac{v^i}{1 - \mathbf{1}^*\mathbf{a}^i} \\ \dfrac{v^c}{1 - \mathbf{1}^*\mathbf{a}^c} \\ \dfrac{v^a}{1 - \mathbf{1}^*\mathbf{a}^a} \\ \dfrac{v^t}{1 - \mathbf{1}^*\mathbf{a}^t} \\ \dfrac{v^d}{1 - \mathbf{1}^*\mathbf{a}^d} \\ \dfrac{v^{nm}}{1 - \mathbf{1}^*\mathbf{a}^{nm}} \\ \dfrac{v^0}{1 - \mathbf{1}^*\mathbf{a}^0} \end{bmatrix}$$

$$\mathbf{1}^*\mathbf{x} = X$$

$$\mathbf{y} = \begin{bmatrix} y^i \\ y^c \\ y^a \\ y^t \\ y^d \\ y^{nm} \\ y^0 \end{bmatrix} = (\mathbf{I} - \mathbf{A}_{68})\,\mathbf{x} + \mathbf{i}$$

where **x** and **y** are the column vectors of gross output and final use by branches, $\mathbf{1^*a}^i$, $\mathbf{1^*a}^c$, . . . are the corresponding column sums of the $\mathbf{A}_{68}$ technological coefficient matrix, **i** is the vector of complementary imports by branches.

C. *Explanation of the variables*

Endogenous variables

v^i = value added in industry,
v^c = value added in the construction industry,
v^a = value added in agriculture, forestry and water conservation,
v^t = value added in transport and communications,
v^d = value added in distribution,
v^{nm} = value added in the non-material branches,
v^o = value added in the "other branches",
V = total value added,
c^m = total material consumption by population,
c^{nm} = total non-material consumption by population,
I = national economic investments,
U = total domestic use,
e = exports,
i = complementary imports,
Y = final use, total,
N = net national product,
x^i = gross output in industry,
x^c = gross output in the construction industry,
x^a = gross output in agriculture, forestry and water conservation,
x^t = gross output in transport and communications,
x^d = gross output in distribution,
x^{nm} = gross output in the non-material branches,
x^0 = gross output in the "other branches",
X = gross national product,
y^i = final use from industry,
y^c = final use from the construction industry,

y^a = final use from agriculture, forestry and water conservation,
y^t = final use from transport and communications,
y^d = final use from distribution,
y^{nm} = final use from the non-material branches,
y^0 = final use from "other branches".

Exogenous (predetermined) variables

a^i = gross value of fixed assets in industry,
a^c = gross value of fixed assets in the construction industry,
a^a = gross value of fixed assets in agriculture, forestry and water conservation,
a^t = gross value of fixed assets in transport and communications,
a^d = gross value of fixed assets in distribution,
a^{nm} = gross value of fixed assets in the non-material branches,
l^i = average employment in industry,
l^c = average employment in the construction industry,
l^a = average employment in agriculture, forestry and water conservation,
l^t = average employment in transport and communications,
l^d = average employment in distribution,
l^{nm} = average employment in the non-material branches,
w = weather variable,
f = variable for fertilizer use,
r = index of real wages,
L = total employment,
p = ratio of earners to dependents,
i^i = stock of incomplete investments (at the end of the previous year),
c^P = total public consumption,
i^s = inventory accumulation,
a^f = depreciation of fixed assets (total).

6. *Using the model.* Following the verification of the stochastic econometric models, in other words, after estimation based on the time series, there is a possibility for analysing the relationship between the variables on the basis of parameters of the reduced form and for making forecasts with the model. The planned model experiment shown here is capable of giving a more complete picture in forecasting, from a certain point of view, than our models elaborated earlier.

Since through its variables and interrelations the planned model also contains the aggregate input–output table for the period, the interindustry relations can also be forecast, which is something former models could not do. After reducing the system of equations, the course of forecasting is as follows. Starting from the assumed values of the exogenous variables (fixed assets, labour, real wages, etc.) we estimate the endogenous variables of the stochastic block: value added formed in the branches, the major directions and sums of final use (consumption by the population, total national investments), exports and imports. After this, using the estimated value added by branches on the basis of the input–output equations, we can determine the estimated gross outputs of the branches and, based on this, also using input–output interrelations, we can compile the estimated vector of final use, which forecasts its origin (composition) by branches (already estimated in total in the stochastic block). Therefore, we obtain a consistent system of forecast values for all endogenous variables, for the intermediate inputs and for the final demand within the model by using the assumed values of the exogenous variables and the 1968 values of the input–output coefficients.

If intermediate inputs are denoted by **Ax** and final demand by **Y**, the estimates **Ax** and **Y** are the following:

$$\overline{\mathbf{Ax}}_t = \mathbf{A}_{68} \begin{bmatrix} \bar{x}_t^i & \dots & 0 & \dots & 0 \\ \vdots & & \vdots & & \vdots \\ 0 & \dots & \bar{x}_t^c & \dots & 0 \\ \vdots & & \vdots & & \vdots \\ 0 & \dots & 0 & \dots & \bar{x}_t^0 \end{bmatrix}$$

$$\bar{y}_t = \mathbf{F}_{68}^x \begin{bmatrix} \bar{f}_t^a & \dots & 0 & \dots & 0 \\ \vdots & & \vdots & & \vdots \\ 0 & \dots & \bar{f}_t^{na} & \dots & 0 \\ \vdots & & \vdots & & \vdots \\ 0 & \dots & 0 & \dots & \bar{e}_t \end{bmatrix}$$

We must emphasize a shortcoming of the model which also appears in the block-recursive structure, in that there is no feed-back between the stochastic block and the input–output (non-stochastic) block. The variables generated by the stochastic block are placed into the input–output block, which prescribes a certain structure of current productive consumption and final use for them, but this has no reciprocal effect on the stochastic block. This phenomenon is a consequence of the fact that we are relying on a technological coefficient matrix assumed to be constant.

On the basis of a programme drafted in the autumn of 1971, we are planning the specification analysis and computation of preliminary estimates, and following that, the use of possibly several alternative methods of estimation, as well as an *ex post* forecasting experiment covering 1971 and an *ex ante* forecast for 1972–1975.

AUTO-REGRESSIVITY ANALYSIS IN THE INPUT–OUTPUT TABLE*

by

GYÖRGY MESZÉNA and MRS. NÓRA SIMON

The research we are now reporting on was aimed at establishing more efficient methods of forecasting input–output coefficients. For this purpose, the occurrence of auto-regressivity in the time series of coefficients was investigated, and the results obtained by the method suggested were compared with those obtained by traditional methods. Our research involved many complementary calculations and produced certain partial results, as well as findings and problems worthy of attention.

The coefficients resulting from complicated economic circumstances are influenced, among other things, by various random factors. Therefore, those sophisticated methods of analysing time series, which emphasize probability variable character, have seemed suitable for our purposes. As a first step, the trend effect was detached from the time series of coefficients, and the residual was assumed to be treatable as an auto-regressive scheme. The checking of this hypothesis and the establishing of the order of auto-regression have required another set of calculation.

Our main objective consisted precisely in checking the validity of this assumption, as a precondition of its further application. In the case of a positive outcome, we intended to utilize the possibilities offered by the method for improving the reliability of forecasting.

As regards the elimination of the trend effect, the following may be stated. Our time series originated in the input–output tables of ten consecutive years, so their length did not make any special approach necessary; the basic linear tendencies seemed to be correct. Considering, however, the results of some fruitful research, completed earlier in Hungary which aimed at investigating other possibilities, we believe that, in order to improve the efficiency of the proposed method, even other tendencies may be taken into account — eventually regarding some groups of coefficients only.

After detaching the trend effects, our hypothetic equation for the time series of the input–output coefficients was the following:

$$X_t = a_0 + a_1 X_{t-1} + \ldots + a_k X_{t-k} + Y_t$$

where the parameters are independent of t, and Y_t is a time series consisting of independent variables of the same distribution:

* Numerical results not figuring in the present paper can be found in the periodical *Szigma*, No. 3, 1971 Budapest.

$$M(Y_t) = 0 \; ; \; D^2(Y_t) = \sigma^2$$

Within this auto-regressive scheme, consistent estimates of the parameters a_i may be made with the least-squares method (the procedure need not be expounded here). Subsequently, we checked the correctness of the estimates by establishing the roots of the characteristic equation, then sifted out the random component of the scheme, estimating also its standard deviation.

Let us now deal somewhat more intensively with the statistical proof of the hypothesis. Here, the steps were the following:

1. We calculated the empirical correlation coefficients:

$$\hat{\varrho}_i = \frac{\sum_{t=1}^{N-i} Y_t Y_{t-i}}{\left(\sum_{t=1}^{N-i} Y_t^2\right)^{\frac{1}{2}} \left(\sum_{t=1}^{N-i} Y_{t+i}^2\right)^{\frac{1}{2}}}$$

$$\hat{\varrho}_0 = \sigma; \quad (i = 1, \ldots, N - 1)$$

2. We calculated the A_i values by assuming that

$$\varrho(z) = \sum_{i=0}^{k} \hat{a}_i z_i$$

and

$$\varrho^2(z) = \sum_{i=0}^{2k} A_i z_i,$$

where an auto-regressivity of the order k figures in the hypothesis; $\hat{a}_i$ means the already estimated basic parameters; z is the root of the characteristic equation which, however, according to what has been said above, need not be determined numerically for determining the A_i-s.

3. We calculated the quantities

$$R_s = \sum_{j=-\infty}^{\infty} A_j \varrho_{s-j}$$

$$(s = k + 1, \ldots, N - i)$$

4. The sum $\chi_f^2 = R_{k+1}^2 + \ldots + R_{k+f}^2$ converges on a χ_f^2 distribution with f degrees of freedom (f is the number of R_s variables obtained).

5. Choosing a value for p, and taking the value of χ_p^2 from the table, we discarded the hypothesis when

$$\chi_f^2 < \chi_p^2$$

Indirectly, the test helps us establish the order of auto-regressivity. By doing the test according to various hypotheses which are compatible with the length of the time series, we may choose, from among the "positive results" the one which is most conspicuously consistent with practical experience.

The set of data for which our analysis was performed was taken from the inner square of the fifteen-sector input–output table for 1959–1968. It is conceivable that some of our statements (including the one relating to the order of auto-regressivity) would take a somewhat modified form, when applied to another set of data.

The test described here was performed by a computer for each of the $15^2 = 225$ cases. Our final hypothesis ($k = 2$) was proven correct in all of them.

Subsequently, extrapolations were made by superimposing the auto-regressive schemes on the trends. This calculation was performed for the years 1969 and 1970.

The table below shows the correction derived from the auto-regressive scheme as a percentage of the total value or, in other words, the share of this component in shaping the time series.

Number of cases investigated	Percentage share of the auto-regressive scheme		
	0.1–10	10–30	over 30
130	+		
70		+	
25			+

The time series investigated were rather short; it may be assumed, therefore, that other effects and perhaps certain periodic components may have blurred the picture to some extent; nevertheless, our results seem to justify the method we have applied.

A very interesting part of the investigation consisted in the comparison of the results obtained by the proposed method with the factual data, e.g., with those derived from the statistical input–output table for 1969. (The results of this comparison will be expounded later.)

We may conclude as to the reliability of the extrapolation obtained by us also from the fact that, although we calculated the individual coefficients independently of each other, i.e., according to their own time series, the matrix obtained had the character of an input–output table, including its character of asymptotic nilpotency, checked by us according to Collantz's criterion. The existence of this possibility of checking suggests that we might attempt an extrapolation for any number of years for which this "test" yields a positive result.

The table below shows the relative variance of the random components sifted out from the time series investigated.

Number of cases investigated	Percentage of relative variance			
	1–10	10–20	20–30	over 30
107	+			
61		+		
55			+	
16				+

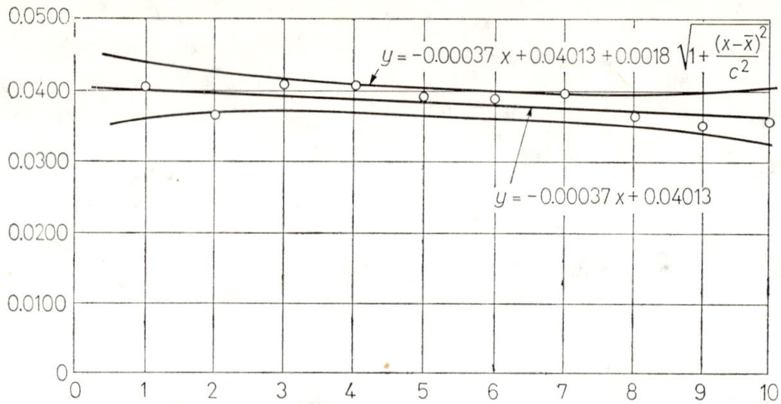

Fig. 1. Regression lines with a confidence interval in case of an auto-regression of three per cent

According to general experience. the relative variance of coefficients having a greater absolute magnitude is but a few per cent, thus they are considerably more stable than the rest.

The questions regarding the reliability of forecasting were investigated also by calculating confidence intervals, for three characteristic categories of trends corresponding to the relative weight of auto-regressivity. Figures 1–3 very tang-

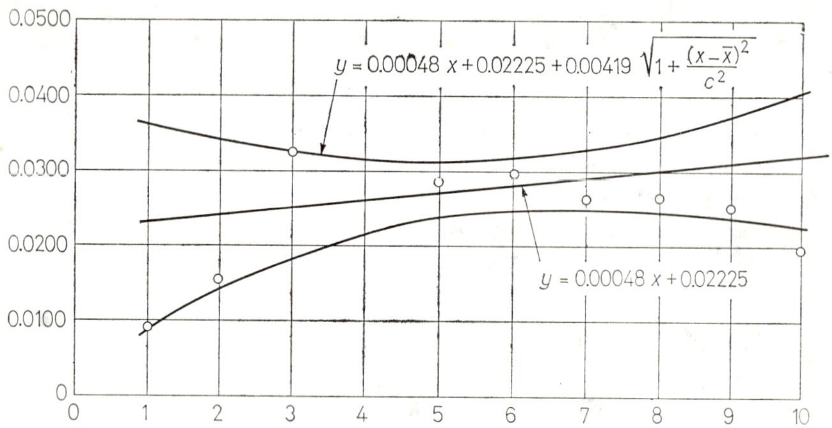

Fig. 2. Regression lines with a confidence interval in case of an auto-regression of fifteen per cent

ibly call attention to the differences between the said categories and to the rapid growth in the breadth of intervals. Thus, they are helpful in drawing our conclusions.

On the grounds of what has been said, it may be stated that the hypothesis of auto-regressivity may be expediently used as a tool of forecasting input–output coefficients.

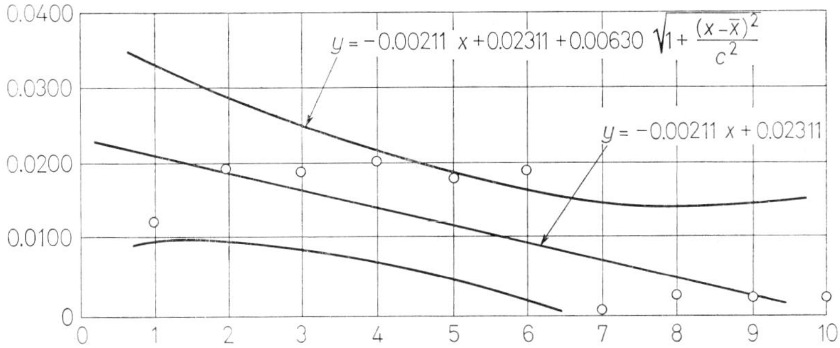

Fig. 3. Regression lines with a confidence interval in case of an auto-regression of ninety per cent

This experience also corroborates the general postulate that even if different types of input–output tables are constructed for various purposes, one defined type has to be calculated continuously, in a constant form, for a considerable length of time. Deeper statistical elaboration becomes impossible when this basic requirement is not satisfied.

As has been already mentioned, it would be an interesting experiment to describe some groups of coefficients separately with trends of different types, according to their different properties appearing even in the short run. In this way perhaps we could obtain even clearer results.

Also the effect of aggregation on the occurrence of auto-regressivity could be investigated separately.

Besides the comparison of our extrapolated results with the table of 1969, we wish to report on another experimental project. We want to investigate what results would be produced if auto-regressive schemes were combined with traditional methods. More closely, how efficient the forecast would be if the "framework" of the balance were built up — according to the above — with the autoregressive schemes, but with the first quadrant filled out with the RAS method.

As regards the comparison with the table for 1969, our final results were the following. In the case of the 20 "big" coefficients, the average deviation of the extrapolated data from the factual ones was 2.675 per cent (in one case it amounted to 10 per cent). Among the smallest coefficients we found 20 for which the average deviation was about 25 per cent.

The combination of the RAS method with auto-regressivity resulted, according to this first experiment, in the figures deviating more from the factual data than in the case of the method based on auto-regressivity only. It is, however, possible that this may be explained by the differences of the 1965 data (used in the RAS calculation) from those of 1969.

Summing up our investigation, it may be confidently stated that the method based on auto-regressivity is a useful tool in forecasting input–output coefficients.

A METHOD ENSURING CONSISTENCY OF FORECASTS REGARDING CERTAIN ELEMENTS OF THE INPUT-OUTPUT TABLE*

by

LÁSZLÓ MIHÁLYFFY

1. INTRODUCTION

This paper is a part of research studies aimed at constructing and improving an econometric model for the purposes of price planning. This research was undertaken by the Enterprise for Systems Engineering (INFELOR), commissioned by the National Office of Materials and Prices. Some of its results, suited for use in short-, medium- and long-term planning, were published in studies by Gy. Szakolczai and P. Vásárhelyi.**

Another previous publication discussed in detail the role of our research results connected with the econometric model of price planning.*** Computations based on this model establish the sectoral price indices, relying partly on labour and

* The author wishes to express his gratitude to J. Réti (INFELOR) and to A. Simonovics (Institute of Economic Sciences of the Hungarian Academy of Sciences) for having contributed valuable advice for this study.

** Szakolczai, Gy. and Vásárhelyi, P.: Az ágazati kapcsolatok mérlege technológiai koefficienseinek előrebecsült matrixai (Extrapolated matrices of technological input–output coefficients). *Közgazdasági Szemle*, Vol. XIV, 1967, pp. 1444–1461, and, by the same authors: Extrapolated Matrices of Input–output Coefficients. *Acta Oeconomica*, No. 3, 1968, pp. 297–318.

Related results can also be found in the following working papers published by the National Office of Materials and Prices, and INFELOR: Az ártervezés ökonometriai modelljének eredményei, I. A magyar népgazdaság ágazati kapcsolati mérlegének előrebecsült koefficiens-matrixai 13 termelő szektorra (Results obtained with the econometric model of price planning, Part One: Estimated coefficient matrices of the input–output table of the Hungarian national economy for 13 productive sectors), September 1968 Budapest.

Az ártervezés ökonometriai modelljének eredményei, II. A magyar népgazdaság ágazati kapcsolati mérlegeinek előrebecsült technológiai koefficiens-matrixai 15 termelő szektorra: 1. kötet: "A" típusú és belföldi koefficiensek. 2. kötet: Import-koefficiensek; 3. kötet: Eredményeink összehasonlítása az OT hagyományos módszerekkel végzett számításainak eredményeivel (Results obtained with the econometric model of price planning, Part Two: Estimated coefficient matrices of the input–output table of the Hungarian national economy for 15 productive sectors; Vol. 1, Type "A" and domestic coefficients, Budapest, November 1969; Vol. 2, Import coefficients, Budapest, November 1969; Vol. 3, Results compared with those obtained by the National Planning Office with the aid of traditional methods, Budapest, April 1970).

*** National Office of Materials and Prices and INFELOR: Az ártervezés ökonometriai modelljének munkaanyagai, I. Az ártervezés ökonometriai modelljeinek rövid ismertetése (The system of data underlying the econometric model of price planning, Part One: A short summary of the econometric model of price planning), Budapest, May 1970.

capital inputs defined with the aid of production functions, and partly on the material inputs calculated on the basis of forecasts of technological coefficients obtained from the input–output table, as well as various other considerations. These price indices, together with other indicators simultaneously obtained, ensure the desired (or permissible) rate of profitability and, at the same time, the material and financial equilibrium of the national economy; in some cases even the assertion of certain optimum requirement is ensured. As regards the use of our results in quantitative planning, no such publication has as yet appeared. It seems evident, however, that any calculation concerning a future period, the breakdown of which conforms to that of the input–output table, may be made more precise by applying, instead of technological coefficients relating to some past period, the expected future values themselves. It is also obvious that the substitution of estimated future coefficients for those observed in the past becomes more recommendable, the longer the period covered by the plan.

The problem of consistently forecasting technological coefficients is twofold. As a first step, the individual elements (future coefficients) have to be estimated *separately*, independently of each other; in the second, the *consistency* of all estimates must be ensured. In the first phase of the work we try forecasting the various elements and aggregates, the material consumption, the interindustry proportions, etc., with the most diverse methods. In the second, we must ensure that all our estimates be consistent with one another, according to the well-known requirements on input–output tables but in such a way that the final value of each element shall deviate to the least possible extent from the original estimate obtained independently. The present paper deals only with the second phase of this work; accordingly, it regards the original estimates of the individual elements and aggregates as previously determined.

The problem in question arises in different forms in connection with "small" and "large" input–output tables. Forecasts made for the small tables involve much less difficulty, partly because the statistical data necessary for the solution of the problem are available in sufficiently long time series, and partly because the coefficients of an aggregated table tend to be more reliable, exactly because they are "comprehensive".

Therefore, we aimed to construct a model in which consistent forecasts, relying on small input–output tables, are applied for making the independent forecasts of the elements figuring in the large table consistent. Thus, the forecasts regarding the individual elements of the large, desaggregated table may be made independently of each other, using perhaps different methods in each sector (e.g., trend calculations, technological forecasts, programming of a branch or of the national economy as a whole, etc.).

Accordingly, the large input–output table may be broken down into blocks, each of which matches one of the elements in the small tables. The latter can be used for checking the independent forecasts used in the former. In addition, forecasts regarding the column totals and the (weighted) row totals of the large table can also be made on the basis of more exact and reliable data than the technological coefficients themselves. Therefore, they may be used for checking the forecasts of technological coefficients figuring in the large table. Our present task now is to build all consistency conditions into a uniform system, taking also into account, of course, the limitations of computer techniques.

The task is rather complicated since, in the case of a large input–output table of 60×60, the number of unknowns amounts to 3600. This would cause serious computational difficulties if standard methods were to be applied. The present paper, however, shows that these difficulties can be circumvented by dividing the task into two steps: in the first one, only the row and column totals of each individual block of the large matrix are considered as unknowns; in the second phase the figures thus obtained are used for estimating the technological coefficients of the large table, separately within each individual block. The solution thus obtained is practically equivalent to one obtained in a single step.

Section 2 deals with the exact mathematical formulation of the problem; Section 3 discusses the method to be applied for determining the row and column totals in the blocks of the large table (requiring the repeated solution of a rather simple quadratic programming problem); Section 4 proposes a solution of this problem suited for exploiting its special features; and, finally, Section 5 proposes three possible ways of determining the elements of the individual blocks.

2. FORMULATION OF THE PROBLEM

Ensuring the consistency of elements, forecast in the framework of an input–output table (for short: consistent forecasting of input–output matrices) may be mathematically expressed as follows: an (α_{ij}) matrix of the size n has to be found that would satisfy certain so-called consistency conditions including, among others, the requirement that its row and column totals must equal certain previously determined values, and that it must approach (in a certain sense optimally) a so-called "target matrix" previously determined by independent forecasts. In order to facilitate the following explanations, it seems convenient to enumerate all "input" data of our problem. We consider as given the following: $(\hat{\alpha}_{ij})$ $n \times n$ matrix, the elements of which are the targets;

$\bar{\bar{\alpha}}_i$ $(i = 1, 2, \ldots, n)$ the weighted row totals of the wanted (α_{ij}) matrix;
$\bar{\alpha}_j$ $(j = 1, 2, \ldots, n)$ the column totals of the matrix wanted;
χ_j $(j = 1, 2, \ldots, n)$ the weights expressing the relative magnitudes of the branches (sectors);
β'_{kl} an $m \times m$ input–output matrix, where $m < n$;
finally, the pairwise disjoint subsets of the indices

$$\varkappa_1 = \{1, 2, \ldots, \nu_1\},$$
$$\varkappa_2 = \{\nu_1 + 1, \nu_1 + 2, \ldots, \nu_1 + \nu_2\}$$
$$\vdots$$
$$\varkappa_m = \{\nu_1 + \nu_2 + \ldots + \nu_{m-1} + 1, \nu_1 + \nu_2 + \ldots + \nu_{m-1} + 2, \ldots, n-1, n\}$$

having the property that by adding them up we obtain the set 1, 2, ..., n. This may be written as

$$\varkappa_i \cap \varkappa_j = \emptyset, \quad \text{for} \quad i \neq j,$$

and

$$\varkappa_1 \cup \varkappa_2 \cup \ldots \cup \varkappa_m = \{1, 2, \ldots, n\}.$$

Obviously, the set $\varkappa_k$ has ν_k elements. Considerations of notation technique justify the introduction of the following:

$$\mu_1 = \nu_1; \; \mu_2 = \nu_1 + \nu_2; \; \ldots; \quad \mu_{m-1} = \nu_1 + \ldots + \nu_{m-1} \; ; \; \mu_m = n.$$

Applying these notations, the consistency conditions can be written as follows:*

$$\sum_{i \in \varkappa k} \sum_{j \in \varkappa l} \chi_j \alpha_{ij} = \beta'_{kl}, \tag{2.1}$$

$$k = 1, \ldots, m; \quad l = 1, \ldots, m;$$

$$\sum_{i=1}^{n} \alpha_{ij} = \bar{\alpha}_j, \tag{2.2}$$

$$j = 1, \ldots, n;$$

$$\sum_{j=1}^{n} \chi_j \alpha_{ij} = \alpha_i, \tag{2.3}$$

$$i = 1, \ldots, n.$$

Regarding equations (2.1) we note that they express the relation between the given matrix (β'_{kl}) and the wanted matrix (α_{ij}). Thus, the matrix (α_{ij}) is obtained by desaggregating the matrix (β'_{kl}).

We illustrate what has been said above with a very simple example starting from a 6×6 matrix:

$$\left[\begin{array}{cc:ccc:c} \alpha_{11} & \alpha_{12} & \alpha_{13} & \alpha_{14} & \alpha_{15} & \alpha_{16} \\ \alpha_{21} & \alpha_{22} & \alpha_{23} & \alpha_{24} & \alpha_{25} & \alpha_{26} \\ \hdashline \alpha_{31} & \alpha_{32} & \alpha_{33} & \alpha_{34} & \alpha_{35} & \alpha_{36} \\ \alpha_{41} & \alpha_{42} & \alpha_{43} & \alpha_{44} & \alpha_{45} & \alpha_{46} \\ \alpha_{51} & \alpha_{52} & \alpha_{53} & \alpha_{54} & \alpha_{55} & \alpha_{56} \\ \hdashline \alpha_{61} & \alpha_{62} & \alpha_{63} & \alpha_{64} & \alpha_{65} & \alpha_{66} \end{array}\right]$$

* Condition 2.2 will be substituted for the condition 2.4 equivalent with it.

Let the sets of indices corresponding to the case investigated be the following:

$$\varkappa_1 = \{1,\ 2\},$$
$$\varkappa_2 = \{3,\ 4,\ 5\},$$
$$\varkappa_3 = \{6\}.$$

We have partitioned the (α_{ij}) matrix according to these sets of indices. Each block of the partitioned matrix corresponds to an element of the (β'_{kl}) matrix; obviously, the latter is now of the size 3×3. Now, specifying (2.1) for the case of $k = 1$ and $l = 2$ we obtain the equation

$$\beta'_{12} = \chi_3(\alpha_{13} + \alpha_{23}) + \chi_4(\alpha_{14} + \alpha_{24}) + \chi_5(\alpha_{15} + \alpha_{25}).$$

It is important to note that, in practice, problems of aggregation or desaggregation do not necessarily arise in such a way that the elements of the individual index sets $\varkappa_k$ are indices *a priori* ranked in sequence. Here, we have assumed the $\varkappa_k$ sets to be such as they have been described in our definition. This, however, does not mean any restriction of the general way of proceeding, since the wanted situation may always be produced by a *transitional* change of the serial numbers of branches (sectors).

In connection with the elements of the (β'_{kl}) matrix it is to be noted that they can be computed from the elements of a matching (β'_{kl}) matrix in the following way:

$$\beta'_{k1} = \sum_{j \in \varkappa_1} \chi_j \beta_{k1},$$
$$\beta'_{k2} = \sum_{j \in \varkappa_2} \chi_j \beta_{k2},$$
$$\vdots$$
$$\beta'_{km} = \sum_{j \in \varkappa_m} \chi_j \beta_{km},$$
$$k = 1, \ldots, m.$$

We now have to deal with the problem of minimizing the deviations between the given matrix $(\hat{\alpha}_{ij})$ and the matrix (α_{ij}) to be obtained. It would appear quite natural to require that either the objective function

$$\sum_{i=1}^{n} \sum_{j=1}^{n} \frac{1}{\hat{\alpha}_{ij}} |\alpha_{ij} - \hat{\alpha}_{ij}|$$

or the other one, namely

$$\sum_{i=1}^{n} \sum_{j=1}^{n} \frac{1}{\hat{\alpha}_{ij}} (\alpha_{ij} - \hat{\alpha}_{ij})^2$$

should be minimized. Since it follows from the nature of the problem that the elements of (α_{ij}) must not be negative, the objective functions in question form, together with the consistency conditions (2.1), (2.2) and (2.3) a linear (or quadratic) programming problem respectively. In view of the very great number of variables, however, its solution would involve serious computational difficulties. Therefore it seems more convenient to resort to another way of interpreting the optimum deviation of our solution from the target matrix; this will be discussed later on.

We now proceed with a slight transformation of the equation system (2.1), (2.2) and (2.3). By multiplying both sides of (2.2) by χ_j we obtain the equation

$$\sum_{i=1}^{n} \chi_j \alpha_{ij} = \chi_i \bar{\alpha}_j, \qquad j = 1, \ldots, n. \tag{2.4}$$

In this way it becomes possible to consider the values $\chi_j \alpha_{ij}$ as unknowns rather than those of α_{ij} and, accordingly, to regard $\chi_j \hat{\alpha}_{ij}$ as target instead of $\hat{\alpha}_{ij}$ $(i = 1, \ldots, n;\ j = 1, \ldots, n)$. This transformation has the advantage that (2.1), (2.3) and (2.4) now constitute a system of equations where the matrix of coefficients contains only 0 or 1 elements. Therefore, in the following we shall always calculate with (2.4) instead of (2.2).

It is easy to recognize that among the equations of this system there occur relations which are the consequences of further equations. Thus, the constants of the problem (i.e., $\beta'_{kl}, \bar{\bar{\alpha}}_i, \bar{\alpha}_j$) cannot be arbitrarily chosen when the system of equations must have a solution. The necessary and sufficient condition of the solution is the satisfaction of the following consistency conditions:

$$\begin{aligned}
\beta'_{11} + \beta'_{21} + \ldots + \beta'_{m1} &= \chi_1 \bar{\alpha}_1 + \ldots + \chi_{\mu_1} \bar{\alpha}_{\mu_1}, \\
\beta'_{12} + \beta'_{22} + \ldots + \beta'_{m2} &= \chi_{\mu_1+1}\, \bar{\alpha}_{\mu_1+1} + \ldots + \chi_{\mu_2} \bar{\alpha}_{\mu_2}, \\
&\vdots \\
\beta'_{1m} + \beta'_{2m} + \ldots + \beta'_{mm} &= \chi_{\mu_{m-1}+1}\, \bar{\alpha}_{\mu_{m-1}+1} + \ldots + \chi_n \bar{\alpha}_n, \\
\beta'_{11} + \beta'_{12} + \ldots + \beta'_{1m} &= \bar{\bar{\alpha}}_1 + \ldots + \bar{\bar{\alpha}}_{\mu_1}, \\
\beta'_{21} + \beta'_{22} + \ldots + \beta'_{2m} &= \bar{\bar{\alpha}}_{\mu_1+1} + \ldots + \bar{\bar{\alpha}}_{\mu_2}, \\
&\vdots \\
\beta'_{m1} + \beta'_{m2} + \ldots + \beta'_{mm} &= \bar{\bar{\alpha}}_{\mu_{m-1}+1} + \ldots + \bar{\bar{\alpha}}_n.
\end{aligned} \tag{2.5}$$

These consistency conditions seem self-evident, and may be proved logically. However, we are not dealing here with their verification. We only note that with the aid of certain corrections it is possible to construct, with equations (2.5), even from inconsistent input data, a consistent system of data. Such correction may consist, e.g., in multiplying the $\bar{\bar{\alpha}}_i$ and $\bar{\alpha}_j$ elements belonging to individual sets of indices $\varkappa_i$ by a conveniently chosen factor.

Our next section deals with the genesis of the collation process. Let us note that, in addition to the method surveyed here, others have also been studied in the course of our research. Some of the results thus obtained were even published* but, since the matrix obtained in this way did not prove satisfactory from every point of view, we had to abandon it and start with a more efficient method.

3. DETERMINING THE ROW AND COLUMN TOTALS BELONGING TO THE BLOCKS OF THE LARGE MATRIX

The blocks of the wanted (α_{ij}) or $(\chi_j\alpha_{ij})$ matrix match the individual elements of the (β'_{kl}) matrix in the sense explained in the introduction. Let us note that the results presented below were obtained with lengthy calculations; *a posteriori*, however, they can be easily verified regardless of how they have been obtained.

Let us consider, within the matrix $(\chi_j\alpha_{ij})$, the block the row indices of which belong to $\varkappa_k$ and its column indices to χ_l:

$$A_{kl} = \begin{bmatrix} \chi_{\mu_{l-1}+1}\alpha_{\mu_{k-1}+1,\ \mu_{l-1}+1}; \dots ; \chi_{\mu_l}\alpha_{\mu_{k-1}+1,\ \mu_l} \\ \chi_{\mu_{l-1}+1}\alpha_{\mu_{k-1}+2,\ \mu_{l-1}+1}; \dots ; \chi_{\mu_l}\alpha_{\mu_{k-1}+2,\ \mu_l} \\ \vdots \\ \chi_{\mu_{l-1}+1}\alpha_{\mu_k,\mu_{l-1}+1}; \qquad \dots ; \chi_{\mu_l}\alpha_{\mu_k,\mu_l} \end{bmatrix}. \tag{3.1}$$

We denote the i-th row total of this matrix $(i = \mu_{k-1} + 1,\ \mu_{k-1} + 2, \dots, \mu_k - 1,\ \mu_k)$ with $\bar{\bar{\beta}}_{il}$, and its j-th column total $(j = \mu_{l-1} + 1,\ \mu_{l-1} + 2, \dots, \mu_l - 1, \mu_l)$ with $\bar{\beta}_{kj}$. To these row and column totals we assign the following targets:

$$\bar{\bar{b}}_{il} = \sum_{s\in\varkappa_l} \chi_s\hat{\alpha}_{is},\quad i \in \varkappa_k \tag{3.2}$$

and

$$\bar{b}_{kj} = \sum_{t\in\varkappa_k} \chi_j\hat{\alpha}_{tj},\quad j \in \varkappa_l. \tag{3.3}$$

It is easy to see that we obtain from relations (2.1)–(2.4) the following systems of equations:

For the row totals $\bar{\bar{\beta}}'_{il}$:

$$\sum_{i\in\varkappa_k} \bar{\bar{\beta}}_{il} = \beta'_{kl};\quad k = 1, \dots, m;\quad l = 1, \dots, m \tag{3.4}$$

$$\bar{\bar{\beta}}_{i1} + \bar{\bar{\beta}}_{i2} + \dots + \bar{\bar{\beta}}_{im} = \bar{\bar{\alpha}}_i \qquad (i = 1, \dots, n), \tag{3.5}$$

* Mihályffy, L.: Megjegyzés egy kvadratikus szélsőérték-feladathoz (On a quadratic extreme-value problem). *Szigma*, No. 3, 1970, pp. 213–223, Budapest.

and for the column totals $\bar{\beta}_{kj}$:

$$\sum_{j\in\kappa_l} \bar{\beta}_{kj} = \beta'_{kl} \qquad (k = 1, \ldots, m;\ l = 1, \ldots, m) \tag{3.6}$$

$$\bar{\beta}_{1j} + \bar{\beta}_{2j} + \ldots + \bar{\beta}_{mj} = \chi_j \alpha_j \qquad (j = 1, \ldots, n). \tag{3.7}$$

In view of the targets defined by (3.2) and (3.3) and the usual non-negativity requirements, we may write up the quadratic programming problems:

– for the row totals $\bar{\bar{\beta}}_{il}$ on the basis of (3.4, 3.5) and of the objective function

$$\sum_{i=1}^{n} \sum_{l=1}^{m} \frac{1}{\bar{\bar{b}}_{il}} (\bar{\bar{\beta}}_{il} - \bar{\bar{b}}_{il})^2, \tag{3.8}$$

– and quite similarly for the column totals $\bar{\beta}_{kj}$ on the basis of (3.6), (3.7) as well as of the objective function

$$\sum_{k=1}^{m} \sum_{j=1}^{n} \frac{1}{\bar{b}_{kj}} (\bar{\beta}_{kj} - \bar{b}_{kj})^2. \tag{3.9}$$

Even these problems, however, would require rather extensive computations. Thus, on technical considerations, it is more convenient to interpret the solution of $\bar{\bar{\beta}}_{il}$ and $\bar{\beta}_{kj}$ in another way. In the following (when not otherwise indicated) we restrict our investigation to the $\bar{\beta}_{kj}$ column totals of the blocks.

Let us consider the system of equations (3.6) and (3.7). Our investigations are centered around the following observation: The $\bar{\beta}_{kj}$ values defined by the following equations:

$$\bar{\beta}_{k1} = \frac{\beta'_{k1}}{\nu_1} + x_{k1}\left(\chi_1\bar{\alpha}_1 - \frac{1}{\nu_1}(\chi_1\bar{\alpha}_1 + \ldots + \chi_{\mu_1}\bar{\alpha}_{\mu_1})\right) \tag{3.10}$$

$$\vdots$$

$$\bar{\beta}_{k\mu_1} = \frac{\beta'_{k1}}{\nu_1} + x_{k1}\left(\chi_{\mu_1}\bar{\alpha}_{\mu_1} - \frac{1}{\nu_1}(\chi_1\bar{\alpha}_1 + \ldots + \chi_{\mu_1}\alpha_{\mu_1})\right)$$

$$\bar{\beta}_{k,\mu_1+1} = \frac{\beta'_{k2}}{\nu_2} + x_{k2}\left(\chi_{\mu_1+1}\bar{\alpha}_{\mu_1+1} - \frac{1}{\nu_1}(\chi_{\mu_1+1}\bar{\alpha}_{\mu_1+1} + \ldots + \chi_{\mu_2}\bar{\alpha}_{\mu_2})\right)$$

$$\vdots$$

$$\bar{\beta}_{k\mu_2} = \frac{\beta'_{k2}}{\nu_2} + x_{k2}\left(\chi_{\mu_2}\bar{\alpha}_{\mu_2} - \frac{1}{\nu_2}(\chi_{\mu_1+1}\bar{\alpha}_{\mu_1+1} + \ldots + \chi_{\mu_2}\bar{\alpha}_{\mu_2})\right)$$

$$\vdots$$

$$\bar{\beta}_{k,\mu_{m-1}+1} = \frac{\beta'_{km}}{\nu_m} + x_{km}\left(\chi_{\mu_{m-1}+1}\bar{\alpha}_{\mu_{m-1}+1} - \frac{1}{\nu_m}(\chi_{\mu_{m-1}+1}\bar{\alpha}_{\mu_{m-1}+1} + \ldots + \chi_n\bar{\alpha}_n)\right)$$

$$\vdots$$

$$\bar{\beta}_{kn} = \frac{\beta'_{km}}{\nu_m} + x_{km}\left(\chi_n\bar{\alpha}_n - \frac{1}{\nu_m}(\chi_{\mu_{m-1}+1}\bar{\alpha}_{\mu_{m-1}+1} + \ldots + \chi_n\bar{\alpha}_n)\right)$$

satisfy the equations (3.6) *and* (3.7) *if and only if with every* l $(1 \leq l \leq m)$ *for which* $\nu_l > 1$, *the following condition is satisfied:*

$$\sum_{k=1}^{m} x_{kl} = 1. \tag{3.11}$$

When, for some l, $\nu_l = 1$, *then regardless of the value of* x_l, $\bar{\beta}_{kj}$ *will equal* β'_{kj} $(k = 1, \ldots, m)$, *where* j *is the only element of the set* $\varkappa_l$. (In other words, when some blocks of the large input–output table consist of a single row, the "column totals" in this block will equal the elements of the row vector.)

Equally important is the observation that the equations of the type (3.11) $(l = 1, \ldots, m)$ *have a solution at which the values determined by* (3.10) *are non-negative*. Namely, in the case of $(k = 1, \ldots, m;\ l = 1, \ldots, m)$

$$x'_{kl} = \frac{\beta'_{kl}}{\beta'_{1l} + \beta'_{2l} + \ldots + \beta'_{ml}} \tag{3.12}$$

it will be seen that the values defined by (3.10) and (3.12) are non-negative.

Since the x'_{kl} values chosen in this way obviously satisfy (3.11), it is enough to prove that in the case of $(k = 1, \ldots, m)$ and $(j = 1, \ldots, n)$ the relations (3.10) and (3.12) involve the inequality $\bar{\beta}_{kj} \geq 0$. Let k and j be arbitrarily chosen (between the given index limits), and let us assume that $j \in \varkappa_l$. Then according to the relations in question,

$$\bar{\beta}_{kj} = \frac{\beta'_{kl}}{\nu_l} + x_{kl}\Big(\chi_j\bar{\alpha}_j - \frac{1}{\nu_l}\sum_{s\in\varkappa_l}\chi_s\bar{\alpha}_s\Big) = \frac{\beta'_{kl}}{\nu_l} + \frac{\beta'_{kl}\chi_j\bar{\alpha}_j}{\beta'_{1l} + \ldots\ldots + \beta'_{ml}} -$$

$$- \frac{\beta'_{kl}}{\nu_l} \cdot \frac{\sum\limits_{s\in\varkappa_l}\chi_s\bar{\alpha}_s}{\beta'_{1l} + \ldots + \beta'_{ml}}.$$

According to the consistency conditions (2.5) the coefficient of $\dfrac{\beta'_{kl}}{\nu_l}$ is zero (after contraction), so that

$$\bar{\beta}_{kj} = \frac{\beta'_{kl}}{\beta'_{1l} + \ldots + \beta'_{ml}}\chi_j\bar{\alpha}_j \tag{3.13}$$

wherefrom the statement follows from the non-negativity of the basic data.

The question arises within what interval can the values x_{kl} be chosen if the corresponding $\bar{\beta}_{kj}$ values must be non-negative?

When fixing a pair of indices k, l it obviously follows from (3.10) that x_{kl} occurs only in the expressions of $\bar{\beta}_{kj}$ column totals when for these latter $j \in \varkappa_l$. These $\bar{\beta}_{kj}$ values will be non-negative if, and only if

$$y_{kl} = \min_{j\in\varkappa_l} \frac{\beta'_{kl}}{\sum\limits_{s\in\varkappa_l}\chi_s\bar{\alpha}_s - \nu_l\chi_j\bar{\alpha}_j} \leq x_{kl} \leq \max_{j\ni\varkappa_l} \frac{\beta'_{kl}}{\sum\limits_{s\in\varkappa_l}\chi_s\bar{\alpha}_s - \nu_l\chi_j\bar{\alpha}_j} = Y_{kl} \tag{3.14}$$

where we may assume that the corresponding denominators are other than zero, since we have to do with deviations of the maximum or minimum of v_l quantities from their arithmetic mean. These deviations, however, may be zero only when all quantities are equal; and in this case we have $\bar{\beta}_{kj} = \beta'_{kl}$ for any value of $j \in \varkappa_l$, regardless of the value of x_{kl}. Except for this trivial case, it similarly follows from the properties of the arithmetical mean that, in (3.14), $y_{kl} < 0$; $Y_{kl} > 0$, and both limits are finite.

Our observations made so far may be summed up in the following: *In the case of $l = 1, \ldots, m$ we have to solve the problem* (P 1) *namely,*

$$(P\ 1): \sum_{k=1}^{m} \sum_{j \in \varkappa l} (\bar{\beta}_{kj} - \bar{b}_{kj})^2 \to \min$$

$$\sum_{k=1}^{m} x_{kl} = 1, \tag{3.15}$$

$$(y_{kl} \le x_{kl} \le Y_{kl};\ k = 1, \ldots, m)$$

where, in the case of $k = 1, \ldots, m$ and $j \in \varkappa_l$ the quantities $\bar{\beta}_{kj}$ are functions of the x_{kl} variables defined by the expressions (3.10). In possession of the optimum values of x_{kl}, the $\bar{\beta}_{kj}$ column totals of the blocks in the large matrix have to be determined with the aid of (3.10); these column totals will be considered as optimal. A possible but non-optimal solution of the problem is given by formulae (3.12) and (3.13).

The objective function (3.15) may be written in a simpler form by substituting the relations (3.10) for $\bar{\beta}_{kj}$. In the case of a fixed k and $j \in \varkappa_l$ we obtain on the basis of (3.10)

$$\bar{\beta}_{kj} - \bar{b}_{kj} = \frac{\beta'_{kl}}{v_l} + x_{kl}(\chi_j\bar{\alpha}_j - \frac{1}{v_l} \sum_{s \in \varkappa_l} \chi_s\bar{\alpha}_s) - \bar{b}_{kj} = \sigma_j x_{kl} - \tau_{kj},$$

where

$$\sigma_j = (\chi_j\bar{\alpha}_j - \frac{1}{v_l} \sum_{s \in \varkappa l} \chi_s\bar{\alpha}_s), \qquad (j \in \varkappa_l;\ l = 1, \ldots, m) \tag{3.16}$$

and

$$\tau_{kj} = \bar{b}_{kl} - \frac{\beta'_{kl}}{v_l}, \qquad (j \in \varkappa_l;\ k, l = 1, \ldots, m). \tag{3.17}$$

Therefore:

$$\sum_{j \in \varkappa l} (\bar{\beta}_{kj} - \bar{b}_{kj})^2 = x_{kl}^2 \sum_{j \in \varkappa_l} \sigma_j^2 - 2x_{kl} \sum_{j \in \varkappa_l} \sigma_j\tau_{kj} + \sum_{j \in \varkappa_l} \tau_{kj}^2 =$$

$$= (a_l x_{kl} - b_{kl})^2 - b_{kl}^2 + \sum_{j \in \varkappa_l} \tau_{kj}^2,$$

and here

$$a_l = \sqrt{\sum_{j\in \varkappa_l} \sigma_j^2}\,, \qquad (l = 1, \ldots, m), \tag{3.18}$$

$$b_{kl} = \frac{1}{a_l} \sum_{j\in \varkappa_l} \sigma_j \tau_{kj}, \qquad (k, l = 1, \ldots, m). \tag{3.19}$$

With these notations, the objective function figuring in (3.15) can be transcribed into the form

$$\sum_{k=l}^{m} (a_l x_{kl} - b_{kl})^2 - \sum_{k=1}^{m} (b_{kl} - \sum_{j\in \varkappa_l} \tau_{kj}^2),$$

but even this form can be further simplified. Since the additive constant has no role in optimization, and since division of the objective function by a positive constant does not change the place of the optimum, we can convert the problem (P 1) into the equivalent problem (P 2):

$$\sum_{k=1}^{m} (x_{kl} - b_{kl}/a_l)^2 \to \min \tag{3.20}$$

$$\sum_{k=1}^{m} x_{kl} = 1 \tag{3.21}$$

$$y_{kl} \leq x_{kl} \leq Y_{kl}, \qquad k = 1, \ldots, n. \tag{3.22}$$

Of course, this problem also has to be solved m times, when the index $l = 1, \ldots, m$. The constants a_l, b_{kl}, y_{kl} and Y_{kl} depend also on the value of l. The optimal $\bar{\beta}_{kj}$ column totals of the blocks have to be defined according to what has been said before. The (P 2) quadratic programming problem may be solved with any of the standard methods. In the next section, however, we propose a special algorithm which can exploit the specific features of this problem.

So far we have dealt with establishing the *column* totals in the individual blocks of the large matrix. The $\bar{\bar{\beta}}_{il}$ *row* totals of the blocks also require that the problem (P 2) be solved m times. Below, we list the cases where the way of computing the constants figuring in (P 2) deviates from what is to be followed when working out column totals. (Here, the serial number of equations is followed by a second one, i.e., by those we have used in the first case.)

$$\bar{\bar{\beta}}_{il} = \frac{\beta'_{kl}}{\nu_k} + x_{kl}(\bar{\bar{\alpha}}_i - \frac{1}{\nu_k} \sum_{s\in \varkappa_k} \bar{\alpha}_s) \qquad (3.23)/(3.10)$$

$$i \in \varkappa_k, \quad k = 1, \ldots, m; \quad l = 1, \ldots, m;$$

$$y_{kl} = \min_{j \in \varkappa_k} \frac{\beta'_{kl}}{\sum\limits_{s \in \varkappa_k} \bar{\alpha}_s - \nu_k \bar{\alpha}_j} \leq x_{kl} \leq$$

$$\leq \max_{j \in \varkappa_k} \frac{\beta'_{kl}}{\sum\limits_{s \in \varkappa_k} \bar{\alpha}_s - \nu_k \bar{\alpha}_j} = Y_{kl} \qquad (3.24)/(3.14)$$

$$k, l = 1, \ldots, m$$

$$\sigma_j = \bar{\alpha}_j - \frac{1}{\nu_k} \sum_{s \in \varkappa_k} \bar{\alpha}_s \quad (j \in \varkappa_k; \quad k = 1, \ldots, m) \qquad (3.25)/(3.16)$$

$$\tau_{kj} = \bar{\bar{b}}_{kj} - \frac{\beta'_{kl}}{\nu_k}, \qquad (j \in \varkappa_k; \; k, l = 1, \ldots, m). \qquad (3.26)/(3.17)$$

Equations (3.8) through (3.22) are invariably used even for establishing the row totals of the blocks.

Finally, we note that, e.g., the (3.6), (3.7) systems of equations have, as a rule, also such solutions that cannot be constructed in the form (3.10). Thus, e.g., when all $\varkappa_k$ sets include at least two indices each, the solutions of the system (3.6), (3.7) will constitute a population having the dimension of $(n - m) \times (m - 1)$ whereas the dimension of the set of vectors which may be constructed in the form (3.10) is $(m-1) \times m$. In this case, evidently, $n \geq 2m$, that is, $(n - m) \times (m-1) \geq$ $\geq (m - 1) \times m$. This means that, when solving the problems (P 1) or (P 2) the *optima* of row and column totals must be chosen from a smaller set than what would be theoretically possible. But it is also evident that the subset of possible solutions defined by formulae (3.10) and (3.23), respectively, still offers sufficient possibilities for optimizing. Among other things, as it has been mentioned before, it is always possible to find a *feasible* solution within each subset. For the narrowing-down of the set of feasible solutions, ample compensation is offered by the advantages of the computing techniques ensured by the proposed algorithm.

4. SOLUTION FOR A SPECIAL QUADRATIC PROGRAMMING PROBLEM

In the preceding section the establishing of row and column totals in the blocks of the large input–output table was reduced to the solution of the problem (P 2) as defined by the relations (3.20) through (3.22). By linear transformation of the variable and by eliminating the index l as a parameter, this problem may be written in the following form:

$$\sum_{i=1}^{m} x_i^2 \to \min, \qquad (4.1)$$

$$\sum_{i=1}^{m} x_i = b, \tag{4.2}$$

$$y_i \leq x_i \leq Y_i; \qquad i = 1, \ldots, m. \tag{4.3}$$

According to Section 3 we may assume that the problem has a solution, that is,

$$\sum_i y_i \leq b \leq \sum_i Y_i.$$

Let us denote the quadratic programming problem defined by (4.1) through (4.3) with $Q(b)$. Let us introduce also the notation $Q(d)$ for the problem in which the total of the variables is d instead of b.

In the following, we deal only with the solution of $Q(b)$.

The solution of $Q(b)$ is initially approached in the following way: in the case of $k = 1, \ldots, m$ let

$$x_k^{(0)} = \begin{cases} 0, & \text{when } y_k \leq 0 \leq Y_k, \\ y_k, & \text{when } 0 < y_k, \\ Y_k, & \text{when } Y_k < 0. \end{cases} \tag{4.4}$$

We denote the sum $\sum_{k=1}^{m} x_k^{(0)}$ with d_0; thus, the first approach of solving $Q(b)$ agrees with the solution of problem $Q(d_0)$.

The basic idea of the proposed algorithm can be formulated as follows. Neglecting the trivial case of $d_0 = b$, we have to solve a finite set of quadratic programming problems $Q(d_0), Q(d_1), \ldots, Q(d_r)$, where (in the case of $d_0 > b$), $d_0 > d_1 > \ldots > d_r = b$ and (in the case of $d_0 < b$), $d_0 < d_1 < \ldots < d_r = b$. For solving the problem $Q(d_p)$ we rely on the solution of the problem $Q(d_{p-1})$. The possibility of this may be shown by the following lemma.

Lemma. When $d_0 < d_1 < d_2$, the value of the objective function belonging to the solution of $Q(d_1)$ is smaller than that of the function belonging to the solution of $Q(d_2)$.

Proof. Let us denote the objective function figuring in (4.1) by $\Phi(x_1, \ldots, x_m) = \Phi(x)$; the solution of $Q(d_1)$, i.e., the vector $(x_1^{(1)}, \ldots, x_m^{(1)})$ by $x^{(1)}$, and the solution of $Q(d_2)$, i.e., the vector $(x_1^{(2)}, \ldots, x_m^{(2)})$ by $x^{(2)}$, but let us assume that — contrary to the statement of the lemma — $\Phi(x^{(1)}) \geq \Phi(x^{(2)})$. Because of $d_0 < d_1 < d_2$, there exists a value λ $(0 < \lambda < 1)$, at which

$$d_1 = \lambda d_0 + (1 - \lambda) d_2 = \sum_{k=1}^{m} \lambda x_k^{(0)} + (1 - \lambda) \sum_{k=1}^{m} x_k^{(2)}.$$

In this case, according to the definition of $x^{(1)}$ and by our indirect assumption, on the one hand,

$$\Phi(\lambda x^{(0)} + (1 - \lambda) x^{(2)}) \geq \Phi(x^{(1)}) \geq \Phi(x^{(2)}),$$

and in view of the strict convexity of the function $\Phi(x)$ as well as by the definition of $x^{(0)}$, on the other,

$$\Phi(\lambda x^{(0)} + (1-\lambda)\, x^{(2)}) < \lambda\Phi(x^{(0)}) + (1-\lambda)\, \Phi(x^{(2)}) \leq$$
$$\leq \max\,\{\Phi(x^{(0)}),\ \Phi(x^{(2)})\} = \Phi(x^{(2)}).$$

This contradiction proves the correctness of our lemma.

According to the lemma, by starting from the solution of $Q(d_0)$ in the sense of (4.4) we may arrive, with the method previously described, i.e., through subsequently solving the $Q(d_p)$ problems, at the solution of $Q(b)$. In the following we assume that $d_0 < b$ (although the problem can be similarly solved in the opposite case). We have to establish the values $d_1, \ldots, d_r$ necessary for solving the individual $Q(d_p)$ problems. Provided that we have already solved $Q(d_{p-1})$, (which is actually the case when $p = 1$), we shall choose the value of d_p in a way that we should be able to find the solution of $Q(d_p)$ by relying on the solution of the preceding problem. In other words, the value of d_p has to be chosen in a way that we should be able to define the particular vector $(x_1^{(p)}, \ldots, x_m^{(p)}) = x^{(p)}$ for which the equation

$$\sum_{k=1}^{m} x_k^{(p)} = d_p,$$

is valid, and the difference between the sums of squares

$$\sum_{k=1}^{m} (x_k^{(p)})^2 \quad \text{and} \quad \sum_{k=1}^{m} (x_k^{p-1})^2$$

is minimum, provided that the (previously obtained) $x^{(p-1)} = (x_1^{(p-1)}, \ldots, x_m^{(p-1)})$ is a solution of $Q(d_{p-1})$.

In the interest of our objective, let us assume that we have already solved the $(p-1)$-th problem, moreover, that the i-th and j-th elements of the objective function are not equal, and finally, that

$$(x_i^{(p-1)})^2 < (x_j^{(p-1)})^2. \tag{4.5}$$

In the solution of $Q(d_{p-1})$ — provided that the proceeding has not ended at this step —, $d_{p-1} < b$. Let us examine what would happen if we augmented or decreased $x_i^{(p-1)}$ or $x_j^{(p-1)}$ by a positive Δx. Evidently, by increasing either $x_i^{(p-1)}$ or $x_j^{(p-1)}$ by Δx the d_{p-1} total value of variables will equally increase by Δx. But we must also know how the objective function $\Phi(x)$ would change if the value of the variables were thus modified. Here we must distinguish two cases. When $x_i^{(p-1)} \geq 0$ and $x_j^{(p-1)} \geq 0$, the value of the objective function will increase, regardless of whether Δx is added either to $x_i^{(p-1)}$ or to $x_j^{(p-1)}$, but, if (4.5) is satisfied, the increment will be *smaller* when Δx is added to $x_i^{(p-1)}$.

Starting from this observation, the following rule of increasing the variables may be formulated.

Let us assume that, after having solved $Q(d_{p-1})$, we obtain t variables satisfying the relations

$$0 \leq x_{i_1}^{(p-1)} = x_{i_2}^{(p-1)} = \ldots = x_{i_t}^{(p-1)} < x_k^{(p-1)}, \qquad (4.6)$$

(although also the case $t = 1$ is conceivable), where all the other non-negative $x_j^{(p-1)}$ members in $\Phi(x)$ are greater than or equal to $x_k^{(p-1)}$. In this case, those $x_{i_1}, x_{i_2}, \ldots, x_{i_t}$ variables which do not reach the upper limit belonging to them can be simultaneously increased by Δx, where

$$0 < \Delta x \leq \Delta x_{\max} = x_k^{(p-1)} - x_i^{(p-1)}. \qquad (4.7)$$

In the case of $\Delta x = \Delta x_{\max}$ the i_1-th, i_2-th, $\ldots i_t$-th and k-th elements of $\Phi(x)$ will be equal.

A similar rule may be formulated regarding a *decrease* in the total of variables, for the case $d_0 > b$.

Let us now return to the investigation of the elements figuring in (4.5). When at least one of $x_i^{(p-1)}$ or $x_j^{(p-1)}$ is negative, then an increase of x_i and/or of x_j causes the $\Phi(x)$ to *decrease*. Because of the lemma, however, the minimum solution of $Q(d_{p-1})$ must be smaller than the minimum solution otained in the next step, so in the case of $x_i^{(p-1)} < 0$ the i-th variable cannot be increased because this would necessarily violate the restrictions included in (4.3). On the other hand, when $x_i^{(p-1)} < 0$, a decrease in x_i involves an increase of Φ (x), and a decrease in the sum total of the variables. It is easy to see that this method of changing the values of the variables is not expedient. Thus, in the case $d_0 < b$ in order to solve the problem $Q(b)$ *we must increase those particular x_i variables for which $x_i^{(p-1)} \geq 0$.*

The rule regarding the increase of variables as defined by (4.6) and (4.7) is yet to be completed by the following.

First, none of the variables $x_{i_1}, x_{i_2}, \ldots, x_{i_t}$ must be increased at the price of violating the corresponding inequalities included in (4.3). Thus, also the inequalities

$$x_{i_1}^{(p-1)} + \Delta x \leq Y_{i_1},\ x_{i_2}^{(p-1)} + \Delta x \leq Y_{i_2}, \ldots, x_{i_t}^{(p-1)} + \Delta x \leq Y_{i_t} \qquad (4.8)$$

must be satisfied. Second, the variables must not be increased in such a way that their total exceed the value of b. Therefore, also the inequality

$$t\Delta x \leq b - d_{p-1} \qquad (4.9)$$

must hold true.

After all this, we may describe the algorithm for the case $d_0 < b$ as follows.

1. On the grounds of (4.4), let is define the vector $x^0 = (x_1^{(0)}, \ldots, x_m^{(0)})$. Let

$$d_0 = \sum_{k=1}^{m} x_k^{(0)}, \qquad d_0 < b$$

where x_0 is the solution of problem $Q(d_0)$.

2. In possession of the solution of the problem $Q(d_{p-1})$, $(p = 1, 2, \ldots)$ let us find the maximum value of $\Delta x^{(p)}$ at which (4.7), (4.8) and (4.9) are fulfilled; the indices $i_1, i_2, \ldots, i_t$ and k have to be defined according to (4.6).

3. Let us assume that

$$d_p = d_{p-1} + t\Delta x^{(p)}.$$

In this case the solution of the problem $Q(d_p)$ is

$$x_i^{(p)} = \begin{cases} x_i^{(p-1)} + \Delta x^{(p)}, & \text{when } i \text{ is equal to one of the indices } i_1, i_2, \ldots, i_t, \\ x_i^{p-1}, & \text{in all other cases.} \end{cases}$$

4. When $d_p = b$, that is, when (4.9) is satisfied as an equality, the procedure is finished; otherwise we must increase the value of p by a unit, and start again from point 2.

The finite character of the procedure follows from the fact that, from among the *finite number* of inequalities (4.7), (4.8), (4.9), *at least one will be an equality for every value of* $\Delta x^{(p)}$ and, in the following, *this equality will no longer appear among the constraints.*

5. ESTABLISHING THE ELEMENTS OF THE LARGE INPUT–OUTPUT MATRIX

After having determined, according to Sections 3 and 4, the row and column totals belonging to the individual blocks of the large matrix, the elements within each of these blocks will be established *exclusively with the aid of the row and column totals of the block in question,* regardless of the other blocks. Evidently, in this second phase of our work we have to deal only with blocks consisting at least of two rows and two columns. When a block has but one row (as, e.g., the one in the example presented in the introduction that consisted of the elements α_{63}, α_{64} and α_{65}), its elements are definitely established already by the end of the first phase, being totals of columns having but one element each. (When a block consists of a single element only — such was α_{66} in the example cited — this one element necessarily equals the corresponding element of the small input–output matrix.)

Thus, in the following we assume that a block to be considered has at least two rows and two columns. Let us take for example the block A_{kl} figuring in (3.1) and, for the sake of simplicity, denote its yet unknown elements with a_{ij} $(i = 1, 2, \ldots, v_k,\ j = 1, 2, \ldots, v_l)$; moreover, we denote the previously defined row total of A_{kl} with $\bar{\bar{c}}_1, \bar{\bar{c}}_2, \ldots, \bar{\bar{c}}_{v_k}$, its column totals with $\bar{c}_1, \bar{c}_2, \ldots, \bar{c}_{v_l}$. With these notations we may write for the elements of the A_{kl} block the following programming problem:

$$\sum_{j=1}^{vl} a_{ij} = c_i, \qquad (i = 1, 2, \ldots, v_k) \tag{5.1}$$

$$\sum_{i=1}^{\nu_k} a_{ij} = \bar{c}_j, \qquad (j = 1, 2, \ldots, \nu_l) \tag{5.2}$$

$$a_{ij} \geq 0; \quad i = 1, \ldots, \nu_k; \; j = 1, \ldots, \nu_l \tag{5.3}$$

$$\sum_{i=1}^{\nu_k} \sum_{j=1}^{\nu_l} s_{ij} \mid a_{ij} - \hat{a}_{ij} \mid^p \rightarrow \min \tag{5.4}$$

where the quantities s_{ij} are conveniently chosen non-negative weights (e.g., $s_{ij} = 1/a_{ij}$; $i = 1, \ldots, \nu_k$; $j = 1, \ldots, \nu_l$), and $\hat{a}_{ij}$ is the target belonging to the element a_{ij}. When, e.g., $a_{ij} = \chi_s \alpha_{rs}$, then $\hat{a}_{ij} = \chi_s \hat{\alpha}_{rs}$. The value of the exponent is either 1 or 2.

Problem (5.1)–(5.2) can be solved by the method of Matuszewski, Pitts and Sawyer.* In the solution provided by this method many of the variables a_{ij} will be identical with the corresponding targets. The number of such variables may attain $v_k \; v_l \times v_k - v_l - 1$. Another solution of the problem (for the case of $p = 2$) was proposed by P. Glattfelder and P. Váczi.**

Sometimes the $\hat{a}_{ij}$ targets are rather inaccurate. It is justified to neglect in such cases the condition (5.4), if by doing so the computation may be substantially simplified. In the following we describe an extremely simple procedure for finding non-negative solutions for the system of equations (5.1), (5.2) which approach the targets satisfactorily, at least when the matching row and column vectors do not deviate extremely from the constants figuring on the right side of (5.1) and (5.2). This, however, seems probable exactly because of the nature of the methods used in the first phase for defining the row and column vectors (see above).

Let us introduce the following notations:

$$C = \sum_{i=1}^{\nu_k} \quad \bar{\bar{c}}_i = \sum_{j=1}^{\nu_l} \bar{c}_j;$$

$$\tilde{\tilde{c}}_i = \sum_{j=1}^{\nu_l} \hat{a}_{ij}, \qquad i = 1, 2, \ldots, \nu_k;$$

$$\tilde{c}_j = \sum_{i=1}^{\nu_k} \hat{a}_{ij}, \qquad j = 1, 2, \ldots, \nu_l;$$

$$\tilde{C} = \sum_{i=1}^{\nu_k} \quad \tilde{\tilde{c}}_i = \sum_{j=1}^{\nu_l} \tilde{c}_j,$$

* Matuszewski, T. I., Pitts, P. R. and Sawyer, J. A.: Linear programming estimates of changes in input coefficients. *Canadian Journal of Economics and Political Sciences*, No. 30, 1964, pp. 203–210. Toronto.

** Glattfelder, P. and Váczi, P.: Egy algoritmus input–output sémák előrebecslésére és korrekciójára (An algorithm for the correction of the forecast of input–output schemes). *Szigma*, No. 3, 1970, pp. 165–172. Budapest.

and define the following matrices:

$$a'_{ij} = \frac{\bar{\bar{c}}_i \bar{c}_j}{C}$$

$$a''_{ij} = \hat{a}_{ij} - \frac{\tilde{\tilde{c}}_i \tilde{c}_j}{\tilde{C}}.$$

Clearly, the elements of the matrix a'_{ij} will satisfy (5.1) and (5.3). On the other hand, it is easy to see from the definitions of $\tilde{\tilde{c}}_i$ and $\tilde{c}_j$ that the row and column total of the (a''_{ij}) matrix are zero. Thus, we may consider as the solution of our problem the (a_{ij}) matrix the elements of which are equal to $a'_{ij} + a''_{ij}$, provided that these values are non-negative. It is obvious that the (a_{ij}) matrix thus defined transforms into the $(\hat{a}_{ij})$ target matrix when (in the case of $i = 1, \ldots, \nu_k$) $\bar{\bar{c}}_i = \tilde{\tilde{c}}_i$, as well as (in the case of $j = 1, \ldots, \nu_l$) $\bar{c}_j = \tilde{c}_j$. When among the values $a'_{ij} + a''_{ij}$ there occur negative ones, we must choose for the figure λ $(0 \leq \lambda \leq 1)$ the highest possible value, so that the values

$$\frac{\bar{\bar{c}}_i \bar{c}_j}{C} + \lambda \left(\hat{a}_{ij} - \frac{\tilde{\tilde{c}}_i \tilde{c}_j}{\tilde{C}} \right)$$

should be non-negative for all i and j indices (this is evidently possible), and consider the obtained $\nu_k \times \nu_l$ matrix as the solution of our problem.

SOME REMARKS ON THE PRODUCT BALANCES IN KIND

by

KAMILLA LÁNYI

INTRODUCTION

It is sometimes inevitable in economic analysis to work with vectors the components of which are defined in terms of different units of measurement. When a given vector of a model is given in terms of some known units of measurement (or dimensions) and this vector is submitted, e.g., to linear transformation, the question may arise what the dimension of the components of its image under the transformation considered will be, since on this depends, among other things, the economic interpretation (within the given model) of the vector obtained. Such a question may arise, for instance, in connection with the dual solution of linear programming problems. On the other hand, when the dimensions of the components of the image are known, we may find a kind of linear transformation that would map the vector with given dimensions into its image with exactly the desired dimensions.

An input–output model describes basic relationships of the economy, which are easily comprehensible. Its mathematical properties are well known, the relation between its mathematical structure and economic interpretation is fairly evident. An input–output table computed in terms of physical units of measurement enables us to check the correctness of the obtained results, but also requires us to formulate the rules of operations with quantities of different dimensions.

It seems fairly evident that these rules have to be formulated in a way ensuring

– that nothing gets disregarded from the information obtainable from the input–output model;

– that the method would be suited for any kind of multiproduct — multisectoral analysis.

The main conclusion of the present paper is that a vector consisting of dimensional quantities can be transformed only by a matrix consisting of dimensional constants. When two (identical or different) sets of dimensions belonging to the components of two different vectors, respectively — transformed and to be transformed — are known, then the dimensions appearing among the elements of the transforming matrix are, with the exception of one (constant) dimension, uniquely defined.

When talking about units of measurement or dimensions, one has to keep in mind that in economics neither is the concept of measurement yet clearly established nor are the units of measurement accurately defined. Or, where they are defined — e.g., in the case of quantities expressed in the dimension of "mass of money" — one cannot uniquely determine coefficients with the aid of which quantities expressed in terms of a given kind of money at a given place could be converted into quantities expressed in another kind of money at another place. This fact is due not so much to the imperfectness of our science as to the characteristics of the economic processes themselves.* This is probably why some economists obstinately return, time and again, to analysis "in kind", i.e., to dealing with physical quantities.

I have summarized under five headings the results concerning the so-called "natural" or "physical" input–output tables and the conclusions which may be drawn. The rules of operations with dimensional quantities are described in the Appendix. One of these deserves attention: the forming of the scalar product (Appendix 1.1). All the rest follows from this, and from the nature of linear transformations.

In the following text, the vectors are designed by **x**, **a** and **X**, independent of whether their components are numbers, dimensional constants, or symbols chosen arbitrarily. The row index is i, the column index is j, transposition is denoted by an *. The exponents are letters of the Greek alphabet. The symbols of dimensions (units of measurement) figure between square brackets.

1

An input–output table — independently of the unit of measurement in which it is expressed — is, essentially, always a balance in kind**

- if the equations included in it are conceived of as production functions, and
- if we consider that it contains no information about the economic nature of interindustry relations.

Authors who — in spite of this — continue to compute input–output tables in terms of genuinely physical units of measurement, generally refer to the inconsistencies of the price system. There are two kinds of such inconsistency: (1) the existence of negative prices: in this case some of the advantageous features of the **A** and (**I** — **A**) matrices get lost; (2) the price system is not uniform: different customers are paying different prices for the same commodity.

Let us consider the second case:

If $\mathbf{B} = (b_{ij})$ is the matrix of natural technological coefficients, $\mathbf{A} = \hat{\mathbf{P}}\mathbf{B}\hat{\mathbf{P}}^{-1}$ is the matrix of technological coefficients in value terms, calculated at average prices, and $\bar{\mathbf{A}}$ is the matrix obtained with non-uniform prices, then by defining

$$\mathbf{W} = \mathbf{B}\hat{\mathbf{P}}^{-1} = (\mathbf{w}_1, \mathbf{w}_2, \ldots, \mathbf{w}_n),$$

* Schumpeter, Joseph: Das Sozialprodukt und die Rechenpfennige. Archiv für Sozialwissenschaft und Sozialpolitik, Vol. XLIV, 3, 1917–1918, pp. 627–715.

** Eckstein, Otto: The Input–Output System — Its Nature and Use. In: Morgenstern, Oskar, Ed.: *Economic Activity Analysis.* John Wiley, Chapman, New York–London 1954.

we obtain

$$\mathbf{A} = (\hat{\mathbf{P}}\mathbf{w}_1, \ldots, \hat{\mathbf{P}}\mathbf{w}_n); \; \bar{\mathbf{A}} = (\mathbf{P}_1 \mathbf{w}_1, \ldots, \mathbf{P}_n\mathbf{w}_n);$$

where $\hat{\mathbf{P}}$ is the diagonal price matrix of the uniform price system (based on average prices), the $\mathbf{P}_j$-s are diagonal price matrices of the inconsistent price system ($j = 1, 2, \ldots, n$ and $n + 1$ will be the index of final use).

Let **x** be the vector of gross output, **y** be the vector of final use (both in value terms), and **q** and **r** the same vectors in terms of physical units of measurement. In this case,

$$\mathbf{x} = \hat{\mathbf{P}}\mathbf{q}; \; (\mathbf{I} - \mathbf{A})\,\mathbf{x} = \mathbf{y} = \hat{\mathbf{P}}\mathbf{r}; \; (\mathbf{I} - \bar{\mathbf{A}})\,\mathbf{x} = \bar{\mathbf{y}} = \mathbf{P}_{n+1}\,\mathbf{r}$$

and $\bar{\mathbf{A}}$ is evidently a matrix from a different transformation as **A** and **B**, and the conclusions we may obtain from it will differ from those that could be drawn from **B** or from an "ideal" **A**.

2

Input–output tables expressed in value terms or in physical units of measurement differ only from the dimensional point of view, but this difference is essential.* Let us draw up the product balance in the form

$$\sum_{j=1}^{n} A_{ij}X_i + Y_i = X_i$$

($i = 1, \ldots, n$; $j = 1, \ldots, n$; the A_{ij}-s are output coefficients); from this one element of the matrix **A** of technological coefficients will be

$$a_{ij} = \frac{A_{ij}X_i}{X_j}$$

and a_{ij} a dimensionless number.

Let us now assume that we have a price system which is consistent in the stated sense. Let

$$X_i = p_iQ_i; \; X_j = p_jQ_j$$

be the dimension of the prices p_i being $[MR_i^{-1}]$ that of the outputs $Q_i[R_iT^{-1}]$, where $[M]$ denotes the mass of money, $[T]$ denotes the dimension of time differences, and $[R_i]$ the output of the i-th industry. From this the natural coefficients b_{ij} may be obtained in two ways:

* Jong, Frits J. (ed.): *Dimensional Analysis for Economists.* North-Holland P. C., Amsterdam 1967.

Either we try to find coefficients z_i, z_j such that

$$B_{ij}z_iQ_i = b_{ij}z_jQ_j$$

holds, while $B_{ij} = A_{ij}$ for the output coefficients (that is the proportions of output in terms of physical units and of value are identical); and with the "real dimension" $[R]$ known from the literature we receive as z_i and z_j: dim $(z_i) = [RR_i^{-1}]$, dim $(z_j) = [RR_j^{-1}]$. It follows that b_{ij} is a dimensionless number, but

$$a_{ij} \neq \frac{p_i}{p_j} b_{ij},$$

because quantities of different dimensions figure on the two sides of the equation.

Or the dimension of b_{ij} is $[R_iR_j^{-1}]$ and for the matrix **B** we obtain

$$\dim(\mathbf{B}) = [\mathbf{RR}^{-1*}],$$

where the expression in the square brackets denotes the diadic product between two dimension-vectors $[\mathbf{R}]$ and $[\mathbf{R}^{-1}]$.

Written out in detail:

$$\dim(\mathbf{B}) = \begin{bmatrix} 1 & R_1R_2^{-1} \dots & R_1R_n^{-1} \\ R_2R_1^{-1} & 1 \quad \dots & R_2R_n^{-1} \\ \vdots & \vdots & \vdots \\ R_nR_1^{-1} & R_nR_2^{-1} \dots & 1 \end{bmatrix}.$$

Under the transformation **B** defined above, the dimensions of the transformed vectors $\mathbf{p}^*[M][\mathbf{R}^{-1*}]$ and $\mathbf{q}[\mathbf{R}][T^{-1}]$ remain unchanged (see Appendix 4).

In this case, there also exists the so-called "natural inverse" $(\mathbf{I} - \mathbf{B})^{-1}$, and its dimension is identical with that of the matrix **B** (see Appendix 4.3).

3

Since

$$\dim(\mathbf{Bq}) = [\mathbf{RR}^{-1*}][\mathbf{R}][T^{-1}] = [\mathbf{R}][T^{-1}]$$

also the computations of contents may be performed in the customary way.

Thus, for instance, the dimension of the wage contents per unit of final use in a given sector is

$$\dim(\mathbf{v}^*\mathbf{Q}^{-1}(\mathbf{I} - \mathbf{B})^{-1}) = [MT^{-1}]_j\ [T][\mathbf{1R}^{-1*}][\mathbf{RR}^{-1*}] = [M\mathbf{R}^{-1*}],$$

where the components of the vector $\mathbf{v}^*\mathbf{Q}^{-1}$ are the direct wage inputs of the industries. It follows that the dimension of the cumulated wages of the sectoral final use is

$$[M\mathbf{R}^{-1*}][\mathbf{RR}^{-1*}][\mathbf{R1}^*][T^{-1}] = [MT^{-1}]_j$$

i.e., its dimension is money per time, identical with what we would obtain by computing with the value of final use expressed in terms of money.

4

Returning now to the inconsistent price system as defined under point 1, it is evidently true for matrix **A** at average prices that

$$\dim(\mathbf{A}) = \dim(\hat{\mathbf{P}}\mathbf{W}) = \dim(\hat{\mathbf{P}}\mathbf{B}\hat{\mathbf{P}}^{-1}) = [M][\mathbf{1R}^{-1*}][\mathbf{RR}^{-1*}][\mathbf{R1}^{*}][M^{-1}] = [\mathbf{11}^{*}].$$

We wish that the elements of matrix **A** (expressed similarly in value terms) should also be dimensionless numbers. Let

$$\bar{\mathbf{A}} = \mathbf{ZW}$$

and (as we know from point 1)

$$\dim(\mathbf{W}) = \dim(\mathbf{B}\hat{\mathbf{P}}^{-1}).$$

From this we have to define the dimension of **Z**. Surely, there exists a transformation **Z**, because we may define **Z** as $\mathbf{Z} = \bar{\mathbf{A}}\mathbf{W}^{-1}$ and **W** as well as $\bar{\mathbf{A}}$ has an inverse. The dimension of $\mathbf{B}^{-1}$ is the same as that of **B** (see Appendix 4.4). It follows, then, that

$$\dim(\mathbf{Z}) = \dim(\bar{\mathbf{A}}\mathbf{W}^{-1}) = \dim(\bar{\mathbf{A}}\hat{\mathbf{P}}\mathbf{B}^{-1}) = [\mathbf{11}^{*}][M][\mathbf{1R}^{-1*}][\mathbf{RR}^{-1*}] =$$

$$= [M]\,[\mathbf{1R}^{-1*}] = \dim(\hat{\mathbf{P}});$$

and from the requirement of

$$\dim(\bar{\mathbf{A}}) = [\mathbf{11}^{*}]$$

we obtain that the **Z** (non-diagonal) matrix creating an inconsistent price system is of the same dimension as the (diagonal) matrix $\hat{\mathbf{P}}$. Accordingly,

$$\dim(\mathbf{AX}) = \dim(\hat{\mathbf{P}}\mathbf{BQ}) = \dim(\mathbf{ZBQ}) = \dim(\bar{\mathbf{A}}\mathbf{X})[T^{-1}]$$

$$\dim(\hat{\mathbf{P}}\mathbf{BQ}) = [M][\mathbf{1R}^{-1*}][\mathbf{RR}^{-1*}][\mathbf{R1}^{*}][T^{-1}] = [M][\mathbf{1\,1}^{*}]\,[T^{-1}] = [T^{-1}]_{ij} =$$

$$= \dim(\bar{\mathbf{A}}\mathbf{X}) = \dim(\mathbf{AX})$$

where the figures of the dimension "money/time" define, in both cases, the intraindustry flows in terms of money, by kinds of inputs. (Here, and in the following, **X** and **Q** mean the diagonal matrices derived from the components of **x** and **q**.)

5

The (static) multi-sectoral analysis makes it inevitable to start, instead of from the uniform $[R]$, i.e. "real dimension" customarily used in the literature, from an appropriately chosen set $\{[R_i]\}$ of n distinct units, and formally to deal with them as truly existing dimensions.*

Let us define the set $\{[R_i]\}$, consisting of a finite n number of different physical outputs and let $[R]$ be the dimension of undistinguished sector performances. Let us find the linear transformation of the vectors the components of which are given in terms of the $[R_i]$ -s into vectors given in terms of only $[R]$.

Let $\mathbf{C}$ be the matrix of transition and $\mathbf{C}'$ its inverse, for which

$$\dim(\mathbf{C}') = [X][\mathbf{1R}^{-1*}] = [X\mathbf{R}^{-1*}]_i$$

$$\dim(\mathbf{C}) = [\mathbf{R1}^*][Y] = [\mathbf{R}Y]_j.$$

If we define $[X] = [R]$; $[Y] = [R^{-1}]$ respectively, then

$$\mathbf{B} = \mathbf{C}'\bar{\mathbf{B}}\mathbf{C},$$

which is exactly the desired matrix, transforming the vectors $\mathbf{C}'\mathbf{q}$ into vectors of dimension $[RT^{-1}]_i$ and the vectors $\mathbf{p}^*\mathbf{C}$ into vectors of dimension $[MR^{-1}]_j$. Accordingly

$$\dim(\mathbf{PC}(\mathbf{C}'\mathbf{BC})\mathbf{C}'\mathbf{Q}) = \dim(\mathbf{P}(\mathbf{C}\bar{\mathbf{B}}\mathbf{C}')\mathbf{Q}) = \dim(\mathbf{PBQ}) = \dim(\mathbf{AX}) = [MT^{-1}]_{ij}.$$

The same is valid for non-consistent price systems, if we write $\mathbf{Z}$ instead of $\mathbf{P}$ or $\hat{\mathbf{P}}$.

With the same procedure we can determine the vectors $\mathbf{q}$ in such a way that the dimension of all their components shall be $[R_jT^{-1}]$, on another basis formed by the columns of a matrix $\mathbf{D}$, if its inverse, $\mathbf{D}'$ has the dimension of $[R_j][\mathbf{1R}^{-1*}]$. Thus, in principle (that is, within the limits of validity of the input–output model), nothing hinders us in expressing the total material production of the national economy in terms of a given dimension, say, in "wheat equivalent" or in an arbitrary product combination,** or even in quantities of gold — provided that gold is produced in the country. It will depend only on the coordinates whether we obtain output proportions identical with, or different from, what could be obtained if calculated in the value of monetary gold.

* A similar kind of procedure is familiar in physics: quantities of the dimension $[L]$ (length) may be determined by coordinates relating to $[L_1]$, $[L_2]$ and $[L_3]$, in which case the unknown dimensions of the constants figuring in the equation have to be defined according to a basis of five (rather than three) elements if the CGS (centimeter-gram-secundum) system or another equivalent system is considered (see D. H. Krantz, D. R. Luce, P. Suppes and A. Tversky: *Foundations of Measurement*. Vol. I, Academic Press, New York–London 1971). For our purposes the set consisting of $n[R_i]$ elements can be better interpreted as a mere $[R]$.

** Sraffa, Piero: *Production of Commodities by Means of Commodities*. Cambridge University Press, London 1960.

APPENDIX

1. Let a_i, b_i be the coordinates of the vectors **a**, **b** with n components, [**X**], [**Y**] the dimensions related to the coordinates and let

$$[X_i][Y_i] = [X_i Y_i] = [Z].$$

The rule of forming the scalar product between the vectors **a** and **b** consisting of dimensional quantities (variables or constants) is the following:

$$(\mathbf{a}^*)[\mathbf{X}^*](\mathbf{b})[\mathbf{Y}] = \mathbf{a}^*\mathbf{b}[Z]. \tag{1.1}$$

This can be verified by

$$(\mathbf{a}^*)[\mathbf{X}^*](\mathbf{b})[\mathbf{Y}] = (\mathbf{a}[\mathbf{X}])^*(\mathbf{b}[\mathbf{Y}]) = a_1b_1[X_1Y_1] + \ldots + a_nb_n[X_nY_n] =$$

$$= a_1b_1[Z] + \ldots + a_nb_n[Z] = (a_1b_1 + \ldots + a_nb_n)[Z] = \mathbf{a}^*\mathbf{b}[Z].$$

2. It follows from (1.1) that dimensional vectors can be transformed only by matrices the components of which are dimensional constants. The dimension-matrix belonging to the matrix of transformation is always the diadic product between two dimension-vectors formed according to (1.1), that is, of the form

$$[\mathbf{X}^\alpha \mathbf{Y}^{\beta *}].$$

Let us have for the elements of the corresponding dimensional vectors*

$$[X_i^{\alpha_i}],\ [Y_j^{-\beta_j}],\ [Y_k^{\beta_k}],\ [Z_l^{\gamma_l}],$$

then

$$[\mathbf{X}^\alpha \mathbf{Y}^{-\beta *}] \quad \text{and} \quad [\mathbf{Y}^\beta \mathbf{Z}^{\gamma *}]$$

are the dimension-matrices belonging to the transformatiions **A** and **B**, and the dimension of **AB** is obtained according to the following chain rule:

$$\dim(\mathbf{AB}) = [\mathbf{X}^\alpha \mathbf{Y}^{\beta -}{}^*][\mathbf{Y}^\beta \mathbf{Z}^{\gamma *}] = [\mathbf{X}^\alpha \mathbf{Z}^{\gamma *}]$$

$$(i = 1, \ldots, m;\ j = 1, \ldots, n;\ k = 1, \ldots, n;\ l = 1, \ldots, p). \tag{2.1}$$

* In the practically relevant cases, the components of the dimension-vectors have only one factor, or, at most, each of them is multiplied by the same factor $[T^{-1}]$ or $[M]$; the exponents may have the values of only 0, or +1 or −1. The results mentioned in the text would not change even if we related them to quantities of the form

$$\dim(a_l) = \left[\prod_{k=1}^{K_l} X_k^{\alpha_{lk}}\right]$$

where X_k is an element of some system of units. (See Quade, Wilhelm: The Algebraic Structure of Dimensional Analysis. *Encyclopaedia Britannica*, 1947 ed. Vol. 7.) In this paper the system

$$[R_1, R_2, \ldots, R_n, M, T]$$

was taken for basis. But also

$$[R_1T^{-1}, R_2T^{-1}, \ldots, R_nT^{-1}, M, T]$$

would have been an equivalent system.

Let us assume, moreover, that

$$\dim(\mathbf{x}^*) = [\mathbf{X}^{-\alpha *}],\ \dim(\mathbf{y}) = [\mathbf{Z}^{-\gamma}],$$

respectively, and that the dimensions of the matrices **A** and **B** are the same as before. Then the dimensions of the transformed vectors will be

$$\dim(\mathbf{x}^*\mathbf{A}) = [\mathbf{X}^{-\alpha *}][\mathbf{X}^{\alpha}\mathbf{Y}^{-\beta *}] = [\mathbf{Y}^{-\beta *}],$$

$$\dim(\mathbf{B}\mathbf{y}) \quad = [\mathbf{Y}^{\beta}\mathbf{Z}^{\gamma *}][\mathbf{Z}^{-\gamma}] = [\mathbf{Y}^{\beta}]. \tag{2.2}$$

3. *Definition:* The dimension-matrix of the transformation is *simple,* when

$$\dim(\mathbf{C}) = [\mathbf{1}\mathbf{X}^{\alpha *}],\ \text{or}\ \dim(\mathbf{C}) = [\mathbf{X}^{\alpha}\mathbf{1}^*]$$

(the dimensions in the rows or in the columns of the matrix **C** are identical).
If the matrix **C** is a diagonal one, and

$$\dim(\mathbf{C}) = [\mathbf{X}^{\alpha}\mathbf{1}^*][Y],\ \text{or}\ \dim(\mathbf{C}) = [Y][\mathbf{1}\mathbf{X}^{\alpha *}],$$

it follows that

$$\dim(\mathbf{C}^{-1}) = [Y^{-1}][\mathbf{1}\mathbf{X}^{-\alpha *}],\ \text{or}\ \dim(\mathbf{C}^{-1}) = [\mathbf{X}^{-\alpha}\mathbf{1}^*][Y^{-1}]. \tag{3.1}$$

The dimension-matrix of a diagonal matrix is always simple or it may be the product of a simple dimension matrix and its inverse.

4. *Definition:* A linear transformation **A** is considered as *dimension-fixing* if there exist some vectors **x** and **x′** so that

$$\dim(\mathbf{x}') = \dim(\mathbf{A}\mathbf{x}) = \dim(\mathbf{x}),$$

that is, the dimension of the appropriate vectors remains unchanged under the transformation **A**.

The dimension-matrices of the dimension-fixing transformations are quadratic and they must have the form of

$$[\mathbf{X}^{\alpha}\mathbf{X}^{-\alpha *}].$$

When applying such a transformation to the vectors $\mathbf{p}^*[\mathbf{X}^{-\alpha *}]$ or $\mathbf{q}[\mathbf{X}^{\alpha}]$ respectively, we obtain vectors of the same dimension.

Furthermore these transformations have the following properties:

a) To any power (with a positive integer exponent) of a dimension-fixing transformation there belongs the same dimension-matrix, that is

$$\dim(\mathbf{A}^k) = \dim(\mathbf{A}).$$

b) If

$$\dim(\mathbf{A}) \quad = [\mathbf{X}^{\alpha}\mathbf{X}^{-\alpha *}]$$

then

$$\dim(\mathbf{A}^*) = [\mathbf{X}^{-\alpha}\mathbf{X}^{\alpha *}]$$

and the transpose of **A** is also dimension-fixing.

c) If we have the matrices of the form

$$\mathbf{C}'[\mathbf{1X}^{-\alpha*}],\ \mathbf{C}[\mathbf{X}^{\alpha}\mathbf{1}^*],\ \mathbf{A}[\mathbf{X}^{\alpha}\mathbf{X}^{-\alpha*}]$$

then

$$\dim(\mathbf{C}'\mathbf{AC}) = [\mathbf{1\,1}^*] = [1]_{ij}$$

$$\dim(\mathbf{C}'\mathbf{C}) = [\mathbf{1\,1}^*] = [1]_{ij}$$

and the following relations hold:

$$\dim(\mathbf{C}'\mathbf{A}) = \dim(\mathbf{C}');\ \dim(\mathbf{AC}) = \dim(\mathbf{C});$$

$$\dim(\mathbf{C}'\mathbf{C}) = \dim(\mathbf{A}).$$

The same is true for those transposed, namely

$$\dim((\mathbf{C}'\mathbf{C})^*) = \dim(\mathbf{C}^*\mathbf{C}'^*) = [\mathbf{1\,1}^*]^* = [\mathbf{1\,1}^*] = [1]_{ij}.$$

The above-defined matrix $\mathbf{C}'\mathbf{AC}$ transforms the row vectors $\mathbf{p}^*\mathbf{C}$ and the column vectors $\mathbf{C}'\mathbf{q}$ into vectors the components of which have dimension one, i.e., they are dimensionless numbers.

The dimension of a (real) characteristic value of a dimension-fixing transformation $\mathbf{A}$ is always one. Namely, if we consider the characteristic equation of $\mathbf{A}$ in the form

$$|\,\mathbf{A} - \lambda\mathbf{I}\,| = 0,$$

then it follows that

$$\dim(|\,\mathbf{A} - \lambda\mathbf{I}\,|) = \dim(\Sigma(-1)^I\bar{a}_{1j_1}\ldots\bar{a}_{nj_n}) = [X_1^{\alpha_1}X_{j_1}^{-\alpha_{j_1}}\ldots X_n^{\alpha_n}X_{j_n}^{-\alpha_{j_n}}] =$$

$$= [X_1^{\alpha_1}\ldots X_n^{\alpha_n}][X_1^{-\alpha_1}\ldots X_n^{-\alpha_n}] = [1] \qquad (4.1)$$

whence the dimension of each of the coefficients and of the unknown λ's is [1]. In (4.1) the number of inversions is I and

$$\bar{a}_{ij_l} = (a_{ij_l} - \delta_{j_l}\lambda); \qquad \delta_{ji} = \begin{cases} 1, & \text{if } i = j, \\ 0, & \text{if } i \neq j. \end{cases}$$

Let us consider the dimension-fixing transformation $\mathbf{A}$ in the canonical form. Because of (4.1), the following relations must exist

$$\dim(\mathbf{A}) = \dim(\mathbf{SJS}^{-1});\ \dim(\mathbf{S}^{-1}\mathbf{AS}) = \dim(\mathbf{J}) = [1]_{ij}. \qquad (4.2)$$

In this case the dimensions belonging to the elements of the inverse of $\mathbf{A}$ can be determined from (4.2) and the known dimensions of the characteristic vectors of $\mathbf{A}$.

If $\mathbf{B}$ is a dimension-fixing transformation and

$$\max_i |\,\lambda_i\,| < 1$$

then prescribing

$$\dim(\mathbf{B}^0) = \dim(\mathbf{B}),$$

we obtain

$$\dim (\mathbf{I} - \mathbf{B})^{-1} = \dim (\mathbf{B});\ \dim (\mathbf{B}^{-1}) = \dim (\mathbf{B}).$$

Namely, for this power series it is valid that

$$\mathbf{B}^0[\dim (\mathbf{B}^0)] + \ldots + \mathbf{B}^N[\dim (\mathbf{B}^N)] + \ldots = \mathbf{B}^0[\dim (\mathbf{B})] + \ldots + \mathbf{B}^N[\dim (\mathbf{B})] +$$
$$+ \ldots = (\mathbf{B}^0 + \ldots + \mathbf{B}^N + \ldots)[\dim (\mathbf{B})] = (\mathbf{I} - \mathbf{B})^{-1} [\dim (\mathbf{B})]. \quad (4.3)$$

Furthermore, in view of (4.2), (3.1) and of the requirement of $\dim (\mathbf{I} - \mathbf{B}) = \dim (\mathbf{B})$ also the requirement of

$$\dim ((\mathbf{C}^{-1}\mathbf{B}\mathbf{C})^{-1}) = \dim ((\mathbf{C}^{-1}(\mathbf{I} - \mathbf{B})\,\mathbf{C})^{-1}) =$$
$$= \dim (\mathbf{C}^{-1}(\mathbf{I} - \mathbf{B})^{-1}\,\mathbf{C}) = \dim\ (\mathbf{C}^{-1}\,\mathbf{B}^{-1}\mathbf{C})$$

is satisfied, and it follows therefrom that

$$\dim (\mathbf{B}^{-1}) = \dim (\mathbf{B}). \quad (4.4)$$

5. Let us form from a quadratic matrix $\mathbf{A} = [a_{ij}]$ consisting of arbitrarily chosen dimensional constants, its inverse $\mathbf{A}^{-1} = (A_{ij})$ — if it exists — using the adjoint of $\mathbf{A}$. Then we obtain the following simple rule regarding the dimension of the elements of $\mathbf{A}^{-1}$

$$\dim (A_{ij}) = 1/\dim (a_{ji}). \quad (5.1)$$

Since it is possible to form the dimension-matrix belonging to any linear mapping by the product of two simple dimension-matrices, we obtain for the dimension-matrix of the inverse a result identical with (5.1) by determining it from such a product and applying the rule of inverting a matrix product. Let

$$\dim (\mathbf{A}) = [\mathbf{X}^\alpha \mathbf{Y}^{\beta *}] = [\mathbf{X}^\alpha \mathbf{1}^*][\mathbf{1}\mathbf{Y}^{\beta *}] = \dim (\mathbf{A}_1\mathbf{A}_2)$$

accordingly:

$$\dim (\mathbf{A}^{-1}) = \dim ((\mathbf{A}_1\mathbf{A}_2)^{-1}) = \dim (\mathbf{A}_2^{-1}\mathbf{A}_1^{-1}) =$$
$$= [\mathbf{Y}^{-\beta}\mathbf{1}^*][\mathbf{1}\mathbf{X}^{-\alpha *}] = 1/\dim (a_{ji}). \quad (5.2)$$

(5.1) and (5.2) are consistent also with (4.1) and (4.2), where we started from the economic interpretation of the elements of the inverse.

6. If the elements of a matrix **A** are dimensional constants, the dimension-matrix related to the matrix of transition to a new basis is either simple or its dimension is identical with that of **A** (in other words, it is dimension-fixing).

AN INTERPRETATION OF THE VARIABLES AND COEFFICIENTS IN THE CLOSED DYNAMIC LEONTIEF MODEL

by

JÓZSEF HORVÁTH

1. In one of his articles János Kovács* puts forth the idea of linking the long-term planning of manpower training with that of production by using a dynamic closed Leontief model. For the implementation of the idea a small team has been formed, in which J. Kovács, Gy. Tényi and the present author took part.

A unique and consistent definition of the variables and coefficients of the said (mathematical) model belongs to the tasks to be solved in the first phase of the work. The adjective "consistent" means in this case that, with the given definitions, the mathematical relations figuring in the model may be interpreted also economically.

2. The form of the closed dynamic Leontief model, that has been used by us, is the following:

$$\mathbf{x} = \mathbf{A}\mathbf{x} + \lambda\mathbf{B}\mathbf{x}$$

where, using general terms,

$\mathbf{x}$ = vector of output levels,
$\mathbf{A}$ = matrix of intermediate inputs,
$\mathbf{B}$ = matrix of capital engagement,
λ = maximum growth rate (see: Kovács, op. cit.).

Vector $\mathbf{x}$ has two parts: $\mathbf{x} = \begin{bmatrix}\mathbf{x}_1\\ \mathbf{x}_2\end{bmatrix}$, where $\mathbf{x}_1$ is the vector of output levels in the closer sense and $\mathbf{x}_2$ is the vector of labour quantities of different categories. Labour can be measured in terms of man-hours worked, but — if we consider the hours put in by a worker as fixed — this can be converted into employment figures and vice versa. According to the division of vector $\mathbf{x}$ matrices $\mathbf{A}$ and $\mathbf{B}$ fall into four blocks each. A more detailed description of the model is therefore:

$$\begin{bmatrix}\mathbf{x}_1\\ \mathbf{x}_2\end{bmatrix} = \begin{bmatrix}\mathbf{A}_{11} & \mathbf{A}_{12}\\ \mathbf{A}_{21} & \mathbf{A}_{22}\end{bmatrix}\begin{bmatrix}\mathbf{x}_1\\ \mathbf{x}_2\end{bmatrix} + \lambda\begin{bmatrix}\mathbf{B}_{11} & \mathbf{B}_{12}\\ \mathbf{B}_{21} & \mathbf{B}_{22}\end{bmatrix}\begin{bmatrix}\mathbf{x}_1\\ \mathbf{x}_2\end{bmatrix}.$$

Block $\mathbf{A}_{11}$ is the well-known technological matrix and block $\mathbf{B}_{11}$ is the capital engagement matrix of material production. These are essentially free of problems.

* Kovács, J.: A munkaerő társadalmi újratermelésének tervezéséhez (On the planning of the social reproduction of labour). *Szigma.* No. 3, Budapest 1969.

So is block $\mathbf{A}_{21}$ comprising the coefficients of direct inputs of live labour into physical production. Also, blocks $\mathbf{A}_{12}$ and $\mathbf{A}_{22}$ are relatively easy to interpret: the first means the per unit consumption, by individual labour categories, from the various material goods, the second are the coefficients of direct "labour input" (services).

The difficulty arises when interpreting the blocks $\mathbf{B}_{12}$, $\mathbf{B}_{21}$ and $\mathbf{B}_{22}$ of matrix $\mathbf{B}$. To see the problems involved in the definition of these coefficients, let us take in turn the definitions hitherto published and test whether they make it possible to interpret the relationships written above. In order to be able to abstract from problems of other types, we assume the technologies as unchanged.

3. For the sake of simplicity, let us consider only the case where $\mathbf{x}_2$ has a single element (in this case, obviously, $\mathbf{B}_{12}$ is a column vector, $\mathbf{B}_{21}$ a row vector and $\mathbf{B}_{22}$ a scalar).

With A. Bródy we have arrived at the following definitions:

Block $\mathbf{A}_{12}$: "the last column comprises the stocks of non-durable and durable consumer goods and other reproducible values held by the population and public bodies".*

Block $\mathbf{B}_{21}$: ". . . the variable capital (embodied in the stocks and semi-finished products engaged in production) . . ."**

Block $\mathbf{B}_{22}$: the costs arising during the training of a person (human investment).***

As regards the components of the product $\mathbf{B} \cdot \lambda\mathbf{x}$, on the grounds of the above definitions they will be the following:

$\mathbf{B}_{12} \cdot \lambda\mathbf{x}_2 =$ increase in the stocks of consumer goods necessary for increasing the quantity of labour power,

$\mathbf{B}_{21} \cdot \lambda\mathbf{x}_1 =$ the amount of labour embodied in the increase of working assets that is required for increasing the output,

$\mathbf{B}_{22} \cdot \lambda\mathbf{x}_2 =$ the input of live labour required for increasing the quantity of labour power.

Accordingly, the vector $\mathbf{x}_1$ would be divided into the following parts: productive consumption ($\mathbf{A}_{11}\mathbf{x}_1$) + other consumption ($\mathbf{A}_{21}\mathbf{x}_2$) + productive accumulation ($\mathbf{B}_{11} \cdot \lambda\mathbf{x}_1$) + increase of stocks in consumer goods.

This would mean, however, that the investments into the training of labour is omitted. They could be accounted for, say, within block $\mathbf{A}_{21}$, by adding them to the consumption by workers, together with the consumption by those being trained.

* Bródy, A.: *Beszámoló a dinamikus ÁKM modellel végzett első magyarországi számításokról* (Report on the first Hungarian computations with the dynamic input–output model,) p. 12. Internal report of the Institute of Economic Sciences, Hungarian Academy of Sciences.

** Bródy, A.: *Érték és újratermelés* (Value and reproduction), p. 88. Közgazdasági és Jogi Kiadó, Budapest 1969.

*** See Bródy: *Beszámoló* . . . op. cit.

This means that the consumption by workers being trained and the investments in their training are proportional with the change in the number of workers. The amount of labour performed in a year ($\mathbf{x}_2$) would then consist of the following components: labour needed for physical production ($\mathbf{A}_{21}\mathbf{x}_1$) + services ($\mathbf{A}_{22}\mathbf{x}_2$) + labour needed for increasing the working assets ($\mathbf{B}_{21} \cdot \lambda\mathbf{x}_2$) + input of live labour required for increasing the quantity of labour power ($\mathbf{B}_{22} \cdot \lambda\mathbf{x}_2$).

But there is already some trouble with our second equation. Namely, the increase of working assets, meaning the accumulation of physical goods, must figure in the product $\mathbf{B}_{11} \cdot \lambda\mathbf{x}_1$. As this latter is a part of $\mathbf{x}_1$, the live labour required for this increase in stocks are already comprised in the product $\mathbf{A}_{11}\mathbf{x}_1$. Therefore, the amount $\mathbf{B}_{21} \cdot \lambda\mathbf{x}_1$ would be doubly accounted.

Also the product $\mathbf{B}_{22} \cdot \lambda\mathbf{x}_2$ requires further inspection. First, the meaning of $\lambda\mathbf{x}_2$ should be made clear. Does it mean the total number of persons newly trained, or only the net increment of the actual labour force (i.e., left over after replacing those dropping out)? In the first case (assuming unchanged methods of training), the amount of labour $\mathbf{B}_{22} \cdot \lambda\mathbf{x}_2$ would mean the amount needed for the number of those being trained which is precisely $\lambda\mathbf{x}_2$ in every class. This, of course, would mean that the rate of growth cannot be λ in this case. In other words, the actual amount of labour required for training must be greater than $\mathbf{B}_{22} \cdot \lambda\mathbf{x}_t$.

In addition, in the first case we must also assume that the increment $\lambda\mathbf{x}$ is a gross one, from which the part used for replacing the scrapped means of production and labour power dropped out must be determined separately. This, again, means that block $\mathbf{A}_{11}$ does not comprise the wear and tear on fixed assets. In the second case, if block $\mathbf{B}_{22}$ continues to represent the labour inputs of training, the quantity $\mathbf{B} \cdot \lambda\mathbf{x}_2$ will be essentially different from (i.e., much smaller than) the labour requirements of training.

4. How could the elements of matrix **B** be given an acceptable definition? The truth is that no fully satisfactory solution has been found yet. I will list here a few approximative solutions regarding the elements of the critical $\mathbf{B}_{12}$, $\mathbf{B}_{21}$, $\mathbf{B}_{22}$ blocks.

Variant 1: $\lambda\mathbf{x}$ denotes the *net* increment:

Block $\mathbf{B}_{12}$ = as defined above according to Bródy, this is the engagement per employee of the stocks of the various consumer goods,

Block $\mathbf{B}_{21}$ = direct inputs of live labour needed for investments, per unit of productive capacity (i.e., per unit of the commodity to be produced), e.g., designing, fitting works, etc., provided that the result of such activity does not figure in any way in the products; in this latter case these elements are zero,

Block $\mathbf{B}_{22}$ = zero.

In this variant, therefore, the training inputs (the consumption by those trained, the investments needed and the live-labour requirements of training) are taken into account in blocks $\mathbf{A}_{12}$ and $\mathbf{A}_{23}$.

Variant 2: $\lambda\mathbf{x}$ denotes the *gross* increment:

Block $\mathbf{B}_{12}$ = consumption and investment of individual products per one person whose training has been completed,
Block $\mathbf{B}_{21}$ = the same as in Variant 1,
Block $\mathbf{B}_{22}$ = labour inputs into training per one person whose training has been completed.

In blocks $\mathbf{B}_{12}$ and $\mathbf{B}_{22}$ the costs of training are computed per persons whose training has been completed because $\lambda\mathbf{x}_2$ means exactly the number of such persons (i.e., of those entering work in the following year). Thus, after multiplication the total inputs of training are arrived at.

The main distortion consists in that the investments into training (as part of the "consumption" by those trained) are supposed to be proportionate with the number of persons whose training is completed in the given year. In reality, it is proportionate with the growth in the number of those trained. This distortion cannot be eliminated here, For this, a model would be needed that comprises the relationships for as many years as needed until the acquisition of the highest qualification (that is, 22–23 years).

In the case of the gross-increment variant it is assumed that replacement equals some δ times the quantity of every product (or of the quantity of labour required for its production, that is, $\delta\mathbf{x}$ meaning that the actual growth rate of each branch is $\lambda - \delta$.

Variant 3: Vector $\mathbf{x}$ will be extended, and training will figure as a separate sector, to be denoted by $\mathbf{x}_3$ so that

$$\mathbf{x} = \begin{bmatrix} x_1 \\ x_2 \\ x_3 \end{bmatrix}, \quad \text{and } \lambda\mathbf{x} \text{ be the net increment.}$$

In this case the matrices $\mathbf{A}$ and $\mathbf{B}$ would fall into 9 blocks each. A possibility for defining the sectors may be the following:

The definition of blocks $\mathbf{A}_{11}$, $\mathbf{A}_{12}$, $\mathbf{A}_{21}$, $\mathbf{A}_{22}$ and $\mathbf{B}_{11}$, $\mathbf{B}_{12}$, $\mathbf{B}_{21}$, $\mathbf{B}_{22}$ should be similar to that in the first variant, with the difference that here the consumption by those being trained, as well as the investments and labour inputs into training are not contained in the products $\mathbf{A}_{12}\mathbf{x}_2$ and $\mathbf{A}_{22}\mathbf{x}_2$;

$\mathbf{A}_{13}$ = consumption coefficients of those being trained (per one school-leaving person);
$\mathbf{A}_{23}$ = labour inputs into training (per one school-leaving person);
$\mathbf{A}_{31}$, $\mathbf{A}_{32}$, $\mathbf{A}_{33}$ = coefficients of labour drop-outs (that is, the sum $\mathbf{A}_{31}\mathbf{x}_1 + \mathbf{A}_{32}\mathbf{x}_2 + \mathbf{A}_{33}\mathbf{x}_3$ gives the number of persons dropping out from the labour force, to be replaced with newly-trained persons);
$\mathbf{B}_{13}$ = coefficients showing the amount of investments required for training purposes (per one school-leaving person);

$\mathbf{B}_{31}, \mathbf{B}_{32}, \mathbf{B}_{33}$ = coefficients showing the amount of labour required for extension, that is, the sum $\lambda(\mathbf{B}_{31}\mathbf{x}_1 + \mathbf{B}_{32}\mathbf{x}_2 + \mathbf{B}_{33}\mathbf{x}_3)$ gives the amount of labour necessary for bringing about the increment $\lambda\mathbf{x}$. In the case of unchanged technology, these blocks evidently agree with blocks $\mathbf{A}_{21}, \mathbf{A}_{22}$ and $\mathbf{A}_{23}$ numerically;

$\mathbf{B}_{23}$ = zero.

The main problem of this variant is the same as that of Variant 2: the inputs into training are proportionate with the number of those leaving school. In addition, also another requirement of proportionality emerges, which is generally not met. Namely, in Variant 3, by definition the following equation must hold:

$$\lambda\mathbf{x}_2 = \mathbf{x}_3 - [\mathbf{A}_{31}, \mathbf{A}_{32}, \mathbf{A}_{33}]\cdot\mathbf{x}\,.$$

I believe there is no guarantee that the vector $\mathbf{x}$ obtained as a solution of the equation

$$\mathbf{x} = \mathbf{A}\mathbf{x} + \lambda\mathbf{B}\mathbf{x}$$

will satisfy the above equation.

In addition to the problems of definition, another serious difficulty arises in connection with the closed dynamic Leontief model. The assumption that the matrices **A** and **B** are constant is strong. If, however, we abandon this assumption, the growth rate λ cannot be interpreted. (Namely, for the $\mathbf{x}_t$ received as a solution of the equation $\mathbf{x}_t = \mathbf{A}_t\mathbf{x}_t + \mathbf{B}_t \cdot \lambda_t\mathbf{x}_t$ it will not necessarily be true that $\mathbf{x}_t = \lambda_{t-1}\mathbf{x}_{t-1}$.)

Therefore, before trying to apply the model on a broad scale, attempts should be made to solve these problems. It depends on the success of these efforts whether we shall continue working with this model or shall have to construct another one.

SIMILARITIES AND DISSIMILARITIES IN THE ECONOMIC STRUCTURE OF THE ECE COUNTRIES

by

GYÖRGY SZEPESI and BÉLA SZÉKELY

INTRODUCTION

The ECE has initiated a joint research programme in order to establish a comparison of the economic structures prevailing in the member countries. For this purpose, the Secretariat constructed *standardized input–output tables* for eighteen European countries as well as for the USA and Japan, covering the period of 1959 to 1961, with the participation of the members of the European Statistical Conference and using materials obtained from the member nations.

The countries participating in this joint effort undertook various tasks of analysis. Hungary has also been participating and several research groups have been occupied in comparing economic structures according to the balance schemes provided by the ECE Secretariat. One of these research groups is working within the department in charge of long-term plans in the Hungarian National Planning Office. This group has been dealing with the questions of comparative analysis in the contest of long-term planning, e.g., the comparison of Hungary's economic structure with other economies, and of the methods serving to plan the development of its various elements.

The research group first published two methodological studies, then with the aid of the methods proposed there it began to process the available data. The present paper is the first report on this work.

RESTRICTIONS AND QUALIFICATIONS

1. The computer program SOS and the description of the DIAD method can be found in Working Paper No. 4 of the meeting, dealing with the comparison of the economic structures of ECE countries, held in Geneva, April 8–10, 1970. The description will not be repeated in this study.

2. Both methods have been applied to a set of input–output tables of the ECE countries. Since computer time and other resources were restricted, the calculations were performed only with the tables of version "A" in the MPS system and of aggregation level C.1. The calculations were restricted to the most simple aspects of structural analysis.

3. The calculations reviewed were run in May and June 1971 and their systematic evaluation could not take place before the Conference.

4. As regards the technical accuracy of the input data used in the calculations, reservations are necessary from at least three points of view:

a) from a few aspects the tables are not fully comparable, e.g., in sector 19, or as regards the treatment of personal incomes in agriculture;

b) the raw material obtained as computer printout seems to be inconsistent in regard to the main diagonal components, and the methods used to correct them need to be checked;

c) a few minor errors were discovered after the programmes had been run and, therefore, a few countries had to be omitted from the comparisons.

5. For these reasons, the present study must not be considered as a report on a completed research project, but rather as a progress report. It contains the outlines of an analysis where some tentative statements can be found which are based on a first approximation.

6. This is the first time in the history of input–output analysis, and even in the history of international economic comparisons when fairly comparable input–output tables are available for a considerable number of countries, expressing the internal structural interdependencies of the economies. This raises the most exciting questions which we always wanted to ask, but which we are only now able to answer in an empirical manner.

7. Obviously, the first question is the following: what is common, what is specific and what is individual in the structure of countries with different social systems and at different levels of economic development, what is similar and what is divergent? If there exist common properties, can they be expressed with the aid of an average structure? What would an average European input–output structure look like?

8. The notion of an average European structure can be relatively well justified if considered simply as an arithmetic mean, a technical tool for disclosing similarities and divergences. What sound economic interpretation can this notion be given or how relevant and realistic it is in reality, remains an open question which cannot be answered merely by an empirical approach. But this empirical test may offer some help: it can show to what extent the individual countries deviate from this average structure and also what the average of the deviations is.

9. Deviations from the average structure may also be explained either with random (or rather individual) factors, or with such as are necessary under certain conditions. If so, there must be something common for individual countries in the extent and direction of the deviations from the average. Do the European countries cluster into groups according to their deviations from the average, and if so, do these groups also show other common characteristics?

In other words: is this classification a useful way of detecting the interrelations between structures and other fundamental economic factors?

10. To characterize the output structures we have chosen
- domestic production,
- individual consumption (of goods of domestic origin),
- total consumption (MPS).

All these were characterized by coefficients, that is, by the share of the individual sectors in the country totals. To characterize the input structure, the following quotients were computed for each sector:
- direct MPS value added per direct primary costs (depreciation plus wages)
- total (direct and indirect) MPS value added per total primary costs (depreciation plus wages)

The sectoral variations in these quotients serve, in a certain sense, to characterize the price system of the country in question.

11. For all five vectors the first diads comprised in Table 1 were computed. The first diad is a vector which condenses the maximum of what is common in the relative structures of the various countries. In this sense it may be considered as the unweighted European average. How well this vector approximates the original set of vectors can be measured with the aid of the quotient of two Euclidean norms; these can be found in the last row of Table 1.

Table 1

The greatest common part of the structures (the first diad)

Sector	Share in domestic production	Share in private consumption	Share in MPS consumption	Value added/cost direct	Value added/cost total
1 Agriculture	0.1309	0.1219	0.1383	2.980	2.543
2 Coal mining	0.0240	0.0087	0.0084	1.294	1.433
3 Other mining	0.0073	0.0002	0.0010	1.539	1.604
4 Food	0.1460	0.3211	0.2919	2.978	2.478
5 Textiles	0.0726	0.0439	0.0474	2.012	1.987
6 Clothes	0.0323	0.0760	0.0747	1.968	2.032
7 Wood, paper industries	0.0425	0.0322	0.0366	1.783	1.918
8 Rubber	0.0106	0.0035	0.0040	2.993	2.033
9 Chemical	0.0380	0.0198	0.0281	2.155	1.950
10 Petroleum refining	0.0221	0.0098	0.0132	5.163	2.258
11 Non-metallic minerals	0.0206	0.0033	0.0039	1.679	1.728
12 Basic metals	0.0447	0.0019	0.0018	1.790	1.745
13 Transport machinery	0.0330	0.0185	0.0221	1.714	1.774
14 Other engineering	0.0790	0.0418	0.0533	1.780	1.799
15 Electricity, gas	0.0214	0.0202	0.0198	1.825	1.698
16 Construction	0.0967	0.0071	0.0139	1.519	1.673
17 Trade	0.1013	0.1953	0.1680	2.716	2.476
18 Transport	0.0663	0.0432	0.0436	1.320	1.401
19 Restaurants, hotels	0.0108	0.0319	0.0299	1.419	1.685
The relative deviation of the two Euclidean norms	94.53	95.35	94.00	93.42	97.71

In general, it may be remarked that the approximation is surprisingly good.

12. Considering the European average, four sectors (agriculture, food processing, distribution and material services) are responsible for almost 40 per cent of production and more than 60 per cent of consumption. The ratio of the four sectors seems to be almost constant while with rising per capita GDP the shares of agriculture and food processing diminish and those of material services are rising (see Fig. 1).

13. The indicator of value added per costs is conspicuously high in oil refining (a well-known fact), then come the food industry, rubber industry and distribution. Transport and communications seem to be the least profitable businesses in Europe.

14. The structure of the individual countries deviates from the average. To measure this deviation we have introduced the indicator $R_k^{(z)}$. For each vector **z** and country k

$$R_k^{(z)} = \frac{1}{N} \sum_{i=1}^{N} | z_{ik}/d_i(z) \tag{1}$$

where z_{ik} is component i of vector **z** in country k, and $d_i(z)$ is component i of the first diad calculated for vector **z**.

The greater the indicator differs from unity, the greater is the deviation, that is,

$R_k > 1$ if some components are characteristically smaller in country k than the corresponding component in the average and the balancing items are distributed among the other components;

$R_k < 1$ if some components are characteristically greater in country k than the corresponding components in the average and the balancing items are distributed among the other components.

In this restricted sense, the indicator R_k also shows the direction of the deviation.

To characterize the average deviation of k number of countries we used the indicator $\bar{R}^{(z)}$

$$\bar{R}^{(z)} = \frac{1}{k} \sum_{k=1}^{k} |R_k^{(z)} - 1|. \tag{2}$$

15. The indicators $\bar{R}_k$ and $\bar{R}$ were calculated for the chosen output and primary input structures (see Table 2). The correlation between two important pairs of vectors is shown in Fig. 2.

16. The values of the indicator $\bar{R}$, which shows the average deviation from the first diad, are smallest with respect to the value added per cost* quotients and are greatest with respect to the pattern of MPS total consumptions.

Is it possible that there are more common properties in the price and cost structures of the European countries than in their output structures? This is

* In spite of the fact that the personal incomes of small-scale agricultural producers figure in some countries as incomes and in others as wages.

Table 2

The average of the relative sectoral deviations from the first diad (the R_k indicators)

Country	Share in domestic production	Share in private consumption	Share in MPS consumption	Value added/cost direct	Value added/cost total
1 Austria	—	—	1.46	1.05	0.98
2 Belgium	1.27	0.99	1.18	1.03	0.98
3 Bulgaria	0.76	0.79	0.71	0.95	1.00
4 Czechoslovakia	0.98	0.77	0.63	0.99	1.00
5 France	1.10	1.09	0.94	0.94	0.98
6 German Federal Republic	1.11	1.40	1.43	1.10	1.00
7 Greece	—	—	1.31	—	—
8 Hungary	1.01	1.42	1.19	0.99	1.03
9 Netherlands	0.92	1.03	1.05	1.08	1.02
10 Norway	0.95	0.98	0.91	1.24	1.01
11 Poland	0.97	0.72	0.63	1.06	0.97
12 Portugal	0.77	0.82	0.91	—	—
13 Spain	1.22	0.92	0.84	1.11	0.99
14 United King-dom	1.24	1.46	1.26	—	—
15 Yugoslavia	—	—	1.11	1.00	1.03
Average relative deviation (R)	0.133	0.201	0.245	0.067	0.016

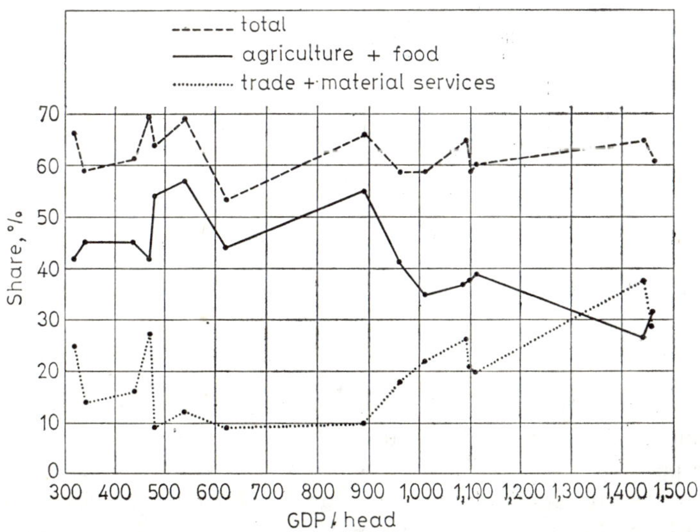

Fig. 1. The share of agriculture, food, trade and material services in MPS consumption

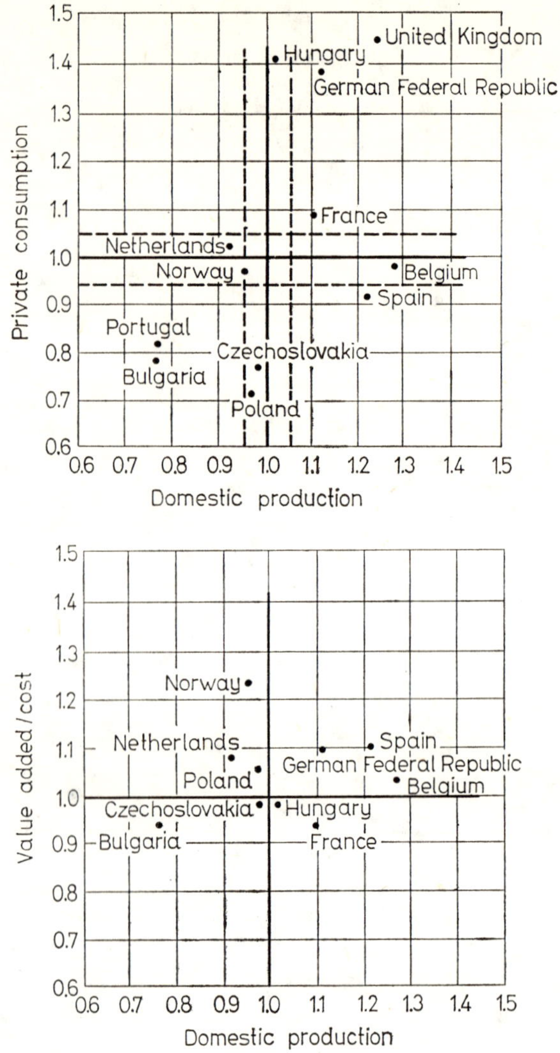

Fig. 2. The average of the relative sectoral deviations from the first diad (the R_k indicators)

a surprising fact, if it is indeed a fact and not the interplay of technical errors. The statement still needs to be verified.

17. The position of the individual countries relative to the European average might be a starting point of some relevant classifications. In the upper part of Fig. 2 most countries are grouped along one of the two axes representing some average. Those which are nearest to the average as regards their production

pattern are farthest from it in the pattern of individual consumption (Czechoslovakia, Hungary, Poland). On the other hand, the countries nearest to the average in the consumption pattern deviate to a greater extent from the average as regards production structure (Belgium, Netherlands, Norway).

In the lower part of Fig. 2, the situation is somewhat different. The countries using the MPS cluster in both directions around the average. Czechoslovakia, Hungary and Poland lie in the heart of Europe. On the other hand, e.g., the Netherlands and Norway differ from the average in the structure of value added per cost more strongly than in either consumption or production patterns. These phenomena call for technical checking and, if proven correct, their interpretation from the aspect of theoretical economics must be sought.

SECONDARY INPUT STRUCTURE — THE MATRIX MULTIPLIER

18. The secondary input coefficients, both direct and total, necessitate an investigation in themselves, similarly their row and column totals, their means, etc. But the present analysis is restricted to the average of the components of the rows in the Leontief inverse, weighted by some existing final utilization pattern. In general, we use the vector

$$\mathbf{x} = \mathbf{Q}\bar{\mathbf{y}} \tag{3}$$

to explore the properties of the matrix multiplier $\mathbf{Q}$ where

$$\mathbf{Q} = (\mathrm{I} - \mathbf{A})^{-1}$$
$$\bar{\mathbf{y}} = [y_i] \tag{4}$$

y_i = the share of sector i in the total MPS final use.

$$\sum_i y_i = 1. \tag{5}$$

19. The most general characteristic of the matrix multiplier is the so-called global multiplier q:

$$q = \mathbf{1}^*\bar{\mathbf{x}} \qquad (\mathbf{1}^* = [1, \ldots, 1]) \tag{6}$$

which shows the total output per unit of final use.

This is, of course, a function of the phenomenon often called "material intensity" but it also reflects the effects of several other factors. Fig. 3 shows the global multipliers of the ECE countries in relation to per capita GDP. The value of the global multiplier ranges from 1.5 to 3.0. (The figure relating to Poland needs to be checked for accuracy.) The multiplier first grows with rising per capita GDP, then it shows a declining tendency.

20. The programme SOS also calculates for k countries ($k = 1, \ldots, k$) the products $\mathbf{Q}_k\bar{\mathbf{y}}_1 \ldots \mathbf{Q}_k\bar{\mathbf{y}}_k$, in other words, the final utilization structure of each country was multiplied by the inverse of every other country. It follows that

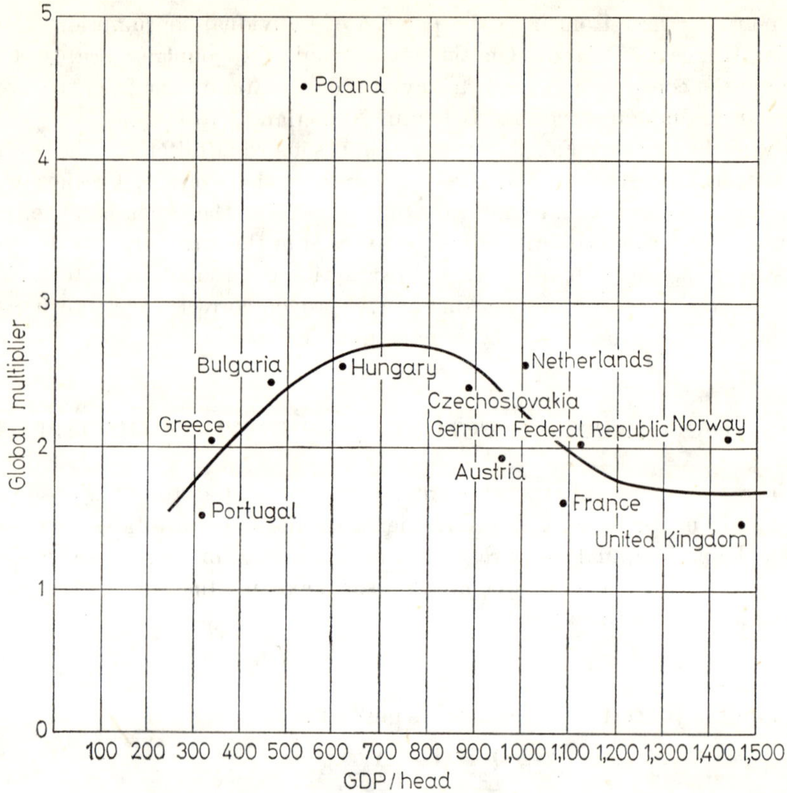

Fig. 3. The global multiplier

for any pair of countries k and m

$$\bar{\mathbf{x}}_k^{(m)} = \mathbf{Q}_k\bar{\mathbf{y}}_m;\ \mathbf{x}_m^{(k)} = \mathbf{Q}_m\bar{\mathbf{y}}_k \tag{7}$$

and the "cross-multiplier":

$$q_k^{(m)} = \mathbf{1}^*\bar{\mathbf{x}}_k^{(m)};\ q_m^{(k)} = \mathbf{1}y\bar{\mathbf{x}}_m^{(k)}. \tag{8}$$

The "cross-multipliers" have been listed in Table 3 and shown in Fig. 4. Even at first sight they reveal some interesting properties:

– the global multiplier is determined mainly by the matrix multiplier and much less by the pattern of final consumption,

– the greater the multiplier, the more sensitive it is to the changes in the pattern of final use (probably because the matrix multiplier is not gradually greater in every column), the final utilization patterns of Bulgaria, Czechoslovakia, Hungary and Poland are characteristically more "material intensive" than those of the other countries. The opposite holds for Greece, Norway and Portugal, as well as the United Kingdom, which are thus not easy to classify.

Table 3

The "cross-multipliers"

y of / Q of	Austria 1	Bulgaria 2	Czechoslovakia 3	France 4	German Federal Republic 5	Greece 6	Hungary 7	Netherlands 8	Norway 9	Poland 10	Portugal 11	United Kingdom 12
Austria	1.89	1.97	2.00	1.90	1.93	1.90	1.96	1.87	1.83	1.94	1.80	1.83
Bulgaria	2.25	2.49	2.47	2.26	2.29	2.28	2.38	2.27	2.17	2.41	2.15	2.19
Czechoslovakia	2.34	2.71	2.47	2.35	2.35	2.63	2.58	2.33	2.20	2.58	2.71	2.25
France	1.78	1.86	1.87	1.77	1.82	1.77	1.84	1.79	1.70	1.83	1.72	1.75
German Federal Republic	2.04	2.12	2.15	2.04	2.08	2.00	2.12	2.07	1.98	2.01	1.96	2.02
Greece	2.09	2.21	2.21	2.08	2.12	2.10	2.17	2.09	2.02	2.16	2.01	2.02
Hungary	2.42	2.67	2.59	2.44	2.47	2.45	2.56	2.45	2.33	2.58	2.47	2.36
Netherlands	2.58	2.77	2.75	2.56	2.72	2.54	2.75	2.58	2.51	2.71	2.46	2.46
Norway	2.36	2.54	2.44	2.27	2.29	2.44	2.33	2.28	2.13	2.42	2.24	2.18
Poland	4.05	4.75	4.38	4.04	4.09	4.38	4.37	4.01	3.65	4.46	4.43	3.84
Portugal	1.72	1.80	1.84	1.72	1.77	1.66	1.81	1.75	1.74	1.79	1.59	1.69
United Kingdom	1.61	1.66	1.65	1.62	1.62	1.63	1.67	1.62	1.60	1.65	1.62	1.60

21. As regards the "cross-outputs" $\mathbf{x}_k^{(m)}$ not only their sum (the "cross-multiplier") is interesting to us, but also the possible variations in their structure. Let us assume that there exists an average European multiplier matrix

$$\mathbf{Q}_E = \frac{1}{k}(\mathbf{Q}_1 + \ldots + \mathbf{Q}_k) \tag{9}$$

then for each country a special "cross-output" also exists:

$$\overline{\mathbf{x}}_E^{(k)} = \mathbf{Q}_E \overline{\mathbf{y}}_k \tag{10}$$

and then for each country the distance between its own inverse multiplied by the final utilization pattern of each country and the average European inverse multiplied by the same can be interpreted as

$$\mathbf{g}_m^{(k)} = \overline{\mathbf{x}}_m^{(k)} - \overline{\mathbf{x}}_E^{(k)}. \tag{11}$$

If we divide the average of each component of the $\mathbf{g}_m^{(k)}$ vectors by the corresponding component of vector $\mathbf{x}_E^{(k)}$, we can apply, instead of the generally used standard deviation, the following measure:

$$\mathbf{s}^{(k)} = \langle \overline{\mathbf{x}}_E^{(k)} \rangle^{-1} \cdot \frac{1}{k} \sum_{m=1}^{k} ||g_m^{(k)}|| \tag{12}$$

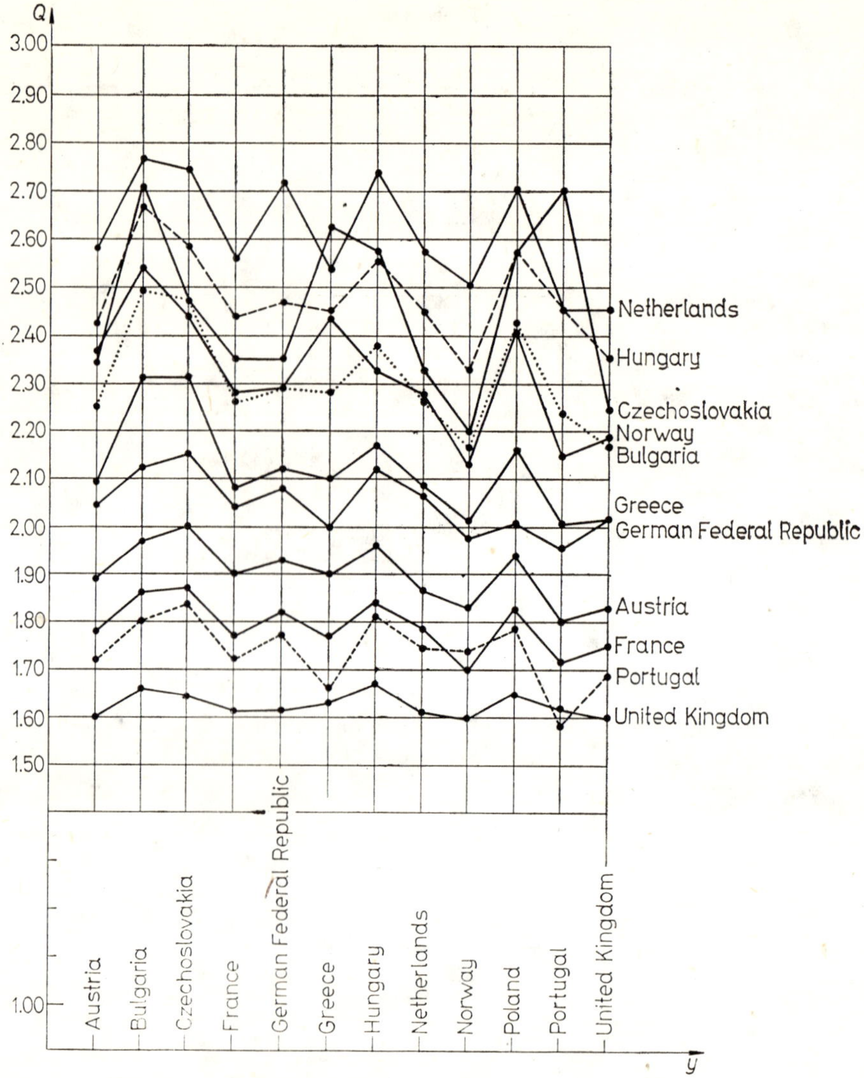

Fig. 4. The "cross-multipliers"

where ⟨**d g**⟩ denotes a diagonal matrix and || || the components of a vector irrespective of their sign.

22. All $\mathbf{s}^{(k)}$ vectors can be found in Table 4. Let us consider, e.g., the component relating to the construction industry of Austria. This shows the following features: the Austrian final utilization pattern multiplied by the inverse matrices of k different countries will result in k number of gross building industry outputs and the value of k will fluctuate around its own average by 7.8 per cent on the

Table 4

"Standard deviation" in "cross-output" structure
(the s_k vectors)

	Austria	Bulgaria	Czecho-slovakia	France	German Federal Republic	Greece	Hun-gary	Nether-lands	Norway	Poland	Portugal	United King-dom	*Mean*
	1	2	3	4	5	6	7	8	9	10	11	12	13
Agriculture	0.467	0.434	0.461	0.454	0.465	0.420	0.435	0.459	0.490	0.437	0.418	0.460	0.449
Coal mining	0.706	0.669	0.631	0.619	0.668	0.640	0.622	0.594	0.699	0.547	0.668	0.600	0.645
Other mining	0.847	0.840	0.912	0.850	0.949	0.707	0.894	0.850	0.879	0.888	0.771	0.891	0.850
Food	0.163	0.146	0.142	0.153	0.150	0.161	0.171	0.147	0.168	0.150	0.202	0.154	0.163
Textiles	0.288	0.282	0.302	0.330	0.322	0.287	0.293	0.294	0.347	0.288	0.246	0.305	0.301
Clothes	0.084	0.074	0.076	0.073	0.089	0.060	0.081	0.089	0.120	0.082	0.138	0.099	0.088
Wood, paper industries	0.157	0.231	0.283	0.201	0.202	0.235	0.245	0.210	0.177	0.242	0.162	0.194	0.209
Rubber	0.480	0.284	0.325	0.361	0.402	0.328	0.394	0.340	0.310	0.341	0.309	0.348	0.351
Chemical	0.225	0.267	0.252	0.222	0.231	0.190	0.228	0.209	0.220	0.237	0.217	0.218	0.228
Petroleum refining	0.534	0.529	0.493	0.417	0.548	0.388	0.521	0.339	0.519	0.509	0.359	0.440	0.474
Non-metallic minerals	0.253	0.277	0.253	0.282	0.281	0.291	0.281	0.286	0.285	0.272	0.295	0.274	0.278
Basic metals	0.840	0.836	0.856	0.849	0.840	0.832	0.848	0.846	0.848	0.844	0.826	0.859	0.842
Transport machinery	0.177	0.176	0.144	0.127	0.148	0.235	0.135	0.138	0.113	0.131	0.154	0.116	0.147
Other engineering	0.202	0.209	0.218	0.206	0.234	0.272	0.206	0.210	0.280	0.227	0.229	0.203	0.231
Electricity, gas	0.403	0.448	0.437	0.397	0.442	0.347	0.439	0.388	0.422	0.454	0.385	0.314	0.408
Construction	0.078	0.071	0.057	0.062	0.071	0.062	0.057	0.075	0.063	0.057	0.109	0.077	0.071
Trade	0.191	0.311	0.292	0.171	0.210	0.553	0.308	0.192	0.157	0.269	0.124	0.166	0.232
Transport	0.265	0.285	0.411	0.349	0.305	0.209	0.349	0.199	0.143	0.296	0.223	0.228	0.260
Restaurants, hotels	0.226	1.333	1.316	0.240	0.301	0.051	1.305	0.558	0.393	0.564	1.301	0.144	0.540
Mean	0.347	0.405	0.412	0.333	0.361	0.330	0.411	0.338	0.349	0.360	0.376	0.321	—

Table 5

Hungary's final structure multiplied by various inverses
(The $\mathbf{x}_m$ vectors)

	Austria	Bulgaria	Czecho-slovakia	France	German Federal Republic	Greece	Hungary	Nether-lands	Norway	Poland	Portugal	United King-dom	*Mean*
	1	2	3	4	5	6	7	8	9	10	11	12	13
Agriculture	0.315	0.449	0.644	0.250	0.230	0.332	0.485	0.367	0.489	1.491	0.292	0.174	0.460
Coal mining	0.025	0.069	0.099	0.048	0.070	0.032	0.108	0.105	0.017	0.184	0.038	0.037	0.069
Other mining	0.030	0.071	0.029	0.027	0.027	0.023	0.029	0.060	0.057	0.092	0.044	0.042	0.044
Food	0.208	0.267	0.265	0.196	0.220	0.202	0.244	0.325	0.324	0.312	0.167	0.206	0.245
Textiles	0.096	0.187	0.096	0.117	0.107	0.108	0.125	0.113	0.090	0.173	0.067	0.071	0.112
Clothes	0.065	0.074	0.064	0.059	0.064	0.059	0.067	0.061	0.058	0.080	0.053	0.056	0.063
Wood, paper industries	0.068	0.078	0.071	0.061	0.091	0.081	0.076	0.106	0.134	0.136	0.047	0.073	0.085
Rubber	0.003	0.020	0.020	0.016	0.013	0.007	0.017	0.012	0.005	0.028	0.006	0.015	0.013
Chemical	0.118	0.097	0.125	0.095	0.123	0.094	0.129	0.129	0.134	0.228	0.105	0.109	0.124
Petroleum refining	0.052	0.053	0.093	0.066	0.067	0.047	0.077	0.102	0.055	0.108	0.047	1.036	0.067
Non-metallic minerals	0.085	0.056	0.053	0.027	0.045	0.033	0.048	0.085	0.028	0.070	0.047	0.034	0.051
Basic metals	0.162	0.168	0.159	0.141	0.206	0.166	0.236	0.389	0.124	0.309	0.229	0.113	0.200
Transport machinery	0.093	0.079	0.113	0.089	0.099	0.108	0.111	0.099	0.082	0.126	0.092	0.082	0.098
Other engineering	0.262	0.338	0.328	0.260	0.259	0.290	0.350	0.336	0.254	0.433	0.220	0.247	0.298
Electricity, gas	0.048	0.050	0.054	0.042	0.074	0.034	0.078	0.046	0.090	0.077	0.043	0.040	0.056
Construction	0.159	0.154	0.157	0.170	0.163	0.158	0.171	0.189	0.155	0.184	0.154	0.164	0.165
Trade	0.097	0.075	0.088	0.089	0.159	0.256	0.093	0.140	0.166	0.150	0.115	0.080	0.126
Transport	0.071	0.095	0.115	0.077	0.100	0.090	0.110	0.082	0.060	0.162	0.044	0.083	0.091
Restaurants, hotels	0.002	0.000	0.000	0.002	0.002	0.045	0.000	0.001	0.000	0.021	0.000	0.002	0.006
Total	1.967	2.387	2.582	1.840	2.127	2.176	2.564	2.754	2.331	4.372	1.818	1.670	—

average. In general: a small value in Table 4 means stability with respect to the corresponding row of the inverse matrix.

23. No systematical analysis of Table 4 was undertaken up to the time of the Conference. At first sight, the following remarks could be made:

– as regards the pattern of final use, the secondary input structure has, in this case, a stronger impact than the pattern of final use itself;

– the most stable sector is the construction industry;

– the next most stable group is the food industry, the wood and paper industries and the production of vehicles;

– there are extreme fluctuations in mining, and in metallurgy, indicating the necessity for a technical check on the data;

– it would be useful to check the data also in agriculture and coal mining, though their development can be economically interpreted.

24. Here an example will be presented to show how this kind of analysis can be used for particular national economic planning purposes. (Not in the sense of directly deriving plan indicators, but in the sense that the position of the country and its long-term development can be described.) Table 5 comprises all the $\bar{\mathbf{x}}_m^{(7)}$ vectors ($m = 1, \ldots, 12$), Hungary being the seventh country. This table shows what the gross output necessary for a unit of final use in Hungary "would be like", if this output were turned out with the cumulated inputs of other countries or with one representing the European average. It can be seen that the Hungarian cumulated inputs are on the average the most "coal and electricity intensive". On the other hand, the inputs of the wood and paper industries, of other mining and commerce are lower than the average.

Of course, such hypothetical statements, taken out of their context, are no substitute for a thorough checking and systematic analysis of the extremely rich material. Both will be undertaken in due course.

BIBLIOGRAPHY

OF HUNGARIAN PUBLICATIONS ON THE SUBJECT OF INPUT-OUTPUT TABLES (1957–1970)

CONTENTS

INTRODUCTION

This compilation surveys the Hungarian publications on input–output tables, beginning with the preparations of the computations and covering about fifteen years. The nature of the subject itself makes the material rather heterogeneous. It seemed, therefore, expedient to group the material according to subject matter. Since a considerable part of the papers included deal with several subjects, the classification was done according to the main topic treated. About 200 books and studies will be reviewed under fourteen headings.

In selecting the headings, the individual phases of constructing and utilizing the tables were delimited so that the whole of research activities and results within the individual themes could be surveyed. With this we wanted to provide useful information for all those who wish to get acquainted with the Hungarian literature on the subject either in particular fields or in its entirety.

The fourteen headings of the compilation can be essentially summed up in four main groups. The first may most aptly be characterized by giving it the title: construction of input–output tables. Here belong all works which, prior to starting the construction of the tables, had clarified the theoretical background or had given answers to the problems of statistical data collection, or mathematical processing emerging in the construction of input–output tables or which clearly assigned the place on the table in the system of national economic balances. Finally, the studies which review the contents and methodology of computations relating to different years are included.

The second group comprises most heterogeneous fields of utilization. The input–output table, by formulating the cumulated indices through mathematical processing, put its own system of indices beside the classical synthetic statistical system of indices, thus establishing a relation between the "product" and the "input". Understandably, for getting acquainted with and judging economic processes, this system of indices is at least as important as the classical one which confronted "production" with "input". This is why the new system of indices has spread quickly in almost every field of economic analysis and in planning, a fact also reflected by the large number of works processed in this group and the most diverse areas covered: researches into efficiency, structural price, money circulation problems and questions of branches and even of enterprises.

The third group comprises the questions related to the construction and utilization of regional input–output tables. As everywhere in the world, in Hungary the computations first covered the whole of the economy. It was only later that the idea emerged that within the comprehensive survey of the economic processes, the regional differences and links should also be expressed. The works included in this group try to give a satisfactory answer or a solution to this wish which is formulated now in increasingly definite terms.

Finally, the international comparisons are a rich field of the input–output work. Although these works cannot be applied to the needs of production, they are nevertheless useful since they give an idea of the place of the Hungarian economy in the world.

If the reader succeeds in obtaining a picture of the development and the level of input–output work in Hungary by studying the individual groups of themes, we believe the compilation has succeeded.

I.1. GENERAL SURVEY OF INPUT–OUTPUT ANALYSIS

Aczél, I.: A marxi újratermelési sémák és az input–output módszer (Oskar Lange tanulmánya alapján) (The Marxian reproduction schemes and the input–output method, based on a study of Oskar Lange), *Közgazdasági Szemle*, 1958, No. 12, pp. 1285–1295.

Aczél starts from the equilibrium conditions of the Marxian reproduction scheme both under simple and extended reproduction. The mathematical implications of the model are reviewed. The technological and value relationships are dealt with separately. Great scope is given to the interrelations between consumption and investment as well as to those between investment and economic growth respectively. Finally, the effect of investment on national income and employment is analysed.

Benedeczki, J., Mrs.: A társadalmi termék termelése és felhasználása során egyes ágazatok között létrejött kapcsolatok vizsgálata. Az ágazati kapcsolatok mérlege (Analysis of the interrelations between individual branches in the course of producing and consuming the social product. The input–output table). In: Zala, J. (Ed.): *Gazdaságstatisztika*, Budapest, Közgazdasági Kiadó, 1959, pp. 461–474.

The problems of the pattern of inputs, the problem of time, the role of chance, and the problem of the so-called "particular scheme" are discussed. The author calls the practical models "particular schemes", and treats their aggregation, the unit of measurement, and periodicity. A considerable part is devoted to the accuracy of the model. The distortions due to error and the economic conclusions to be drawn are reviewed. The author surveys in detail the numerical investigations carried out in Hungary and elsewhere. The investigation results are generalized and conclusions drawn. Finally, the mathematical error limits of the calculations are discussed. The reasoning about the accuracy of results is supported from the economic point of view and proved mathematically.

Bródy, A.: Az input–output módszer a nemzetgazdasági folyamatok elemzésére (The input–output system; a method for the analysis of national economic processes), *Közgazdasági Szemle*, 1957, No. 2, pp. 145–165.

Bródy also surveys the opinions and the objectives. With the aid of a process diagram, he presents the interrelations of the major sectors of production and consumption. He stresses the importance of the matrix method and its advantages over others. Reviewing the 1919 model for the USA, the relations between the rows and the columns are described. An analysis of the productive sectors and in this framework, of the homogeneity of final output and costs and one of the "non-productive" sectors are also given. The general problems of a model to be used in case of extended reproduction are also dealt with, and the ideas of Leontief are reviewed. In conclusion, the accuracy of the model and the expediency of its use are investigated.

Bródy, A.: *Az ipar ágazati termékmérlegei. Az input–output rendszer. Időközi beszámoló* (Interindustry tables. Interim report on the input–output method), Budapest, MTA Közgazdaságtudományi Intézet, 1958, 115 pp.

This paper deals with some theoretical and practical problems, deriving the equations on the basis of the theory of value. The problem of possible distortions due to measurement is raised. Then the method of computing the volume and value of production is shown. Some proposals are put forward for a purposeful modification of industrial statistics. The schemes elaborated for the years 1952–1954 are presented. Finally, the coefficients, prices and the volume of production are dealt with in detail.

Bródy, A.: Az ágazati kapcsolatok mérlegének elméletéhez (On the theory of the input–output analysis), *Közgazdasági Szemle*, 1958, Nos. 8–9, pp. 923–935.

The evaluation of the method is connected here with Marxist research. The author first deduces a system of equations, essentially corresponding to the equation system of the input–output tables, from the labour theory of value and from the fact of the division of labour. The ideas in the works of Marx which point to such schemes are then summarized. The five-sector scheme of Marx and his attempts at establishing a system of equations are reviewed. According to Bródy the system of equations presented can be established on the basis of the labour theory of value and corresponds to the reproduction scheme of Marx. In his opinion, Marx has essentially — though not formally — drawn up the equation system and even carried out calculations with its aid.

Bródy, A.: *Az ágazati kapcsolatok modellje. A felhasznált absztrakciók, azok korlátai és a számítások pontossága* (The input–output model. Its abstractions, limitations and the accuracy of computations), Budapest, Akadémiai Kiadó, 1964, 214 pp.

The results of the author's economic and mathematical investigations are systematically surveyed. At first economic models in general are treated. Then, the input–output model is introduced and discussed in detail with various theoretical considerations.

Kenessey, Z.: Az input-output módszer (The input–output method), *Gazdasági Figyelő*, 1957, No. 8, p. 11.

Kenessey surveys the origins of the system and its fundamental hypotheses. The mathematical handling and usefulness of the model are presented in a logical framework.

Kenessey, Z., Nemény, V. and Szakolczai, Gy.: A ráfordítás-kibocsátás (input–output) rendszer vázlatos ismertetése (A general outline of the input–output system), *Statisztikai Szemle*, 1957, Nos. 1–2, pp. 23–48; 1957, No. 3, pp. 196–213.

This is a survey of the input–output method on the basis of Leontief's theory, using also the works of several other economists. The major stages of evolution of the subject are reviewed from Quesnay to Leontief. The general form of the model, the matrix of coefficients and the fundamental mathematical relations are described. First the closed model, then the principles of the open model are given and its advantages over the closed type are stressed. The model is presented first as a logical structure and later also its mathematical apparatus is shown. Due consideration is given to the dynamic model. Possible practical uses of the closed and the open model are discussed. Results achieved with the aid of the method in the USA and Western Europe are reviewed. A detailed evaluation is followed by analysis of the criticism of the method, their application in socialist countries is also touched upon.

Rácz, A.: On Bródy, A.: Az ágazati kapcsolatok modellje (The input–output model). *Acta Oeconomica*, 1966, Nos. 1–2, pp. 224–225.

This is a critique of Bródy's book.

Ujlaki, L., Mrs.: On Bródy, A.: Az ágazati kapcsolatok modellje (The input–output model. Reviewed), *Közgazdasági Szemle*, 1964, No. 10, pp. 1263–1265.

This is a critique on Bródy, A.: Az input–output módszer a nemzetgazdasági folyamatok elemzésére (The input–output system; a method for the analysis of national economic processes), *Közgazdasági Szemle*, 1957, No. 2, pp. 145–165.

Kornai, J.: On Bródy, A.: Az ágazati kapcsolatok modellje, Budapest, 1964 (The input–output model. Reviewed). *Statisztikai Szemle*, 1965, No. 7, pp. 762–763.

This is a critique on Bródy, A.: *Az ágazati kapcsolatok modellje.* Op. cit.

Morva, T.: A népgazdasági mérleg (The balance of the national economy), *Népgazdasági tervezés*, Vol. 1, Manuscript. Budapest, Közgazdasági Kiadó, 1963, pp. 87–124.

This was prepared for educational purposes, and is based on the planning point of view.

Rácz, A.: Az ágazati kapcsolatok vizsgálata (Analysis of the input–output relationships). In: Drechsler, L. (Ed.): *Gazdaságstatisztika,* Budapest, Közgazdasági Kiadó, 1966, pp. 345–379.

This paper was prepared for educational purposes. The input–output tables are treated under the statistical aspect. It is an extended study of Benedeczki's work.

I.2. THE INPUT–OUTPUT TABLES COMPILED IN HUNGARY

(1) *Az ágazati kapcsolatok mérlege,* 1957 (The table of input–output relations, 1957), Budapest, Statisztikai Kiadó, 1959, 56 pp.

(2) *Баланс межотраслевых связей* (The table of input–output relations, 1957), Budapest, 1958, 53 pp.

(3) Az ágazati kapcsolatok mérlege, 1957 (The table of input–output relations, 1957), *Statisztikai Évkönyv, 1958,* Budapest, 1960, Statisztikai Kiadó, pp. 376–387.

(4) *A magyar népgazdaság ágazati kapcsolatainak mérlege, 1959* (The table of input–output relations of the Hungarian economy in 1959), Budapest, 1961, Statisztikai Kiadó, 39. pp.

(5) A népgazdaság ágazati kapcsolatainak mérlege, 1959 (The table of the input–output relations of the economy in 1959), *Statisztikai Évkönyv, 1960,* Budapest, Statisztikai Kiadó, pp. 386–391.

(6) *A magyar népgazdaság ágazati kapcsolatainak mérlege, 1961* (The table of input–output relations of the Hungarian economy in 1961), Budapest, Statisztikai Kiadó, 1964, 208. pp.

(7) *A magyar népgazdaság ágazati kapcsolatainak mérlegei 1959–1964, 13 termelő szektorra* (The input–output tables of the Hungarian economy 1959–1964 in 13 productive sectors), Budapest, Statisztikai Kiadó, 1966, 54 pp.

The seven publications listed contain the numerical material of the Hungarian input–output tables up to 1964. Those under (1), (2) and (6) comprise all variants and, in addition to the basic data, also the major indices computed, as, e.g., the technological and the inverse coefficients. The publications (3) and (5) present only the basic data of the tables.

All publications contain the three variants of the tables, namely, those denoted by A, B and C, but the inverse matrix is given only for the type B, showing the interrelations of domestically produced materials. The variants A, B and C differ from one another in their handling of import materials within the inner quadrant of the tables. The model of type A does not distinguish domestically produced and imported materials. Type C shows domestic and import materials separately in each row and column of the table, according to origin and use, respectively. In the inner quadrant of the table of type B, only the use of domestically produced materials is shown and imported materials are added in a separate row. The table for 1957 contains 39 sectors, the 1959 table 95 and the 1961 table 54 sectors. Publication (6) also contains the data for 1959 aggregated into 54 sectors allowing some comparisons between 1959 and 1961. Paper (7) contains the tables for six consective years in a comparable form, by 13 productive sectors, of which seven are industrial ones. The basic data are not presented but several cumulated coefficients are given in addition to the technological and inverse matrices. Thus, the direct and cumulated coefficients are given for the wage, fixed assets and import contents. The inverse matrices of the A and the B type are given. All coefficients are worked out with both inverses. (7) also contains a detailed analysis of the dispersion work and changes in the coefficients, and the most important coefficients are separately investigated for their behaviour. The most important characteristics of the direct and cumulated (inverse) coefficients of tables A and B are described.

(8) *A magyar népgazdaság ágazati kapcsolatainak mérlegei, 1964–1966 (16 termelő szektorra)* (Input–output tables of the Hungarian economy, 1964–1966, in 16 productive sectors), Budapest, Statisztikai Kiadó, 1968, 42 pp.

(9) *A magyar népgazdaság ágazati kapcsolatainak mérlege 1965 évben* (The input–output table of the Hungarian economy in 1965), Budapest, Statisztikai Kiadó, 1969, 49 pp.

(10) A magyar népgazdaság ágazati kapcsolatainak mérlege, 1968 (The input–output table of the Hungarian economy in 1968), *Statisztikai Időszaki Közlemények*, No. 178, Budapest, Statisztikai Kiadó, 1970, 135 pp.

(11) A magyar népgazdaság ágazati kapcsolatainak mérlege 1965–1968 (14 termelő szektorra) (The input–output tables of the Hungarian economy for 1965–1968, in 14 productive sectors), *Statisztikai Időszaki Közlemények*, No. 180, Budapest, Statisztikai Kiadó, 1970, 42 pp.

(12) *A Nehézipari Minisztérium ágazati kapcsolatainak közgazdasági-matematikai modellje* (Economico-mathematical model of the input–output relations of the Ministry of Heavy Industry), Budapest, NIM Ipargazdasági és Üzemszervezési Intézet, 1967, 242 pp.

(13) *A NIM ágazati kapcsolatainak 1965 évi természetes mértékegységű közgazdasági-matematikai modellje* (Economic-mathematical model of the input–output relations of the Ministry of Heavy Industry in 1965, in physical units of measurement), Budapest, NIM Ipargazdasági és Üzemszervezési Intézet, 1968, 691 pp.

The six publications (8–13) contain the numerical material of the Hungarian input–output tables based on factual data since 1965. The publication comprise all variants of the table, and the most important indicators computed from them, with short methodological notes. The two series, for 1964–1966 (16 sectors) and for 1965–1968 (14 sectors), are not directly comparable, but within each booklet the tables are shown at comparable prices and in comparable structure. Both the 1965 and the 1968 tables comprise 83 sectors, but only at current prices. The last two publications show a detailed breakdown of the sectors belonging to the Ministry of Heavy Industry and comprise a thorough analysis in both physical and value terms.

I.3. STATISTICAL PROBLEMS INVOLVED IN COMPILING INPUT–OUTPUT TABLES

Gelei, A.: Az ágazati kapcsolati mérlegek összeállításának és felhasználásának kérdései (Input–output tables, their compilation and use), *Ipargazdaság,* 1963, Nos. 2–3, pp. 55–56.

The volume contains 21 papers delivered at the Statistical Scientific Conference, Branch A in Budapest, June 1961. The individual studies are reviewed under the corresponding group-headings.

Kenessey, Z.: A társadalmi termék részletes sakktáblaszerű mérlegének összeállításáról tartott értekezlet (KSH vitája) (A conference on the compilation of the detailed "chess-board-type" table of the social product. Discussion held in the Central Statistical Office). *Statisztikai Szemle,* 1958, Nos. 1–2, pp. 138–143.

Kenessey, Z.: A magyar népgazdaság ágazati kapcsolatainak mérlege (The input–output table of the Hungarian economy), *Statisztikai Szemle,* 1959, No. 12, pp. 1174–1190.

Kenessey describes the circumstances under which the first Hungarian model was compiled, presents the basic data of the table, surveys its formal characteristics, comparing it with tables compiled abroad. Separate treatment is given to the unallocated sector, the secondary activities of the accounting units and to the various model types.

Kupcsik, J. and Rácz, A.: Az ágazati kapcsolatok mérlege (A dinamikai összehasonlítás főbb problémái) (The table of input–output relations. Major problems of dynamic comparisons). *Módszertani Füzetek* No. 1, Budapest, Central Statistical Office, 1966, 76 pp.

Kupcsik and Rácz summarized the major statistical-methodological problems of the Hungarian input–output tables based on factual data as well as those of dynamic comparison. The formal characteristics of the tables, the contents of the productive and non-productive sectors in the tables, the types of the tables prepared, the prices used as well as the methods of handling the secondary activities of the enterprises are surveyed. In connection with comparison over time, the problems of organizational and price changes are reviewed on the basis of the practical experiences. Practical examples show in a generalized form how the various organizational changes affect the model and the computations performed. The role of price changes in a dynamic comparison is illustrated by examples drawn from the re-pricing techniques used in the compilation of the 1959–1964 tables.

Lendvai, B. and Mányi-Szabó, I.: A közlekedési szektor problémái az 1957. évi ágazati kapcsolatok mérlegében (Problems of the transport sector in the 1957 table of input–output relations), *Statisztikai Szemle,* 1959, Nos. 8–9, pp. 887–891.

Lendvai and Mányi-Szabó discuss, relying on the experiences gained in compiling the 1957 model, the special transportation problems and their solutions. Emphasis is laid on the accounting methods relating to export transportation as well as on separating transportation from other activities. The individual input items are determined by branches of transportation. Detailed consumption data are, however, given only for the most important materials. In the absence of the output rows of the individual transportation branches, the various opinions on how to determine the distribution data are reviewed.

Lendvai, B. and Mányi-Szabó, I.: Ankét az ágazati kapcsolatok mérlegének közlekedési problémáiról (Conference on the problems relating to transportation in connection with the compilation of the table of input–output relations), *Közlekedési Közlöny,* May 31, 1959, pp. 429–430.

This paper also deals with the transportation problems. An aggregate form for the 1957 table is presented and its contents as well as its main interrelations are explained. Some uses of the model are also briefly reviewed.

Lukács, O.: Az első magyar ágazati kapcsolati mérleg összeállítása és felhasználása (The first Hungarian table of input–output relations: its compilation and use), *Közgazdasági Szemle,* 1960, No. 2, pp. 168–175.

Lukács views the first Hungarian model for 1957. The problems of compiling the model, mainly those of data collection, are treated in detail and so are the prices and the problem of homogeneity. Some examples are given of the utilization of the model; the preparations for compiling the 1959 table are surveyed briefly.

Lukács, O.: A magyar ágazati kapcsolati mérlegek és összeállításuk statisztikai alapjai (The Hungarian input–output tables and the statistical sources of their compilation), *Statisztikai Szemle,* 1961, No. 7, pp. 701–711.

Lukács reviews the statistical sources of compiling the input–output tables. The author surveys in turn the individual branches of the economy and the final consumption. The industrial data necessary for the model were taken from the regular annual industrial censuses but material consumption and marketing data were taken from other sources. The data for the agricultural sector were elaborated on the basis of the activity principle. For other branches, it was necessary to make sample surveys and to draw in field specialists.

Lukács, O. (ed.): *Input–output tables, their compilation and use* (Scientific conference on statistical problems, Budapest, 1–5 June, 1961, Branch A). Budapest, Akadémiai Kiadó, 1962, 292 pp.

The volume contains 21 papers delivered at the Statistical Scientific Conference, Branch A, in Budapest, June, 1961. The individual studies are reviewed under the corresponding group-headings.

Nyitrai, F., Mrs.: Az 1957. évi ágazati kapcsolatok mérlege összeállításának tapasztalatai (Experiences in drawing up the input–output table for 1957), *Statisztikai Szemle*, 1959, No. 2, pp. 179–197.

Nyitrai surveys in detail the experiences gained in the course of compiling the input–output tables for 1957. The theoretical points of view and the practical solutions are described. The process of compilation, the organizations and institutions participating are described. The difficulties connected with compiling cost and allocation data are cited with several practical examples, e.g., the trade margin, the problems of transports and exports. The problems of agriculture, machine building, non-productive consumption and other sectors are dealt with in detail.

Nyitrai, F., Mrs.: *Az ágazati kapcsolatok összevont mérlegeinek szerepe az ÁKM-ek rendszerében* (The role of aggregated input–output tables in the system of input–output tables), Budapest, Statisztikai Kiadó, 1967, 28 pp. (Papers of the Centenary Statistical Session.)

Nyitrai scrutinizes the utilization possibilities and limitations of highly aggregated input–output tables, reviewing also the practical problems of compilation.

Rácz, A.: Az ágazati kapcsolatok 1961. évi mérlege (The table of input–output relations for 1961), *Statisztikai Szemle*, 1964, No. 6, pp. 571–591.

The readers get acquainted with the major characteristics of the 1961 model and the deviations from the 1959 table. Aggregation and the accuracy of data are discussed. Some characteristic data of the two models are compared. Beside the production-type model, the so-called turnover-type model is also described, prepared for the specific needs of planning. The major deviations from the general input–output scheme and some problems of compilation are reviewed. The economic conclusions to be drawn from such comparisons are made. Information is given on a variant, worked out at prices net of turnover tax; the necessity and problems of compilation are discussed.

Kéri., E., Mrs, and Kiss, F.: Az ágazati kapcsolati mérleg készítésének tapasztalatai a NIM Ipargazdasági és Üzemszervezési Intézetben (Experiences in drawing up the input–output table in the Institute for Industrial Economics and Business Organization of the Ministry of Heavy Industry), *Ipari és Építőipari Értesítő*, 1969, No. 11, pp. 408–415.

The authors describe the special input–output table detailing the activities of the enterprises belonging to the Ministry of Heavy Industry, reporting on the experiences in the course of work and on the methodological problems encountered.

Román, Z.: A magyar népgazdaság 1957. évi ágazati kapcsolati mérlege (The input–output table of the Hungarian economy for 1957), *Ipargazdaság*, 1959, No. 8, pp. 3–8.

Román stresses over and above the general problems for the input–output table, the special industrial relationships. Besides a formal and conceptual description some industrial relationships are also illustrated.

Román, Z.: Az ágazati kapcsolatok mérlegeinek számviteli alapjai (Accounting bases of the input–output table), *Pénzügy és Számvitel*, 1959, No. 11, pp. 410–414.

Román analyses the fundamental accountancy requirements of the input–output tables. The purposes and techniques of recording sales are discussed in detail. In order to establish the input structure, a proper grouping of material costs in the accounts is required. However, it is difficult to establish the material part of the overheads by the major material types. Similar difficulties arise in accounting for returns in accordance with the principles of the model.

I.4. MATHEMATICAL PROCESSING OF THE TABLES; ACCURACY OF DATA AND COEFFICIENTS; INDICES COMPUTED

Ács, L.: Az ágazati kapcsolatok mérlege és az életszínvonal mérése (The input–output table and measurement of the standard of living), *Bankszemle*, 1961, No. 7, pp. 114–123.

Ács analyses a special case of the application. Since the model comprises the volume and pattern of consumption, it offers a way to analyse the standard of living, or, at least, to link the household sector of the model with analyses of the standard of living based on other methods.

Balsay, É.: Népgazdasági szintű ráfordítások meghatározása (Determination of economic inputs on the national level), *Statisztikai Szemle*, 1965, No. 11, pp. 1115–1126.

This is dealt with more fully in Miss Balsay's paper. She starts from the assumption that the input in one unit of imports (e.g., total labour input) equals the average input of the export goods given in exchange. The input elements of depreciation are determined by the inputs into the investment goods. Limitations of these assumptions are stressed, and it is justified why it is necessary to carry out export–import calculations not only in the domestic currency but also in foreign exchange. The mathematical methods are presented with which the national-level inputs of a unit of exports (in terms of foreign exchange) and of a unit of investments may be determined. Essentially we have as many equations (and as many unknowns) as there are sectors in the model for exports and investments.

Bod, P.: Néhány gyakorlati megjegyzés az ágazati kapcsolatok formális elemzéséhez. Az ágazati és igazgatási rendszerű sakktábla (input–output) mérlegének kapcsolatáról (Some practical remarks on the formal analysis of input–output tables. The connection between the input–output tables with a sector-breakdown and with a breakdown according to administrative units). *Az ágazati kapcsolati mérlegek összeállításának és felhasználásának kérdései* (Problems of the compilation and utilization of input–output tables), Budapest, Akadémiai Kiadó, 1962, pp. 89–97.

Bod examines the mathematical possibilities of transforming the input–output table originally compiled in a breakdown by standard classification into a system broken down by administrative units (ministries). The mathematical solution of the transformation is the following. First, the elements of the matrix aggregated according to the pattern by industries are established. Next, this matrix is desaggregated into an assumed matrix of the size $N \times N$, the matrix thus obtained is re-arranged by means of a permutation operator — thus another form of the assumed matrix is arrived at; from this, by means of an aggregation operator the, desired matrix is established in a breakdown by administrative units.

Bródy, A.: Vállalati és népgazdasági megtakarítás (Savings on the enterprise and the national level), *MTA Matematikai Kutató Intézetének Közleményei*, 1959, No. 1, pp. 11–14.

Assuming a price system proportionate to values, Bródy determines savings on the enterprise and on the national economic level. He deduces and establishes that the real savings at the national level are always smaller than those computed at enterprise level. He also proves that from the national point of view it is not immaterial, in which industry or enterprise or in connection with which product the savings are reached even if they should appear identical as computed at the enterprise level.

Bródy, A.: Az ágazati kapcsolati mérlegszámítás hibakorlátairól (The error limits of input–output computations), *Statisztikai Szemle,* 1961, No. 1, pp. 31–47.

Bródy discusses in detail the exactness of statistical sources. He introduces the matrix of errors (H) and expresses the "true" matrix by means of the inaccurate inverse (Q) and the error matrix (H). He points out that for practical purposes a linear approximation of the "true" matrix will suffice if the value of error matrix H is not too high. From this point of view, he deals separately with the "norm" of the error matrix. He proves that the average error in the end result is smaller than the average error in the initial data. He stresses that first of all the bill of goods (Y) should be rendered more exact and then further errors in data collection can be practically neglected.

Csepinszky, A.: Hibameghatározás az ágazatok kapcsolatának elemzésénél (Determination of errors in input–output analysis), *Statisztikai Szemle,* 1961, No. 1, pp. 6–29.

Csepinszky analyses the structure of the input–output table particularly from the aspect of aggregation of products and industries, and describes the major mathematical interrelations of the matrix of technological coefficients. Then the errors are analysed according to their causes (uncertain basic data, aggregation, approximation, rounding off, etc.). The mathematical approximation procedure by means of which the maximum extent of the error can be established is presented. The problem is also numerically illustrated by a simple three-sector model. The errors due to the third and fourth causes are treated mainly as problems of computation techniques.

Ganczer, S. and Veidinger, L.: A sakktábla-szerű társadalmi termékmérleggel kapcsolatos számítások (Computations connected with the "chessboard-type" table of the social product), *M-3 elektronikus számítógép,* Budapest, 1960, pp. 49–56 (MTA Számítástechnikai Központja. Tájékoztató 5).

Ganczer and Veidinger are dealing with problems similar to Balsay and Rácz and Ujlaki. In addition, they give a mathematical description and an economic interpretation of the planned input–output tables. They also discuss the interrelations between the net output and the inverse matrix and between the vectors of value added and the inverse matrix.

Glattfelder, P.: Mit is mutat az inverz-matrix? (What does the inverse matrix show?), *Szigma,* 1969, No. 2, pp. 124–126.

The author treats the economic interpretation of the Leontief inverse. He reaches the conclusion that, in view of the economic meaning of the A matrix, the elements of the inverse matrix $(I - A)^{-1}$ relate to the unit of gross output and not to net output.

Kóos, A., Mrs: *Az ágazati kapcsolatok mérlegének dinamikus modellje. Kísérlet a mérleg dinamizálására, 1959–1965 évi adatok alapján* (Dynamic model of the input–output table. An attempt at dynamization based on 1959–1965 data), Budapest, Statisztikai Kiadó, 1969, p. 115.

Nyitrai, F., Mrs.: Az ágazati kapcsolatok mérlegének inverzéről (The inverse of the input–output table). *Az ágazati kapcsolati mérlegek összeállításának és felhasználásának kérdései,* Budapest, Akadémiai Kiadó, 1962, pp. 81–88.

Nyitrai surveys the economic contents of the different variants of the inverse matrices A, B and C. It is found that the inverses of the individual types serve different tasks. She also reviews the mathematical methods by means of which — considering the capacity of computers available in Hungary — the inversion can be performed. The problems of the verification of the inverse matrix are also shown.

Rácz, A.: Az árak szerepe és a forgalmi adó torzító hatása az ágazati kapcsolatok mérlegében (The role of prices and the distorting effects of turnover taxes in the input–output table), *Statisztikai Szemle,* 1965, No. 6, pp. 536–548.

Rácz analyses the distortions in computational results caused by the turnover tax, based on experiences with the 1961 Hungarian model drawn up at producers' prices both inclusive and net of turnover tax. The distorting effects are analysed in two major fields: the influence on the various input indicators per unit output of the individual productive sectors and the effect on the input elements of the individual items of final use. The author surveys the magnitude of the errors and makes a proposal to eliminate the distorting effects. He proves that the computations starting from (or relying on) final utilization are but slightly affected (distorted) by the turnover tax. He reaches the conclusion that the existence of the turnover tax does not substantially affect the proportions of secondary effects (those of the inverse coefficients).

Rácz, A.: Az ágazati kapcsolati mérlegek technikai koefficienseinek sajátosságai (Properties of the technological coefficients of input–output tables). Budapest, Statisztikai Kiadó, 1967, 24 pp.

The author investigates the changes of coefficients over time, and, in this context, their usability for model-building. Also the consequences of the linearity assumption are discussed.

Rácz, A. and Ujlaki, L., Mrs.: Az ágazati kapcsolatok 1957. évi mérlegének inverze (The inverse of the 1957 input–output table), *Statisztikai Szemle,* 1960, No. 12, pp. 1216–1229.

Rácz and Ujlaki survey the practical methods of computing the inverse. Reviewing the method of power series expansion, the inverse coefficients are interpreted also economically. The actual inversion of the 1957 model — the Gaussian elimination process — is also described. The possibilities of verifying the inverse both from a mathematical and an economic point of view and the actual verification of the 1957 model are presented. The full inverse is published.

Rácz, A. and Ujlaki, L., Mrs.: A népgazdasági költségszint és termelékenység alakulásának elemzése az ágazati kapcsolatok mérlege alapján (Analysis of cost and productivity on the national level, based on the input–output table), *Statisztikai Szemle,* 1962, No. 5, pp. 533–549; 1962, No. 6, pp. 643–658.

Rácz and Ujlaki expound the economic interpretation and methodology of national (total) wage inputs and labour inputs. They compare the direct and total wage inputs of the individual productive sectors. They show the connection between the national cost level and prime costs and then proceed to analyse the major proportions of total wage inputs in the industrial sectors and in those of final utilization. The method is used by the authors in the analysis of productivity. The changes in materialized labour are also treated. On the basis of total labour inputs a so-called national economic index number of productivity is constructed. The factors affecting this index are analysed and a consistent system of factors is formulated to be computed by means of the input–output table.

Román, Z.: A népgazdasági ráfordítások és költségek mérése ágazati kapcsolati mérlegek segítségével (Measurement of the national economic inputs and costs with the aid of the input–output table), *Közgazdasági Szemle,* 1966, No. 2, pp. 182–196.

Román reviews the contents of the most important national economic indices. The difference between direct and total (direct plus indirect) coefficients is shown and their names as used in international terminology are described. The contents of the following indexes are reviewed in detail: total wage inputs, total labour inputs, total import inputs, total depreciation allowance inputs. Possible uses in the analysis of prices and price formation as well as productivity and efficiency computations are also treated.

Román, Z.: Népgazdasági és ágazati termelékenység, elemzésük az ÁKM segítségével (National and sectoral productivity, their analysis based on input–output tables), Budapest, *Statisztikai Kiadó,* 1967, 19 pp. (Papers of the Centenary Statistical Session.)

Román investigates from many aspects the role of input–output tables in computations of labour productivity. The illustrations are taken from the 13-sector aggregated input–output tables compiled by the Central Statistical Office for 1959–1964.

Ságoly, F.: Some economic and mathematical problems of an input–output model for the Hungarian heavy industry. Budapest, 1966, 16 pp. (International Conference of the Econometric Society and the PIMS in Warsaw.)

The study reviews the model of the Ministry of Heavy Industry and its complete mathematical processes.

Simon, Gy.: Matematikai módszerek közgazdasági alkalmazása (Application of mathematical methods in economics), *Társadalmi Szemle,* 1963, No. 11, pp. 72–79.

Simon surveys in simple terms the possibilities of the application of mathematical tools in economic analyses. Among the various mathematical methods, he devotes much space to practical analysis with the input–output table. The use of the input–output method in planning is particularly stressed.

Szabó, L.: Az inverzmatrix értelmezéséről (The interpretation of the inverse matrix), *Statisztikai Szemle,* 1963, No. 4, pp. 369–384; 1963, No. 5, pp. 463–476.

Szabó surveys analytically the contents of the inverse matrix. Its economic contents are examined on the basis of the fundamental product flows. The basic product flows are presented by means of a simple three-sector model, process diagrams and generalized mathematically. The interpretation of the inverse of a model containing also non-homogeneous sectors called the inverse matrix of costs is also treated. Considerable space is devoted to the characteristics of the technological and the inverse matrices. The author asks whether the character of the technological matrix A unequivocally determines also the character of the inverse matrix; whether any kind of A matrix with non-negative elements secures an inverse matrix with non-negative elements. The following problems are treated: the character of material inputs and the production system; determination of a definitely favourable production program; the behaviour of the inverse matrix if material inputs are exactly equal to production results or exceed them.

Szabó, L.: Az ágazati kapcsolatok mérlege alapján számítható főbb mutatók újszerű értelmezése (A novel interpretation of the major indicators to be worked out from the input–output table), *Statisztikai Szemle,* 1970, No. 6, pp. 677–698.

The paper examines the frequent inaccuracies in the practical interpretation of the indicators of the input–output model. The author defines a few indicators which enable a satisfactory interpretation as regards contents and also secure the building up of a consistent system of indicators.

Szakolczai, Gy.: The pattern of investments and the rate of growth, *Acta Oeconomica,* 1967, No. 2, pp. 187–211.

The author applies the economic model of Lange to the Hungarian economy and investigates with its aid the relations between production and investment. His conclusions are:

the output/investment ratio is not constant in the Hungarian economy, the growth of production is hindered not by the manpower available nor by the scarcity of capital, but by the difficulties of realization.

II.1. UTILIZATION OF THE INPUT–OUTPUT TABLES IN GENERAL

Augusztinovics, M.: Az ágazati kapcsolati model általánosításához (On the generalization of the input–output model), *Közgazdasági Szemle,* 1968, No. 5, pp. 583–589.

The author presents a generalized input–output model. Her purpose is a comparative analysis of the Hungarian input–output table for 1961. By circumventing the price system, the problems of structural stability are analysed.

Kupcsik, J.: *Az ágazati kapcsolatok mérlegének felhasználása a gazdasági részfolyamatok vizsgálatában* (Utilization of the input–output table in the analysis of partial economic processes), Budapest, Statisztikai Kiadó, 1967, 30 pp. (Papers of the Centenary Statistical Session.)

The author investigates the problem how processes restricted to certain areas of the economy can be analysed with the input–output table in a satisfactory manner. The various processes: monography, complementary series and partial balance methods are treated in turn. The possibilities inherent in a further breakdown of the right-hand side and the lower wing of the table are also dealt with.

Kupcsik, J. and Rácz, A.: Az ágazati kapcsolati mérlegek dinamikai összehasonlítása (Dynamic comparison of input–output tables), *Statisztikai Szemle,* 1969, No. 4, pp. 339–368.

The study treats the comparability problems of input–output tables drawn up for different years. The most important solutions worked out for comparing such table-series are reviewed.

Lukács, O.: *Népgazdasági összefüggések statisztikai feltárása az ágazati kapcsolatok mérlegének segítségével* (Statistical examination of economic interrelations with the aid of the input–output table), Budapest, Statisztikai Kiadó, 1960, 10 pp.

Lukács first points out that a substantial general improvement of the statistical service was reached, which is an achievement in itself. Then he stresses the importance of widening the scope of national economic analysis. For example, the connections between consumption and production, the pattern of investments, etc., should be subjected to analysis. Finally, he evaluates the possible uses of the model in planning, and in economic efficiency and related computations.

Nyitrai, F., Mrs.: Az ágazati kapcsolatok mérlege és a mérleg felhasználása (The input–output table and its utilization), *Ipari és Építőipari Statisztikai Értesítő,* 1960, Nos. 1–3, pp. 53–56.

Nyitrai illustrates some fields where the table can be utilized. She deals with the broad possibilities of analysing the cost pattern. Analyses of the allocation of production and material inputs according to sources are also shown. The practical importance of investigating import requirements and of the interpretation of inverse coefficients is stressed.

Nyitrai, F., Mrs.: Az ágazati kapcsolatok mérlegének felhasználása a statisztikában (Utilization of the input–output table in statistics), *Statisztikai Szemle*, 1965, No. 10, pp. 998–1009.

Nyitrai states that the analytical tools offered by input–output tables complement the traditional methods in an advantageous manner. The application of the model in statistical analysis promotes a national viewpoint even if individual fields are explored. Statistical methods in connection with drawing up the input–output table have lately also improved. The new types of indices, the cumulated coefficients are also reviewed. The author finally analyses the export performances of industrial sectors, their labour inputs and capital intensity.

Ollé, L.: Die Zuverlässigkeit der bei der Messung der wirtschaftlichen Zusammenhänge benutzten Kennziffern unter besonderer Berücksichtigung der bei der Verflechtungsbilanzierung benutzten Kennziffern. *Wissenschaftliche Zeitschrift der Humboldt Universität zu Berlin. Gesellschafts- und Sprachwirtschaftliche Reihe*, 1967, No. 6, pp. 819–821.

Ollé points out the importance of direct and indirect relations in analysing economic processes. These relations are shown to exist within the input–output system.

Rácz, A. and Ujlaki, L., Mrs.: Mire jó az ágazati kapcsolatok mérlege? (What is the use of the input–output table?), *Figyelő*, Dec. 20, 1961, pp. 3–4.

Rácz and Ujlaki give a brief survey of the uses of the input–output table, meant for newspaper readers. However, they are also dealing with the evaluation of direct and indirect inputs, and with material inputs of domestic and import origin. The analysis of the pattern of final utilization is separately surveyed.

II.2. UTILIZATION OF THE INPUT–OUTPUT TABLES IN PLANNING

Augustinovics, M.: *Input–output methods in analysing and planning foreign trade*, Geneva, 1967.

The study reviews the application of the input–output method in the analysis and planning of foreign trade.

Cserba, L.: *Использование шахматного даланса одщественного продикта базисного года при составленни годовых планов* (Use of the input–output table of the social product of the basc-year in drawing up the annual plans, Budapest, 1967, 21 pp. Gosplan–UNR.)

The author reviews the methods with the aid of which the Hungarian National Planning Office drew up the annual plan for 1967 by relying on the statistical input-output table for 1965.

Csernok, A.: *A nemzeti jövedelem elosztásának és újraelosztásának vizsgálata az input–output mérleghez kapcsolódóan* (Investigation of the distribution and redistribution of national income related to the input–output table), Budapest, Statisztikai Kiadó, 1967, 17 pp. (Papers of the Centenary Statistical Session.)

Csernok proves that the analysis of the input–output table is important in investigating the distribution of national income. He also draws up a matrix of redistribution and emphasizes its significance for economic analysis and planning, particularly in the short run.

Cukor, Gy.: Az ágazati kapcsolatok mérlegének felhasználása a távlati tervezésben (Utilization of the input–output tables in long-term planning), *Közgazdasági Szemle*, 1961, No. 8–9, pp. 934–945.

Cukor, Gy.: Az ágazati kapcsolatok mérlegének felhasználása a távlati tervezésben (Az ipar és a kereskedelem kapcsolatainak tervezése) (Utilization of the input–output table in long-term planning. The planning of the relations between industry and trade). In: *Az ágazati kapcsolati mérlegek összeállításának és felhasználásának kérdései*, Budapest, Akadémiai Kiadó, 1962, pp. 117–126.

The two studies by Cukor emphasize that the input–output table ensures a harmony between the various partial plans as parts of the complex plan of the economy. This is illustrated by planning the relations between industry and foreign trade. Though the model cannot be used for solving the specific foreign trade problems of planning, the major proportion can be worked out. The changes in production and export–import patterns are analysed in detail. For their measurement the author proposes the inverse coefficients. Finally, the import-intensity of production is investigated by productive industries and also with respect to the items of final consumption.

Denke, G.: A sakktábla-szerű ágazati kapcsolatok mérlegéről (Input–output tables of the "chessboard-type"), *Bankszemle*, 1961, No. 7, pp. 103–108.

Denke surveys the planned "chessboard-type" tables briefly and in principle only, presenting the schemes and the most important relations.

Gerő, M.: Az 1965. évi sakktáblamérleg (The "chessboard" table for 1965), *Közgazdasági Szemle*, 1961, No. 10, pp. 1156–1168.

Gerő surveys the type of input–output table first used in the course of drawing up the second five-year plan for the year 1965. She presents the general scheme of the planning model, a part of the scheme also in detail, together with the approximate computations and estimations. She states that the planned "chessboard-type" table for 1965 could be well used in drawing up the second five-year plan.

Glattfelder, P. and Váczi, P.: Egy algoritmus input–output sémák előrebecslésének korrekciójára (An algorithm for correcting the forecasts of input–output schemes), *Szigma*, 1970, No. 3, pp. 165–172.

The study seeks an answer to the following problem: We have some future or past estimated technological matrix A, and the vectors x of gross output and y of net output; the elements of these are available from individual estimates. Therefore, the volume equation $Ax + y = x$ is generally not satisfied. The procedure is sought by which the equation can be met and deviations from the original components A, x, y are minimal. After clarifying the theoretical problems, the study reviews the various application possibilities of the method in planning.

Glattfelder, P.: A Nehézipari Minisztérium ágazati kapcsolati modelljének előrebecslése (Forecasting the input–output model of the Ministry of Heavy Industry), *Statisztikai Szemle*, 1969, No. 3, pp. 282–298.

The author reviews the method with which the inner quadrant of an input–output table was extrapolated. The results achieved with the input–output model of the Ministry of Heavy Industry are outlined. Three methods are employed for forecasting the coefficients: the system of unchanged coefficients (the so-called "primitive method"), the RAS method, and a combined system of RAS and supplementary information (the so-called "global procedure").

Kádár, I.: A tervezés és az ágazati kapcsolatok mérlege (Planning and the input–output table), *Pénzügy és Számvitel*, 1959, No. 6, pp. 219–221.

Kádár enumerates the major fields where the input–output table may be utilized. He states that knowing certain parameters, the maximum of national income and social product can be determined on the basis of the model and that in this sense the input–output table may be considered an additional tool of national economic planning.

Kornai, J. (in collaboration with T. Lipták and P. Wellisch): *Mathematical Planning and Structural Decisions*, Budapest, Akadémiai Kiadó — North Holland Publishing Co., 1966.

Kornai examines the possibilities of further development in long-term planning methods with the aid of modern mathematical methods and computers. He refers to the utilization of the input–output table for checking the consistency of the plan, and to the results achieved in Hungary with the input–output method. He indicates the relationship between input–output and the programming models. He qualifies the programming models as being superior to the input–output models. The volume sums up the author's previous investigations and comprises thus several results already published.

Kornai, J. and Martos, B.: Az ágazati kapcsolatok mérlegének felhasználása az alumíniumipar optimális fejlesztési programjának meghatározására (The utilization of the input–output table to work out an optimum development program for the aluminium industry), *Ipargazdaság*, 1961, Nos. 8–9, pp. 17–22.

The input–output table was first used for programming in the aluminium industry. Kornai and Martos give an account of this experiment. The model, its major characteristics and activities are described. Also the mathematical formulation of the equations, constraints and other conditions is given. The input–output table was used to determine indirect investments as well as the real costs of domestically produced materials.

Morva, T.: A társadalmi termékmérleg szerepe a népgazdasági tervezésben (The role of the balance of social product in national economic planning), Budapest, 1962, pp. II, 166. Candidate's dissertation. Manuscript.

Morva points out that the role of the balance of social product in planning practice is much less significant than would be desirable on the basis of theoretical considerations. The application of mathematical tools, with input–output analysis among them, may have a favourable effect both on the development of economic science and on the elaboration of more advanced planning methods. The author presents the Soviet model for 1923–1924, the actual Hungarian practice and points out that in order to fulfil its role the table must become a tool of planning the material flow of products. He also confronts the input–output scheme established in Hungarian planning with the tables of the Central Statistical Office.

Morva, T.: A társadalmi termékmérleg szerepe az 1959. évi terv átárazásában és felhasználásának további lehetőségei (The role of the balance of national product in re-pricing the plan for 1959 and its possible further utilization), *Közgazdasági Szemle*, 1960, No. 4, pp. 436–451.

The input–output tables were used also for re-pricing the annual plan for 1959. This is reviewed by Morva, presenting the theoretical structure of the model and also a numerical example. For all items of the table, two-sided estimates were made: both from the aspect of inputs and from that of allocation. In addition to the general problems, practical difficulties arose when the table had to be drawn up at new prices, mainly because of uncertainties and inaccuracies in the values of social product and national income. The author also treats the possible uses of the input–output table in establishing the harmony between the value indexes and those expressed in natural units; in securing the consistency of various partial plans and in coordinating simultaneously the financial and material coverage of the latter.

Németh, S.: On Simon, Gy. and Kondor, Gy.: Az ágazati kapcsolatok mérlege és a tervezés egyes kérdései (The input–output table and some problems of planning), *Közgazdasági Szemle,* 1962, No. 6, pp. 760–763.

A critique on Simon and Kondor.

Németh, S.: *Az összevont sakktáblamérleg alkalmazása az éves tervezésben* (Use of the aggregated "chessboard"-table in annual planning). (Papers of the Centenary Statistical Session.) Budapest, Statisztikai Kiadó, 1967, 19 pp.

Németh shows the many-sided applicability of the aggregated input–output tables in the formulation of coordinated plan conceptions, in drawing up plan variants, and preparing comprehensive analyses of the major economic proportions — both in the preparatory period of planning and later, when comprehensive analysis and information are needed on short notice.

Nyitrai, F., Mrs.: Ankét az ágazati kapcsolatok mérlegének tervezésbeni felhasználásáról (A conference on the utilization of the input–output table in planning), *Közgazdasági Szemle,* 1961, No. 3, pp. 365–370.

Nyitrai analyses the ideas put forward on a conference organized to discuss the utilization of the input–output table in planning the structural pattern of industry, the equilibrium of the national economy, and in other fields, e.g., in assessing economic efficiency.

Rácz, A. and Ujlaki, L., Mrs.: A munkatermelékenység indexének tervezése és mérése az iparban (Planning and measurement of labour productivity in industry), *Közgazdasági Szemle,* 1963, No. 8, pp. 916–931.

Rácz and Ujlaki review the utilization of the input–output table for planning the index numbers of productivity. The model makes it possible to account for the combined effect of changes in the productivity of both live and materialized labour. An index of productivity is computed on the national level and the methods used in the analysis of various factors affecting this indicator are discussed. Also a method is presented to determine the index of productivity (by sectors) for the years when no input–output table is compiled. Various methods — differing in accuracy — are shown which are suited for planning.

Rajnik, J.: A könnyűipar 1960. évi sakktáblamérleg-rendszerű terve (The light industry's "chessboard-type" plan for 1960), *Textilipari Tervgazdaság,* 1960, No. 3, pp. 5–14.

Rajnik reviews the 1960 "chessboard-type" plan of the light industry. Technological coefficients worked out from the model are presented and the partial plans on which the main table rests are reviewed. From among these, the most important ones are the allocation plans for the light industry as a whole and for the Ministry of Light Industry, separately.

Román, Z.: Tervezés, statisztika és ágazati kapcsolatok mérlege (Planning, statistics and the input–output table), *Közgazdasági Szemle,* 1961, No. 11, pp. 1135–1148.

Román surveys the most important fields where the widely known open static model is used in capitalist countries. He devotes a separate section to the utilization of the model in socialist planning. He states that the model is suited for planning computations in a socialist economy and usefully complements the planning methods.

Szakolczai, Gy. and Vásárhelyi, P.: Az ágazati kapcsolatok mérlege technológiai koefficienseinek előrebecsült matrixai (Forecast matrices of technological coefficients of input–output tables), *Közgazdasági Szemle,* 1967, No. 12, pp. 1444–1461.

The authors review, by starting from practical aspects, the methods worked out for forecasting the matrices of input–output technological coefficients, and the results achieved.

Besides reviewing the methods of forecasting the coefficients and the other indicators to check the former, they also present the method that may be used for collating the various forecasts.

Simon, Gy. and Kondor, Gy.: Az ágazati kapcsolatok mérlege és a tervezés egyes kérdései. Iparági és kombinált mérlegek (The input–output table and some problems of planning. Tables for individual industries and combined tables), *MTA Közgazdaságtudományi Intézetének Közleményei*, No. 12, Budapest, Közgazdasági Kiadó, 112 pp.

Simon and Kondor intend to use the input–output table for solving the problem of "proportionate" planning. They outline how the volume of final bill of goods may be determined from the volume of production planned for a given period, and also the reverse procedure. They also deal with the combined application of the two methods and indicate that in certain sectors it is more useful to start from final demand while in others from the pattern of production. In connection with foreign trade for the purpose of volume planning it is expedient to use a scheme where the imported products which have a domestic equivalent are grouped together with the corresponding domestic products. This scheme differs from model "B" generally used in Hungary. The authors investigate the necessity of drawing up separate tables for individual industries, substantiating their findings by computations for ferrous-metal industry. The substance of the method is a detailed breakdown of some individual sector of the national model. The authors finally deal with the methods of combining the sectoral tables with the national ones. The combined application of the two types of table enables the investigations to be conducted at a national level. An advantage of the method is its flexible adaptation to the established planning practice.

Simon, Gy. and Kondor, Gy.: A gazdasági részfolyamatok népgazdasági összefüggéseinek elemzési módszereiről (The methods of analysing the interrelations of partial economic processes on a national level), *Közgazdasági Szemle*, 1961, No. 3, pp. 312–328.

Simon and Kondor deal with theoretical economic problems. Presenting the model for 1957 they treat in detail the theoretical problem of the total labour and wage content of products, their accumulation contents, as well as the methodological problems of computing these indices. Further parts of the study deal with the theoretical problems of export efficiency, the comparison of technological variants, the international division of labour, manpower planning and the planning of final demand, prices and volumes.

Ujlaki, L., Mrs.: Ágazati kapcsolat és tervezés (Interindustry relations and planning), *Figyelő*, May 23, 1962, p. 7.

Ujlaki points out that the input–output model offers an opportunity to work out a reasonable and efficient structure of the national economy. She reviews Soviet practice and presents some comparable data on the economies of the USA and the Soviet Union. Intersectoral and intrasectoral relations as well as the degree of their concentration are also analysed.

Ujlaki, L., Mrs.: A forgalmi jellegű és a termelés anyagi-műszaki kapcsolatait tükröző ágazati mérlegekről (Input–output tables reflecting flows and the material and technical relations of production). *Az ágazati kapcsolati mérlegek összeállításának és felhasználásának kérdései*, Budapest, Akadémiai Kiadó 1962.

Ujlaki discloses the major formal and substantial differences between the empirical tables and the planned ones. She calls the planned tables used in annual planning "turnover" tables and the empirical tables "material-technical" ones. She analyses the two major differences: the first is the turnover as opposed to the production approach, the second is the breakdown according to administrative (addressed) units as opposed to the standard activity classification.

Ujlaki, L., Mrs.: Ágazati kapcsolatok mérlege és a gyakorlati tervezés (The input–output table and practical planning), *Figyelő*, January 8, 1963.

Ujlaki reviews here the practice of planning in the Soviet Union in the use of the input–output table. She stresses that the first experimental table of interindustry relations (for 1962) was drawn up with planning purposes in mind. She examines the major conclusions to be drawn from that table.

Плановые шахматные балансы на 1959—1965 гг. (Planned input–output tables for 1959—1965). Budapest, 1966, 24 pp. (Венгерская Народная Республика, Государственное Плановое Управление, Институт народного хозяйства).

The publication was prepared for a CMEA session held in 1966 in Moscow. It comprises the aggregated planned balances for 1959–1965 as well as the one drawn up for 1970.

II.3. USE OF INPUT–OUTPUT TABLES IN STRUCTURAL ANALYSIS AND EFFICIENCY COMPUTATIONS; THEIR PLACE IN NATIONAL ACCOUNTS

Ausch, S.: A népgazdasági mérlegrendszer néhány főbb problémája (Some major problems of the national system of economic balances), *Közgazdasági Szemle*, 1958, No. 6, pp. 561–574.

Ausch emphasizes that the system of national economic balances should comprise the whole reproduction process into a uniform framework. If the system of balances is not a closed one in this sense, it is not suited for determining the equilibrium of the economy and much less for planning it. The Hungarian system of balances does not satisfactorily show where individual products are used. To make up for this deficiency, he thinks the input–output well suited for complementing the balances of global social product and of national income.

Csernok, A.: A népgazdaság pénzügyi mérlege (The financial balance of the economy), Budapest, 1963, 98 pp. Manuscript.

Csernok describes briefly how the financial balance of the economy can be used to link the lower wing (primary inputs) and the sector of final use in the input–output table. He essentially deals with fitting into the model the redistribution of national income.

Cukor, Gy. and Román, Z.: Az ágazati kapcsolatok mérlegének felhasználása az ipar ágazati szerkezetének vizsgálatára és tervezésére (Utilization of the input–output table for the analysis and planning of the pattern of industry by branches), *MTA Közgazdaságtudományi Intézetének Közleményei*, No. 8. Budapest, Közgazdasági Kiadó, 1960, p. 85.

Cukor and Román extend their methods for the analysis of the pattern of industry. They define the concept of the pattern of industry and its determining factors, and treat the planning method for determining a suitable pattern of industry with the aid of the input–output table. They introduce the investigations based on the pattern of final output and final utilization. Relying on the 1957 table, they characterize the criteria for establishing a suitable pattern of industry with the aid of several indices. They also survey some problems of economic policy. The effects of the progress in engineering and in the chemical industry on the national economy as a whole are analysed from the point of view of foreign exchange earnings, capital intensity and other factors. The improvement in overall economic efficiency to be expected from the substitution of fuel oil for coal is also discussed.

Cukor, Gy. and Román, Z.: Az ágazati kapcsolati mérlegek felhasználása az ipar célszerű ágazati szerkezetének vizsgálatában (Utilization of the input–output table for working out a suitable pattern for industry), *Közgazdasági Szemle*, 1960, No. 11, pp. 1289–1304.

This study is based on the more detailed material of the previous paper and stresses its major bearings. It deals with the system of indicators proposed for the comparative analysis of industries and with the results to be gained from the substitution of fuel oil for coal.

Havas, P.: Az ágazati kapcsolatok mérlegének felhasználása exportgazdaságossági számításokhoz (Utilization of the input–output table for computing the efficiency of exports), *Statisztikai Szemle*, 1960, No. 3, pp. 236–251; 1960, No. 4. pp. 352–363.

Havas, P.: Az exportgazdaságosság átlagos színvonala és határértékei (The average level of export efficiency and its marginal level), *Közgazdasági Szemle*, 1962, No. 11, pp. 1346–1364.

Havas treats in general the possible computation of gross and net export efficiency indicators. He illustrates the method and analysis with a three-sector model, with special regard to the relative ranking of industries. He specifies the assumptions about homogeneity, prices, the pattern of exports, production and depreciation, all of which determine the scope of the indices and computations when using the model. He proceeds to construct a full system of efficiency indices to be worked out from the input–output table. The relative merits and deficiencies of the various indices are analysed and compared with those of the traditional ones. Also the reckoning of the tied-up assets is dealt with. On the basis of the 1959 table, the export efficiency indices for socialist and capitalist markets are analysed by industries. On the basis of national economic interrelations and values, various marginal values for export efficiency are established. Finally, the author draws some general conclusions.

Huszár, I.: On Cukor, Gy. and Román, Z.: Az ágazati kapcsolatok mérlegének felhasználása az ipar ágazati szerkezetének vizsgálatára és tervezésére (Utilization of the input–output table for the analysis and planning of the pattern of industry by branches), *Ipargazdaság*, 1961, No. 2, pp. 34–35.

Mód, A., Mrs.: A szocialista és kapitalista mérlegrendszerek összehasonlítása (A comparison of the socialist and capitalist balance systems), *Statisztikai Szemle*, 1960, No. 11, pp. 1134–1141.

Mód reports on the Conference of European Statisticians discussing the ways of making the balance systems of socialist and capitalist countries comparable. Here the author proposed a model, which she called "the third system of balances", and which is to an extent suitable also for input–output analysis.

Rácz, A.: Az ágazati kapcsolatok mérlege és a társadalmi termékmérleg, valamint a nemzeti jövedelem-mérleg főbb összefüggései (Major interrelations between the input–output table, the balance of the social product and the balance of national income). In: *Az ágazati kapcsolati mérlegek összeállításának és felhasználásának kérdései*, Budapest, Akadémiai Kiadó, 1962, pp. 61–71.

Rácz treats the subject on the basis of the methodology and the computation material of the 1957 and 1959 tables. He presents both the differences and the connections between the balances. While defining the sectors of material production he warns that in the input–output table they are not homogeneous while in the other two balances they are. This is illustrated by examples. Also the differences between the balances as regards accounting the social product of foreign trade, exports and imports, are surveyed. The necessary deviations due to the special requirements of the input–output table are expounded. Finally, the differences in the degree of "double counting" are analysed.

Rácz, A.: Konzultáció W. W. Leontief professzorral az input–output módszerről (Consultation with Prof. Leontief on the input–output method), *Statisztikai Szemle*, 1964, No. 5, pp. 531–536.

Professor Leontief paid a visit to Hungary early in 1964. Rácz reports on his meeting with Hungarian economists. Prof. Leontief spoke of the possibilities of analysing the economic structure of a country with the aid of the input–output table. This structure is influenced by the country's size and development level. He compared the economic pattern of the USA with that of other countries. In the course of the discussion, Prof. Leontief analysed the changes in technological coefficients and also the planning of changes.

Rácz, A.: Az ipari termelés szerkezetének elemzése több dimenzióban (Multi-dimensional analysis of the pattern of industrial production), *Ipargazdaság*, 1966, No. 3, pp. 35–37.

Rácz states that — alongside with other methods — the input–output table is suited for characterizing the structure of industrial production. The substance of the method is an analysis conducted along the lines laid down by Leontief. The author applies this method to industry.

Rácz, A.: Az ágazati kapcsolati mérlegek technológiai koefficiensei (The technological coefficients of the input–output tables), *Statisztikai Szemle*, 1967, No. 6, pp. 507–528.

The paper analyses the behaviour and development over time of the technological coefficients, based on the detailed tables of 1959 and 1961, comprising 54 productive sectors.

Rácz, A. and Ujlaki, L., Mrs.: A népgazdasági költségszint és termelékenység alakulásának elemzése az ágazati kapcsolatok mérlege alapján (Analysis of the national economic cost level and of the development of productivity on the basis of the input–output table), *Statisztikai Szemle*, 1962, No. 5, pp. 533–548; 1962, No. 6, pp. 643–658.

Rácz and Mrs. Ujlaki present the methodology of computing the index number of productivity on a national level and the factors which influence it. Relying on the 1959 and 1961 tables they analyse the development of cumulated labour inputs embodied in industrial products.

Román, Z.: A munkatermelékenység nemzetközi összehasonlítása az iparban (International comparison of the productivity of industrial labour), *MTA Közgazdaságtudományi Intézetének Közleményei*, No. 4, Budapest, Közgazdasági Kiadó, 1959, p. 82.

Román reviews briefly and only in principle the computation method based on the input–output table and the advantages to be gained from the compilation of a table with a sectoral breakdown by products.

Román, Z.: Az ágazati kapcsolati mérlegek felhasználása gazdaságossági számításokhoz (Utilization of the input–output tables in computations of economic efficiency), *Statisztikai Szemle*, 1961, Nos. 8–9, pp. 831–850.

Román, Z.: Az ágazati kapcsolati mérlegek felhasználása gazdaságossági számításokhoz (Utilization of the input–output tables in computations of economic efficiency). *Az ágazati kapcsolati mérlegek összeállításának és felhasználásának kérdései*, Budapest, Akadémiai Kiadó, 1962, pp. 147–156.

The papers by Román deal with the role of prices, with the elimination of their distorting effects, and with the necessity of accounting for indirect effects. It is shown how the indirect effects can be worked out and an example is given for the computation of the labour inputs on the national level. The input–output table can also be used in investment and export efficiency computations, to determine indirect investments, total national economic wage inputs and the factors of total import inputs. A system of indices to be worked out from the input–output table and suited for giving help in drawing up plan variants and in assessing the effect of plan modifications is presented.

Román, Z.: A munka termelékenysége és a munka technikai felszereltsége (Productivity and the technical equipment of labour), *Közgazdasági Szemle*, 1963, No. 3, pp. 272–288.

Román deals here with the theoretical aspects of the problems treated in the above two studies.

II.4. USE OF INPUT–OUTPUT TABLES IN PRICE ANALYSIS AND IN INVESTIGATING MONEY FLOWS

Augustinovics, M.: A pénzügyi-pénzforgalmi kapcsolatok mérlegéről (The balance of financial and money-flow relations), *Közgazdasági Szemle*, 1962, No. 6, pp. 40–54.

Augustinovics, M.: A pénzforgalmi kapcsolatok mérlegéről (The balance of money-flow relations), *Közgazdasági Szemle*, 1962, No. 10, pp. 1223–1239.

Augustinovics illustrates in her papers the internal structure of money-flows, the interrelations of the money-flows between various holders of money. This table differs from the other national economic balances in compilation and accounting. The table expresses also the reasons for the flow of money. After a review of the general scheme of the model, the economic contents of its major sectors (the State, enterprises, investments and renewals, population, foreign countries, etc.) are explained. The types of analysis to be carried out by the aid of the model are discussed. Starting from an analysis of commodity flows, the author treats the possibilities of analysing output and material inputs. The differences between this model and the generally known input–output table of the national economy are emphasized.

Augustinovics, M. and Sári, J.: A pénzforgalom adatainak közgazdasági elemzésre való fokozottabb felhasználása a bank számviteli és statisztikai rendszerének továbbfejlesztése alapján. 4. rész. Matematikai modellek (Increased utilization of money-flow data in economic analysis, based on the improved accounting system of the National Bank. Part 4. Mathematical models). In: *Tanulmányok*, No. 16, Budapest, MNB Tanulmányi és Elvi Főosztály, 1965, p. 104.

Augustinovics and Sári outline an econometric model which constitutes a further development resulting from their experiments and investigations based on the balance of money-flow relationships. They remark that the analogy with the input–output model is only formal.

Ausch, S. and Madarasi, A.: Kísérlet a nemzeti jövedelem újrafelosztásának ábrázolására a pénzügyi mérlegek alapján (An attempt at illustrating the redistribution of national income with the aid of financial balances), *MTA Közgazdaságtudományi Intézetének Évkönyve 2. 1958–1959*, Budapest, Közgazdasági Kiadó, 1959, pp. 11–38.

Ausch and Madarasi stress the importance of the system of these financial balances. They point out that a closed system of balances should be established for ascertaining the equilibrium of the national economy, and for illustrating the interrelations of the social product in terms of use values. In their opinion, the input–output table is suited for this purpos. Accordingly, they deduce from this model the system of balances showing the distribution and redistribution of national income.

Biró, K., Mrs. and Sári, J.: A pénzkapcsolatok mérlegének problémái a Német Demokratikus köztársaságban (Problems of the balance of money relationships in the German Democratic Republic), *Pénzügyi Szemle,* 1965, No. 7, pp. 598–604.

Mrs. Biró and Sári report on the draft table of money flows in the GDR. Similarly to the input–output table, this table illustrates the reproduction process at the national level and at the level of the various economic bodies. It is expected to lend itself to use in economic control and financial management. The possible uses in analysis are also surveyed.

Bródy, A.: A termelési árak és az átlagprofitráta unicitásáról. Egy konvergens számítási eljárás (On the unicity of production process and the average rate of profit. A convergent method of computation), *Az ágazati kapcsolati mérlegek összeállításának és felhasználásának kérdései,* Budapest, Akadémiai Kiadó, 1962, pp. 211–215.

Bródy analyses the problem whether the general definition of the production-type price will lead to an unequivocally determined practically computable price system. He finds that the input–output table is suited also for computations of this type. The general description of the model is followed by a Marxian formulation of the rules pertaining to the transformation of values into production prices. The author works out the solution and gives a convergent method of computation.

Bródy, A.: Az importszorzóról és alkalmazásáról (On the conversion rate of imports and its application), *Közgazdasági Szemle,* 1964, Nos. 7–8, pp. 808–820.

Bródy, A.: Három árrendszerről (On three price systems), *Közgazdasági Szemle,* 1964, No. 12, pp. 1426–1436.

Bródy discusses the problems connected with the practical application of the import coefficient. He describes how the input-output table can be used for the determination of the coefficient of foreign-exchange returns. He proves that the so-called net coefficient of foreign-exchange returns is equal to the gross coefficient which will be obtained after the completion of a full and consistent price reform. In the second paper the author presents some characteristic features of three price-system types, viz. the value-type prices, the production prices and the two-channel prices. The author proves that under simple reproduction value-type prices yield proper orientation and it is not absolutely necessary to start from labour inputs in their formation. His next two theses are that even production prices orient correctly only in a special case of reproduction — that of extensive expansion — and that the system of Marxian production prices valuates the individual products in proportion to the full amount of capital tied up in their production. Finally, he proves that the theses expounded in connection with the above price types are also valid for the two-channel type prices. In a price system of this type the assets directly tied up in the expanded reproduction of labour are also taken into account.

Bródy, A. and Rényi, A.: Az árrendezés problémájáról (On the problem of price reform), *Matematikai Kutató Intézet Közleményei,* March, 1956, pp. 325–337.

Bródy and Rényi analyse the possibilities of restoring the equilibrium of the price system under conditions of distorted prices which fail to reflect actual inputs. A model is described which is suited for successive price adjustments. The authors also deal with the planning possibilities arising out of the model.

Cságoly, F. and Szabó, A.: Az első világpiaci árakkal képzett népgazdasági model (The first Hungarian model drawn up by using world-market prices), *Közgazdasági Szemle*, 1969, No. 5, pp. 549–568.

The authors give information about the methodological problems and the results achieved in connection with drawing up the 1961 input–output table at world market prices, inclusive of 110 products of national importance.

Csepinszky, A.: *Az input–output modellek szerepe a normativ jellegű árrendszerek kidolgozásában* (The role of input–output models in working out normative price systems) Budapest, Statisztikai Kiadó, 1967, 26. pp. (Papers of the Centenary Statistical Session.)

The study analyses, from the theoretical and methodological points of view, the valuation system of economic analyses performed by relying on the computations of national economic balances. A separate chapter is devoted to the problem of transformation of the price system.

Csernok, A.: Hungary's national income established on the basis of the system of national accounts, *Acta Oeconomica*, 1968, No. 3, pp. 403–417.

The author has worked out a system for comparing the national income data of Hungary with those of non-socialist countries. He first computes Hungarian national income according to the SNA and then converts it to dollars at the official rate of exchange, approximating thus the actual purchasing-power parity. Relying on the results arrived at, he gives per capita national income and per capita GDP in Hungary between 1959–1965.

Csepinszky, A.: A népgazdasági ágak közreműködése a végső felhasználásban (The contribution of the branches of the economy to final use), *Statisztikai Szemle*, 1968, No. 5, pp. 487–499; No. 6, pp. 606–627.

The study interprets the net output of individual sectors in the major fields of final use (consumption, capital formation and exports). Also a price-transformation model is worked out and applied.

Csikós-Nagy, B., Esze, Z. and Rácz, L.: Ipari termelői árrendszerünk problémái (Problems of the Hungarian industrial producers' price system), *Közgazdasági Szemle*, 1965, Nos. 7–8, pp. 785–799.

Csikós-Nagy, Esze and Rácz analyse the system of industrial producers' prices, mainly relying on the data and interrelations of the input–output table for 1959 and 1961. They emphasize the great difference between the 1959 producers' prices and social inputs as well as between the domestic supply prices of imported goods and their social input requirements.

Csikós-Nagy, B., Ganczer, S. and Rácz, L.: Az első termékrendszerű ármodell (The first price model based on product breakdown), *Közgazdasági Szemle*, 1964, No. 1, pp. 17–35.

Csikós-Nagy, Ganczer and Rácz describe the price model based on the analysis of the input–output table, the theoretical structure and its major characteristics. They review the methodology of computations performed with the aid of the model, especially that applied in the numerical calculation of the various price types. A programme for further computations with the price model is given and, in conclusion, the price structure of private consumption is analysed.

Ganczer, S.: Árszámítások modern matematikai módszerekkel (Price computations with modern mathematical methods), Budapest, 1962, 240. pp. Candidate's dissertation. Manuscript.

Ganczer, S.: Az árváltozások kölcsönhatásai és vizsgálatuk módszerei a szocializmusban (Mutual effects of price changes and methods of their analysis under socialism), *Közgazdasági Szemle*, 1960, No. 3, pp. 276–292.

Ganczer deals with the price computations that can be performed on the basis of the "chessboard-type" table of the social product. He builds up a system, analyses the problems of their compilation and shows finally what price computations and price-type computations can be performed with these balances and what specific methods can be used in the course of the computations. He treats the product price computations and the price model which serves this purpose. The latter problem is discussed also in his earlier paper.

Ganczer, A.: Árszámítások, népgazdasági arányok (Price computations and the analysis of proportions within the national economy), *Közgazdasági Szemle*, 1965, No. 11, pp. 1289–1307.

Ganczer, S.: Price calculations and the analysis of proportions within the national economy, *Acta Oeconomica*, 1966, Nos. 1–3, pp. 55–68.

Ganczer performed price computations and analysed the proportions of the national economy on the basis of the input–output for 1961. He treats in detail the production type prices. Reviewing several variants, he takes a stand in favour of the price type which best reflects social inputs. To analyse the proportions of the economy in 1961, he aggregates the 1961 model of 54 productive sectors into seven. He presents the distribution of national income by branches of economy at various types of computed prices. He deals separately with imports (at domestic supply prices and based on the average coefficient of foreign-exchange earnings). The proportions of the economy are analysed also from the point of view of capitalization. Finally, the cost pattern of the sectors of final use is analysed. The author deals mainly with the relative proportions of industry and agriculture. He briefly reviews the methods of price-type computations with the aid of the input–output table.

Glattfelder, P.: Some Methods of Price Planning by Multiperiodical Models. (Second World Congress of the Econometric Society, Sept. 8–14, 1970, Cambridge, England. Programme and Abstracts of Papers, 175 pp.)

The study, written for the World Congress, treats the behaviour in time of the shadow prices of single and multi-periodic models. The proposal is advanced to use for the purposes of price planning not only multi-periodic *ex-ante* models, but shadow price forecasts should also be made with the aid of *ex-post* models drawn up for various dates in the base period.

Glattfelder, P. and Mátéffy, P.: Az árszámítások tapasztalatai és új irányai (Experiences with and new trends in price computations), *Közgazdasági Szemle*, 1970, No. 11, pp. 1320–1331.

The authors report on the experiences and results of a working panel created in the National Office of Materials and Prices with the aim of performing price-type computations.

Havas, P.: Az árrendszer vizsgálata az ágazati kapcsolatok mérlegével (Examination of the price system with the aid of the input–output table), *Az ágazati kapcsolati mérlegek összeállításának és felhasználásának kérdései*, Budapest, Akadémiai Kiadó, 1962, pp. 166–179.

Havas discusses the characteristic features of the actual Hungarian price system. He shows the effects of the price system on the distribution of the national income and on the extent of changes in the national product. The effects of the general adjustment of producers' prices on January 1st, 1959, on the extent of accumulation and on the relative proportions of industries as well as of price components in various industries are analysed. It is found that as a consequence of the 1959 price adjustments a high rate of accumulation is realized in products for productive consumption, in some industries higher than justified. The national economic cost factors — imports, amortization and live labour — are shown separately for the industries. The cost pattern according to these factors is presented both at the actual current prices in 1957 and at value proportionate computed prices.

Havas, P.: Az ár- és értékarányok eltérése a jelenlegi árrendszerünkben (Deviation of the price relations from value relations in the present Hungarian price system), *Közgazdasági Szemle*, 1965, No. 5, pp. 537–552.

Havas analyses in detail the average deviations of relative prices and relative values, as shown by the data of the input–output table for 1959. The method of computing prices proportionate to value is reviewed. Economic interpretation is given to the price structure of imports and amortization, and the methods of their computation as well as its deficiencies are explained. The price structure of one Forint gross price-sum is given for 1959. The price structure of the individual items of the final bill of goods is analysed. Finally, the price structures of exports to socialist and capitalist countries are compared.

Kondor, Gy.: Megjegyzések Bródy András "Három árrendszerről" c. cikkéhez (Some comments on Bródy's paper "On three price systems"), *Közgazdasági Szemle*, 1965, No. 6, pp. 746–749.

Kondor questions in the first place the justification of Bródy's (1964) coupling the concept of surplus production with a reduction of the eigenvalue of the matrix of technological coefficients. A second problem is whether it is possible to take into account more than one scarce resource when treating prices proportionate to value.

Kovács, J.: A munkaerő értékelése a többcsatornás árrendszerben (The evaluation of labour in a multi-channel price system), *Közgazdasági Szemle*, 1965, No. 3, pp. 313–317.

Kovács criticizes Bródy (1964) because in the model for the two-channel type of prices the social labour inputs necessary to create the material and personal conditions of labour are not given equal weight. In a multi-channel price system wages must first be adjusted for the socially necessary cost of manpower reproduction and the remainder of the surplus value should then be allocated to prices in proportion to the full amount of tied-up social labour.

Morva, T.: A társadalmi termék sakktábla-mérlegével végzett árvizsgálatok néhány tapasztalata (Some experiences of price investigations carried out with the "chessboard-type" table of the social product), *Az ágazati kapcsolati mérlegek összeállításának és felhasználásának kérdései*, Budapest, Akadémiai Kiadó, 1962, pp. 180–192.

Morva surveyed in great detail the experiences gained in the course of re-pricing the model. Within the framework of the evaluation he deals with the necessary extent of details needed, and with the problem of aggregation. He also gives a general mathematical formulation of the method employed.

Sári, J.: A pénzforgalmi (pénzügyi) kapcsolatok mérlege. A termék és jövedelemmozgás ábrázolása a pénzfolyamatok modellezésével (The balance of monetary [financial] circulation. Illustration of product and income flows by modelling the monetary processes) In: *Tanulmányok*, No. 32, Budapest, Magyar Nemzeti Bank, 1968, 112 pp.

The study treats the problems related to the system of monetary balances, mainly theoretical in nature. The balance of money circulation is considered to be a payment matrix illustrating the relations, economic processes between the economic units.

Sári, J. (ed.): A pénzforgalom adatainak közgazdasági elemzésre való fokozottabb felhasználása a bank számviteli rendszerének továbbfejlesztése alapján. 2. rész. A pénzforgalmi kapcsolatok mérlege (Increased utilization of currency data in economic analyses, based on the improved accounting system of the National Bank. Part 2. The balance of money-flow relations). In: *Tanulmányok*, No. 13, Budapest, MNB Tanulmányi és Elvi Főosztály, 1964.

The comprehensive study deals with the general problems of compiling and utilizing the balance of money-flow relationships. Its three parts are: major theoretical problems of the table, its individual parts and possible uses. In the first part the model of flows is outlined and its concrete form is described. On the basis of the table of money-flows a table of financial relations can be compiled which reflects the monetary aspect of material processes in a given period not only in qualitative but also in quantitative terms. Then the place of the table of financial relationships in the framework of national economic balances is defined. Also the financial balance of enterprises is discussed. The connection between the input–output table and the table of financial relations is shown. Other parts of the input–output table (those relating to foreign trade, the State, investments and renewals, population, foreign countries, other bodies, credits, changes in the stock of money, etc.) are similarly treated. In the third part the uses and the mathematical treatment of the table of money flows in economic analysis and planning are investigated.

Simon, Gy. and Kondor, Gy.: *Gazgasági hatékonyság, árnyék-árak* (Economic efficiency, shadow prices), Budapest, Közgazdasági Kiadó, 1965, 255 pp.

Simon and Kondor perform their computations and prove their statements generally on the basis of the input–output table. The authors present a method of the mathematical programming of economic interrelations. This is followed by an interpretation of shadow prices and a survey of some of their possible uses. Of the various fields where the method may be employed, detailed treatment is given to the efficiency of investment decisions, the solution of multiregional tasks and the problems of price formation. In conclusion, the authors sum up the problems of price deviations (from value proportions), the deficiencies of the Hungarian price system and, in general, the results of the Hungarian price debate. In an appendix a summary is given of the views of Soviet economists on the price problem and of the discussions which have taken place in the USSR.

Szilágyi, Gy.: Árváltozások elemzése az ÁKM segítségével (Analysis of price changes with the aid of the input–output table), *Statisztikai Szemle*, 1969, No. 6, pp. 620–642.

The article presents a new system and methods for price-statistical analyses. The various price index numbers are fitted into a system arranged according to the input-output table and two kinds of price-scissors are formulated on this basis.

Világpiaci áras népgazdasági modell. Elemzés (Models of the national economy at world market prices. Analysis), Budapest, Nehézipari Minisztérium Ipargazdasági és Üzemszervezési Intézet. 1969, 142 pp.

The publication reviews the models drawn up at world market prices and the analyses performed with their aid.

II.5. USE OF INPUT–OUTPUT TABLES IN FOREIGN TRADE ANALYSIS

Augustinovics, M.: A comparative analysis of foreign trade impacts on the Hungarian economy, *Acta Oeconomica*, 1968, No. 3, pp. 145–164.

The article analyses the impact of foreign trade on production, on the distribution of production by branches, on primary inputs (labour, fixed capital), on foreign trade itself and on final use. The study is centred on the Hungarian economy and foreign trade, but comparisons are made also with the countries of the EEC.

Augustinovics, M.: A külkereskedelem az ágazati kapcsolatok nyílt statikus modelljében (Foreign trade in the open static input–output model), *Szigma,* 1969, No. 1, pp. 1–10.

The author presents a generalized input–output model to illustrate the situation of a national economy, where domestic production and foreign trade complement each other in securing the product-mix for final use.

Cukor, Gy.: A külkereskedelem gazdaságosságának ágazati számítása (Computing the efficiency of foreign trade as an industry), *Külkereskedelem,* 1960, No. 8, pp. 6–9.

The study by Cukor calls the reader's attention to the fact that with the input–output table an opportunity is offered to compute export efficiency indices on the industry level and describes the advantages of the input–output table from this point of view.

Nyitrai, F., Mrs.: Külkereskedelmi kapcsolataink vizsgálata az ágazati kapcsolatok mérlege alapján (Examination of Hungarian foreign trade relations on the basis of the input–output table), *Statisztikai Szemle,* 1960, No. 6, pp. 588–603.

Nyitrai illustrates the suitability of the various types of the table (A, B and C) for examining external trade relations. She analyses the data for 1957 in respect of the pattern of additional imports, utilization of imports and material utilization in general. She defines the concepts of direct and total import requirements and then examines their differences by industries. The author illustrates the effects of increased production for export or for domestic use on foreign trade and on the increase of import. Finally, the import requirements of the individual sectors of final demand are briefly analysed (consumption by the population, investment, stockpiling, export).

Rácz, A.: Magyarország külkereskedelmének jellege a munkaráfordítás és állóeszköztartalom figyelembevételével (The character of Hungarian foreign trade in view of labour and capital inputs), *Közgazdasági Szemle,* 1966, No. 2, pp. 197–210.

Rácz analyses the character of Hungary's foreign trade relation, the efficiency of export–import conversion. The analysis is performed by using the cumulated labour and fixed asset inputs for exports and the assumed ones for the competitive imports. The author deals with the substitution possibilities of imports and the character of conversion in relation to socialist and non-socialist countries. He also examines the changes in the character of foreign trade over time, as characterized by the distribution of exports and imports over a longer period and by the dispersion of total inputs by sectors.

Rácz, A. and Wiesel, I.: Az ágazati kapcsolatok mérlegének szerepe a külkereskedelem gazdasági kapcsolatainak elemzésében (The role of the input–output table in analysing the economic relations of foreign trade), *Külkereskedelem,* 1964, No. 10, pp. 13–15.

Rácz and Wiesel deal with using the input–output table for evaluating foreign trade, illustrating its advantages and disadvantages over other methods. The share of exports and imports in national income, in the final bill of goods; the role of direct and indirect exports, the labour inputs of exports and the concentration of exports are analysed. The paper extensively deals with the problems of imports: the utilization of imported materials, the "import-content" and "additional" imports.

II.6. USE OF INPUT–OUTPUT TABLES IN INVESTMENT ANALYSIS

Bródy, A.: Az ágazati kapcsolatok mérlege és a közvetett beruházások (The input–output table and indirect investments), *Közgazdasági Szemle,* 1960, No. 5, pp. 561–580.

The inverse matrix computed from the input–output table makes it possible to work out the level of indirect investments, taking into consideration the production relationships between industries. A method for this purpose is outlined by Bródy based on the data of the engineering sectors in the input–output table for 1957. The author interprets the inverse matrix using the method of expansion into power series. After a definition of investment and of direct and indirect investments, he stresses the differences between the various sectors with respect to the two types of investment. The author complements the matrix used up to now with a sector for the "investment industry" and determines the direct and indirect material and technical composition of investments. He establishes the direct and indirect demand for the products of the engineering sectors due to investment activity.

Bródy, A.: A gazdasági növekedés üteme (The rate of economic growth), *Közgazdasági Szemle,* 1965, No. 11, pp. 1354–1368.

Bródy believes that the closed dynamic model of the Neuman–Leontief type is suited for describing the growth of an economy. He gives the mathematical formulation of the model and surveys the problems of its practical application. Then he interprets the recovery period, its statistical approximation and surveys the possibility of drawing up an investment matrix. He aims at a model in which the effects of changes in technology or in capital requirements on the rate of growth, on the desired proportions, etc. can be established. The author explains the economic contents and interrelations of the rate of growth and of its changes, giving also a mathematical formulation of the problem. He also performs computations based on US data.

Hoós, J.: A beruházások elemzési lehetőségeinek bővítése az ágazati kapcsolatok mérlege segítségével (Improved possibilities for investment analysis with the aid of the input–output table), *Ipargazdaság,* 1965, No. 10, pp. 25–28.

Hoós discusses the theoretical contents and possible uses of an investment matrix. This is a detailed breakdown by origins of the data in the investment column of the input–output table. The relation between the general scheme of the input–output and the investment matrix is presented for use in planning. It lends itself, among other purposes, for the analysis of the allocation methods to minimize the social input necessary for a given volume of investments, or of the production increase necessitated or rendered possible by an increase of investments. The theoretical dicussions and general review are illustrated by simple examples.

Kornai, J.: Az indirekt hatások — az ágazati kapcsolatok mérlegének felhasználása (Indirect effects — the utilization of the input–output table), *A beruházások matematikai programozása,* Budapest, Közgazdasági Kiadó, 1962, pp. 110–127.

Examining the mathematical programming methods of investments, Kornai uses the input–output table in his analysis of the indirect effects which present themselves in connection with investments. He attempts to determine the indirect costs of investments which he uses in a programming model. The investigations are based on the model for the aluminium industry.

Nagy, J.: Beruházásstatisztikai adatszolgáltatás az 1965. évi ÁKM kidolgozásához (Statistical data collection on investments for drawing up the 1965 input–output table), *Ipari és Építőipari Statisztikai Értesítő,* 1966, No. 2, pp. 41–51.

The author reports on the full-scope data collection necessary to compile the investment matrix. The questionn aire is reviewed and a practical example presented.

Nemény, V.: *Az ágazati kapcsolatok mérlegének felhasználása a beruházások tervezéséhez* (Utilization of the input–output table in investment planning), Építésügyi Minisztérium, Építésügyi Dokumentációs Iroda, Budapest, 1964, 40 pp.

Nemény surveys the investment plan computations which can be carried out with the input–output table in the construction industry. He reviews the general methods of plan computation performed with the model of the combined input–output table of construction (the construction sub-matrix) and presents in an appendix the numerical data. He deals also with the statistical conditions and methods of drawing up the model. It is shown how the data should be transformed or complemented to suit the plan computations based on econometric methods. The "content" of the cost coefficients is analysed by the author to establish their suitability for plan computations.

Nyiri, Gy., Mrs.: A beruházások az 1968. évi ágazati kapcsolatok mérlegében (Investments in the 1968 input–output table), *Ipari és Építőipari Statisztikai Értesítő,* 1969, Nos. 8–9, pp. 331–338.

The author discusses the technical problems related to the compilation of the investment column of the input–output table and the necessary statistical data collection. Also the role of the questionnaire in drawing up the investment matrix related to the input–output table is mentioned.

II.7. USE OF INPUT–OUTPUT TABLES IN ECONOMIC ANALYSIS OF INDIVIDUAL SECTORS

Benet, I.: A mezőgazdaság az ágazati kapcsolatok rendszerében (Agriculture in the system of input–output tables), *Statisztikai Szemle,* 1968, Nos. 8–9, pp. 817–832.

The study summarizes the major characteristics of Hungarian agriculture in the first half of the sixties, based on the 1965 input–output table.

Bródy, A.: A nehézipar néhány fajlagos mutatójának alakulása, kísérlet az input–output módszer alkalmazására (Trends of some specific coefficients in the heavy industry; an attempt at input–output analysis), *MTA Közgazdaságtudományi Intézetének Évkönyve,* Budapest, Közgazdasági Kiadó, 1958, pp. 135–155.

Bródy, A.: *A gépipar kooperációs kapcsolatainak néhány problémája, különös tekintettel a beruházási igényekre* (Some problems of cooperation in the engineering industry, with special regard to investment requirements), Budapest, MTA Közgazdaságtudományi Intézet, 1958, 49 pp.

Bródy gives an account of the first experimental analysis of specific material input, and of the results obtained. The basic data and the coefficients of a five-sector model covering several years are discussed, and the limitations of the model and the difficulties encountered in its compilation are also dealt with. The intensity of sectoral relations, the changes in coefficients as well as the proportions between external output and total production are discussed. Bródy starts here from the 1957 input–output table of the Central Statistical Office and suitably enlarges its engineering sectors. Discussing the various kinds of cooperation, he proves that cooperative activity between enterprises is in practice partly of too low and partly of too high intensity. Then the economic content of the inverse matrix is surveyed on the basis of expansion into power series and the direct and indirect relationships, their volume and direction are discussed. The author treats also the problem of direct and indirect investments and describes the direct and indirect demands on the engineering sectors arising from investment activities.

Bródy, A.: A gépipar anyagfelhasználási mutatóinak vizsgálata (Analysis of the material input norms of the engineering industry), *MTA Közgazdaságtudományi Intézetének Évkönyve 2., 1958–1959*. Budapest, Közgazdasági Kiadó, 1959, pp. 153–166.

The author confronts the principles relating to the stability of coefficients and to their diminishing over time and analyses how these seemingly contradictory principles assert themselves in practice. This involves an analysis of the stability of coefficients. Examining the material input norms of some engineering products, the author finds that these are not constant, nor can the direction of changes be generalized, and that the direction of changes in actual input is not always identical with those in input norms. He stresses that the dispersion of norms among enterprises was much greater than the changes over time.

Ságoly, F. and Kiss, F.: A vegyipar fejlődésének elemzése az ÁKM alapján (Analysis of the development of the chemical industry, based on the input–output table), *Közgazdasági Szemle*, 1969, No. 4, pp. 443–456.

The authors examine the development of the chemical industry and its role in the economy between 1959–1966. Mainly the aggregated input–output tables for 1959–1964 and 1964–1966 are used, but also the more desaggregated tables of individual years are examined.

Csepinszky, A.: A termelő ágazatok kapcsolatainak néhány kérdése a mezőgazdaságban (Some problems of the interrelations of productive branches in agriculture), *Statisztikai Szemle*, 1962, No. 2, pp. 188–197.

A detailed breakdown offers wide possibilities for analysing the internal relationships of agriculture and its connections to the economy as a whole. The author surveys the results obtained from the computations performed with such tables for 1957. The agricultural model for 1957, or rather the combined sector table, comprises 32 agricultural and 7 industrial sectors; each of the other branches of the economy represents one sector. This special model shows several productive branches which do not always appear separately in everyday practice. The author presents the evaluation method applied and its connections with that used in the balance of national income. He deals with the meteorological factors and with the stability of price proportions and cost patterns. The study presents also the numerical material of the 1957 agricultural model.

Csepinszky, A.: *Исследование участия отраслей народного хозяйства в конечном использовании* (An examination of the role of economic branches in final use). Budapest, Statisztikai Kiadó, 1968, 79 pp.

The publication examines the role of the branches of economy in economic processes, with the aid of input–output techniques.

Kádár, I.: Építőanyagtervezés és a népgazdaság ágazati kapcsolatainak mérlege (Building material planning and the input–output table), *Építőanyag*, 1959, No. 6, pp. 209–210.

Kádár reviews here the building material and construction sectors of the 1957 input–output table, their interrelations and the direct input coefficients. Then the advantages of practical application are treated, particularly as regards building material production. Possible uses are exemplified also by numerical examples.

Kádár, I.: Az ágazati kapcsolatok mérlegének építőipari felhasználásáról (Utilization of the input–output table in the construction industry), *Az ágazati kapcsolati mérlegek összeállításának és felhasználásának kérdései*, Budapest, Akadémiai Kiadó, 1962, pp. 204–210.

Kádár analyses the utilization of the sector table — or sub–matrix, as the author calls it — prepared for the purposes of the construction industry. He deals with the problems of investment and economic growth. He reviews the contents of the investment matrix, gives its mathematical description and a method for the determination of investment coefficients. The use of the sub-matrix in investment efficiency computations is also demonstrated.

Kéri, E. and Kiss, F.: Az ÁKM készítésének tapasztalatai a NIM Ipargazdasági és Üzemszervezési Intézetében (Experiences with compiling the input–output table in the Institute for Industrial Economics and Business Organization of the Ministry of Heavy Industry), *Ipari és Építőipari Statisztikai Értesítő*, 1969, No. 11, pp. 408–415.

The authors describe the special input–output tables detailing the activities of the enterprises subordinated to the Ministry of Heavy Industry. The experiences and methodological problems related to compiling the model are reviewed beginning with 1961.

Kornai, J. and Holló, J., Mrs.: *A ruházati ipar ágazati kapcsolatainak mérlege. Az operatív mérleg táblázatai. Az összeállítás statisztikai problémái* (The input–output table of the clothing industry. The tables of the operative balance. Statistical problems of compilation), Budapest, Textilipari Kutató Intézet, 1962, 638 pp.

Kornai and Holló present the detailed numerical data of the 1960 table for the clothing industry, with methodological explanations. The authors also describe the functions the table has to fulfil. The publication contains the general scheme of the model. A list of products and their major characteristics, the input coefficients in terms of *forints* and in physical units are also given. Also a detailed mathematical description of the model and a general formulation of the relationships is presented.

Nyitrai, F., Mrs.: A termelés energiaigényének vizsgálata az ágazati kapcsolatok mérlege segítségével (Analysis of the energy requirements of production, based on the input–output table), *Ipargazdaság*, 1960, No. 5, pp. 18–20.

Nyitrai believes that variant B of the table is suited for this type of analysis. She emphasizes that the analysis in value terms is rendered difficult by the fact that the price of electric energy differs by users and this can be eliminated only by means of physical units. The method of computing direct and total per unit electric energy consumption is shown and the data for 1957 are presented. For purposes of illustration the direct and total indicators are computed also on the basis of physical indicators. A short analysis covers the inter-industrial proportions and those between direct and total indicators.

Nyitrai, F., Mrs.: Iparunk fejlesztésének összefüggései az ipar importigényességének alakulásával (Industrial development and the import intensity of industry), *Közgazdasági Szemle*, 1965, No. 2, pp. 229–237.

Nyitrai analyses the import requirements of industry and their changes, on the basis of the 1959 and 1961 input–output tables. She deals in great detail with the changes in the patterns of export and import and works out the relationship between these changes and those in the intensity of import requirements. Import intensity is characterized by detailed numerical examples and both direct and total import requirements are analysed. The industries are ranked according to their import intensities. On the basis of this analysis, the author shows that the increase in the volume of imports was in part due to the growth of the chemical industry, a sector of relatively high import intensity. The author thoroughly analyses the importance of the progress of certain industries from the point of view of exports and imports.

Papp, I. and Réczei, G.: Az energiagazdálkodás elemzése az ágazati kapcsolatok mérlege alapján (Energy economic analysis based on the input–output table), *Statisztikai Szemle,* 1958, No. 12, pp. 1133–1144.

Papp and Réczei analyse the economics of energy in the 1957 input–output table of the Central Statistical Office. The authors take the six energy sectors of the 1957 model, desaggregate them and obtain thus a special model which is already well suited for the analysis of energy economy. The system of indices to be collected from enterprises is reviewed. Finally the proposed method is exemplified also in numerical terms in a four-sector model; the major interrelations and the computation method of the major indices of energy consumption are surveyed.

Román, Z.: Az ipar ágazati kapcsolatai (Inter-sectoral relations in industry), *Ipargazdaság,* 1962, Nos. 8–9, pp. 74–77.

Román analyses the mutual relationships of industry as a whole using the 1957 input–output table. He briefly reviews the distribution of industrial production, the relations within heavy industry, the structure of final demand, the relations between direct and total coefficients. The data are presented for industry as a whole and for individual industrial groups.

Réczei, G.: Energiagazdálkodási kérdések megoldása az ágazati kapcsolatok mérlegével (Solution of energy economy problems with the aid of the input–output table), *Energia és Atomtechnika,* 1961, No. 8–9, pp. 351–356.

Réczei devotes greater space to general relationships and connections. The author stresses mainly the output pattern of the five energy sectors. Then he reviews the substitution possibilities among the sources of energy and presents an analytical method of establishing the technical and economic conditions of substitution. The 1957 table is transformed to conform to this method and the general basis of certain computations is worked out.

Rimler, J.: A ruházati ipar ágazati kapcsolatainak mérlegéről (The input–output table of the clothing industry), *Ipari és Építőipari Statisztikai Értesítő,* 1961, No. 12, pp. 446–452.

A survey is given of the data collection, the contents of the data required as well as the structure of the questionnaire sent to enterprises. The author also gives an example of filling in the questionnaires.

Sebestyén, J.: Az ágazatközi kapcsolatok vizsgálata kölcsönös összefüggéseket tartalmazó rendszerekben (An examination of interindustry relations in systems comparing mutual relations), *Matematikai módszerek alkalmazása a mezőgazdasági termelés szolgálatában,* Budapest, Akadémiai Kiadó, 1962, pp. 79–99.

Sebestyén analyses an input–output table constructed for an individual agricultural plant. He reviews the scheme, shows the major mathematical relationships of the model as well as the general forms of mathematical methods to be applied in the analysis. He is engaged mainly in the examination of the efficiency and the prime cost of production.

Simon, Gy., Ságoly, F. and Kiss, F.: A magyar nehézipar input–output modelljéről (On the input–output model of the Hungarian heavy industry), *Közgazdasági Szemle*, 1967, No. 4, pp. 459–472.

The article reports on the work related to constructing the economic-mathematical model of the production and consumption relations of industries under the supervision of the Ministry of Heavy Industry. The authors deal with the inverse tables, the possibilities of computation and analysis and illustrate the study with the coefficients of five products.

Simon, Gy. and Kondor, Gy.: Az ágazati kapcsolatok mérlege és a termelő ágak közötti közvetett összefüggések (The input–output table and the indirect connections between productive branches), *MTA Közgazdaságtudományi Intézetének Évkönyve 2., 1958–1959,* Budapest, Közgazdasági Kiadó, 1959, pp. 107–131.

Simon and Kondor modified the table of the Central Statistical Office for 1957. The most important modification was to transfer depreciation to the quadratic matrix. Various other modifications finally led to an 18 sector model instead of the 40 sectors of the original. With the aid of the new model the direct and total material inputs of the individual industries are analysed and the interindustrial relations of productive sectors are disclosed. They also deal with the specific labour inputs, and analyse the relations between direct, indirect and total inputs.

Simon, Gy. and Kondor, Gy.: Az ágazati kapcsolati részmérlegek és kombinált alkalmazásuk (Partial input–output tables and their combined application), *Közgazdasági Szemle,* 1961, No. 6, pp. 684–701.

Simon, Gy. and Kondor, Gy.: Ágazati kapcsolati részmérlegek és kombinált alkalmazásuk néhány kérdése (Some problems of partial input–output tables and their combined application), *Az ágazati kapcsolati mérlegek összeállításának és felhasználásának kérdései,* Budapest, Akadémiai Kiadó, 1962, pp. 108–116.

Simon and Kondor emphasize that the sectoral tables enable the analysis and the evaluation of both intra- and interindustrial relations on a national level. By connecting the sectoral table to a national economic model, a combined model will be obtained. The interindustrial relations of the sectoral tables are broken down into vertical relations when the product is not used in earlier production phases, and into circular connections when also a feedback utilization occurs. The internal production relations are also characterized by schemes. The mathematical relationships of the sector balances and the combined table as well as the possibilities for analysis are also reviewed through the example of ferrous metallurgy.

The Contribution of Agriculture and the Food Industry to National Income. *Bulletin,* No. 27, Research Institute for Agricultural Economics, Budapest, pp. 7–76.

Relying on the input–output tables, the publication analyses the relative proportions in production of agriculture, the food economy and industry, as well as in the utilization of output. The first part treats the characteristics of development in the sixties. The second shows, in a price system proportionate to social inputs, the size and relative proportions of the net output of agriculture, the food industry and industry.

A Nehézipari Minisztérium ágazati kapcsolatainak közgazdasági-matematikai modellje (Econometric model of inter-sector relations under the Ministry of Heavy Industry), Budapest, NIM Ipargazdasági és Üzemszervezési Intézet, 1965.

For the year 1961, a sectoral or rather combined table was constructed for the Ministry of Heavy Industry. The general scheme and mathematical description of the model are given; the major interrelations of the model are defined and the model is connected to the

1961 model of the national economy. The publication describes how the necessary additional data were obtained; the scope of the latter is also defined. The model comprises 98 productive sectors, of which 70 belong to the Ministry. The basic data are worked out for both variants A and B. Also the import table corresponding to the scheme of the balance was constructed. In addition to the basic data both the direct and the inverse coefficient matrices are given.

II.8. USE OF INPUT–OUTPUT TABLES IN ENTERPRISES

Iványi, T.: Az ágazati kapcsolatok 1965. évi mérlegének összeállításából adódó vállalati feladatok (The tasks of the enterprise in connection with drawing up the 1965 input–output table), *Ipari és Építőipari Statisztikai Értesítő*, 1965, No. 1, pp. 24–27.

Iványi is particularly concerned with the problems of sales statistics necessary to draw up the 1965 input–output table.

Nagy, L.: A mezőgazdasági üzem ágazati kapcsolati mérlege (The input–output table of the agricultural plant), *Statisztikai Szemle*, 1966, No. 5, pp. 491–513.

Nagy, L.: Ágazati kapcsolati üzemi mérleg a mezőgazdaságban egy állami gazdaság példáján (Application of the input–output table in agriculture as exemplified by a state farm), *Keszthelyi Agrártudományi Főiskola Kiadványai*, Keszthely, Vol. VIII, Fasc. 1, 1966, 44 pp.

Nagy treats the general theoretical problems of the input–output table of a farm. He stresses the specific features of agricultural plants and the effects of ownership relations on the structure of the model. The problems of computation and analysis are discussed. The measuring of profitability and the problems of efficiency are also treated. In his other study, Nagy presents the input–output table of a state farm and shows the uses of the model in agriculture.

Rácz, A.: Az ágazati kapcsolatok mérlegének alkalmazási lehetőségei az iparvállalatoknál (The application possibilities of input–output tables in enterprises), *Ipari és Építőipari Statisztikai Értesítő*, 1966, Nos. 3–4, pp. 81–91; 1966, No. 5, pp. 156–168.

Discussing the applications of the model in industrial enterprises, Rácz demonstrates the practical problems by a numerical example. He describes the enterprise contents of the parts of the general model, and the major theoretical and practical points of view of the sector breakdown. He also deals with the external data which, connected with the model, may enlarge the possibilities of analysis. He builds a four-sector industrial enterprise model and reviewing its figures explains the contents of the technological coefficients, inverse coefficients and other indices which can be computed with the aid of the model as well as the methods of computation. He shows how the various indices can be worked out even in complex enterprises. The author also points out the advantages of the model over the planning methods applied up to now.

Román, Z.: A ráfordítás-kibocsátás tábla összeállításának vállalati feladatai (The tasks of the enterprise in compiling the input–output table), *Ipari és Építőipari Statisztikai Értesítő*, 1958, No. 5, pp. 141–147.

The problem relating to the compilation of input–output tables may arise at the enterprise level under two aspects: partly, in connection with securing the enterprise data required for the table of the national economy and partly in connection with the application of this model, at the enterprise level. The construction of the input–output table involved the necessity of supplementing the statistical data collection. Some data became necessary in greater detail and also new data had to be compiled. The data of enterprises on material utilization and sales had to be broken down and supplemented according to the sector breakdown of the input–output table. The sources of the required investment, export and consumption data had also to be created. Of course, only a part of the data needed for the model could be supplied by the enterprise. A smaller part of the data had to be procured by means of estimations or representative surveys. Román advises the enterprise's statisticians on these problems.

III. REGIONAL INPUT-OUTPUT TABLES

Csepinszky, A.: Gazdasági közösségekre szerkeszthető input–output sémák (Input–output schemes for economic communities), *Statisztikai Szemle,* 1964, No. 5, pp. 490–506; 1964, No. 6, pp. 619–633.

Csepinszky discusses the principles and methodology of multi-regional models, their patterns and fundamental relationships. Though the input–output tables relate to a spaceless economy, space influences the development of production processes and their organizational framework in several ways. The role of space in the model is more important than the mere appearance of transportation and trade activities. A practical interpretation of the mathematical model is followed by a mathematical formulation of the basic relationships within the model. The author distinguishes two basic types of multi-regional model and several variants within the first type — according to the various methods of handling turnover relations. The first starts from the entirety of the economic community while the second starts from a given region. The various types are reviewed in detail.

Csepinszky, A.: Multiregionális input–output analízis (Multi-regional input–output analysis), *Megyei és Városi Statisztikai Értesítő,* 1965, No. 1, pp. 1–11; 1965, No. 2, pp. 53–64.

Csepinszky stresses the usefulness of multi-regional input–output tables. The possibilities for analysing the consistency of the model and the efficiency of production processes are surveyed. A type of multi-regional model, which can be constructed for the individual regions of a country, is reviewed and its scheme outlined. The problems of aggregation which differ from the general problems of constructing the model of a country, are also discussed.

Csepinszky, A.: Input–output analízis a területi statisztikában (Input–output analysis in regional statistics), *Területi Statisztika,* 1969, No. 2, pp. 212–231.

The author stresses the usefulness of input–output analysis in regional statistics and outlines the characteristics of regional input–output tables. In his opinion, there are two major fields of utilization: one is to create links between the sectoral and the regional approaches, the other the analysis of price systems and relative prices.

Kenessey, Z.: A területi ágazati kapcsolati mérlegekről (Regional input–output tables), *Megyei és Városi Statisztikai Értesítő,* 1962, No. 2, pp. 61–66.

Kenessey illustrates the theoretical possibilities of building a regional input–output model. He reviews the computations performed by Nemchinov in the Soviet Union in 1958–1959 and the similar experiments of Leontief in the United States. He outlines the major characteristics of models for big cities and mentions the Stockholm model. He proposes to construct a model for Budapest.

Korodi, J.: Input–output módszer alkalmazása a hazai ipar-földrajzi kutatásokban (Kazincbarcika példáján) (Use of the input–output method in Hungarian industrial-geographical research (the example of Kazincbarcika)), *Földrajzi Értesítő*, 1968, No. 4, pp. 429–446.

In the article the industrial model of the Kazincbarcika region is presented using 1965 data.

Kovács, T.: Vas megye ÁKM-jének tervezete és a kidolgozása problémái (Project of an input–output table for Vas county and related problems), *Területi Statisztika*, 1968, No. 6, pp. 640–671.

By way of introduction, the viewpoints necessitating the construction of an experimental input–output table for a country are reviewed and then the structure of the table for Vas county is presented.

IV. INTERNATIONAL COMPARISON OF INPUT–OUTPUT TABLES

Augustinovics, M.: *Использование межотраслевых балансов для международных сопоставлений* (The utilization of input–output tables for international comparisons), Budapest, 1966, 37 pp.

The author proposes a method for international comparisons of input–output tables that is independent of the price systems.

Augustinovics, M.: Methods of Intertemporal Comparison of Structure. *Input–Output Conference*, Geneva 1968.

By comparing the data of the EEC countries with those of Hungary, the author discusses the problem of international and intertemporal comparison.

Ausch, S. and Bródy, A.: Az ágazati kapcsolati mérleg összehasonlítható rendszerben való kidolgozása (Drawing up the input–output table in a comparable system), *Közgazdasági Szemle*, 1961, No. 2, pp. 171–179.

In the opinion of Ausch and Bródy the model of interindustry relations is suited for a complex comparative analysis of the economies of socialist countries. They are aware of the causes owing to which a direct comparison of the tables in different countries is difficult. They stress the differences in the statistical data supply systems and the problem of a uniform price. The fields are surveyed where a table drawn up at national prices for international comparisons can be utilized.

Bródy, A.: Beszámoló egy tanulmányútról (Report on a study-tour), *MTA Filozófiai és Történettudományi Osztályának Közleményei*, 1966, Nos. 1–2, pp. 129–140.

Bródy gives an account of his study-tour in the United States and England. He gives a detailed historical survey of the input–output model and of the development of mathematical input–output analysis, outlining the activities of the most outstanding economists and mathematicians who contributed to the development of the method. The theoretical and practical state of research in Hungary is surveyed and both the results achieved and the major deficiencies are dealt with.

Ćságoly, F.: Price Problems in International Input–Output Comparison, Geneva, UNO 1970, 51 pp. (ECE).

The first part of the study reviews the price problems emerging when comparing the input–output tables of countries with different price systems and the possibilities of solution, in the second part it offers a new proposal for solution.

Fáy, J.: Input–output számítások Lengyelországban. K. Romaniuk professzor ankétja a Marx Károly Közgazdaságtudományi Egyetemen (Input–output computations in Poland. Report on the conference held by Prof. K. Romaniuk at the Karl Marx University of Economics), *Statisztikai Szemle*, 1958, Nos. 1–2, pp. 143–148.

Fáy surveys the work in process in Poland. In the course of the work started by Oscar Lange, the model was drawn up along the lines of the Leontief model. The author shows the general schemes of the models compiled and the major relationships in the cases both of simple and expanded reproduction. He also touches on the problems of aggregation and the prices used.

Lukács, O.: Az ágazati kapcsolatok mérlege összeállításának és felhasználásának tapasztalatai Norvégiában (Experiences in the compilation and utilization of the input–output table in Norway), *Statisztikai Szemle*, 1958, No. 10, pp. 963–970.

Lukács gives an account of the organizational conditions under which the Norwegian input–output table is compiled. He describes the models prepared and their formal characteristics, the major methods used in drawing up the tables, as well as the theoretical problems encountered. He also deals with the statistical sources of the data used in the model. The author sums up the Norwegian experiences and presents also the numerical material of the 1950 input–output table of Norway broken down by aggregate sectors.

Kenessey, Z.: A szovjet népgazdaság 1923–1924. évi mérlege (The balance of the Soviet economy in 1923–1924), *Statisztikai Szemle*, 1958, No. 4, pp. 315–322.

Kenessey gives a detailed survey of the Soviet model for 1923–1924. He outlines the circumstances which gave birth to the model and presents contemporary comments. He also publishes the numerical material of part of the table, and reviews the part of the system of balances which may be considered the precursor of the input–output model.

Kenessey, Z.: Az ágazati kapcsolatok mérlege összeállításának nemzetközi összehasonlítása (International comparison of the compilation and utilization of input–output tables), *Az ágazati kapcsolati mérlegek összeállításának és felhasználásának kérdései*, Budapest, Akadémiai Kiadó, 1962, pp. 43–53.

Kenessey reviews the formal characteristics of the input–output tables drawn up in 27 countries. He deals separately with the work carried out in the socialist countries in connection with input–output tables. He quotes foreign expert opinion on the problem arising in the course of constructing such tables.

Kozma, F.: On the International Comparison of Input–Output Tables, *Acta Oeconomica*, 1966, Nos. 1–2, pp. 107–119.

Kozma qualifies the input–output table as the system best suited for comparisons between nations in respect of the structure and efficiency of the economy. In his opinion, the model provides a firm basis for the coordination of plans, for disclosing the internal relationships of the reproduction process as well as for pointing out the interrelations between various economies. The author mainly deals with the comparability of physical volumes, and with the comparable prices which can be used in the model. For the comparison of interindustry tables the author proposes the use of prices and price ratios which constitute actual means of measurement in international relations.

Rácz, A.: A bolgár és a magyar népgazdaság néhány fontosabb területének összehasonlítása (Comparison of some of the more important fields of the Bulgarian and the Hungarian economies), *Gazdaság*, 1969, No. 3, pp. 89–105.

The input–output table is used by the author to compare some important fields of the two economies, with particular emphasis on national income, economic structure and foreign trade.

Rácz, A.: Az ágazati kapcsolatok mérlegének nemzetközi összehasonlítása (International comparison of input–output tables), *Statisztikai Szemle*, 1967, No. 1, pp. 52–60.

The study examines, on the one hand, how the existing input–output tables can be used for direct comparative analyses, and, on the other, the possibilities for working out the input–output tables in the individual countries in a manner providing opportunity for more exact comparisons.

Rácz, A. and Román, Z.: Az ágazati kapcsolatok mérlegének összehasonlíthatósága (The comparability of input–output tables), *Statisztikai Szemle*, 1964, No. 11, pp. 1149–1155.

In May 1964, a conference of European statisticians examined the problems of the international comparison and standardization of input–output tables. An account of this conference is given by Rácz and Román. Suggestions were adopted for standardization of the tables. The problems involved in uniformly delineating productive activities render it difficult to formulate uniform points of view on aggregation. The construction of standardized tables, on the other hand, affects the standardization of statistical reports. The paper reviews a more detailed and more aggregate variant of the proposed uniform sector breakdown.

Román, Z.: Nemzetközi input–output konferencia (International conference on input–output tables), *Statisztikai Szemle*, 1962, No. 1, pp. 80–83.

Román gives an account of the conference organized jointly by Harvard University and the Secretariat of the United Nations (September 11–15, 1961) with the aim of promoting the international comparability of input–output tables.

Ujlaki, L., Mrs.: A munkaráfordítások első ágazati mérlege a Szovjetunióban (The first interindustry table of labour inputs in the Soviet Union), *Figyelő*, March 13, 1963, 7 pp.

Ujlaki reviews the Soviet interindustry table of labour inputs drawn up for the year 1962. The model comprises 83 productive sectors. With the aid of the table, the social labour input of production can be established. As an example, the author presents the proportion between the live and materialized labour input in some industries in 1959.

A Bolgár és a Magyar Népköztársaság népgazdaságának összehasonlítása az ÁKM alapján (Comparison of the economies of the Bulgarian and Hungarian People's Republics with input–output tables), (in the series: Statisztikai Időszaki Közlemények), No. 136, Budapest, Statisztikai Kiadó, 1969, 147 pp.

The publication comprises the analysis performed as a joint venture of the two statistical offices of the countries concerned. The main purpose of the exercise was to establish to what extent input–output tables of relatively uniform pattern and contents are suited for international comparison, to what extent they are able to offer deeper and more detailed results than the traditional analyses.

LIST OF PERIODICALS

Acta Oeconomica. Multi-lingual periodical of the Hungarian Academy of Sciences.

Bankszemle (Bank Review). Edited by the Economic Research Department of the National Bank of Hungary.

Energia és Atomtechnika (Energy and Nuclear Technology). Journal of the Society for the Supply and Use of Energy.

Építőanyag (Building Materials).

Figyelő (Observer). Economic and political weekly.

Gazdasági Figyelő (Economic Observer). Economic and political weekly. No longer published.

Ipargazdaság (Industrial Economics). Journal of the Union of Technical and Scientific Associations.

Ipari és Építőipari Statisztikai Értesítő (Statistical Review of Industry and of the Construction Industry). Journal of the Central Statistical Office's Department for Industry and the Construction Industry.

Közgazdasági Szemle (Economic Review). Journal of the Institute of Economic Sciences of the Hungarian Academy of Sciences.

Közlekedési Közlöny (Transportation Bulletin). Official record of the Central Transport Council.

Külkereskedelem (Foreign Trade). Journal of the Hungarian Chamber of Commerce.

MTA Filozófiai és Történettudományi Osztályának Közleményei (Proceedings of the Section of Philosophy and Historical Sciences of the Hungarian Academy of Sciences).

MTA Matematikai Kutató Intézetének Közleményei (Proceedings of the Mathematical Research Institute of the Hungarian Academy of Sciences).

Megyei és Városi Statisztikai Értesítő (Statistical Review of Counties and Towns). Periodical of the Hungarian Central Statistical Office.

Pénzügy és Számvitel (Finance and Bookkeeping). No longer published.

Statisztikai Szemle (Statistical Review). Periodical of the Hungarian Statistical Office.

Szigma (Sigma). Periodical of the Hungarian Academy of Sciences.

Társadalmi Szemle (Social Review). Theoretical and political journal of the Hungarian Socialist Workers' Party.

Textilipari Tervgazdaság (Planned Economy in the Textile Industry). Journal of the Hungarian Technical and Scientific Society of the textile industry.